SHINGON REFRACTIONS

SHINGON
REFRACTIONS

MYŌE AND THE
MANTRA OF LIGHT

•

MARK UNNO

Wisdom Publications • Boston

Wisdom Publications
199 Elm Street
Somerville MA 02144 USA
www.wisdompubs.org

09 08 07 06 05 04
6   5   4   3   2   1

Library of Congress Cataloging-in-Publication Data
Unno, Mark.
  Shingon refractions : Myōe and the Mantra of light / Mark Unno.
    p. cm.
  Includes bibliographical references and index.
  ISBN 0-86171-390-7 (pbk. : alk. paper)
  1. Myōe, 1173–1232. 2. Buddhist mantras. 3. Shingon (Sect)–Prayer-books and
devotions–History and criticism. I. Title.
  BQ8249.M967U56 2004
  294.3'926—dc22

                              2004002602

Cover design by Rick Snizik
Interior designed by Potter Publishing Studio. Set in Adobe Garamond 11/16

Wisdom Publications' books are printed on acid-free
paper and meet the guidelines for the permanence and
durability set by the Council of Library Resources.

Printed in the United States of America.

CONTENTS

ACKNOWLEDGMENTS

THIS WORK HAS BENEFITTED from the prodding, assistance, advice, and encouragement of many. It is not possible to list all of those people here, but I would like to express my heartfelt appreciation to the following: Carl Bielefeldt, Lisa Blasch, Karen Brock, Bernard Faure, Robert Felsing, Andrew Goble, Peter Gregory, Paul Ingram, P.J. Ivanhoe, Miyashita Seiki, Nabeshima Naoki, Pori Park, Richard Payne, Robert Rhodes, Harold Roth, George Tanabe, Yanagida Seizan, and Lee Yearley.

In addition, the following organizations have provided invaluable support for research related to this project:
Asian Studies Program, University of Oregon
Center for Asian and Pacific Studies, University of Oregon
College of Arts & Sciences, University of Oregon
Department of Religious Studies, University of Oregon
East Asian Collection, Knight Library, University of Oregon
Fukakusa Library, Ryukoku University
Harvard-Yenching Library
Open Research Institute, Ryukoku University
Reischauer Institute of Japanese Studies, Harvard University

Special thanks to editor Josh Bartok and production manager Tony Lulek of Wisdom Publications for their expertise and professionalism.

To Megumi, I wish to express my appreciation for her remarkable patience, support, humor and wisdom, and of course, to Taata, and Onyx, too.

ABBREVIATIONS

BGDJ   *Bukkyōgo daijiten.* By Nakamura Hajime. Condensed version. Tokyo: Tokyo Shoseki, 1980.

BGJ   *Butten gedai jiten.* 2d ed. Edited by Mizuno Kōgen, Nakamura Hajime, Hirakawa Akira, and Tamaki Kōshirō. Tokyo: Shunjūsha, 1977.

DNBZ   *Dai Nihon Bukkyō zensho.* Edited by Takakusu Junjirō et al. 150 vols. Reprint. Tokyo: Dai Nihon Bukkyō zensho kankōkai, 1931.

IBJ   *Iwanami Bukkyō jiten.* Edited by Nakamura Hajime, Fukunaga Mitsuji, Tamura Yoshirō, and Konno Tōru. Tokyo: Iwanami Shoten, 1989.

IKJ   *Iwanami kōgo jiten.* Edited by Ōno Susumu, Satake Akihiro, and Maeda Kingorō. Tokyo: Iwanami Shoten, 1974.

KKB   *Kamakura kyū Bukkyō.* Edited by Kamata Shigeo and Tanaka Hisao. Nihon shisō taikei 15. Tokyo: Iwanami Shoten, 1971.

KOJ   *Kōjien.* 4th ed. Edited by Shinmura Izuru. Tokyo: Iwanami Shoten, 1991.

MJ   *Mikkyō Jiten.* Edited by Sawa Ryūken et al. Kyoto: Hozokan, 1975.

MSH   *Myōe Shōnin hen*. In Kōsō meicho zenshū, vol. 9.
Edited by Yamamoto Isao. Tokyo: Heibonsha, 1930.

MSS   *Myōe Shōnin shiryō*. Edited by Kōzanji tenseki monjo
sōgō chōsa dan. 3 vols. Tokyo: Tokyo Daigaku
Shuppankai, 1971–87.

NBSJ *Nihon Bukkyō shi jiten*. Edited by Ōno Tatsunosuke.
Tokyo: Tokyōdō Shuppan, 1979.

NDK   *Nihon daizōkyō*. Edited by Nakano Tatsue. 48 vols.
Tokyo: Nihon daizōkyō hensan kai, 1919–21.

SAZ   *Shingonshū anjin zensho*. Edited by Hase Hōshū. 2 vols.
Reprint. Kyoto: Daigakudō Shoten, 1973.

T   *Taishō shinshū daizōkyō*. Edited by Takakusu Junjirō
and Watanabe Kaigyoku. 100 vols. Tokyo: Taishō
Issaikyō Kankōkai, 1924–32.

NOTES ON ROMANIZATION AND TRANSLATION

THE GENERAL PRINCIPLE in rendering Asian proper nouns and dates is to strike a balance between readability in any given context and consistent usage throughout.

In citing dates, years are given according to Western convention, but months and dates are given according to the lunar calendar used in medieval Japan. Thus, the twenty-fourth day of the tenth month of 1211 refers to the tenth month of the lunar calendar, not October.

Personal names are given whenever possible in terms of the native pronunciation: Fazang for the Chinese Huayan patriarch, Wŏnhyo for the Korean Huaŏm patriarch, and Myōe for the Japanese Kegon and Shingon monk. East Asian names are given in native order with surnames first and given names last. Exceptions to this rule are made in the case of modern scholars who regularly publish works in Western languages and list their names following Western convention.

Titles of texts, names of Buddhist sects, and the like are given with pronunciation according to multiple Asian languages wherever appropriate to facilitate ease of identification for a diverse readership.

The language to which a particular foreign word belongs is generally identified by an abbreviation, such as "Ch. Chan" or "Skt. dhyāna," indicating that *Chan* is a Chinese word and *dhyāna* a Sanskrit one. All foreign terms in parentheses without such an identifier are Japanese. An asterisk precedes reconstructed Sanskrit titles of sacred scriptures.

Chinese terms have been transliterated in Pinyin. The convention in Pinyin transliteration is not to separate semantic units within a word by the use of the hyphen, as is the case with Wade-Giles; however, in the case of longer words and especially titles, semantic units within a word are separated by a space.

Terms of art have been translated as consistently as possible, but depending on the context, different translations have been used for the same term in Japanese. For example, *hō* (Skt. *dharma*) has been rendered as "dharma," "dharmas," and "phenomena," depending on the context. Myōe, following conventional Buddhist usage, employs the term to mean both the Buddhist teachings about reality and the phenomena comprising reality, since in many instances the two coincide: To talk about sentient beings implies their suffering and impermanence; impermanence and suffering imply sentient beings. In some cases he is emphasizing the fact that there are phenomena involved, such as grasses, trees, or sky. In others, he is emphasizing the aspect of teaching, as when he critiques a particular understanding of the dharmas of the five *skandha,* the five constituent factors of reality and consciousness. Depending on the context, either the singular or plural usage is more appropriate. Also, "syllable" has been used variously to translate *ji, ku,* and *jiku;* although strictly speaking, *ji* means "character" and thus refers to the written form rather than the phoneme. In most cases, *ji* refers to the phoneme either directly or indirectly, because in Myōe's Shingon Buddhism the meaning of a syllable is inseparable from its sound.

Tenses are rendered as consistently as possible. However, there are instances in which adjustments have been made for the sake of readability and logical consistency from one statement to the next. These often involve cases where the conditional present and the past perfect have been substituted for one another, and where past and past perfect have been substituted for one another.

Whenever appropriate, gender-specific pronouns have been used alternately in female and male forms to (1) translate the neutral pronoun *hito* and (2) to insert pronouns where English syntax makes them necessary. This choice has been made because women were known to be present in Myōe's intended reading audience. Most of the translated texts refer to events that occurred while Myōe was abbot of Kōzanji and after he built Zenmyōji nunnery; many of his lay followers at the time were women.

Where there are missing or illegible characters in the original text, this is indicated in the English translation by ellipses within brackets: "[…]." My own elisions or abbreviations are indicated by bracketed ellipses, according to standard usage. Where the text quotes a source in which an elision has already been made (usually indicated by the term *naishi*, "up to," in the source text), this elision is also signified by unbracketed ellipses.

In the *Lectures on the Commentary on the Significance of the Syllables of the Mantra of Light (Kōgonku gishaku chōjūki),* the bullet in the recurring phrase "• The passage…" replicates the original manuscript in Japanese, which contains this sign "•" marking the topic of discussion.

Where annotations are included in the original text upon which the present translations are based, these are indicated by parentheses.

Paragraphs do not follow divisions in the original text but have been inserted for the sake of readability.

INTRODUCTION

The earth and sand of the Mantra of Light constitute the great secret dharma of all of the buddhas. The Mantra of Light spreads throughout the world and protects all people, lay and ordained.

If this sand is sprinkled on the corpse or grave of the deceased, then, even if the deceased had committed grave sins throughout her life, had failed to cultivate the slightest good, and had fallen into the Avīci Hell, the sand will immediately release the light of the mantra and reach the place of sin and suffering. The sin will dissipate spontaneously, and the deceased will attain birth in the Land of Bliss.

—Myōe Kōben

•

THE MANTRA OF LIGHT AND MYŌE KŌBEN

THE KŌMYŌ SHINGON, or the Mantra of Light, is a practice of the Shingon sect of Japanese Buddhism. It consists of a series of incantatory syllables, and the mantra in Japanese is: "On abogya beiroshanō makabotara mani handoma jimbara harabaritaya un," a transliteration of the Sanskrit "Oṃ amogha vairocana mahāmudrā maṇi padma jvāla pravarttaya hūṃ." Its meaning is, roughly, "Praise be to the flawless, all-pervasive illumination of the great *mudrā* [the seal of the Buddha]. Turn over to me the jewel, lotus, and radiant light."[1] The first existing references to this practice, which originated in India in the early history of Mahāyāna Buddhism, can be found in a Chinese translation made by

1

Bodhiruci, a monk of northern Indian birth of the sixth century.[2] The descriptions of this practice tell us that it has the power to effect the karmic purification of practitioners on many levels—spiritual, moral, and physical—thus leading them to everything from physical well-being to enlightenment.

The same scriptural translation contains a curious reference to sand: One can transfer the power of such buddhas as Dainichi (Skt. *Mahāvairocana*), or the Cosmic Buddha, and Amida (Skt. *Amitābha* or *Amitāyus*), or the Buddha of Infinite Light or Immeasurable Life, to the sand by chanting the mantra and infusing grains of sand with its power. Furthermore, this sand has the power to cure illnesses, if, for example, its grains are simply placed near the head of the bedridden. Even after people have died, one can sprinkle sand on their corpses or graves, and the power of the mantra will then reach the deceased, purify their karma, and lead them to birth in the Pure Land of Amida Buddha.

Such an apparently arcane practice may have some interest for scholars, but what significance does it have for us today? Many would be surprised to learn that the Mantra of Light is one of the most widely disseminated practices of the Shingon, one of the largest sects of Japanese Buddhism. Fewer are aware that it has spread to other sects. Fewer still, even among its adherents, know that arguably the most important proponent of this practice, the one who first advocated the use of sand as its cornerstone, was Myōe Kōben (1173–1232), a monk of thirteenth-century Japan.

Japanese Buddhist sects. Broadly speaking, the sects of Japanese Buddhism may be chronologically categorized into four groups: the Six Nara schools; the Heian schools of the Tendai and Shingon; the Kamakura schools of the Zen, Pure Land, and Nichiren; and the New Religions of the nineteenth through the twenty-first centuries:

- Nara 710–94: Sanron, Jōjitsu, Hossō, Kusha, Kegon, and Ritsu.

- Heian 794–1185: Tendai and Shingon.
- Kamakura 1185–1333: Zen—Sōtō, Rinzai; Pure Land—Jōdo, Jōdo-Shin, Ji; Nichiren.
- Modern 1800– : Reiyūkai, Risshō Kōseikai, Sōka Gakkai, and others.

This classification, though widely used, is an artificial construction insofar as no sanctioning body has approved it; nevertheless, it serves our purposes well, for the reason why the Mantra of Light has been overlooked is due in part to the same biases that have produced this classification.

In the West, Zen Buddhism is so well known that most people have heard of the Zen *kōan* (question for meditative inquiry), "What is the sound of one hand clapping?" even though they do not know its meaning. The word "Zen" has achieved such cultural currency that it is used to market books: the Zen of golf, the Zen of cooking, the Zen of business. One home-building article even criticizes the installation of a set of kitchen cabinets as "not very Zen" without any further explanation. There has also been a steady stream of publications on Pure Land Buddhism, and its most widespread form Jodo-Shin or more simply Shin Buddhism, has gained increasing notice in the mainstream press since the 1990s. Finally, Nichiren Buddhism, in particular Soka Gakkai International (SGI), which has the largest number of adherents of any Buddhist organization outside of Asia, has also been gaining wide notice. SGI has not only produced numerous publications but recently opened Soka University, its own accredited institution of higher education in the United States.

The Zen, Pure Land, and Nichiren sects, all originating during the Kamakura Period (1185–1333), also constitute the dominant institutional presences in Japan, with Zen and Pure Land having the largest religiously affiliated universities and divinity schools there. Due in part to the influence of scholars from these sects, the start of a truly distinctive

"Japanese" Buddhism has often been defined as beginning during the Kamakura Period, even though Buddhism was first introduced into Japan in the sixth century.

Although there may be some truth to the image of "Kamakura Buddhism" as a critical turning point in the establishment of Japanese religious life, there have certainly been many important figures, institutions, and events before the emergence of the Kamakura schools. In particular, the Tendai and Shingon sects originating during the Heian Period have been and continue to be influential in the development of Japanese religion. Yet, while scores of Western-language books have been published on new developments initiated during the Kamakura Period, there have only been a handful of works on Tendai and Shingon. There are, for example, just two major studies on the Shingon founder Kūkai (774–835) and only one of the Tendai founder Saichō (767–822).[3]

The Tendai traces its origins to Chinese Tiantai, so named because of the location of its headquarters on Mount Tiantai. Shingon is the Japanese pronunciation for the Chinese "Zhenyan," meaning literally "mantra"; thus the Shingon is the Mantra sect. It is the esoteric or tantric branch of Japanese Buddhism, the counterpart to the Vajrayāna in Tibetan Buddhism and traces its origins to Indian tantra. There is generally a much better understanding of Tendai Buddhism than of Shingon for the simple reason that the Kamakura sects of Zen, Pure Land, and Nichiren emerged out of the matrix of the Tendai; virtually all of the figures who came to be regarded as the founders of these Japanese sects studied at or near the Tendai headquarters on Mount Hiei just northeast of the ancient capital of Kyoto. Most recently, Jacqueline Stone has published a detailed study of *hongaku,* or Original Enlightenment, a major Tendai doctrine, as it evolved from pre-Tendai phases and into later sects.[4]

The Shingon headquarters was established on Mount Kōya, relatively far removed from the capital of Kyoto, for centuries the political, cultural, and religious center of Japan. The Shingon founder Kūkai had located it on Mount Kōya for good reason, in part to establish the religious and institutional independence of this esoteric form of Buddhism in Japan. Yet, this did not mean that Shingon thought and practice had no influence on the Tendai or later sects. In fact, as Stone recounts in some detail, the very notion of Original Enlightenment, so central to Tendai thought and a cornerstone of later sectarian developments, is influenced by the tradition of the secret or hidden transmission of Shingon esotericism in which the "original enlightenment" of the Buddha is said to be transmitted from master to disciple through secret ritual initiations.[5]

As we will see, Myōe's formulation of the Mantra of Light as found within the medieval milieu of Original Enlightenment both strongly reflects its mysterious tantric origins and the trend to innovate that is considered characteristic of new forms of practice to emerge during the Kamakura Period. Yet, precisely because it does not follow the stereotypical story about the practice of the "founders" of the "New Kamakura Buddhism" as told by the dominant Zen, Pure Land, and Nichiren sects, Myōe's advocacy of the Mantra of Light during the same period has gone virtually unnoticed, even as it has stealthily made its way into the twenty-first century Buddhism of the West. Thus, the study of this Shingon practice promises to offer keys to understanding major themes at the core of Japanese Buddhism. These include: the buddha mind, emptiness and the twofold truth, sudden versus gradual enlightenment, ritual purity, and the role and status of women.

The Mantra of Light, Kūkai's Shingon Buddhism, and Myōe. Contemporary accounts of Japanese Buddhist sects have tended to focus on sectarian founders and additional key figures in the development of religious thought and practice. In the case of Zen Buddhism, these include the Sōtō sect founder Dōgen and such Rinzai sect figures as the founder Eisai (or Yōsai) and the eighteenth-century reformer Hakuin. In Pure Land, there are Hōnen, the Jōdo sect founder; Shinran, Hōnen's follower and founder of the Jōdo-Shin or Shin sect; Rennyo, the major revivalist of the Shin tradition during the fifteenth century; and Ippen, founder of the Ji school. Nichiren eventually came to be regarded as the founder of the Nichiren sect as well as an inspirational figure to many of the new religions of modern Japan.

The term "founder" *(shūso, kaiso)* is used loosely here, as the question of whether these figures intended to establish independent sects with all of the attendant institutional and ritual trappings is an issue of continuing debate. Ippen, for example, went to such an extreme as to oversee the destruction of all documents recording his sayings, stating that his teaching was for his time only. Regardless of these figures' intentions, however, sectarian accounts continue to regard them as founders on a par with the Buddha himself. This is no less true in Tendai and Shingon.

Certainly, in the case of the Shingon, Kōbo Daishi Kūkai stands as a towering figure. *Kūkai* means "ocean of emptiness." *Kōbo Daishi*, meaning "Great Master of the Vast Dharma," is the posthumous title given to Kūkai by the emperor Daigo in 921, in recognition of his achievements. A renowned scholar-monk, educator, architect, and man of letters, Kūkai was something like a renaissance figure. By the time of his death in 835 he had established a remarkable complex of temples at Mount Kōya as the seat of the Shingon sect as well as other temples; he is famous for his public works, having established schools, refurbished a major reservoir on the island of Shikoku, and built bridges. As an author he composed numerous treatises on Buddhist thought and practice and was widely recognized for the beauty of his poetry and calligraphy. Such was his fame that among the numerous legends that have grown around his name is one that (falsely) attributes the invention of the Japanese syllabic writing system *(kana)* to him.

Above all, however, he was the founder of Shingon Buddhism, the student of the esoteric traditions in China who returned to Japan in 806 to transmit his own understanding of them along with a store of sacred writings and objects from the continent. If the title "founder" fits anyone, surely it is Kūkai. Certainly, no one in the Shingon tradition since has attained even one-tenth of his stature, and in this sense Kūkai *is* in many ways Shingon Buddhism. Today, tens of thousands of pilgrims to Mount Kōya annually visit his shrine in the belief that he somehow lives on in eternal meditation watching over the faithful.

Japanese Buddhism has historically had strong sectarian boundaries—boundaries that have been at times contested with strong rhetoric, political maneuvering, and even military might, with monks taking up arms against one another. Yet, such is the power of Kūkai devotionalism that even today multitudes of followers of various Buddhist sects undertake the pilgrimage to the Eighty-Eight Temples of Shikoku commemorating Kūkai's attainments.

Buried among the treasures that Kūkai brought back with him from China was a copy of the *Bukong zhuansuo shenbian zhenyan jing* (Sutra of the Mantra of Divine Transformation of the Unfailing Rope Snare),[6] a translation made by Amoghavajra (705–74), a tantric monk of North Indian and Central Asian descent, from Sanskrit into Chinese only decades before Kūkai made his trip to China.[7] This Mantra of Divine Transformation is none other than the Mantra of Light; it would become one of the central practices of Shingon Buddhism, and so it would seem to further reinforce Kūkai's place as the preeminent formulator of Shingon practice.

But there is a slight problem here: Although Kūkai may have brought the scripture of the Mantra of Light to Japan, he seems not to have employed the practice, not even once. Nowhere is it mentioned in any of his writings or in any mention of Shingon practices associated with Kūkai. Rather, the practice of the mantra seems to have gained momentum haphazardly, as it was employed at first only occasionally, mostly at state funerals, and then gradually more often over the centuries until the early thirteenth century, when Myōe made the critical move to disseminate the practice widely among the laity as well as ecclesiastics through focusing on the empowerment of sand.

Myōe was a Buddhist monk ordained in the Shingon tradition, but this was not his only sectarian affiliation. In the latter half of his career, he served as abbot of Kōzanji, a temple of the Kegon (Ch. *Huayan*) sect. This may strike some as being rather odd. Although it would generally be impossible, for example, for a Christian minister to be simultaneously ordained and active as both a Methodist and a Baptist minister, it was not uncommon for Buddhist monks in medieval Japan to be ordained in multiple sectarian lineages. Thus, Myōe had a dual sectarian affiliation; lineage charts tracing his religious ancestry exist for both sectarian identities, and he alternately signed his treatises and correspondence as a monk of the Kegon sect or the Shingon sect through much of his career. As abbot of Kōzanji, however, and due to the strong influence of Kegon thought, Myōe has more often been regarded as a monk of the Kegon sect. Conversely, there is virtually no mention of Kūkai in all of Myōe's doctrinal works—unusual, to say the least, among prominent Shingon scholar-monks.

It is easy to understand, then, why Myōe might not figure so prominently in the sectarian accounts of Shingon tradition or of the history of the Mantra of Light, even though Myōe devoted upward of ten works to its explication during the final decade of his life. His story and his contributions to the practice and dissemination of the mantra neither amplify Kūkai's legacy nor reflect mainstream Shingon doctrine. Rather, Myōe emerges as an idiosyncratic figure in Shingon history who nonetheless played a crucial role in the development of one of its key practices.

•

MYŌE AND THE BUDDHISM OF THE KAMAKURA PERIOD

IN THE STUDY OF Japanese Buddhism, the definition of Buddhism during the Kamakura Period is one of the most contested arenas of scholarship. As noted above, sectarian scholars have argued divergent interpretations based on their individual doctrinal perspectives, reflecting debates that can be traced all the way back to their medieval origins in the Kamakura Period. Since the opening of Japan to the West, much work has been done to revise the dominant founder-centered approach based on new forms of Buddhism. Interestingly, Myōe has become an important figure in helping to redefine this period, both as someone of significance who has been hitherto overlooked and as a religious figure representing the best of the older, established traditions. Yet, because he has often been presented as a foil to the paradigm of the "New Kamakura Buddhism," his distinctive role has not been accurately assessed or fully appreciated. Nowhere is this more evident than in the fact that few are aware, even in Japan, that Myōe dedicated much of the final decade of his life to the formulation and practice of the Mantra of Light. This mantra practice does come out of the established milieu of medieval Japanese Buddhism; yet Myōe's advocacy of the mantra may also be characterized as a response to the challenges of the "New Buddhisms," as an attempt to formulate a practice in their mold, responsive to the needs of the age. Ultimately, however, Myōe's implementation of the mantra really cannot be pigeonholed as either an older, established practice nor as a copycat of the new. This is true philosophically, in terms of such key notions as emptiness and enlightenment, and socially and culturally, relative to such factors as gender and relations with the state.

Thus, Myōe's contributions should be considered on their own terms; when understood in this way, the mantra can be seen as reflective of his own creative engagement with Buddhism and a lens through which to view the many forces that shaped the Buddhism of his time. Traditions are rarely static; innovation necessarily draws on past traditions. The present exists in the interstice between the urge to conserve the past and what the sociologist Peter Berger calls the "heretical imperative" to break out.[8]

In recent decades, there has been something of a mini-boom in scholarship on Myōe. Including the present study, there have been four works devoted to Myōe in Western languages and three in Japanese. In addition there have been several major articles and book chapters. All of the books devoted to Myōe compare and contrast him with his Pure Land contemporary Hōnen, and for good reason. Myōe composed a two-volume sequence, the *Zaijarin* (Breaking the Circle of Heresy) and *Zaijarin shōgonki* (Breaking the Circle of Heresy—Elaboration),[9] widely regarded as the most learned and scathing criticism of Hōnen's major work on Pure Land Buddhism, *Senchaku hongan nembutsu shū* (Passages on the Selected Primal Vow of Amida Buddha).[10]

Two of the recent works in Japanese make the Myōe/Hōnen comparison the main topic of inquiry: Machida Sōhō's *Hōnen tai Myōe: Kamakura Bukkyō no shūkyō taiketsu* (Hōnen versus Myōe: The Religious Confrontation of Kamakura Buddhism) and Hakamaya Noriaki's *Hōnen to Myōe: Nihon Bukkyō shisōshi josetsu* (Hōnen and Myōe: Prologomena to an Intellectual History of Japanese Buddhism).[11] In all cases, both Japanese and Western, the discussions focus on problems in religious thought. With the exception of Hakamaya's work, all scholars seek to either defend Myōe against the history of pro-Hōnen scholarship or present a more balanced view of the strengths and weaknesses of both Hōnen and Myōe's views. Hakamaya reiterates in a new form the usual claim made by Hōnen's supporters: Hōnen's socially inclusive and liberal Buddhist vision, with its criticism of existing institutional structures and religious ideologies, is superior to Myōe's.

Of the Western-language studies, George Tanabe's *Myōe the Dreamkeeper* deals most extensively with the Myōe/Hōnen comparison, placing the religious thought of the two figures in historical context.[12] Frédéric Girard's *Un Moine de la secte Kegon à l'époque de Kamakura: Myoe (1173–1232) et le "Journal de ses rêves"* also provides substantial discussion on this matter.[13] Both Tanabe and Girard's works contain translations of Myōe's *Yume no ki* (Chronicle of Dreams), with Girard providing a more comprehensive collection of Myōe's dream records found in a wide range of sources. Hayao Kawai, *The Buddhist Priest Myōe: A Life of Dreams,* a translation from the Japanese, analyzes the *Chronicle of*

Dreams from the perspective of Western depth psychology and places greater emphasis on a comparison of Myōe with Shinran than with Hōnen.[14] In addition, I have published an article on the Mantra of Light that compares Myōe and Hōnen.[15] All of these Western-language studies seek to provide a balanced description of the approaches taken by Myōe and Hōnen.

This present study deliberately avoids debates about the merits of Myōe's views on Hōnen because too much of Myōe's identity has been subordinately defined in relation to Hōnen. Those interested in a comparison between the two are directed to the works listed above. What this does attempt is to place Myōe's mature thought and practice in historical context free from the strictures of sectarian scholarship previously imposed upon it. That does not mean that it is entirely without bias. Historiography, bound by the rigorous methods of textual and historical analysis, is nonetheless a specific kind of storytelling. As is the case of any story or discursive account, this historiography of Myōe represents just one viewpoint and as such is bound by the categories and characters that appear on its pages. Yet, it does not simply replace one biased account with another. Rather, it adds another viewpoint with which to round out the whole picture of Myōe and his times; in this sense, all the accounts should be seen as complementing as well as correcting one another. What sets this account apart from the others is first, that it depicts Myōe not in terms of categories that find their center in the doctrines of other schools and (later) sects but by the logic of categories he and his disciples saw as central to his own sense of history, and second, that it depicts Myōe in terms of the Mantra of Light, the primary focus of his thought and practice during the final decade of his life.

•

MYŌE'S APPROACH TO THE
MANTRA OF LIGHT

SINCE THE PRACTICE OF the Mantra of Light developed gradually and somewhat haphazardly, it is necessary to begin with an overview of the practice in Japan. In the following chapter I provide a history of the textual sources and records of practice of the mantra from India through Japan during the Kamakura Period, placing Myōe's contributions in historical context. As I examined these sources, I saw that the traditional categories of analysis were insufficient to understand his particular formulation and practice. Unlike the founders of the New Kamakura Buddhism, Myōe was ordained in and remained within the established institutions of Japanese Shingon and Kegon. At the same time, he almost entirely rejected their authority over him, declaring that there was not a single qualified master to lead him on the Buddhist path. Intellectually and institutionally, he faced a great challenge in finding and articulating legitimate sources of religious knowledge and authority.

The manner in which Myōe sought to establish the legitimacy of his understanding and practice is the subject of chapter 2, which examines the various sources of Myōe's knowledge concerning the Mantra of Light. I give special attention to the problem of sectarian lineages of transmission and Myōe's view that the Kegon and Shingon sects lacked legitimate lineages. Myōe appealed to the authority of cosmic buddhas and other celestial beings such as bodhisattvas, an appeal that I analyze in terms of the three buddhabodies (Skt. *trikāya*), the three mysteries *(sanmitsu kaji)* of body, mind, and speech found in Shingon Buddhism, and the three learnings (Skt. *trīṇiśikṣāṇi*) of precepts, meditation, and wisdom. Other sources of religious knowledge such as scripture and doctrine are also examined. Some readers may find it easier to gain entreé into Myōe's world through this discussion of lineage and knowledge than through attempting to digest the historical details of the previous chapter on textual sources.

Among the various Buddhist doctrines Myōe invoked, he placed particular emphasis on the classic Mahāyāna notion of emptiness, first formulated by Nāgārjuna. This provided Myōe with a widely accepted basis for his Buddhist thought; ironically, very few other Buddhists of his time made it the cornerstone of their thought. In chapter 3 I delineate the content and rationale behind Myōe's articulation of emptiness. In this regard, there are some striking similarities with the Daoist thought of the fourth-century, B.C.E. figure Zhuangzi. In particular, both Myōe and Zhuangzi closely analyze the use of language, its limits and possibilities, and its relation to illusion and reality. The *Zhuangzi* was a standard part of the classical education of monks in medieval Japan, as evinced by the existence of a commentary on the *Zhuangzi* in the archives of Kōzanji dating back to the Kamakura Period. As much as this comparison between Myōe and Zhuangzi helps to illuminate points of resonance between them, it also delineates the clear differences, bringing into relief the strict monastic framework of daily practice at Kōzanji, in which the Mantra of Light played a central role.

The context of Myōe's monastic practice as it relates to the Mantra of Light and the strict hierarchy of ritual practices within which the mantra was invoked are taken up in chapter 4. Emptiness, the basis of the mantra, signifies the equality of all beings and things; everything is equally empty of any conceptually specifiable qualities, and all beings are equally embraced in the practice of the mantra. Yet, each practitioner differs with respect to the attachments that he must overcome; thus there is a hierarchical dimension to the practice of the mantra. Myōe, who has been called "a pure monk his whole life," placed great emphasis on the purity of ritual conduct in monastic life and in the practice of the mantra. At the same time, the mantra was designed to lead the practitioner beyond hierarchical distinctions.

This creative tension, between the strict boundaries established by monastic practice and the potentially transgressive boundlessness that opens up in the practice of the mantra, is treated in chapter 5. In particular, Myōe came to form close relationships with a number of women, both historical and mythic. These relationships raise questions about the relationship between form and emptiness, samsāra and nīrvāṇa, eros and compassion. For Myōe, who largely rejected the dominant patriarchy of his day, women came to play crucial roles both in his mantra practice and in his life as a whole.

•

TRANSLATIONS

THE KAMAKURA PERIOD IS one of the most extensively researched epochs of Japanese Buddhist history, and a great variety of texts from this period have been translated, analyzed, and interpreted by Japanese and Western scholars. In terms of the total number and range of documents available, however, only the tip of the iceberg has been uncovered. The original manuscripts of countless ritual manuals, transcripts of lectures on the precepts, posthumously recorded statements, and other materials from the medieval period remain stored in university libraries, public and private archives, and Buddhist temples.

Myōe was a prolific scholar-monk of this period who composed over fifty works, of which approximately twenty-five are extant,[16] and there are numerous additional documents that purport to record his statements in the form of transcripts, chronicles, and hagiographies. Myōe wrote in a wide variety of genres, including philosophical treatises, meditation manuals, oracular chronicles, travel itineraries, codes of conduct, letters, and polemics. He was recognized by the foremost contemporary authority on *waka* poetry Fujiwara Teika as a preeminent poet,[17] and he kept a diary of his dreams and visions for over thirty-five years.[18]

The first modern attempt to catalog the texts composed by Myōe was made by Murakami Sodō in 1937. Since then, the most comprehensive compilation of his writings has been published in three volumes: the *Myōe Shōnin shiryō* (Primary Texts Concerning Myōe Shōnin), a project carried out by the Comprehensive Research Group for Texts Stored at Kōzanji.[19] However, the task of cataloging and annotating Myōe's opus is far from complete.

This study of the Mantra of Light contains six translations: a one-panel wooden tablet that places the Mantra of Light in the context of daily practice at Myōe's monastery, Kōzanji; four titles on the Mantra of Light; and a record of Myōe's statements that places the Mantra of Light in the context of his disciples' view of the essential Myōe.

TEXTS TRANSLATED IN THIS VOLUME

TITLE OF WORK	DATE
Arubekiyōwa ([Act] as Appropriate)	> 1221
Fukū kenjaku birushana-butsu daikanjō kōmyō shingon kugishaku (Commentary on the Significance of the Syllables of the Mantra of Light of the Baptism of the Buddha Vairocana of the Unfailing Rope Snare)	1222
Kōgonku gishaku chōjūki (Lectures on the Commentary on the Significance of the Syllables of the Mantra of Light), 2 fascicles	< 1229
Kōmyō Shingon dosha kanjin ki (Recommending Faith in the Sand of the Mantra of Light), 2 fascicles	1228
Kōmyō Shingon dosha kanjin bekki (Recommending Faith in the Sand of the Mantra of Light—Supplement)	1228
Kyakuhai mōki (Chronicle of Things Not to Be Forgotten)	1235

The six documents listed here are significant for what they add to our knowledge of the Buddhist literature of that period as a whole as well as their relevance for the topic of the present study, and it is worth noting the different ways in which they may contribute to our understanding.

These works can be grouped into two main types: works by Myōe (items 1, 2, 4, and 5) and records of his statements (items 3 and 6). They also represent various genres: a daily schedule of temple life, a doctrinal commentary on the Mantra of Light in *hentai kambun* or classical Chinese form, a transcript of Myōe's lectures on this commentary, two works on the Mantra of Light in Japanese syntax written in a more informal style than the commentary and making extensive use of parables and metaphors, and a posthumous record of Myōe's collected sayings. All of the works by Myōe and transcribed lectures date from the final decade of his life, and the *Chronicle of Things Not to Be Forgotten* was compiled just three years after his death. Thus, these texts also constitute a concentrated body of work representing the mature phase of Myōe's life and thought. *Act as Appropriate,* the wooden tablet listing the daily regimen of Kōzanji, and the *Chronicle of Things Not to Be Forgotten* are not solely about to the Mantra of Light. These works, however, contain references to it and are invaluable in placing Myōe's practice of the mantra in the larger context of his pluralistic vision.

Arubekiyōwa, Kōmyō Shingon dosha kanjin ki, and *Kyakuhai mōki* appeared for the first time in English in my dissertation on Myōe and the problem of the precepts in the Kamakura Period.[20] The translation of the *Kōmyō Shingon dosha kanjin ki* has been considerably refined and updated for this publication. The rest of the translations appear here for the first time in English.

•

APPENDIXES

THREE APPENDIXES ARE included. The first provides information concerning the dating, editions, and authenticity of the original texts forming the basis of the translations. The second is a list of works purported to be composed by Myōe on the Mantra of Light. Only about

half of these works are known to be extant, and it is impossible to determine at this date the authenticity or even existence of all of the texts.
The list has been compiled from various sources of modern scholarship,
and endnotes are provided for all listings. The third provides a list of
translations of Myōe's works into Western languages.

•

1   Translation adapted from George Tanabe, *Myōe the Dreamkeeper: Fantasy and
    Knowledge in Early Kamakura Buddhism* (Cambridge: Council on East Asian Studies
    at Harvard University, 1992), 137.
2   *Bukong zhuansuo shenbian zhenyan jing,* T, 20:227, #1092.
3   Paul Groner, *Saicho: The Establishment of the Japanese Tendai School,* Berkeley
    Buddhist Studies Series 7 (Berkeley: Center for South and Southeast Asian Studies,
    University of California, 1984); Yoshito Hakeda, *Kūkai: Major Works* (New York:
    Columbia University Press, 1972); Ryūichi Abe, *The Weaving of Mantra: Kūkai and
    the Construction of Esoteric Buddhists Discourse* (New York: Columbia University
    Press, 1999).
4   Jacqueline Stone, *Original Enlightenment and the Transformation of Medieval Japanese
    Buddhism* (Honolulu: University of Hawai'i Press, 1999).
5   Ibid.; see especially chapter 3.
6   T, 20:227, #1092.
7   Information regarding Chinese sources in this and the following paragraphs were
    gleaned from *Bussho kaisetsu daijiten,* ed. Ono Genmyō (Tokyo: Daitō Shuppansha,
    1938), 8:185–188, 335.
8   Peter Berger, *The Heretical Imperative: Contemporary Possibilities of Religious
    Affirmation* (Garden City, N.Y.: Anchor Press, 1980).
9   *Zaijarin,* KKB, 43–106; *Zaijarin shōgonki,* MSH, 335–397.
10 *Hōnen's Senchakushū,* trans. and ed. *Senchakushū* English Translation Project
    (Honolulu: University of Hawai'i Press, 1998).
11 *Machida Sōhō, Hōnen tai Myōe: Kamakura Bukkyō no shūkyō taiketsu* (Tokyo:
    Kōdansha, 1998); Hakamaya Noriaki, *Hōnen to Myōe: Nihon Bukkyō shisōshi josetsu*
    (Tokyo: Daizō Shuppan, 1998).
12 George Tanabe, *Myōe the Dreamkeeper: Fantasy and Knowledge in Early Kamakura
    Buddhism* (Cambridge: Council on East Asian Studies, Harvard University, Harvard
    University Press, 1992).
13 Frédéric Girard, *Un Moine de la secte Kegon à l'époque de Kamakura: Myoe (1173–1232)
    et le "Journal de ses rêves"* (Paris: École Française d'Extrême-Orient, 1990).
14 Hayao Kawai, *The Buddhist Priest Myōe: A Life of Dreams* (Venice, Calif.: Lapis
    Press, 1992).
15 Mark Unno, "Myōe Kōben and the *Kōmyō Shingon dosha kanjinki:* The Ritual of
    Sand and the Mantra of Light," in *Re-visioning "Kamakura" Buddhism,* ed. Richard
    Payne (Honolulu: University of Hawai'i Press, 1998), 167–218.

16 The following sources have been helpful in locating extant texts: Murakami Sodō, "Shōnin chosaku mokuroku," in *Toganoo-zan Kōzanji Myōe Shōnin* (Kyoto: Kōzanji, 1937), 313–316; "Myōe, Kōzanji kankei sankō bunken mokuroku," in *Myōe Shōnin to Kōzanji* (Kyoto: Dōbōsha, 1981), 535–543; MSS, vols. 1–3.

17 See Akamatsu Toshihide, "Kajin to shite no Myōe Shōnin," *Myōe Shōnin to Kōzanji*, 57–66.

18 For translations of Myōe's dream diary, the *Yume no ki*, see Tanabe, *Myōe the Dreamkeeper*, 159–198; Girard, *Un Moine de la secte Kegon*, 109–200. Girard's French translation includes many fragments not contained in Tanabe's translations. See also Kawai, *The Buddhist Priest Myōe*, which focuses on the dreams.

19 *Myōe Shōnin shiryō*, 3 vols., ed. Kōzanji tenseki monjo sōgōchōsadan (Tokyo: Tokyo Daigaku Shuppankai, 1971–87).

20 Mark Ty Unno, "As Appropriate: Myōe Kōben and the Problem of the Vinaya in Early Kamakura Buddhism" (Ph.D. diss. Stanford: Stanford University, 1994).

PART I

INTELLECTUAL AND CULTURAL HISTORY: REFRACTIONS OF LIGHT

CHAPTER 1

THE MANTRA OF LIGHT, A TEXTUAL HISTORY

On abogya beiroshanō makabotara mani handoma jimbara harabaritaya un. The Tathāgata Vairocana, seeking to bestow the mudrā and the sanmaya, gave primacy to the divine dharma entity [i.e., cosmic truth, realized teachings]. Even though there are the various sins of all of the ten evils, five transgressions, and four grave offenses from past [lives], their embers are all extinguished. If sentient beings attain this baptism and mantra anywhere so that it reaches their ears just two, three, or seven times, then all evil hindrances will be eliminated.

If sentient beings commit the various sins of the ten evils, five transgressions, and four grave offenses—so many as grains of dust needed to fill the world—then their bodies will be broken, their lives will come to an end, and they will fall into the various evil paths [of rebirth]. [In that case], one should empower the sand with the mystic power of the mantra by repeating it one hundred and eight times, and the sand should be sprinkled on the corpses in the charnel grounds or on the graves of the deceased; one should sprinkle the sand wherever one encounters them.

The deceased may be in hell, in the realm of hungry ghosts, of angry gods, or of beasts. However, they will attain the body of light according to the needs of time and circumstance by means of the mystic power of the sand of the divine power of the Mantra of Light.... The karmic retribution of their sins will be eliminated, they will discard their suffering bodies, and they will

21

go to the Western Land of Bliss [the Pure Land of Amida]. They will be re-born in the lotus blossom [of Amida] and will not fall back until they attain bodhi [awakening].

After many years and many moons come to pass, sentient beings may be stricken with frailty, illness, and myriad other hardships. This is the karmic retribution suffered by the ill due to [their actions in] past lives. If one sits before the stricken for one, two, or three days and intones this mantra one thousand and eighty times every day with a full voice, then the hindrance of illnesses from past karma will be destroyed.

Suppose one is tortured by a demonic spirit and loses one's voice. Although one does not say a word, if one holds the hand of someone who maintains the mantra and rubs her face one hundred and eight times…then one can get rid of [the spirit]….

—*Bukong zhuansuo piluzhenafa daguanding*
guangming zhenyan jing
(Sutra of the Mantra of Light of the Baptism
of Vairocana of the Unfailing Rope Snare)

•

BACKGROUND OF INDIAN, CHINESE, AND KOREAN SOURCES

ALTHOUGH THE PRESENT STUDY focuses on the Mantra of Light as advocated and practiced by Myōe in thirteenth-century Japan, the story would be incomplete without an account of its prior history.

There is much that remains unknown about the early practice of this mantra, but we do know that there were Sanskrit texts in India, probably composed in the first few centuries of the Common Era, advocating the practice of intoning the mantra and empowering the sand for the purpose of extinguishing sins, curing illnesses, and leading the practitioner to birth in the Pure Land of Amida. This cosmic buddha originated as two separate but closely associated buddhas in India: Amitābha, the Buddha of Infinite Light, and Amitāyus, the Buddha of

Eternal Life. Each cosmic buddha has his own buddha-land *(buddha-kṣetra)*. Amida's is known as the Land of Bliss (Skt. *Sukhāvatī*) or the Western Pure Land, so named because, in the cosmology of the Mahāyāna, the buddha-land of Amida is trillions of miles to the west of the buddha-land of Śākyamuni, which is our own solar system, as it were.

The origins of the myths that appear in Mahāyāna sutras are often rather murky. There are those who are apt to think that the sutras are pure expressions of religious experience, and while such experience may be important and even central in some cases, we now know that many sutras were compiled over several centuries, reflecting various influences including climate, geography, culture, local politics, and indigenous pre-Buddhist beliefs. This does not preclude reading any given sutra as a sacred text in its entirety, with its own internal religious logic. However, the fact that a sutra may be interpreted in terms of its religious meaning should not lead blindly to any conclusions about its historical origins. Mythic or cosmic figures such as Amida and Maitreya, the future buddha, often appeared as secondary or auxiliary figures in sutras featuring other cosmic deities before they had their own sutras, perhaps like backup singers to a famous band before they made it big and had their own marquee shows.

Some agreement has emerged that, prior to the compilation of the first sutras devoted to Amitābha worship, the symbology of Amitābha is likely to have been shaped by ancient Indo-Iranian religion, in particular the Zoroastrian cult of Mithra, a deity of light closely associated with Sun worship, and eclectic cultural influences from the Kushan empire, which extended from central Asia and northern India into present-day Iran.[1] Scriptures describing practices leading to birth in the Sukhāvatī (Land of Bliss) of Amitābha belong among the earliest layers of Indian Mahāyāna and pre-Mahāyāna sutra literature[2]; the first full-fledged sutras devoted to Amitābha (and Amitāyus) appeared around the beginning of the Common Era, the first being the *Larger Sukhāvatīvyūha Sūtra* and the *Smaller Sukhāvatīvyūha Sūtra*.[3]

Much of the research on the literature and practices of Amitābha worship has centered on Chinese and Japanese developments, where the majority of extant documents are found. The first extant record of Amitābha worship in Indian society is located in the pilgrimage reports of the Chinese monk Huizhi (d. 748)[4], made long after practices had developed in the South Asian subcontinent. When Huizhi inquired about the most expedient means of seeing the Buddha, the reply he received was that he should seek the Pure Land.

As little as we know about practices involving Amitābha in early Indian Buddhism, there are some important clues. As Gregory Schopen suggests, there is evidence of the dissemination of Sukhāvatī as a religious goal independent of any actual Amitābha-centered religious community of practice. This is indicated by a number of references to Sukhāvatī in Sanskrit sutras that do not focus on Amitābha worship.[5] Schopen hypothesizes that, in such instances, the idea of Sukhāvatī functioned symbolically in a manner similar to that of Mount Sumeru, center of the Mahāyāna universe. That is, such images have symbolic resonances that were useful in amplifying themes common to early Indian Mahāyāna as a whole. Thus, Mount Sumeru signifies imperturbability, and Sukhāvatī, as the land of enlightenment, exalts the virtues and rewards of the bodhisattva path to awakening.[6] In addition to this, there may have been some sectarian concerns at work; due to the early prevalence of this cult, it may have been advantageous for various schools or cultic centers to incorporate the idea of Sukhāvatī.[7] In any case, the fact that references to Amitābha and Sukhāvatī appeared independently in sacred literature predating the Pure Land sutras indicates their popularity.

Sutras expounding the Mantra of Light were a part of this history of devotion to Amitābha and Sukhāvatī. The *Sutra of the Mantra of Light of the Baptism of Vairocana of the Unfailing Rope Snare* translated by Amoghavajra specifically advocates birth in the Sukhāvatī of Amitābha and not other buddha-lands, even though the main deity is actually Mahāvairocana. This shows that practices leading to birth in Amitābha's

Sukhāvatī constituted a substantial cult, so much so that worshippers of other buddhas and bodhisattvas may have sensed a need to recognize and institute practices leading to the realm of Amitābha even for their own followers.

It is difficult to go beyond anything more than speculation on this point, but the spread of devotional cults is an important issue because Myōe appears to have advocated the Mantra of Light in part as a response to the rising popularity of Pure Land devotionalism in medieval Japan. Myōe further complicated the picture by interpreting the available scriptural sources to convey an ambiguous or ambivalent message: According to the sutras he cites, the Mantra of Light is especially effective for attaining birth in Amida's Pure Land, but he interpreted the scriptural sources to mean that one is not limited to birth there; the Mantra of Light could equally be the means to birth in other buddha-lands. This ambiguity or ambivalence is manifest in Myōe's own life. Although he devoted much of the last decade of his life to composing works on the Mantra of Light, he himself sought birth in yet another realm, the Tuṣita Heaven of Bodhisattva Maitreya, the future buddha, which he rarely mentions in connection with the Mantra of Light. The problem of the relation between the Mantra of Light, Myōe's own practice, and that of his religious community is one to which I will later return.

Although there are no Sanskrit texts extant, sutras describing the Mantra of Light practice can be counted among this early group of Indian Mahāyāna scriptures. From the Chinese translations it appears that there were one or two primary sources, which were eventually redacted into several versions. From these texts it is also apparent that the basic elements of the ritual were in place from quite early on: the specific powers of the mantra, the use of the sand, and the ritual intoning of the mantra as an alternative means of birth in the Pure Land of Amida.

The earliest record of the Mantra of Light (Ch. *Guangming zhenyan*) in Chinese sources is Bodhiruci's (ca. sixth century) *Bukong zhuansuo shenbian zhenyan jing* (Sutra of the Mantra of Divine Transformation of the Unfailing Rope Snare),[8] a translation from Sanskrit *(*Amoghapaśa-vikriṇita-mantra Sūtra)*;[9] the Mantra of Light is described at the end of the twenty-eighth fascicle. Amoghavajra (705–74) translated just this portion devoted to the Mantra of Light as the *Bukong zhuansuo piluzhenafa daguanding guangming zhenyan jing* (Sutra of the Mantra of the Unfailing Rope Snare of the Buddha Vairocana's Great Baptism).[10] There is also the *Guangming zhenyan yigui* (Ritual Protocols for the Mantra of Light), another translation attributed to Amoghavajra, a work, however, whose supposed Indian origins have been regarded as apocryphal since the Kamakura Period and which was likely to have been composed in Japan during the eleventh century.[11]

Other related scriptures include *Bukong zhuansuo shenzhou wang jing* (Sutra of the King of the Divine Incantation of the Unfailing Rope Snare), translated by Bao Siwei (673–706),[12] and the *Bukong zhuansuo tuoluoni jing* (Sutra of the Dhāraṇī of the Unfailing Rope Snare), translated around 700 by Li Wuzhao.[13]

In addition, a few commentaries were composed on the Mantra of Light, including the *Bukong zhuansuo jing su* (Commentary on the Sutra of the Unfailing Rope Snare) by Wen Gui.[14] However, the sparsity of the commentarial literature suggests that the Mantra of Light may not have developed into a major practice in China.[15]

In Korea the *Yusim Allakto* (Path of Ease of the Playful Heart) recommended the efficacy of the Mantra of Light, a work erroneously attributed to Wŏnhyo (617–86) and referenced by Myōe in his *Kōmyō Shingon dosha kanjin ki* (Recommending Faith in the Mantra of Light and Sand).

•

THE MANTRA OF LIGHT IN JAPAN

AMOGHAVAJRA'S TRANSLATION, *The Sutra of the Mantra of the Unfailing Rope Snare of the Buddha Vairocana's Great Baptism*, was first

brought to Japan by the Shingon founder Kūkai (774–835) not long after its translation into Chinese,[16] but there is virtually no mention of
the text or the ritual in Kūkai's own writings or those of his disciples,
thus supporting the idea that it may not have been prominent on the
continent. In any case, it apparently did not initially receive much attention in Japan.[17] It is also worth noting that, five centuries later, Myōe
rarely mentioned Kūkai in his writings on the Mantra of Light.[18]

The earliest known use of the Mantra of Light in Japan took place
in 880 for a memorial service for the emperor Seiwa. At that time, fifty
monks are said to have gathered to recite the mantra from the eleventh
day following the funeral until the forty-ninth-day memorial service.
There is little mention of the Mantra of Light from that time until the
mid to late Heian Period (794–1185), mostly the eleventh century onward, when references to the Mantra of Light began to appear with some
regularity. Gradually, the mantra was used with greater frequency in funerary rituals until it became codified for such use. Then there was an
increasing recognition of the mantra's usefulness for its effects in this
world, and the mantra was regularized as a regimen of practice. There was
also doctrinal systematization of its various aspects of efficacy.

Initially, the Mantra of Light appears mostly to have been auxiliary to Amida *nembutsu*—the invocation of the Name of Amida Buddha,
meditative visualization, and other practices as a means of attaining birth
in Amida's Pure Land.[19] According to the Tendai monk Genshin's
(942–1017) *Nijūgo zammai kishō* (Twenty-Five-Day Samādhi Pledge),
the main practice of cultivating *nembutsu* samādhi was followed by the
chanting of the Mantra of Light and the empowerment of sand at the end
of the practice period. In the *Ōjōyōshū* (Collected Sayings on Birth in
the Pure Land) Genshin states, "One who seeks the Land of Bliss does
not necessarily focus solely on the *nembutsu*. Each should abide in the
realm of pleasurable ease by illuminating one of the other practices in a
sustained manner. For example, there are practices of such dhāraṇīs as
the Zuigu (Following Desire), Sonshō (Victorious), and [Mantra of]

Light of the Unfailing Rope Snare. By receiving, maintaining, invoking, and intoning them, all of which are within the various Mahāyāna teachings, one may attain birth in [Amida's] Land of Bliss."[20]

As the following instances illustrate, implementation of the Mantra of Light as the primary rather than auxiliary practice first took place at funeral rites for the nobility in an attempt to expiate evil karma on behalf of the deceased.

Raishō, a monk of the Taimitsu or Tendai esoteric tradition, was the first to codify the ritual protocol of the *Kōmyō Shingon hō* (Method of the Mantra of Light) and performed a service on the occasion of Fujiwara Yorimichi's death in the second month of 1074. The term "Taimitsu" contrasts with "Tōmitsu"; the former reflects Shingon practices appropriated by the Tendai, and the latter the development of Shingon practices within the Shingon sect.[21] In the tenth month of the same year, Raishō and Ōhara Chōen (1016–81),[22] another Taimitsu monk who was a preceptor and founder of the Ōhara-style of Tendai esotericism, performed the Mantra of Light ritual for the funeral of Fujiwara Akiko, otherwise known as Jōtōmon'in, Emperor Ichijō's consort. In 1084, Gihan (1023–88),[23] a Shingon monk of Fujiwara descent and innovator of the Ono style of Tōmitsu or Tōji-based Shingon esoteric practice, performed the ritual for the death of Fujiwara Katako, one of Emperor Shirakawa's wives.

The Shingon monk Ejū performed the ritual in 1107 at the time of Emperor Horikawa's death. In 1176 Shōken (1136–96),[24] another Shingon monk of Fujiwara descent and abbot of Daigoji, invoked the Mantra of Light on the occasion of the death of Taira Shigeko, or Kenshunmon'in, future mother of Emperor Takakura.

As these examples illustrate, members of the Fujiwara clan were often involved in the performance of the mantra at funerals. The prevalence of the Fujiwara is to be expected given the aristocratic clan's dominant presence at the imperial court. Myōe was himself affiliated with the Fujiwara clan, and the role of the Fujiwara in Myōe's life is a theme to which we will later turn.

Hanjun (1038–1112), a cohort of Gihan, made a study of the Mantra of Light within the Tōmitsu tradition in order to apply its powers to curing illnesses and increasing longevity. He specified different ritual protocols for these purposes from those for the funerary use of the ritual. This marked the beginning of the use of the mantra for purposes other than funerals. Mandalas, circular diagrammatic depictions of Buddhist cosmology or mythosphere, were also used in conjunction with performance of the mantra; the type and ritual location of the mandala to be used were specified as well, and these practices were transmitted to Shōkaku of Sambō'in, who was the abbot of Daigoji and preceptor to Emperor Shirakawa.[25] Shōkaku also studied Gihan's method, and he eventually combined the two styles of Hanjun and Gihan.

The differences between Hanjun and Gihan concerned the correspondences between the functions of the ritual, the deities worshipped, and the arrangement of sacred space. There were three types of mandalas, corresponding to three aspects of Mahāvairocana: the mandalas of the Kongōkai, Taizōkai, and Hosshō-funi (Diamond-Realm, Womb-Realm, and Nondual Dharma-Nature; Skt. *Vajradhatū, Garbhakośadhatū,* and *Dharmatā*). The Diamond-Realm and Womb-Realm mandalas were variously placed on the eastern or western walls of the ritual hall. Shōkaku's innovation was to bring together all the functions of the mantra, whether for expiating sins of the deceased or for curing illness in this life, under the all-encompassing purview of the Dharma-nature Mahāvairocana, who symbolized the nonduality of the other two mandalas.

Shōkaku transmitted his understanding to his younger brother Jitsu'un, who in turn transmitted it to his own disciple Jōkai.[26] When Jōkai performed the ritual in honor of his deceased teacher for one hundred days, Amoghavajra is said to have appeared to him in a dream extolling Jōkai's virtue. Because of this Jōkai adopted the Mantra of Light as the standard practice for the funeral of all his monks. In 1159, Jōkai was chosen to perform the Mantra of Light in the palatial hall of the Ninshōden, whereupon the nobleman Chūnagon Tomotaka dreamt that his entire being was suffused with light. From this point on Jōkai's fame spread further, and along with it the renown of the ritual. Jōkai transmitted the ritual protocol to Jōken.

The record of this protocol indicates a complex ritual of seven stages and sixty-eight steps. The seven major stages along with some of the steps in each are these:

1. Entering the ritual enclosure: supplication before the deity, purification of the three karmic actions (of body, speech, and mind) corresponding to the visualization of the three mysteries (of body, speech, and mind) or mystic powers of the cosmic buddhas[27]— declaration to the kami (local gods), repentance, and *bodaishin* (arousing the mind of aspiration for enlightenment; Skt. *bodhicitta*).

2. The *sanmaya* (Skt. *samaya*) precepts (see below for explanation): further visualizations, overcoming transgressions, removing karmic hindrances, and completing *bodaishin* (as the force propelling one to enlightenment).

3. Adornment of the ritual enclosure.

4. Requesting and sealing (the boundaries of the ritual space).

5. Offerings, hymns of praise: symbolic and material offerings and the worship of the buddhas.

6. Recitation cultivation: visualization of the supplicant becoming one with the main deity, visualization of seed syllables, and recitations.

7. Second offering: hymns of praise, aspiration to enlightenment, worship of buddhas, transfer of merit, unsealing the ritual boundaries, and release.

The entire ritual is designed to effect a deity yoga, the union of the supplicant with the main deity, in this case the Dharma-nature

Mahāvairocana. Particularly noteworthy in this process are the purification of karma, declaration to kami, arousing *bodaishin*, and the *sanmaya* precepts. The emphasis on purifying karma and giving rise to *bodaishin* helps to delineate key elements in the process of the supplicant uniting with the deity. The inclusion of the kami, nonexistent in the sutra descriptions, reveals an adaptation to Japanese cosmology. The *sanmaya* precepts, also known as the bodhicitta precepts, were central to both Shingon and Tendai esotericism:

1. The precept to never cast aside the true dharma
2. The precept to never cast aside *bodaishin*
3. The precept to never resent the demands of the dharma
4. The precept to never cease working for the benefit of all beings[28]

The *sanmaya* precepts, like the bodhisattva precepts of the Tendai, focused more on the enlightening spirit of the precepts rather than the day-to-day regulations that constituted the actual forms of behavior. For Myōe as for Jōkai, the practice of the mantra and the practice of the precepts went hand in hand. For Myōe, however, both the spirit of the precepts as found in the *sanmaya* precepts and the letter of the law as found in the classical Dharmaguptaka Vinaya (Ch. *sifenlu*) were important. The Dharmaguptaka Vinaya, dating back to early Indian sources, contained monastic regulations governing everything from allowable mealtimes and possessions (robe and bowl) to relations with lay followers.

In the Kamakura Period, Dōhan (1178–1252), a contemporary of Myōe (1173–1232), advocated the Mantra of Light in his *Kōmyō Shingon shijūshaku* (Fourfold Commentary on the Mantra of Light) as a simple practice accessible to all, whether good or evil, lay or ordained.[29] Dōhan was a prominent Shingon monk who studied on Mount Kōya, received the transmission of several styles of practice, and held numerous prominent posts at prestigious Shingon temples.[30] One of these was the Daidenpōin, originally founded by Kakuban in 1131. When Kakuban became the abbot of Daidenpōin, the emperor Toba also appointed him abbot of Kongōbuji, the head temple of Mount Kōya, but this caused strife with those who were already in charge of Kongōbuji. Tensions surrounding these two temples continued for some time; Dōhan became embroiled in the ensuing conflict during his appointment at Daidenpōin, and he was exiled to Sanuki on the island of Shikoku in 1243. He was pardoned in 1249 and returned to a grand welcome but died just three years later. Dōhan's Pure Land contemporaries Hōnen and Shinran are famous for having been exiled as the leaders of a heretical movement; as Dōhan's case illustrates, exile was a punishment meted out regardless of religious affiliation. Another Shingon monk, Mongaku, who was the teacher of Myōe's uncle Jōgaku at the Shingon temple of Jingoji, similarly suffered exile; Mongaku had something of a "wild man" reputation, as he has been portrayed as conniving and politically ambitious, but he may also have been subject to partisan circumstances.

Both Myōe and Dōhan lived during what many Buddhists regarded as *mappō*, the final, degenerate age of the dharma. Under such circumstances, the aid of cosmic buddhas and bodhisattvas was deemed necessary to overcome the accumulated effects of negative karma. Myōe enlisted the mystic power of Dainichi and Amida through the Mantra of Light in order to overcome to karmic limitations of his age. Dōhan may have been similarly impelled.

•

MYŌE AND THE MANTRA OF LIGHT

As Tanaka Kaiō notes, it was really with Myōe that the Mantra of Light began to attract attention in its own right as a superior and even preferred practice over Amida *nembutsu* for attaining a favorable birth:

> The general propagation of the Mantra of Light took place after Myōe Kōben began to advocate it. Myōe Shōnin [began with] the simple intent of reviving the Kegon [school], and [from there worked] to harmonize the Pure Land and Kegon [doctrines]. Furthermore,

[he worked] to unify Kegon and Shingon, and out of this arose the
Kugishaku (Commentary on the Syllables of the Mantra of Light)
[in which he advocated] the Mantra of Light. [He also composed]
the *Dosha kanjin ki* (Recommending Faith in the Sand) in which
he sought to harmonize Pure Land and Shingon, to free the Mantra
of Light from its subordinate status in relation to Amidism, and in-
troduce the Mantra of Light to the common people.[31]

Initially, Myōe drew scholars' attention because of his sharp criticism of Hōnen, the prominent Pure Land teacher. Tanaka suggests that
Myōe was not merely reacting to the rising popularity of Pure Land devotionalism but was synthesizing many strands of Buddhist thought and
practice with the Mantra of Light as the focus. Certainly, the fact that
Amida symbolism was already present in the sutra literature helped Myōe
to address Pure Land themes. However, his engagement with the Mantra
went beyond addressing Pure Land sectarian issues or attempting intellectual syntheses. He was seeking an embodied practice that would lead
him out of the darkness of karmic evil. He recorded his first major vision in which the mantra appeared in 1220:

> In the summer of 1220, I was practicing the samādhi of the Buddha's
> Radiance. On the twenty-ninth day of the seventh month of the same
> year, I received auspicious signs in the midst of meditation. That is,
> a sphere of white light appeared before me. Its shape was like that of
> a white jewel of approximately one foot in diameter. To the left there
> was a white light that grew from one foot [in length] to two feet and
> then three. To the right there was a light like a mass of fire. There
> was a voice that said, "This is the Mantra of Light."
>
> When I emerged from my contemplation and thought about it,
> its profound meaning became apparent. The light, like a mass of
> flames, was the light to illuminate the evil paths [of rebirth]. [32]

From the following year he began to compose works on the Mantra
of Light. In all, ten works devoted to the Mantra of Light have been attributed to Myōe.[33] All ten works are thought to have been composed
during the final decade of Myōe's life, which indicates the importance
of the Mantra of Light as a subject of his intensive study and practice

as well as a mature expression of his religious thought. His disciples also compiled a record of his lectures on the ritual.

Like Dōhan, Myōe advocated the Mantra of Light as a simple, accessible practice available not only to the priesthood and nobility but all people. At first most of Myōe's concern lay with the Mantra and not with the empowerment and use of the sand. References to the sand began appearing sometime around 1227, just five years before his death, but by the end the great importance Myōe placed on the sand is clearly evident.[34] As Ueda Reijō states, "This method [of using the sand] in our country [Japan] seems first to have been advocated by Myōe Shōnin (High Priest Myōe)."[35]

Toganoo Shōun provides the following description of the ritual sequence involved in Myōe's empowering the sand:

At the beginning of the Doshakaji Ritual (Ritual of Empowering the Sand), each of the ritually purified monks makes seven mudrās and empowers the sand while reciting the Mantra of Light. These mudrās are said to have been revealed to [Myōe] Kōben personally by the Bodhisattva Mañjuśrī on Mount Makio and were to have been made while reciting the Mantra of Light as follows:

1. *Oṃ bhuh khaṃ amogha*—Wisdom Fist Mudrā [both hands in a fist with the right hand above the left, except that the right hand fist grabs the index finger of the left]
2. *Vairocana*—Outer Five-Pronged Vajra Mudrā
3. *Mahāmudrā*—Five-Colored Rays of the Light Mudrā, which is identical to the Bestowing Fearlessness Mudrā [right hand facing out near right shoulder, fingers together]
4. *Maṇi*—Maṇi Jewel Mudrā: an outer fist with two middle fingers in the shape of a jewel
5. *Padma*—Amitābha Mudrā: an outer fist with the two middle fingers in the shape of a lotus
6. *Jvala*—Wisdom Fist Mudrā
7. *Pravarttaya hūṃ*—Eight-Petaled Lotus Mudrā [hands facing each other; wrists, thumbs, and pinkies touching, with all fingers slightly separated to form an upward cup-like lotus blossom][36]

Myōe's use of the sand eventually became central to his advocacy of the Mantra of Light because Myōe saw the efficacy of the sand as a means of extending all the benefits of the mantra to everyone, lay or ordained, male or female. The sand thus signified two kinds of inclusivity: temporal inclusivity for effects in this life as well as the next, and social inclusivity of gender, social, and religious status.

Once the sand had been empowered, it could be sprinkled on corpses and graves, or it could be given to the ill and stricken to cure various ailments and to provide spiritual relief from the burden of evil karma. Although the full ritual of the mantra may have been quite involved, Toganoo's description of the mudrās indicates that the sand did not require elaborate ritual for it to take effect. As long as the sand was maintained in a ritually purified container, it retained its power and could be used at any time. How this empowered sand actually worked is another matter; the logic of its efficacy is examined later in this book.

Myōe used the mantra in several ways: in the complex rituals of a deity yoga, through which the mystic powers of the buddhas and bodhisattvas entered into the practitioner; in funeral rites; in the preparation of sand for alleviating karmic suffering, both physical and mental, in this life and the next; and in simple recitations as part of the daily monastic regimen at Kōzanji where Myōe served as abbot.

•

EIZON AND THE MANTRA OF LIGHT

THE SHINGON MONK Eizon (1201–90), also known as Kōshō Bosatsu (Bodhisattva Righteous Revival) according to the posthumous title given under imperial decree, was a later contemporary of Myōe and well known for his contributions in four areas: the revival of the precepts, a theme with which Myōe was also concerned; the protection of the state; the revival of the order of nuns;[37] and what might be characterized as social welfare activities involving criminals and outcasts, through attending to their physical and material needs as well as administering

precepts and otherwise propagating the dharma among these groups.
Eizon used the Mantra of Light as well as longer incantations including
dhāraṇīs so as to complement the administration of precepts.
Administering the precepts was designed to initiate and instruct people
in "right living," the moral conduct becoming of a Buddhist and con-
ducive to enlightenment; the Mantra of Light was the necessary inspiration and antidote to the karmic evil of the times and the particular
plight of outcasts and criminals, who were regarded as especially "defiled."

Eizon propagated the practice of the Mantra of Light by institut-
ing an annual seven-day assembly for chanting the mantra, the Kōmyō
Shingon-e (Mantra of Light Assembly), which over time grew to be a
major event held at Saidaiji of Nara. As Ryūichi Abe notes, at first the
service was designed to memorialize the deceased members of his order,
their relatives, and patrons of the order. This became an annual event that
was key to the broadening influence of Eizon's movement.[38]

Tanaka Kaiō states, "On the fourteenth day of the tenth month of
1264, [Eizon instituted the annual] seven-day assembly of engaging in the
esoteric cultivation of the uninterrupted chanting of the Mantra of
Light…which since then has become standard practice and continues
to this day."[39]

The following excerpt from the *ganmon*, or vow-decree, dictated
by Eizon to his disciple Shōkai in 1265, conveys Eizon's sense of the
Mantra of Light as the fundamental expression of Śākyamuni's enlightenment.

> In the southern province in the great nation of Japan at Saidaiji, Ga'un
> Shamon Eizon and others were united in placing their palms together
> and in unison reciting that all of them took refuge in the buddha-
> treasure, all took refuge in the dharma-treasure, and all took refuge
> in the three treasures.
>
> Then he said, as for the Mantra of Light of the Great Baptism of
> the Buddha Vairocana of the Unfailing Rope Snare, when our orig-
> inal master the Tathāgata Śākyamuni was still at the causal stage [of

bodhisattvahood],[40] he concentrated his mind [on this mantra] and illuminated ten quintillion worlds by releasing innumerable, boundless rays of light. He vanquished the armies of Mara the Tempter and liberated all sentient beings. He realized the stage of buddhahood by single-mindedly relying on the power of this divine incantation. This [was realized] with the wisdom of the dharma-realm as its basis.

The moon attains its pristine state of equality in the illumination of its great circular mirror[-like character]. Dewdrops glisten with the hue of the *mani* jewel. The fine white hairs in the brow of the great compassionate Kannon (Skt. *Avalokiteśvara*) sparkle as he expounds this mantra. The Tathāgata Vairocana expounds this mantra and pours the jeweled light on the heads [of all beings].

It goes without saying that all sins are eliminated just as the morning sun evaporates the dew; [the mantra's] benefits are incalculable.[41]

Despite all that Eizon did to propagate the Mantra of Light, his focus on the single annual assembly, which was primarily a memorial service, and on the mantra itself rather than on the sand, signaled somewhat of a return to earlier practices. Eventually, it would be the sand that would become the mantra's vehicle of greater participation, thus indicating Myōe's pivotal role. Within Shingon circles, however, Eizon was better known and therefore more renowned for his role in advancing the practice of this mantra.

•

THE MANTRA OF LIGHT IN THE LATE KAMAKURA AND BEYOND

SUCH EMINENT MONKS as Mujū Ichien (1226–1312) and Yoshida Kenkō (ca. 1283–1350) attested to the increasing popularity of the Mantra of Light. In an interesting reversal of earlier practice in which the likes of Genshin advocated the Mantra of Light as auxiliary or secondary to Amida *nembutsu,* by the thirteenth century there were Pure Land monks who in the context of funerals advocated the Mantra of Light rather than the *nembutsu.* As Mujū states,

When Jōganbō (1168–1251) of Takedani in Daigo, a noted scholar of the Jōdo sect, was asked by the emperor for the best method to console the spirits of the dead, he recommended the Jewel-Box Spell (Hōkyōin Darani) and the Mantra of Light. He defended this view against the criticism of a disciple who said that as a teacher of Pure Land doctrine he should not praise the methods of another sect. The *Sutra of the Unfailing Rope Snare* (Ch. *Bukong zhuansuo jing*), where the Mantra of Light is revealed, states that if it is chanted while sand is sprinkled on the body of a dead person, the spirit of the dead person will be born in Amida's Land of Bliss. Such written proof is not available concerning the efficacy of the *nembutsu* in these circumstances, and one should not reply to the emperor without written proof.... The Shingon and *nembutsu* teachings are compatible. It is said that at the present time, members of the Seizan branch of the Jōdo sect study Shingon.[42]

Initially, this popularity was centered on funerary rites; only later would it become one of the most widespread practices of Shingon Buddhism. The vehicle of this popularity would not be primarily Eizon's annual assembly but the flexible application of the sand as first fully articulated by Myōe.

•

ICONOGRAPHIC REPRESENTATIONS FROM THE NARA TO THE KAMAKURA

IN TERMS OF the iconography, it is difficult to establish hard evidence for the connections between the Mantra of Light and images from medieval Japanese Buddhist history. The main deities for the mantra—Mahāvairocana of the mandalas of the Nondual Dharma-Nature, the Diamond-Realm, and Womb-Realm; Amida; and Fukūken-jaku Kannon (Bodhisattva of Compassion of the Unfailing Rope Snare; Skt. *Amoghapāśa Avalokitesvara*)—were all objects of worship common to different sects and practices.[43] In most cases there is not enough documentary evidence to establish a specific connection with the Mantra of Light.

Nevertheless, Fukūkenjaku Kannon has particularly strong associations with the Mantra of Light. This due to the fact that (1) he is specifically featured in *The Sutra of the Mantra of Divine Transformation of the Unfailing Rope Snare* (Ch. *Bukong zhuansuo shenbian zhenyan jing*), translated by Bodhiruci, as well as in related sources,[44] and (2) this deity is not as widespread as Amida or Mahāvairocana as the object of devotion, either textually or institutionally. Fukūkenjaku Kannon appears wearing a deerskin wrap and for this reason is also known as the Rokuhi Kannon (Deerskin Kannon). He is one of the *henge Kannon* (Transformation-Kannon), so called because his appearance has been transformed in order to bring forth various salvific powers, and often manifests with one or three heads and two, four, or eight arms. Typical of Japanese representations is the main deity of the Hokkedō at Tōdaiji, a single-faced, three-eyed, eight-armed statue made by the *datsukanshitsu* (evacuated dry lacquer) method.[45] Apart from this there is a Nara Period statue at Kōfukuji and a Heian Period statue at Kōryūji. The statue at Kōfukuji was lost in the great fire of 1180 and recreated by Kōkei at the beginning of the Kamakura Period. The fact that Myōe is known to have frequented Tōdaiji and Kōfukuji, both in Nara, indicates that he had occasion to worship before these statues.

One of the most significant local representations of the Fukūkenjaku Kannon, however, is not associated with any concrete image or statue but with the kami of the Kasuga Shrine, also in Nara, with which Myōe had close ties. Worship at the Kasuga Shrine follows the Japanese practice of *honji suijaku*, essence and manifestation, wherein a particular kami is regarded as the manifestation of a Buddhist deity as its essence. *Honji suijaku* literally means "fundamental ground and flowing traces," and this conveys better the organic relation between the kami and the buddha or bodhisattva as its "ground"—and we will return to a more detailed examination of this notion later. It was not unusual for the Buddhist "ground" of the kami to change identities or even to have dual identities. This was the case with the kami of the

Kasuga Shrine, which was associated with two deities, the Buddha Śākya-muni and the Fukūkenjaku Kannon.

Myōe was intensely devoted to both Śākyamuni and the Fukūken-jaku Kannon, and the presence of the latter as the deity in not only Kasuga but also the temples of Tōdaiji and Kōfukuji would have formed a natural source of inspiration for Myōe's practice of the Mantra of Light. All three institutions were also intimately related to the Fujiwara clan: The Kasuga Shrine was the exclusive clan shrine of the Fujiwara. Kōfukuji was founded in honor of the original Fujiwara, Katamari, and the abbot was always a Fujiwara. Tōdaiji, the center of Buddhism as the state re-ligion, was founded under the influence of the Fujiwara. The Mantra of Light had often gained impetus at the instigation of the Fujiwara, ei-ther as the deceased at a funeral or as the monk performing the ritual. It might well be possible, then, to view Myōe's practice of the Mantra of Light partly as the crystallization of Fujiwara influence both in terms of the history of its practice and as the vehicle of clan representation through the deity of the Fukūkenjaku Kannon.

•

IN RETROSPECT

KŪKAI FIRST BROUGHT to Japan the sacred texts of the Mantra of Light, but it would be left to others to find its applications. At first, it was invoked at funerals and memorial services as a means of relieving the karmic burdens of nobility in the afterlife. As it gained increasing recog-nition, it was used to cure illnesses and to propel the practitioner to en-lightenment in this life. Then, Shōkaku helped to integrate the various functions of the mantra, and Jōkai helped to regularize the practice; his disciple Jōken codified the ritual practices in textual form.

In the Kamakura Period Dōhan advocated the Mantra of Light as a simple practice accessible to all. Myōe's implementation represented a piv-otal turning point as he emphasized the efficacy of the sand for the living and the dead, lay and ordained, men and women. Myōe demonstrated that the sand was easily applied and transportable across all kinds of cultural boundaries. Eizon also propagated the practice of the Mantra of Light as a vehicle of his religious activities that carried him into the social arena. By focusing on the Kōmyō Shingon-e, the annual memorial assembly focused on chanting the mantra, however, he tended to reemphasize its funerary function.

From quite early on, both Tendai and Shingon monks engaged in its practice, and the practice only grew as time passed, so much so that monks such as Jōganbō who were followers of Hōnen's Pure Land movement also adopted it. For other forms of practice, such as those of Zen and Pure Land *nembutsu,* the Japanese adopted and adapted Chinese forms that had been well established on the continent for some time. The Mantra of Light, however, was introduced to Japan not long after the initial translations into Chinese were made by Bodhiruci and Amoghavajra, and the practice reached a level of popularity in Japan that may have never been attained elsewhere in East Asia.

Today, the Mantra of Light is one of the most important and widely practiced mantras in Japanese Shingon. The use of sand, which has become integral to its application and the mantra, has been incorporated into the contemporary practices of other schools including Tendai and Zen.[46] The specifics of this practice in other sects remains obscure because the Mantra of Light is treated as an esoteric transmission. In Sōtō Zen, for example, all monks ordained with full teaching authority are taught the mantra as an oral esoteric tradition. Due to its esoteric nature, no textual evidence exists for this. Yet, Japanese Sōtō monks overseas have brought this practice to the West, including the United States, with hardly any notice. A history of the Mantra of Light since the Kamakura Period will have to await further study, but this brief accounting of its early history should suffice to indicate its importance for our understanding of Buddhism and the pivotal role played by Myōe in its formulation and implementation.

•

1   See, for example, Fujita Kōtatsu, *Genshi Jōdo shisō no kenkyū* (Tokyo: Iwanami Shoten, 1970); and Alice Getty, *The Gods of Northern Buddhism: Their History and Iconography* (New York: Dover, 1988). Sōhō Machida has summarized some of the findings regarding the origins of Amitābha symbology in his "Life and Light, the Infinite: A Historical and Philological Analysis of the Amida Cult," *Sino-Platonic Papers* 9 (December 1988).

2   My remarks here are focused on Amitābha since, with respect to the Pure Land, the Mantra of Light is associated with this Buddha of Infinite Light rather than Amitāyus, the Buddha of Eternal Life. Although in East Asia Amitābha and Amitāyus were often combined into the single Buddha Amitofo or Amida in China or Japan, respectively, other terms differentiating the two continued to be used, such as Muryōju Nyorai and Mugekō Nyorai, Japanese for Tathāgata of Eternal Life and Tathāgata of Unhindered Light, respectively. Much of what can be said about Amitābha can also be applied to Amitāyus.

Kenneth Tanaka provides a helpful summary of findings regarding the scriptural records of Amitābha in his *The Dawn of Chinese Pure Land Buddhist Doctrine: Ching-ying Hui-yüan's Commentary on the Visualization Sutra* (Albany: State University of New York Press, 1990), 1–9.

3   For a summary of these issues see ibid., 1–19.

4   Ibid., 3.

5   Gregory Schopen has identified several of these sources and provided an analysis of this phenomenon in his "Sukhāvatī as a Generalized Religious Goal in Sanskrit Mahāyāna Literature," *Indo-Iranian Journal* 19 (1977): 170–210.

6   Ibid., 199.

7   Schopen suggests that the dissemination of Sukhāvatī as a generalized religious goal independent of any actual Amitābha cult took place not long after the appearance of the *Larger Sukhāvatīvyūha-sūtra*. He further suggests this as a factor contributing to the nonappearance or disappearance of a large Amitābha following in India (ibid., 201–205).

8   T, 20:227, #1092. Information regarding Chinese sources in this and the following paragraphs were gleaned from *Bussho kaisetsu daijiten,* ed. Ono Genmyō (Tokyo: Daitō Shuppansha, 1938), 8:185–188, 335.

9   The asterisk indicates a Sanskrit title reconstructed from later translations, in this case Chinese.

10 T, 19:606, #1002.

11 T, 20:432, #1098. For a detailed discussion of the origins of the *Guangming zhenyan yigui,* see Tanaka Kaiō, *Kōmyō Shingon shūsei* (Kisarazu, Japan: Tokuzōji Shuppanbu, 1968), 47–52; and Taira Masayuki, *Nihon chusei no shakai to shūkyō* (Tokyo: Hanawa Shobō, 1992), 402.

12 T, 20:421, #1097.

13 T, 20:409, #1096.

14 *Bussho kaisetsu daijiten,* 9:185.

[15] There has been a paucity of scholarship on Chinese esoteric Buddhism, and future research may reveal that the practice of the Mantra of Light was more widespread than current scholarship shows.

[16] Amoghavajra's translation is listed in Kūkai's *Goshōrai mokuroku* (Catalogue of Sutras and Ritual Implements That Came from the Continent). See Taira, *Nihon chūsei no shakai to shūkyō*, 402. Kūkai studied with Amoghavajra's successor Huiguo.

[17] I am indebted to the following sources for information regarding the practice of the Mantra of Light in Japan prior to the time of Myōe as described in the following paragraphs: Tanaka, *Kōmyō Shingon shūsei* (1958), 67–72; Toganoo Shōun, "Shingon: The Japanese Tantric Tradition," trans. Leo Pruden (unpublished), 287–298, originally published as *Himitsu jisō no kenkyū* (Wakayama-ken Koyasan: Koyasan Daigaku Shuppanbu, 1940).

[18] In all of the documents containing Myōe's statements that are examined in this study, there are only two brief references to Kūkai. In the *Kōgonku gishaku chōjūki*, Myōe is said to have made a reference to Kūkai's *Jūjūshinron* (Ten Stages of the Abiding Mind), and in the *Kyakuhai mōki*, he is said to have studied the teachings of Kūkai.

[19] Tanaka, *Kōmyō Shingon shūsei*, 63.

[20] *Eshin sōzu zenshū*, ed. Eizan Gakuin (Kyoto: Shibunkaku, 1971) 1:341–342, 350; cited in Koizumi Haruaki, "Myōe Shōnin kankei kikigakirui no Bukkyō-shigakuteki ichizuke," MSS, 3:743–744.

[21] "Taimitsu," a term applied by modern Japanese scholars, refers to the incorporation of Shingon esoteric practices and ideas into the Japanese Tendai school. I have not translated this term, which means roughly "Tendai esotericism," because it does not refer so much to an elite, esoteric lineage within the Tendai as it does to the appropriation of Shingon ritual and doctrine for a variety of complex ideological reasons. Eventually, however, Shingon scholars also began to use the term "Taimitsu" in what they saw as the legitimate transmission of esoteric traditions within the Shingon, the "Tōmitsu," the latter so named because the center of much of the formalization of Shingon ritual took place at Tōji (and not the official seat of the Shingon school on Mount Kōya).

[22] NBSJ, 347a.

[23] NBSJ, 104b.

[24] NBSJ, 241b.

[25] NBSJ, 234c.

[26] According to the NBSJ, 234b, Jōkai lived from 1074 to 1149. However, Toganoo Shōun has him performing the ritual at the Ninshōden in 1159 ("Shingon: Japanese Tantric Tradition," 292–293).

[27] The three mystic powers are explained in detail in the next chapter.

[28] Toganoo, "Shingon: Japanese Tantric Tradition," 180–181.

[29] SAZ, 2:74.

[30] NBSJ, 371c, 326b.

[31] Tanaka, *Kōmyō Shingon shūsei*, 68.

[32] Nichizō: Shin 74, 107a; cited in Sueki Fumihiko, *Kamakura Bukkyō keisei ron* (Kyoto: Hōzōkan, 1998), 257–258.

[33] See "Appendix: Works on the Mantra of Light by Myōe."

34 According to the hagiographic records of the *Kōzanji Myōe Shōnin gyōjō* (The Acts of Myōe Shōnin of Kōzanji), he first began the use of the sand in 1228 (MSS, 1:60; cited in Sueki, *Kamakura Bukkyō keisei ron,* 267). As Sueki Fumihiko notes, however, since the *Kōmyō Shingon kaji dosha gi* (The Significance of the Mystic Power of the Sand and the Mantra of Light), composed in 1227, records Myōe's use of the sand, his practice of empowering the sand must have begun earlier (SAZ, 2:15–54. See Sueki, 267).

35 Ueda Reijō, *Shingon mikkyō jisō gaisetsu—shosonhō, kanjōbu (jō)* (Kyoto: Dōbōsha, 1989), 367.

36 *Makio Myōe Shōnin shichijū'in kuden,* transcribed by Raiyū; cited in Toganoo, *Himitsu jisō no kenkyū,* 205. Translation adapted from Toganoo, "Shingon: Japanese Tantric Tradition," 300–301.

37 Eizon's work in these areas is well known. However, Ryūichi Abe's study of Eizon provides a new perspective on his work to revive the nuns' order. Beyond rebuilding nunneries, ordaining nuns, and authenticating their attainments through the usual monastic hierarchy, Eizon also oversaw the administration of the *dembō kanjō,* the highest level of attainment in the Shingon school, granting thereby independent authority to the highest ranking nuns. This point was made by Ryūichi Abe, "Mantra, Hinin, and the Feminine: On the Salvational Strategies of Myōe and Eizon," presentation at the 1999 Evans-Wentz Conference, "Buddhist Priests, Kings, and Marginals: Medieval Japanese Buddhism," Stanford University, May 29, 1999.

38 Ryūichi, "Mantra, Hinin, and the Feminine."

39 Tanaka, *Kōmyō Shingon shūsei,* 88.

40 "Causal stage" (Jpn. *in'i*) refers to the stage of bodhisattvahood as the cause of becoming a buddha.

41 Tanaka, *Kōmyō Shingon shūsei,* 85–86.

42 Translation adapted from Robert E. Morell, *Sand and Pebbles (*Shasekishū*): The Tales of Mujū Ichien— A Voice for Pluralism in Kamakura Buddhism* (Albany: SUNY Press, 1985), 118. Yoshida Kenkō recounts the same episode in his *Tsurezure gusa;* see Donald Keene, trans., *Essays in Idleness: The Tsurezuregusa of Kenkō* (New York: Columbia University Press, 1967), 184.

43 Tanaka, *Kōmyō Shingon shūsei,* 71–72.

44 The information in this and the next paragraph has been gleaned from the entry on Fukū Kenjaku Kannon in IBJ, 687a.

45 KOJ, s.v. *"kanshitsu,"* 577a.

46 Tanaka, *Kōmyō Shingon shūsei,* 55.

CHAPTER 2

KNOWLEDGE OF ENLIGHTENMENT AND RELIGIOUS AUTHORITY

It is not what you know that counts, but how you know it.

THE RELATIONSHIP BETWEEN what enlightenment is and how one comes to know it is at once simple and complex. Anyone seeking to study Buddhism today can go to the bookstore, library, or museum, browse the Internet, take a class at the local college or university, visit a Buddhist temple or center, or attend a public lecture by a Buddhist priest, scholar, or museum curator, and so forth. Unlike knowledge of matters based primarily on information or on the intellect, however, knowledge concerning enlightenment requires the further step of engaging in practice. Although there are books or manuals about meditation, mantras, and other Buddhist practices, study under the guidance of a qualified master is generally regarded as necessary for proper cultivation of the Buddhist path. In the West, it is not difficult to obtain instruction from recognized masters and teachers from Buddhist sects originating all over Asia. In such an open society, theoretically all one needs is a sincere commitment to practice in order to attain enlightenment.

In traditional Asian societies including medieval Japan, such was not the case. Women were not allowed in major centers of Buddhist learning. Those who came from karmically "impure" backgrounds, who engaged in occupations deriving income from the death of sentient beings such as hunting, fishing, grave-digging, and weapon-smithing were likewise excluded. Generally, only members of the aristocracy and nobility had access to the literacy and social connections required to study at major temples and monasteries. Even then, one could obtain copies of sacred scriptures—sutras and commentaries—only by permission of the priest in charge and by hand-copying them using brush and ink. Deciphering the meaning of these texts further required years of study and practice under a teacher. In esoteric traditions such as those of the Shingon, higher stages of practice, and thus higher stages of knowledge, required confidential, secret initiations at the hands of a qualified *ajari,* or master.

Although many of these hierarchical structures of religious authority and knowledge remain in place even in today's marketplace of religious ideas and practices, a far greater number blocked the path to enlightenment in medieval Japan. Thus, the knowledge of enlightenment cannot be treated apart from matters of religious authority.

The question of religious authority was an especially pressing issue for Myōe. He believed that he lived in a time of *mappō,* the final degenerate age of the dharma, the culmination of millennia of devolution in Buddhist understanding, stranded in a tiny island nation far removed from the birthplace and center of Buddhism, India. So isolated did he perceive himself to be, he declared that no one in Japan was qualified to transmit the knowledge of enlightenment to him. He became so desperate that twice he made elaborate plans to leave Japan and travel to India, only to abandon his dreams at the last minute. As we shall see, the Mantra of Light became for him a key means to overcome the gap that lay between what he considered the authentic practice of the dharma and his perceived historical situation.

Traditionally, three interrelated triads have defined the framework of Buddhist knowledge and practice: the three treasures (buddha, dharma, and sangha) as the context of practice; the three baskets of sacred literature (sutra, śāstra, and vinaya) as the sources of knowledge; and the three learnings (monastic precepts, meditation, and wisdom) with enlightenment as their culmination. Without entry into the sangha, one could not meet the buddha and receive his teachings, the dharma. With the historical Buddha long gone, the three baskets of sutra, śāstra, and vinaya (words of the Buddha, commentaries, and monastic regulations) became the critical source of the dharma. Dharma, in turn, was internalized and embodied through the three learnings. Historical continuity with the Buddha was maintained through lineage. Each temple within each branch of the various sects has lineage charts that trace the transmission of enlightenment from one master to another all the way back to the Buddha Śākyamuni. In many sects, recitation of the names of this purportedly unbroken lineage is part of the daily liturgy.

In East Asia, different schools or sects developed based on different sutras,[1] and various masters within their lineages composed commentaries based on the particular sutra or group of sutras considered to transmit the essence of the Buddha's enlightenment. Thus, there developed traditions of intellectual and personal lineages, of doctrinal orthodoxy and embodied orthopraxy, and of intellectual continuity through personal transmission. The one-to-one transmission from master to disciple carried not just individual significance but formed the conduit to communal, institutional sanction, authority, and knowledge. With each transmission, the three baskets, three treasures, and three learnings were all entrusted to the succeeding generation—including mentorship or transmission of religious virtues; robes, rank, and institutionalized charisma; and documents and knowledge pertaining to everything from the workings of doctrine and institutional offices to the cleaning of toilets. In many ways, the master-disciple transmission crystallized the transmission of all components of tradition as a whole.

Just as there is a genealogical lineage in biological families, there is a genealogical lineage in the Buddhist family of each sect. In Shingon, the term *shuzoku* (Skt. *gotra*), signifying "family," is used to denote the community of each cosmic buddha. Myōe describes the Mantra of Light as a means of joining the buddhas' families, and of expressing familial connection to the buddhas: "By maintaining this mantra, foolish, ordinary beings fulfill the immeasurable virtues of the tathāgatas, transcending the realm of foolish beings and followers of the two vehicles [of Hīnayāna Buddhism]. Thus, they join the jewel of the family of the tathāgatas. The first character [*shu*] of [the Sino-Japanese compound] *shuzoku*, 'family,' refers to species, and the second [*zoku*], to genus."[2]

•

LINEAGE—CONTINUITY AND DISCONTINUITY

IN CONTRAST WITH religions where only one ultimate savior appears in this world, Mahāyāna Buddhism depends upon the unbroken succession of adepts who transmit undiminished the enlightenment of the Buddha. In terms of the actualities of history, however, there have inevitably been twists and turns in the stories of succession. The most thorough research to date has been done on Zen (Ch. *Chan*) Buddhism. Current scholarship indicates that the accounts of master-disciple transmission involving such key figures as the founder Bodhidharma and Sixth Patriarch Huineng are at least partly legendary, and that records of transmission have often been subject to amplification and distortion.[3]

During the Kamakura Period, the problem of lineage became acute as increasing numbers of learned monks no longer had faith in the established lineages. The best-known accounts involve those who studied at the Tendai headquarters on Mount Hiei and left to found new lineages that eventually became the basis of some of the largest sects of Japanese Buddhism. The problem faced by these renegade figures was twofold: First, one had to find a source of religious authority alternative to the existing monks, who were perceived to be less than enlightened; second, once a new source was found, one had to establish the legitimacy of the new lineage.

Zen masters Eisai and Dōgen both traveled to China in search of authentic practice under recognized masters. Eisai went twice and returned from the second trip having received the Chan transmission of the Linji lineage of Xu'an Huaichang. His founding of Shōfukuji in 1191 is celebrated as the beginning of Rinzai Zen in Japan. Dōgen is said to have received the Chan transmission of the Caotong (Jpn. *Sōtō*) lineage of Rujing in 1225 at the age of twenty-five, when he realized "dropping off body-mind, body-mind dropping off" (Jpn. *shinjin datsuraku, datsuraku shinjin*). He returned to Japan in 1227 and eventually built the mountain monastery of Eiheiji, which is still the headquarters of the Sōtō sect today. Less well known is the Daruma school of Nōnin, who established his own Rinzai lineage in 1189 even before Eisai. Rather than travel to China himself, he sent two of his disciples to China with his understanding of enlightenment written in verse; they returned with the seal of approval of Zhuoan Deguang of Mount Ayuwang. Nōnin's movement was eventually outlawed by imperial decree, he himself was assassinated by his nephew, and his community of followers disintegrated. Recognition by Chinese authorities was not enough to guarantee the survival of his lineage, but Nōnin's case nevertheless illustrates the importance of obtaining official sanction for the legitimacy of one's own lineage.

In the case of Pure Land Buddhism, Hōnen, who like his counterparts in Zen Buddhism studied on Mount Hiei, also rejected his Tendai roots, comparing those who engaged in traditional meditative practices to a band of robbers. Rather than leave Japan physically, Hōnen took a literary journey to the continent, finding inspiration in the words of the Chinese Pure Land master Shandao (613–81).[4] Having read the entire Buddhist canon five times, he is said to have read the sections on Pure Land an additional three times. At the age of forty-three, reading a line from Shandao's *Commentary on the Sutra of the Meditation on the Buddha of Eternal Life* (Ch. *Guan wuliangshoufo jing shu*) exhorting him to focus single-mindedly on Amida Buddha, Hōnen's doubts dissolved, and for the rest of his life he followed the Pure Land practice of chanting the *nembutsu,* the Name of Amida Buddha. Shinran, putative founder of the Shin sect of Pure Land, did not have to look to continental sources for a lineage because he had his teacher Hōnen.

When the orthodoxy of their new Pure Land movements was called into question, Hōnen and Shinran formulated lineages of five and seven masters, respectively, seeking to demonstrate the legitimacy of their version of Buddhism and the community of their followers. That they traced these lineages back to recognized Japanese, Chinese, and Indian masters after the fact—that is, after they had already arrived at their understanding of Buddhism independently of actual face-to-face transmission from earlier teachers (excepting Shinran's encounter with Hōnen)—again demonstrates the importance that lineage held for the medieval Japanese.

For the purposes of articulating their visions of spiritual liberation, historical accuracy was not necessarily important; Hōnen, Shinran, Dōgen, and others are well known for their creative "misreadings" of sacred texts. Shinran turned a passage in Amida Buddha's Eighteenth Vow, found in the *Larger Sutra of Eternal Life,* from an exclusionary clause stating that those who had committed grave transgressions against the dharma could not be born in the Pure Land, into an inclusionary statement stating that those who had committed the same karmic evils were precisely the object of Amida's boundless compassion.[5] Dōgen took liberties with the syntax of the Chinese version of the *Nirvāṇa Sūtra;* what had previously been understood to read, "All beings *have* buddha-nature," he now read, "All beings *are* buddha-nature."[6] The latter reading accorded with his view that "practice *is* enlightenment," rather than that "practice leads to enlightenment" based on each person *having* the potential of buddha-nature.

Of course, much of the literature of the Mahāyāna including the sutras is built not on historical literal truths but on the idea of discerning the highest truth (Skt. *paramārtha-satya*) of emptiness beyond the artificiality of fixed ideas. Nevertheless, appeal to the language of lineage at least partly depends on historical grounding in the world of conventional truth (Skt. *saṃvṛti-satya*). Thus, questions about historical inaccuracies in the language of lineage might be used to raise issues about institutional legitimacy. In Pure Land Buddhism, Hōnen and Shinran attributed ideas to earlier Indian and Chinese masters that are now regarded as inaccurate. For example, there seems to be no historical basis for references to Pure Land Buddhism that Shinran ascribes to the Indian masters Nāgārjuna and Vasubandhu. In Zen Buddhism, Dōgen's accounts of his transmission from Rujing seem to vary with changes in Dōgen's own views.[7] Nevertheless, even in these cases, literal historical accuracy alone may not determine the legitimacy of lineage; as long as the highest spiritual truth takes priority over conventional historical truth, fidelity to the enlightening spirit of Indian and Chinese sources would outweigh literal fidelity. Such an appeal is precisely what we will see in Myōe's case, as he invokes transcendent, cosmic deities expressing the highest truth as the very source of immanent, earthly lineages.

Thus, there is a complex interplay between these two aspects of sacred lineage—as sources of theoretical or liberating knowledge and as sources of religious authority. What is said is distinct from, yet related to, who said it, both in meaning and the weight that it carries.

•

SCHOLARLY CONFUSION OVER QUESTIONS OF LINEAGE

ALTHOUGH MODERN SCHOLARSHIP has helped to uncover historical problems with the lineage accounts of various sects, scholars can also unwittingly fall into the trap of adopting unsupported assumptions about lineage. In particular, scholars have sometimes tended to confuse images of earlier sources as seen through the present with historical realities in the past. As William Bodiford states with respect to Zen studies, "Scholars writing about Zen, many of whom are themselves Zen

monks, naturally have been influenced by the self-image promoted by
the Zen school…. This has helped to engender an idealized image of
the classical Chinese teachers and of their initial Japanese students."[8]
Even when Japanese innovations were trumpeted, they were often presented as the essential expression of what had been received from China.[9]
As Bodiford observes, such scholarship has tended to portray Zen
Buddhism as a rather static and monolithic entity, thus failing to convey the actual conditions of changing circumstances:

> Most discussions of Japanese Zen proceed from the assumption that
> it can be explained best as a continuation of Chinese traditions, to-
> tally severed from the religious and cultural context of Japan. Such
> discussions follow the lead of early Japanese Zen leaders who strongly
> emphasized their connections to China…. [However,] we must bear
> in mind that Chinese traditions, the way in which these traditions
> were perceived by Japanese monks, and the actual conditions of
> Japanese Zen cannot automatically be equated.[10]

With regard to lineage, scholars still persist in assuming that the
important thing is to identify the authentic Chinese sources and then
to place a given Japanese figure within the context of the established
Chinese lineage; this is often done in such a manner as to actually begin
with a given Japanese figure and then to pose the question of lineage so
as to arrive at a preconceived answer. While the case of Zen Buddhism
has been most closely examined in this regard, this holds true for other
sects as well. It has certainly been the case with Myōe; for reasons given
above as well as others, this preconceived approach to defining Myōe's
sources of knowledge and authority has significant limitations.

•

MYŌE AND HIS LINEAGES

As Myōe was ordained in both the Kegon and Shingon, there
are lineage charts tracing his spiritual ancestry for both. During the early
part of his life, he devoted more of his time and energy to studying and

writing about Kegon thought rather than Shingon, and he was appointed abbot of Kōzanji in order to revive the fortunes of the Kegon. Most students of Myōe have therefore focused on his Kegon lineage and have paid little attention to his Shingon connections. Yet, in the final decade of his life he concentrated on the Mantra of Light, a Shingon practice. Nevertheless, due to scholarly biases even the Mantra of Light has been interpreted through the lens of his Kegon lineage. By reinterpreting the mantra through his Shingon inheritance, a different understanding of Myōe emerges, one that has broader implications for seeing how religious thought and practice meld in the synergy of the present moment.

Myōe's Kegon lineage. An outline of the scholarship on Myōe's Kegon inheritance will help us understand the limitations of focusing primarily on this lineage. Institutionally, Myōe entered the Kegon lineage by receiving the full monastic precepts at the ordination platform of Tōdaiji, the seat of the Kegon school, in 1189 at the age of sixteen.[11] He also began receiving formal instruction under a qualified Kegon master, Rinkanbō Shōsen, thus initiating his intellectual succession within the Kegon order. Yet, while he studied with various monks, Myōe ultimately found his Japanese teachers lacking and turned elsewhere to solidify his understanding.

Traditionally, Kegon thought traces its origins to Chinese Huayan, where the lineage begins with the first five patriarchs of Dushun (557–640), Zhiyan (602–68), Fazang (643–712), Chengguan (738–839), and Zongmi (780–841). Of these, Myōe refers several times to the work of Fazang, the great synthesizer of Huayan, but makes virtually no mention of the others. Instead, he makes extensive use of the work of the lay Huayan master Li Tongxuan (d. 730). Some have argued that Myōe thus took an idiosyncratic approach to Japanese Kegon thought and that the Kegon scholar-monk Gyōnen (1240–1321), who followed and documented the standard lineage of the first five Chinese patriarchs and beyond, was the one who transmitted the orthodox understanding in Japan.[12]

Recently, however, Sueki Fumihiko has argued that Li Tongxuan in fact represents mainstream Huayan thought and that thereby Myōe is following a well-established intellectual lineage.[13] George Tanabe attempted to clarify what is at stake by suggesting that Myōe, rather than being concerned with the status of Li's pedigree, became interested in his work because Li, like Myōe, sought to realize the vision of Huayan in practice rather than nit-pick over doctrinal matters. The *Flower Ornament Sutra* (Ch. *Huayan jing;* Jpn. *Kegon gyō;* Skt. *Avataṃsaka Sūtra*), the main sutra of Chinese Huayan and Japanese Kegon, is a massive work that is filled with images of light. According to Tanabe, Myōe turned to Li because he provided a way for Myōe to translate his many dreams and visions of light into a practical understanding of Huayan thought: "[Li's] appeal was not to reason but to the faculty of mind that translates internally created images [of light] into inner understanding.... It was this style of manipulating images that Myōe learned from Li."[14] Li's Huayan thought became an important source for Myōe's practice of the Samādhi of Contemplating the Buddha's Radiance *(Bukkōkan zammai),* a practice developed by Myōe prior to the period of his advocacy of the Mantra of Light.[15]

Tanabe's point is significant because he shifts the discussion from the orthodox legitimacy of Myōe's doctrinal lineage to his concern with the immediate practicalities of realization. Tanabe shows that the attempt to justify Myōe's Kegon interpretation by arguing for the orthodoxy of his lineage according to traditional accounts fails to grasp his use of sources. As Bodiford suggests in the case of Zen, some scholars may have fallen into preconceived notions of lineage in seeking to understand Myōe. This is particularly important to keep in mind with respect to the Mantra of Light; although Myōe may have drawn upon his Kegon heritage in formulating and implementing this practice, the Mantra of Light is also based in other sources, not the least of which is his Shingon background.

Myōe's Shingon lineage. Just as in the case of other sects and schools, Shingon has its own lineage charts, including Myōe's. Due to Kūkai's dominant role in the tradition, virtually all lineages within Japan trace their origins to him. Thus, Myōe appears as a sixteenth-generation descendent in Kūkai's lineage who received the transmission from Jōshin, who in turn was a key disciple of Kōnen, a fourteenth-generation descendent in Kūkai's main line of succession.[16]

In China, Tantric Buddhism was first introduced by the Indian monk Vajrabodhi (671–741), who translated key sutras, introduced methods of practice, and won the favor of many Chinese from the emperor on down. Vajrabodhi ordained Amoghavajra (705–74), a monk of North Indian and Central Asian descent. Amoghavajra traveled from China to India and returned with an enormous store of sacred scripture. This, of course, included the *Sutra of the Mantra of the Unfailing Rope Snare of the Buddha Vairocana's Great Baptism* with its exposition of the Mantra of Light, which he translated into Chinese.[17] He was a prolific translator, scholar, and practitioner who garnered the patronage of three successive Chinese emperors. His successor was Huiguo (746–805), the first native Chinese Tantric master and mentor to Kūkai (774–835).

When we turn to the case of India, however, the Tantric lineage quickly becomes more obscure. Vajrabodhi's master was Nāgabodhi, who in turn was tutored by Nāgārjuna. Now, Vajrabodhi lived during the seventh and eight centuries, and Nāgārjuna approximately during the second. This would mean that Nāgabodhi would have to have lived at least five hundred years. To make matters even more complicated, the Tantric Nāgārjuna, scholars now believe, differed from Nāgārjuna the Mādhyamika (Middle Way) dialectician, the first Mahāyāna exponent of emptiness.[18] Nāgabodhi, then, is a legendary figure of mythic proportions, and his master Nāgārjuna may also have been legendary.[19]

The Tantric Nāgārjuna's master was an even more mythical figure, Vajrasattva, who purportedly heard Mahāvairocana expound the dharma, compiled what he heard, and stored it in a great tower in southern India.

Mahāvairocana, the Great Sun Buddha, the most cosmic of cosmic buddhas, is the primal buddha at the head of the Tantric lineage and the
most mythical figure of all.

Unlike Zen and most other schools, then, Indian and Chinese
Tantric Buddhism, the ancestors to Japanese Shingon, do not appeal to
a purely historical lineage originating with the person of Buddha Śākya-
muni; instead they trace their ancestry to ever more legendary and mythic
figures until one reaches the cosmic scale of the Buddha Mahāvairocana.
This is also the case for Myōe's Kegon heritage; back up through
Vasubandhu and Nāgārjuna, the Kegon traces its lineage to human masters, but beyond that it shifts suddenly to the celestial bodhisattvas
Mañjuśrī and Samathabhadra and then, fortuitously for Myōe, to
Vairocana, short for Mahāvairocana.[20] Thus, the two lineages in which
Myōe was ordained both trace their lineages to the same cosmic buddha. This certainly seems to make it easier for Myōe to have viewed him-
self as uniquely situated to be empowered by Mahāvairocana's wisdom
and virtue.[21]

The three buddhabodies and the three mystic powers of the buddhas.
Despite the fact that Shingon tradition has conflated or blended the historical dimensions of lineage with those of the cosmic or mythical, it is
difficult to believe that the likes of Kūkai or Myōe thought of Mahāvairocana and Vajrasattva as historical personages akin to themselves. How,
then, did they conceive of the relationship between the cosmic dimensions of Mahāvairocana and the human figures who constituted their
immediate predecessors? Two key concepts provide important clues to
the answer: the theory of the three buddhabodies (Skt. *trikāya*) and the
three mystic powers *(sanmitsu kaji)*.

The theory of the three buddha bodies is a general Mahāyāna notion that distinguishes three levels of embodiment: the physical body,
the blissful body, and the dharma body (Skt. *nirmāṇakāya, saṃboghakāya,*
and *dharmakāya*). The *nirmāṇakāya,* meaning literally "transformation

body," is the body of form, or the physical body in human form; it changes, or transforms, from one life to the next. The *saṃboghakāya* is the body of bliss, or alternately, the body of recompense, so named because, when the accumulated merit of positive karma is recompensed or realized, the blissful body of the cosmic buddhas is manifest. The *dharmakāya*, or truth body, constitutes the deepest of the three levels of the buddhas' existence, equivalent to emptiness as such. Myōe's view of emptiness is examined in detail later on, but a brief word on the topic is in order here. Emptiness, meaning "empty of any fixed characteristics" (Skt. *alakṣaṇa*), is the highest or deepest level of reality; in and of itself it is colorless, odorless, formless, and so on. However, the act of being released from attachment to form, from emotional entanglement with preconceived ideas, is a blissful one. In personalized terms, it is the realization of emptiness manifest as the blissful body of liberation. Thus the practitioner who enters the samādhi of liberation realizes the bliss body of the cosmic buddhas, which in turn gives rise to bodhisattvas and other celestial beings. Myōe's *Chronicle of Dreams (Yume no ki)* contains numerous accounts of deep, blissful samādhi conveyed to him by various celestial beings. In Shingon Buddhism, the one exception is the Buddha Mahāvairocana who is regarded as the dharma body, not the bliss body, and as containing all other buddhas and bodhisattvas. Vairocana is similarly all-encompassing in Kegon Buddhism, wherein all phenomena interpenetrate,[22] and all deities are found in one another. Vairocana is merely the most cosmic expression of this vast web of interpenetration.

Since *kāya*, literally "body," here includes more than just the material body but the total embodied personality of the buddhas, *kāya* might be understood as "personhood" or "personality" as well as "body." *Dharmakāya*, for example, might be rendered "dharma personality" just as well as "dharma body." Thus embodied in the personality of the cosmic buddhas, the dharma takes shape as their virtues, as various aspects of wisdom and compassion. Myōe speaks repeatedly of these virtues as found in "the secret mantra [the Mantra of Light] that is used by all buddhas and bodhisattvas. All buddhas are included in the five [cosmic] buddhas,...[and t]heir virtues are contained in the five wisdoms.[23]

In Shingon esotericism, the mechanism by which the cosmic buddha personalities and their virtues infuse the personalities of the practitioner is the three mystic powers. As Myōe explains,

> When there are sentient beings who even hear just some of the syllables of this mantra, all of the virtues of the tathāgatas' great wisdom and compassion are bestowed on them. [In the Sino-Japanese compound *kaji*, "mystic power," the first character] *ka* signifies "adding" to sentient beings the virtue of the tathāgatas' great wisdom and compassion. [The second character] *ji* signifies that the tathāgatas "grasp and hold" the sentient beings. The meaning of ji, "to hold," should also be applied to the sentient beings [who hold what has been added to them].[24]

The "three mysteries" *(sanmitsu)* refers to the body, speech, and mind of the practitioner becoming infused with the body, speech, and mind of the buddhas. The mystery lies in the esoteric nature of this infusion. It is imperceptible to the conventional senses, that is, senses conditioned by conventional linear logic. The mystery of the buddhas' power yields only to those who are able to enter into and harness the samādhi of the cosmic buddhas. Thus, the dharma body or body of highest truth, synonymous with emptiness, is conveyed to the practitioner through the mystic empowerment of the buddhas.

In explaining the Mantra of Light, Myōe likens the action of the buddhas upon the practitioner to a master sculptor working on raw wood. Thus, for example, when one forms an esoteric hand gesture, or mudrā, in meditation, it is the buddhas working upon the body of the practitioner. When one intones the syllables, *"mahāmudrā"* (great mudrā), from the Mantra of Light, it is the buddhas chanting these syllables through the speech of the practitioner. The Tathāgata Vairocana contains the virtues or powers of all of the buddhas, and he leaves his imprint on the practitioner like a seal (mudrā) being pressed into wood.

Myōe explains the effect of Tathāgata Vairocana's mystic power by setting up the following dialogue.

QUESTION: What is the meaning of "great mudrā"?

ANSWER:

> It is to press on the hands. It is customary with respect to the mudrās that one press red clay on the hands; then the hands manifest the [proper] form [of the mudrā]. It is also like this in carving the image of the Buddha in wood. Anything carved into wood will manifest that shape, and this is called a mudrā or seal. It is like the fact that if one presses a piece of wood with the shape of a horse or an ox [carved into it], then the shape of a horse or an ox will appear. The unfailing great mudrā of the Tathāgata Vairocana signifies the Tathāgata, the one whose very being is great compassion, great wisdom, the various virtues.
>
> Thus, this Tathāgata impresses broad and great samādhi-wisdom and virtue on sentient beings like a wood-seal and makes manifest the virtue of great wisdom and compassion. That is why it is called the unfailing great mudrā of the Tathāgata Vairocana.[25]

In Shingon, Mahāvairocana, as the dharmakāya or body of truth, is regarded as the constant source of all buddha bodies, and all teachings are considered to come from Mahāvairocana. Whether one is studying an exoteric or esoteric source, there is always an esoteric level of understanding. When one discerns this esoteric level, one sees the source's true significance, including the origin of the source or teaching in Mahāvairocana.[26] Kūkai explains this with his notion of the dharma body expounding the dharma *(hosshin seppō),* wherein Mahāvairocana as the dharma body is continually expounding the deepest level of truth. Thus, what at first appears as a shallow, exoteric teaching reveals its profundity when seen in light of the body of truth. According to Myōe, the "profundity of the profound dharma is constant. The Shingon is profound because it expounds the shallow as profound."[27] No matter what the scriptural source is, to see the deepest level of dharma exposition, one only has to plumb its esoteric depths.

The authority of celestial beings. Myōe, having rejected the authority of existing historical lineages, could appeal to the cosmic dimension of Mahāvairocana's exposition at the level of the dharma body. Such concepts as the buddha bodies and the mystic power of the buddhas and their associated practices enabled Myōe to bring to life his own sense of belonging to the lineage of celestial beings. The appeal to the cosmic or mythic dimension within the existing Shingon view of lineage made it easier for him to take the next logical leap in terms of religious authority, which was to appeal directly to the buddhas and bodhisattvas, those divine figures who appeared so frequently in his thoughts, dreams, and visions. He may have been ordained in orthodox historical lineages, but he considered that the real dharma was transmitted to him by cosmic and celestial beings.

In the *Overview of the Zen School (Zenshū kōmoku)*, Myōe's disciple Shōjō addresses the problem of lineage, and he quotes directly from his master's own writings to confirm Myōe's celestial heritage.[28] After noting that the human master-to-disciple transmission is the basis for all of the lineages of Zen Buddhism, Shōjō sets up the following dialogue:

QUESTION: "From whom is your transmission [received]?"
ANSWER: "I received it from the holy man, my late master [Myōe]."
QUESTION: "From whom, then, is the holy man's transmission?"
[Shōjō answers by citing Myōe's own words from his *Kegon bukkō zammai kan meikan den:*] "I, a foolish monk, have been deeply fond of actual practice since my youth, and make nothing of floating splendor. Sometimes going deep into the mountains, sometimes living by the seashore, I made the wind in the pines my friend in meditation, and the bright moon a lamp for recitation. With flowing sweat and strings of tears, alone I recited, alone I practiced. To Mañjuśrī I turned and asked for wisdom and understanding; on Samantabhadra I relied in seeking

practice.... By the majesty of Maitreya Bodhisattva I regard him as my teacher of meditation."[29]

With the all-inclusive cosmologies of the Shingon and Kegon with Mahāvairocana as the center, circumference, and everything in between, as it were, virtually any celestial deity could infuse Myōe with its mystic power, empowering him with a charisma that transcended this world. Indeed, Myōe invoked all kinds of deities, including those mentioned above as well as other deities such as various expressions of Kannon, the bodhisattva of compassion of the Mantra of Light: "This Kannon is the result of uniting all sentient beings as one to make Kannon. All sentient beings attain virtue when they hear this Mantra of Light."[30] Indeed, even Mahāvairocana appeared before Myōe. He had the following dreams around 1221, just when he was beginning to focus all his energy on the Mantra of Light:

> Between four and six in the afternoon on the third day of the eleventh month, I went to sleep as planned. In a dream I saw the figure of the Buddha Vairocana [seen in meditative contemplation]. On either side of the image there were ornaments of golden beads strung together that shone forth from under the raiments draped over the ears.
>
> In a dream seen on the night of the sixth day of the eleventh month (during my early evening meditation when I wished to perform esoteric practices) there was a dignified and beautiful lady in a room. She was dressed exquisitely, but she showed no sign of worldly desire. I was in the same place, but I did not feel any affection for her. She was quite fond of me and did not wish to be separated. I ignored her and left. She still showed no sign of worldly desire. The lady was holding a mirror around which she wrapped some wire. She also had a large sword.
> *Interpretation:* The woman was Vairocana; she was no doubt the queen.[31]

The second dream is especially striking because Vairocana appears as a woman, "the queen," a matter to which we shall later return. For now, it is worth noting that Myōe "ignored her and left." Why he would leave the presence of the ultimate deity one can only guess. One might say that any concrete manifestation of Vairocana is not the true Vairocana of the dharma body. Paradoxically, only the unseen Vairocana can be grasped directly, in the midst of practice, because the dharma body is directly embodied in the mantra. Even if the dream-image is of an embodied Vairocana, if the deity is disembodied from the practitioner and objectified, this is not the true Vairocana that Myōe sought. Yet, it may be insufficient to examine this dream solely in terms of Myōe's religious thought. It can also be seen in terms of lineage and institutional authority, in which case a consideration of the social context will also be necessary.

In any case, the story of Myōe's lineage does not end here, for ultimately, he did not entirely abandon the earthly, historical lineage as a source of religious self-understanding. There was one teacher in this world whom Myōe recognized as his true master: the Buddha Śākyamuni. He longed so much for Śākyamuni that he considered himself to be the Buddha's long-forgotten orphan:

> Many centuries have passed since the Parinirvāṇa of the Tathāgata Śākyamuni, my great merciful father, my great blessed master. I, the inhabitant of this tiny land on the periphery of the great continent, the child of the teachings left [by the Buddha], have been abandoned by my merciful father, alone with no opportunity to escape from this burning house [called samsara].... Yet, in the long sleep [of ignorance] I gave rise to the mind of awakening,...aroused a great sense of compunction, with love for the merciful father, the Tathāgata Śākyamuni.[32]

Myōe sought to trace his lineage back to Śākyamuni, but finding that the human lineage had been broken by the ravages of *mappō,* the final degenerate age of the dharma, in medieval Japan, he described an arc, a leap over the chasms of time carried on the shoulders of celestial beings. How this leap was effected in such a way as to be convincing to the Buddhist institutions of his day is a matter to which we shall return.

•

SCRIPTURAL AUTHORITY

ANOTHER SOURCE OF AUTHORITY, closely related to that of
lineage, is scripture. Myōe was a voracious student of scriptural sources
including the traditional triad of sutra, śāstra, and vinaya. In writing
about the Mantra of Light, he drew upon the key sutra literature of the
Kegon and Shingon, such as the *Mahāvairocana Sūtra* and the *Flower
Ornament Sutra,* as well as the main sources regarding the Mantra of
Light available to him, the *Sutra of the Mantra of Divine Transformation
of the Unfailing Rope Snare* (Ch. *Bukong zhuansuo shenbian zhenyan
jing*),[33] translated by Bodhiruci and partially translated by Amoghavajra
as the *Sutra of the Mantra of the Unfailing Rope Snare of the Buddha
Vairocana's Great Baptism* (Ch. *Bukong zhuansuo piluzhenafa daguanding guangming zhenyan jing*).[34] In addition, Myōe drew upon the *Ritual
Protocols for he Mantra of Light* (Ch. *Guangming zhenyan yigui*),[35] a manual for the Mantra of Light (this work is now widely considered to be
apocryphal). The translation is attributed to Amoghavajra, but the work
was probably originally composed in Japan.

Myōe also gleaned ideas from other sources such as the Korean
work *The Playful Heart and the Path of Repose (Yusim Allakto),* another
apocryphon erroneously attributed to Wŏnhyo. There are other sources
Myōe cites that do not mention to the Mantra of Light, such as the
Vajrasamādhi Sutra, another apocryphon, probably of Korean origins,[36]
and the *Sūtra of the Ultimate Meaning of Principle* (Ch. *Liqu jing*),[37] an
important sutra in Chinese Tantric Buddhism and Japanese Shingon. In
one sense, the idea of apocrypha is an oxymoron in Mahāyāna Buddhism
because the whole corpus of Mahāyāna sutras was composed with the
idea that the highest truth of emptiness, expressing the true spirit of enlightenment, took priority over literal fidelity to the words of the Buddha.
Yet the fact that sutras continued to be manufactured in China, Korea,
and Japan with the pretense that they were of Indian origin shows that

scriptural authenticity was an issue.[38] In fact, in the well-established East
Asian practice of classifying the teachings *(kyōhan,* Ch. *panjiao),* different schools or sects of Buddhism have ranked one another in accordance
with a hierarchical view of the sutras. Each school places its own canonical sutra or sutras at the top and ranks the rest of the schools in accordance with its view of the authenticity and profundity of each sutra.

Myōe, however, generally did not subscribe to such a hierarchical
view and used his sources freely to formulate his own understanding of
the Mantra of Light. He pieced together his understanding from diverse
sources, and he justified his method of *bricolage* by appealing to precedent in his own Shingon tradition: "The doctrines of the Shingon are for
the most part at the level of the teachings of the three vehicles [of śrāvaka,
pratyekabuddha, and bodhisattva]. However, just as an artisan collects
odd pieces from here and there and creates something, so too do [these
sundry teachings of the various schools] become the functioning parts of
the esoteric school."[39] Just as in the case of lineage, Myōe seems to have
taken liberal license with his scriptural sources to formulate what he saw
as appropriate.

The practice of synthesizing new interpretations is nothing new;
however, more than a few of his contemporaries would have been uncom-
fortable with his open avowal that his chosen textual sources were cob-
bled together to fit the occasion.

•

THE THREE LEARNINGS

TRADITIONALLY, THE THREE LEARNINGS *(sangaku,* Skt.
triṇiśikṣāṇi) of precepts, meditation, and wisdom define the elements
of practice in Buddhism. They are often presented as a progression from
precepts to meditation and wisdom with enlightenment as the pinna-
cle. The Kamakura Period was a time that many saw as *mappō,* the degenerate age of the dharma, the third and final stage in a declining series.[40] The theory of the three declining stages of the dharma begins

with an initial period of five hundred or one thousand years following the death of the historical Buddha Śākyamuni. This was said to be the age of the true dharma *(shōbō),* during which scriptural study, practice, and enlightenment were regularly realized. During the next five hundred or one thousand years, the age of the so-called semblance dharma *(zōbō),* there was a semblance of study and practice but rarely enlightenment. In the age of the final dharma *(mappō),* widely held to last ten thousand years, a state of degeneracy settled in where only the superficial study of scriptures took place, and enlightenment was all but impossible. This concept of *mappō* described not only the failure of religious institutions but the breakdown of society as a whole, entailing the proliferation of crime, widespread famine and disease, threats to the integrity of the state, and, of course, undesirable destinations in the hereafter.

Myōe made clear his views on the degenerate condition of Buddhist practice on numerous occasions. The following are among his most pointed statements:

> If we priests were living in the age of the Buddha, we would never dare regard ourselves as equal to even the lowliest novice-monk. We should be ashamed, therefore, to put on airs of being great masters.
>
> Most monks these days envisage the buddha dharma they have chanced to learn not as the key to emancipation but as a means for attaining high rank, a trivial, contemptible thing.... What has become of Buddhist practice in this land, so remote from India, in these depraved latter days [of the final dharma]?[41]

Of the three learnings, people still had access to the scriptures, and there were still attempts at meditation. Yet when monks and nuns failed to observe the monastic precepts, their practice was like a tripod missing a leg. Thus in Myōe's opinion it was especially important to observe the precepts. Furthermore, the precepts were not merely the first step to mastering the other two learnings. Rather, they formed the cornerstone of practice and sustained one throughout the cultivation of the path. The precepts might seem like a stepping stone at first, but ultimately they are expressions of the enlightened lifestyle, and at the deepest level the three learnings are inseparable:

> Within the three learnings of precepts, meditation, and wisdom, the two dharmas of meditation and wisdom are profound and complex. The one gate of the precepts is the way to enter the buddha-dharma without too much ado. It stops the evil karma of sentient beings who are at the first gate of practice; it is not complex but easy. It is like a doctor who knows where the moxacautery points are and marks them.[42] As one reaches deeper levels, so too, do these precepts become more profound and [eventually] come to interpenetrate meditation and wisdom. Thus, it is said that the way is [one] with meditation and [one] with the precepts.[43]

As I have described in detail elsewhere, there was a movement during the Kamakura Period to revive the observance of the precepts.[44] As one of its proponents, Myōe is said to have uttered on his deathbed the words, "I come from among those who maintain the precepts."[45] In the historical context of the Kamakura Period, such a statement signified not merely Myōe's satisfaction with his individual attainment and religious authority but also a criticism of his times.

In order to implement the precepts in his own life and in the lives of his followers, Myōe made use of a wide range of resources.[46] These included (1) the classical precepts from early Buddhism, the 250 regulations for monks and 348 for nuns of the Dharmaguptaka Vinaya (Ch. *sifenlu*) that covered everything from rules of etiquette to offices held by the ordained, (2) the sutra precepts of the Nikaya literature that addressed basic rules of morality for both lay and ordained, (3) the fifty-eight bodhisattva precepts of the *Brahma-net Sutra* (Ch. *Fanwang jing*) that focused on the spirit of enlightenment, (4) the threefold pure precepts that were administered prior to the bodhisattva precepts, and (5) the *sanmaya* (Skt. *samaya*) precepts of the Shingon.

The *sanmaya* precepts, as explained in the previous chapter, are also known as the *bodaishin* (Skt. *bodhicitta*) precepts due to their emphasis on the mind of aspiration for enlightenment rather than on specific regulations regarding monastic behavior. In this regard they are similar to the bodhisattva precepts of the *Brahma-net Sutra* but are even less specific than the latter. Myōe also formulated his own set of monastic codes similar to the *shingi* of the Zen schools. Myōe's own codes for Kōzanji are examined in detail later.

The Mantra of Light, furthermore, went hand in hand with the precepts. In the age of the final dharma, when the practitioner was stained by the defilements of the age, one could not reverse the momentum of corruption on one's own. Faith in the cosmic buddhas, and the embodiment of this faith through the mantra, became the engine through which the cosmic forces of the buddhas could be harnessed to counteract the negative momentum of communal karma: "Eventually the precepts and the mantra arise together within the mind and form of the buddhadharma. If one is mindful of this [seed-]syllable [of the mantra], then one will realize the yoga of the main deity."[47]

Thus, just as the cosmic buddhas carved the seal of the mantra into the practitioner through their mystic power, so too, did they sculpt the ethical life of the practitioner through the precepts:

> Although we are but temporary manifestations of the five aggregates [forming the mind and body], that we are able to realize the wondrous fruit of the four wisdoms and three [buddha-]bodies means we are like things made of cypress. We should think of ourselves as pieces of cypress being fashioned into buddhas by those skillful artisans, the various buddhas, bodhisattvas, and spiritual guides. Their first act [in this capacity] is to bestow us with the ten major and forty-eight minor bodhisattva precepts.[48]

•

UNTANGLING THE STRANDS: AN ILLUSION

IN SEEKING TO UNTANGLE the influences that helped to shape Myōe's Buddhist thought and the sources of religious authority that he himself appealed to, one is confronted with a complex situation. On the one hand, he made use of the traditional categories of lineage, scripture, and practice, and he was certainly influenced by the various movements and trends of his day, including the rising popularity of Pure Land *nembutsu, mappō* sensibility, and precept revival. On the other hand, the sheer multiplicity of sources he drew upon, the improvisational character of his use of these sources, and the limitations of defining him in terms of traditional categories makes it difficult to define the parameters of his thought.

Some have even said that Myōe tried out so many different ideas and practices and changed them so often that he confused his disciples:

> As for Myōe Shōnin practicing the teachings of various buddhas and bodhisattvas, Master [Kōshū] said, "This priest did not limit himself to [the practices of one deity] but changed time and again trying out various deities until his disciples became confused. The priest would tell them that they would each enter the complete vehicle by following their own main practices; since the main practices differed, the complete vehicle was not singular. According to which deity should one manifest *samādhi?* [As there was no single right answer, he told them] the practices of the multitude of main deities were to be followed."[49]

Kōshū (1276–1350) was a Tendai monk who might have had some sectarian biases against Myōe, but his point is well taken. Some of Myōe's disciples may very well have been confused by the plethora of practices and ideals that were presented to them. This confusion may or may not have extended to Myōe himself.

If, however, as Bodiford suggests in the case of Zen, there are limits in Myōe's to applying the conventional idea of tracing intellectual and institutional lineages to earlier Japanese and continental sources, and if there are serious limitations to the attempt to define Myōe in terms of the external influences as well as traditional canonical sources such as the Vinaya, then how should one proceed in seeking to define the parameters of Myōe's thought as it relates to the Mantra of Light?

Perhaps part of the answer lies in the most obvious place: Myōe's thought itself. Over the last decade of his life, Myōe devoted much of his energy to the Mantra of Light—its practice, exposition, and propagation. The documents he composed, several of which are included here in translation, were meant to stand on their own, albeit within their historical milieu. Especially in the case of *Recommending Faith in the Mantra of Light* and its sequel, the *Supplement,* which were written for laypeople, he sought to formulate his understanding in succinct, accessible terms. And in the case of the *Lectures on the Significance of the Commentary on the Syllables of the Mantra of Light* we have a transcript of his lectures that effectively provides a commentary on his own work. This is not to say that the various genealogical influences on his work are unimportant, or that a linear view of external sources cannot add significant knowledge.

The particular problems and ambiguities associated with institutional and textual lineages, however, suggest that it might be helpful to look within Myōe's thought for the ways in which he attempted to lay the foundations. As we shall see in the next chapter, Myōe turned to the classical Mahāyāna notion of emptiness *(kū,* Skt. *śūnyatā)* as the intellectual basis of his Buddhist self-understanding.

•

1 Within East Asian Mahāyāna, only Zen Buddhism declares that its authority lies outside of the sutras; but then Zen Buddhism has invented its own sacred literature, the "sayings of the masters" *(goroku,* Ch. *yulu),* even going so far as to call one of them a sutra, the *Platform Sutra of the Sixth Patriarch.* See Philip Yampolsky, trans., *The Platform Sutra of Hui-neng* (New York: Columbia University Press, 1967).

2 *Kōmyō Shingon dosha kanjinki,* SAZ, 2:29.

3 See, for example, Bernard Faure, *The Will to Orthodoxy: A Critical Genealogy of Northern Chan Buddhism* (Stanford: Stanford University Press, 1997); John R. McRae, *The Northern School and the Formation of Early Ch'an Buddhism* (Honolulu: University of Hawai'i Press, 1986).

4 Harper Havelock Ellis and Ryūgaku Ishizuka, trans., *Hōnen the Buddhist Saint— His Life and Teaching, by Shunjō Hōin* (Kyoto: Chionin, 1925), 162–163.

5 *Passages on the Pure Land Way: A Translation of Shinran's* Jōdo monrui jushō, ed. Yoshifumi Ueda, trans. Dennis Hirota, Shin Buddhism Translation Series (Kyoto: Honganji International Center, 1982).

6   Dōgen, "Busshō," in *Shōbōgenzō*, Iwanami Bunkō 319-20, ed. Mizuno Yaeko (Tokyo: Iwanami Shoten, 1990), 72–73.

7   Carl Bielefeldt, "Recarving the Dragon: History and Dogma in the Study of Dōgen," in *Dōgen Studies*, ed. William LaFleur, Kuroda Institute Studies in East Asian Buddhism 2 (Honolulu: University of Hawai'i Press, 1985), 21–53.

8   Will Bodiford, *Sōtō Zen in Medieval Japan*. (Honolulu: University of Hawai'i Press, 1990), 3.

9   Ibid.

10 Ibid., ix–x. Tanaka Hisao, *Myōe* (Tokyo: Yoshikawa Kōbunkan, 1961), 15. For several centuries, the practice of the full Dharmaguptaka Vinaya, the classical monastic precepts that had been handed down from the earliest times, had gradually been falling into disuse. During the eleventh and twelfth centuries, a number of prominent monks sought to revive the practice of the full precepts, 250 for monks and 348 for nuns. Myōe was both a beneficiary of this revival as well as one of its major proponents.

11 Tanaka Hisao, *Myōe*, 15.

12 Kamata Shigeo, "*Nanto kyōgaku no shisōshiteki igi*," KKB, 528–569.

13 Sueki Fumihiko, *Kamakura Bukkyō keiseiron* (Kyoto: Hōzōkan, 1998), 218–219.

14 Tanabe, *Myōe the Dreamkeeper: Fantasy and Knowledge in Early Kamakura Buddhism* (Cambridge: Council on East Asian Studies, Harvard University, Harvard University Press, 1992), 150.

15 The transition between these two practices is evident in Myōe's *Kegon bukkō zammai kan hihōzō*, DNBZ, 13.

16 *Myōe Shōnin kankei kechimyaku shū*, MSS, 2:1131–1133.

17 *Bukong zhuansuo piluzhenafa daguanding guangming zhenyan jing*, T, 19:606, #1002.

18 The Mādhyamika philosopher Nāgārjuna is rendered as "Ryūju" (Ch. *Longshu)* in Sino-Japanese while the Tantric Nāgārjuna is rendered as "Ryūmyō" (Ch. *Longmeng*) in Sino-Japanese.

19 According to Kūkai's *Shingon fuhō den* (Record of the Transmission of the Shingon [Lineage]), Nāgabodhi is another name for Dharmagupta, who taught Śubhakarasiṃha (637–735), an Indian monk who studied Tantric Buddhism at the famed Nālandā Buddhist University and transmitted Indian Tantra to China (IBJ, 831a, 507a). There is now an argument that the Tantric Nāgārjuna lived much later, shortening Nāgabodhi's mythic longevity, but it is difficult to gather sufficient textual evidence to make the case conclusively either way.

20 *Kegon kechimyaku*, MSS, 2:1147–1149.

21 Vairocana and Mahāvairocana are not always synonymous. In Myōe's case, however, they would be. In both the *Flower Ornament Sutra* of the Kegon School and the *Mahāvairocana Sūtra of the Shingon*, Mahāvairocana appears as the buddha of the dharma body (body of the highest truth of emptiness) rather than the body of recompense or bliss (body of skillful means). A discussion of the theory of the buddha bodies follows the numeral for this endnote in the body of the text (IBJ, 682b).

22 dharma-realm of the mutual interpenetration of phenomena and phenomena: *jiji muge hokkai*, Ch. *shishi wu ai* (Chengguan, *Huayan fajie xuanjing*, T, 45:672–683, #1883).

23 *Kōmyō Shingon dosha kanjinki*, SAZ, 2:15.

24 *Kōgonku gishaku chōjūki*, MSS, 2:831.

25 Ibid., 814.

26 Kūkai, *Ben kenmitsu nikyō ron, Kōbō daishi zenshū* I, ed. Mikkyō Bunka Kenkyūjo (Osaka, Japan: Mikkyō Bunka Kenkyūjo, 1968), 474–505.

27 *Kōgonku gishaku chōjūki*, MSS, 2:852.

28 The fact that Myōe, a monk of the Kegon and Shingon, had a disciple studying the teachings of Zen is emblematic of Myōe's doctrinal inclusivity. According to Myōe's *Biography*, "In the Latter Age [of the buddha dharma] there is no one who grasps the entire truth. If there is something that one cannot understand by studying one's own school, then one may obtain the view [of the matter as taught in] the Zen school and thus benefit by consulting a Zen priest, or by relying on the Buddhist teachings, or [some other] person. Do not be confined to one-sided views." Cited in Kawai, *The Buddhist Priest Myōe*, 48.

29 The translation is excerpted from Tanabe, *Myōe the Dreamkeeper*, 53. Passages from the *Zenshū kōmōku* are taken from KKB, 187. The passage from the *Kegon bukkō zammai kan meikan den* is excerpted from NDK, 41:141. As Tanabe notes, the last line of the original from the *Meikan den* is slightly different.

30 *Kōgonku gishaku chōjūki*, MSS, 2:866.

31 *Myōe Shōnin yume no ki*, MSS, 2:154–155.

32 Myōe, "*Zui'i betsugan mon*," in Tanaka Hisao, *Kamakura Bukkyō zakkō* (Kyoto: Shimonkaku Shuppan, 1982), 309. Cited in Sueki, *Kamakura Bukkyō keiseiron*, 231.

33 T, 20:227, #1092.

34 T, 19:606, #1002.

35 T, 20:432, #1098.

36 See Robert Buswell, *The Formation of Chan Ideology in China and Korea: The Vajrasamādhi-Sūtra, a Buddhist Apocryphon* (Princeton, N.J.: Princeton University Press, 1989).

37 T, 8:784–786, #243.

38 On the relation between apocrypha and religious authority, see Robert Buswell, ed. *Chinese Buddhist Apocrypha* (Honolulu: University of Hawai'i Press, 1990).

39 *Kyakuhai mōki*, KKB, 109.

40 There are several models of decline ranging from three to five historical periods, but the most common was three. For detailed descriptions of *mappō* theory in medieval Japan, see Kazue Kyōichi, *Nihon no mappō shisō—Nihon chūsei shisōshi kenkyū* (Tokyo: Kōbundō, 1961); Takagi Yutaka, "Kamakura Bukkyō ni okeru rekishi no kōsō," in *Kamakura Bukkyōshi kenkyū* (Tokyo: Iwanami Shoten, 1982); and Michele Marra, "The Development of Mappō Thought in Japan," parts 1 and 2, *Japanese Journal of Religious Studies* 15, nos. 1 & 4 (1988): 25–54, 287–305.

41 Rebecca Rasmus, "The Sayings of Myōe Shōnin of Togano-o," *Eastern Buddhist* 15, no. 1 (spring 1982): 97, 100–101.

42 Moxacautery (or Moxibustion) is a medical treatment originating in China and developed alongside acupuncture, often used to stimulate the same meridian points on the body as the latter. Instead of inserting needles, an incenselike herbal remedy (mugwort) is burned along the same points as those for acupuncture.

43 *Toganoo Sekkai nikki*, MSS, 3:639.

44 Mark Ty Unno, "As Appropriate: Myōe Kōben and the Problem of the Vinaya in Early Kamakura Buddhism" (Ph.D. diss., Stanford University, 1994).
45 *Kambun gyōjō*, MSS, 1:144.
46 Unno, "As Appropriate," 50–51.
47 *Kōgonku gishaku chōjūki*, MSS, 3:850.
48 *Toganoo sekkai nikki*, MSS, 3:637.
49 Kōshū, *Keiran shūyō shū*, T, 76, #2410; cited in Takeuchi Yoshinori, *Kyōgyōshinshō no tetsugaku*, Gendai Bukkyō meicho zenshū—fukyūban (Tokyo: Ryūmonkan: 1987), 90.

CHAPTER 3

EMPTINESS AND ILLUSION IN THE MANTRA OF LIGHT

When I say you are dreaming, I am dreaming, too.

—Zhuangzi

"Clearly see the nature of the various phenomena." Such statements are the expressions for the two kinds of emptiness, of person and dharmas, of which I so often speak.

—Myōe

•

THE LOGIC OF EMPTINESS

ONE OF THE STRIKING features of Myōe's Buddhist thought is his emphasis on emptiness, a cornerstone of East Asian Mahāyāna thought. For all its doctrinal and ritual diversity, virtually all sects of Japanese Buddhism identify Nāgārjuna as a pivotal figure in its lineage charts and make some reference to his theory of the twofold truth of form and emptiness, or conventional truth and highest truth. It is also worth noting, however, that during the Kamakura Period few of the figures who have traditionally been identified as seminal, either during that time or subsequently, even mention emptiness. Among them Dōgen, Hōnen, Shinran, Nichiren, Jōkei, Jien, Shunjō, and Kakukai make virtually no reference to the concept of emptiness, although the twofold truth appears in their work in one form or another. This is not as strange

73

as it might seem, since the *concept* of emptiness is not necessary to articulate the *logic* of emptiness. As Nāgārjuna's Mādhyamika notion of the emptiness of emptiness (Skt. *śūnyatā-śūnyatā*) indicates,[1] attachment to the concept of emptiness is said to hinder the proper understanding of emptiness. Nonetheless, there may be potential pitfalls in formulating Buddhist doctrine without an explicit reference to emptiness.

Just as Nāgārjuna's critical notion of emptiness was directed toward what he perceived to be the dogmatism of his contemporaries regarding the teachings of the Nikaya literature, his emptiness critique also became applicable to the various teachings of the Mahāyāna schools. No teaching, no matter how profound, could be absolute since each situation demanded a unique response. In the Mahāyāna this point regarding the provisional status of all teachings has been expressed positively in the notion of *upāya*, or the skillful means of flexibly adapting the teachings to the particular circumstances and abilities of each practitioner, time, and culture. In fact, it is this very idea that has served as the rationale for much of East Asian Mahāyāna thought and its hierarchical systems of doctrinal classification *(kyōhan;* Ch. *panjiao)* alluded to in the previous chapter. These systems were usually correlated against scriptural hierarchies: for the Tiantai, the teaching of the *Lotus Sutra* was the highest and most appropriate for its context; for the Huayan, it was the *Flower Ornament Sutra;* for the *Zhenyan,* or Chinese esoteric school, the *Mahāvairocana Sūtra,* and so forth. However, in these classification systems, assertions of appropriateness often went beyond the idea of specific times and places. In the case of such figures as Tiantai Zhiyi and the Huayan patriarch Fazang, the hierarchies they established were often presented as the distilled essence of the Buddhist teachings, not a temporary or provisional phase.[2] In that sense, the *panjiao* systems tended to be characterized by a certain degree of sectarianism and dogmatism that may have stood in tension with the spirit of emptiness.

While these hierarchies were well established in China, they became further solidified along sectarian lines in Japan, especially during the thirteenth century, a period characterized by much doctrinal polemics and by the formation of religious communities requiring doctrinal loyalty.[3] The more that various schools asserted the superiority of their own doctrinal position and institutional affiliations, however, the less likely they were to expound at length on the emptiness of all doctrines as the basis of orthodoxy and orthopraxy. There was an emptiness school in Japan, the Sanronshū, which had made an effort to reestablish itself in the Heian Period after an earlier decline, but it never did flourish intellectually or institutionally in the Kamakura Period in the way that the other schools did.[4] This may have been because the Sanron lacked both the positive doctrinal practices and the political and institutional affiliations needed to carve out a niche in Japanese religion.

Whatever the actual causes of the absence of emptiness discourse, it is noteworthy that Myōe spent much time expounding and emphasizing the centrality of emptiness throughout his career. This correlates well with his pluralistic approach to practice, which left the question of salvific paths and practices open to individual choice and proclivity, even as he advocated the Mantra of Light. As we will see, however, his pluralism was not without its own issues of doctrinal exclusion and hierarchical classification.

It is also worth noting that in discussing emptiness Myōe makes virtually no direct textual references to earlier scriptural or commentarial sources. While the logic by which he expounds emptiness conforms to various past formulations, Myōe's interpretation is very much his own. In particular he articulates his views at length in the *Kōgonku gishaku chōjūki* (Lectures on the Commentary on the Significance of the Syllables of the Mantra of Light) and the *Kōmyō Shingon dosha kanjin ki* (Recommending Faith in the Sand of the Mantra of Light) included in the present study in translation. The former contains a more abstract, theoretical discussion. The latter takes an anecdotal approach that conveys the concrete flavor of Myōe's ideals. For the purposes of the present, the *Lectures* provide a helpful framework with which to begin.

In the *Lectures* and the *Commentary* that it accompanies, Myōe enunciates four broad aspects of emptiness theory: the emptiness of the phenomenal world, in particular that of the self; the intimate interrelatedness of self and other as mutual manifestations of interdependent origination and emptiness; the inconceivability of emptiness as the unborn basis of mind; and the relation between emptiness and the distinctions between esoteric and exoteric, sudden and gradual.

Emptiness of the self and the phenomenal world. An important aspect of emptiness critique is to point out the impermanent, provisional nature of the phenomenal world: "Truly [such a thing as] one's own body does not [really] appear, for the body [one] acquires is nothing more than a temporary assemblage. [One attains] the realm of buddhas and bodhisattvas by abandoning this [temporary abode] and manifesting the original nature of mind." Emptiness in this regard applies to the body, the self, and all phenomenal reality that is constituted by various causes and conditions. Ultimately, there is no conceptually identifiable essence: "There is originally no master among the four great elements [of earth, water, fire, and air] or the five aggregates [of form, sensation, thought, volition, and consciousness that constitute the self]. For whom are the ten directions established? Their original nature is the body of emptiness that is self-evident."[5]

Self and other as mutual manifestations of emptiness. As Myōe's reference to the "body of emptiness" suggests, emptiness is not merely a critical notion but also discloses the positive reality of things. "Body of emptiness" is a paradoxical expression that reflects the complex character of Myōe's Buddhism: Given its constant state of flux, reality cannot be grasped in substantial terms, yet there is an "original nature" beyond the ever changing, illusory facade of things. However, it is deceptive to speak of such a reality, because discursive, linear thought tends to posit it as existing in a dichotomous, substantial opposition to the impermanent world of form. Emptiness is real, but in emptiness all oppositions including that of "real" versus "not real" are dissolved; what appears in the manifest world of form derives from emptiness, but in emptiness itself there is neither "emptiness" nor "form." "The provisional explanation is given of self and other, this and that, even in [the eyes] of sagely wisdom, because they [those distinctions] inform one another in the emptiness of mind. When there are no [distinctions between] self and other, this and that, self and other inform one another in [their mutual] emptiness."[6]

The inconceivability of emptiness. In order to attain a proper understanding of emptiness, it is not sufficient to merely recite the formal structure of the logic of emptiness. As long as the dichotomous presuppositions embedded in discursive logic remain hidden, the mind that seeks to grasp emptiness merely perpetuates the endless chain of propositions by which it further binds itself. Applying the classical Indian *tetralemma* (Skt. *catuṣ-koṭi*), or fourfold logic, Myōe seeks to unmask the pretensions of the linear, dichotomous intellect.

> [Although dharmas can be said to exist,] the various dharmas arise from causes and conditions, and their fundamental natures are empty. When one comes to know this, *bodhicitta* [the aspiration to realize emptiness] arises provisionally. "Provisionally" means arising from causes and conditions. Thus, the various dharmas are provisional and empty. To say upon hearing this that the entirety transcends nonbeing constitutes the slander of denial [because this would be to posit emptiness as a fixed reality]. Thus, to speak of being and nonbeing is already in error [because one is trapped in discursive logic]. Next, to think that the various dharmas exist or do not exist constitutes the slander of difference. Furthermore, to think based on this that the various dharmas neither exist nor do not exist is [the exercise of] the useless rhetoric of nonduality.[7]

These ideas can be schematized according to the *catuṣ-koṭi* as follows:

A. *Dharmas (phenomenal particulars / Buddhist teachings) exist (being)* at one level, yet

B. *Dharmas do not exist (nonbeing);* they are provisional and empty. To think, however, that emptiness as nonbeing exists independently of and transcends the phenomenal world is slanderous insofar as it denies the conditioned character of emptiness itself.

C. *Dharmas both exist and do not exist;* to attempt to conclude that they merely either exist or do not exist is to be bound to the terms of discursive difference. All things both exist at the level of conventional distinctions and do not exist in the sense that they are empty.

D. *Dharmas neither exist nor do not exist.* To be bound, however, to the discursive proposition or *idea* that "dharmas both exist and do not exist" is also erroneous.

In this way, nondiscursive logic is used to expose the erroneous, "slanderous" assumptions of discursive logic and to release the mind to the inconceivability of its own reality. Thus, in the paragraph that immediately follows the one just cited, the four levels of the *catuṣ-koṭi* are revived in light of boundless, inconceivable awareness. In this awareness all aspects of phenomenal reality are affirmed:

> If one frees oneself from these four types of slander, then the being of the various dharmas inconceivably exists, and the nonbeing also inconceivably exists (being and nonbeing inconceivably exist when one is freed from the four types of slander. This means that, with respect to a single dharma there is the meaning of being and the meaning of nonbeing, the meaning of both being and nonbeing, and the meaning of neither being nor nonbeing. Because all of these meanings are realized, [the various dharmas are] inconceivable.)[8]

Problems arise not from any given phenomenal particular in and of itself, then, but rather from a one-sided, deluded understanding of reality. When ideas, things, and teachings are seen in terms of all aspects of their multiple, mutual manifestations in emptiness, the practitioner is freed from the constrictions of deluded consciousness. This view of emptiness is not merely a theoretical stance but is reflected in Myōe's pluralistic attitude toward practice. "If there is something that one cannot understand by studying one's own school, then one may obtain the view [of the matter as taught in] the Zen school and thus benefit by consulting a Zen priest, or by relying on the Buddhist teachings [in the scriptures], or [some other] person. Do not be confined to one-sided views."[9]

Thus far, Myōe's articulation of emptiness logic does not differ significantly from the traditional East Asian formulations of the Sanron (Ch. *Sanlun*) or even the basic notions of classical Indian Mādhyamika.[10] This logic takes on a different hue, however, when one considers that it is being expressed in the context of Myōe's exposition on the Mantra of Light.

Esoteric and exoteric, sudden and gradual. The mind, according to Myōe, that is free from the four types of slander and manifests the inconceivable significance of emptiness is the "pure mind of self-nature, and this is the inconceivable"; this is the mind purified of attachments to one-sided views, and this inconceivable, pure mind is said to be the true principle behind the incantation of the Mantra of Light: "Thus, it is said that the meaning of the cause of the syllable hūṃ [of the Mantra of Light] is for the nature of mind to be free of the four types of slander.... This is the being of the pure mind of self-nature." This true principle of the esoteric Shingon mantra is contrasted with the teaching of the exoteric provisional schools: "The provisional schools [teach] the suchness of the manifestation of the two emptinesses, and the true teaching is that the two emptinesses [of self and dharmas] are none other than suchness.... In the former the two tenets of the provisional and the true share a common basis, but in the latter the true teaching stands alone."[11]

Here we see that, based on his interpretation of the Mantra of Light, Myōe begins to articulate his own doctrinal hierarchy from a

Shingon perspective. The distinction he draws between the true and the provisional is subtle and seems almost insignificant. He merely states the relation between suchness and emptiness in reverse order, where in any case suchness is the positive expression of emptiness: "The provisional schools [teach] the suchness of the manifestation of the two emptinesses, and the true teaching is that the two emptinesses [of self and dharmas] are none other than suchness."

Nevertheless, there is a difference between the two predications. It lies in the fact that the provisional interpretation posits a transition from emptiness to its manifestation as suchness, whereas the "true" interpretation in accordance with the Mantra of Light is to see emptiness and suchness in immediate identity: "the two emptinesses are none other than suchness."

However, this appears to contradict the foregoing discussion of emptiness, which seems to describe a transitional or gradual understanding; the four levels of the *catuṣ-koṭi* and the entire practice of the mantra describe a gradual process of becoming free of discursive entanglements before one realizes suchness as the positive expression of emptiness. Indeed, Myōe combines the idea of the fifty-two bodhisattva stages found in Huayan with the progression of practice according to the Shingon to formulate his own view of gradual practice.[12] How can Myōe's gradualism, which is mediated by a complex set of ritual practices and formulated in terms of a logical progression, be reconciled with his view that the true teaching of the Mantra of Light points to the immediate identity of emptiness and suchness?

The answer he offers is that the truly sudden realization is to be found in gradual practice, and true immediacy in mediation. That is, the very *immediacy,* the sudden identity of suchness and emptiness, of form and emptiness, is realized in the *mediation* of the gradual cultivation of ritual practice. "In the exoteric schools, according to the explanation of the *Sutra of the Jeweled Necklace* (Ch. *Yingluo jing*), the ten [culminating] stages are profound, and the three [groups of the preceding] wisdom [stages] shallow, and this is constant.[13] Since the *Flower Ornament Sutra* is the complete teaching, it teaches that the ten [culminating] stages are shallow, and the three [groups of the] wisdom [stages] are profound."[14]

In other words, the exoteric teachings identify themselves with the ten culminating *bhūmi* stages (stages 41–50) and speak of the sudden realization of the *bhūmi* stages.[15] According to Myōe's interpretation of the Shingon mantra, the preceding wisdom stages (stages 11–40) are more profound because, in his gradualist thinking, there is no culmination without proper preparation. Yet, these preceding stages are not merely a means to an end, preparation for something greater. The progression is sustained from beginning to end by the fact that the entirety of emptiness/suchness is present at each point of gradual practice. More precisely, the progress of gradual self-cultivation only takes place to the extent that the pure mind of self-nature,[16] the reality of emptiness, informs each moment of practice. Paradoxically, the goal only becomes a real possibility when one lets go of one's obsession with it as an external object.

In the *Lectures*, Myōe does not mention the first ten bodhisattva stages, the stages of faith, although he discusses the eleventh through fiftieth stages (of the total fifty-two). Elsewhere, however, he does identify the faith stages as being even more important than the wisdom and *bhūmi* stages they precede. This is confirmed by a vision Myōe had in the eighth month of 1220, the same year that he had the pivotal vision of the Mantra of Light. In this vision, recorded in his *Yume no ki* (Chronicle of Dreams), he speaks of the sudden, simultaneous realization of cause and effect, faith and enlightenment. Again, paradoxically, it is only at the end of a long process of self-cultivation that the real significance of initial faith becomes apparent, that faith and enlightenment were always one, mutually sustaining.

> During my early evening meditation, I prayed for the extinction of sins and received the body which maintains the precepts.... My body and mind became quiescent in the midst of samādhi as had happened

in the sixth month. There was a pole made of lapis lazuli hanging from the sky, and I think it was hollow like a tube.

I grabbed the end, and someone pulled me up. I maintained my hold and seemed to have reached the Tuṣita Heaven.

There was a jewel at the top of the pole. Pure water poured forth, washing my entire body. After that the thought arose in my mind that I would like to see my actual body.

My face suddenly became like a bright mirror. My entire body gradually became like one. I felt completely whole, like a bead-jewel of quartz.

I rolled and moved to another place. I was waiting for a voice, and someone said, "All the Buddhas have entered. You have now attained purity."…

Before this, however, I exited the gate of True Wisdom and traversed the Fifty-Two Stages. The mind that arises at the stages of Faith is Mañjuśrī [himself]. The Wisdom of the Buddha is then divided into [the next] ten levels, [all of] which manifest the wisdom of emptiness. The principles [of enlightenment] and the phenomena [of existence] are contained within these Ten Abiding Stages [11–20] which exhaust all dharmas…. The production of the fruit of the Abiding [Stages] through True Wisdom signifies the production of the fruit of Buddhahood through [the power] of Mañjuśrī. The arising of a portion of the initial [stage] of Abiding in the stages of Faith means that Mañjuśrī becomes the disciple of the fruit of Buddhahood. In other words, this is the mutual correspondence of cause and effect…. When the meaning of this is suddenly grasped in the midst of samādhi, *cause and effect are simultaneous*. This should be contemplated. It is difficult to express in words.[17] [italics added]

An analogy can be drawn with the process of learning to play music. Suppose that there is a young woman, call her Anne, who attends a performance of Beethoven's piano sonata, say the *Appasionata*, and is deeply inspired, so much so that that night, she makes up her mind to pursue a musical career as a pianist. Disregarding the advice of others against going into such a difficult profession, she holds the image of perfection she experienced that night in her mind as she begins the process of learning the piano. The image she holds, however, is not literal or photorealistic. It is not that she forgets all the visual and auditory details, but what is important about her experience does not lie in the sense data. She does not aspire to mimic the soloist. Rather, it is an indefinable quality that emanated from the music that inspires her. It is whole, complete, yet indefinable. It cannot be reduced to a visual or musical description. If, along the way, Anne becomes preoccupied with the end result—a concert career, peer recognition, a recording contract—then she is less likely to be fully focused on her musical discipline and to achieve her aims. Even if she does become a successful soloist, the original source of inspiration is likely to be obscured and her creative spirit diminished. Conversely, regardless of the external goals she might attain, if her heart has been true to her beginnings, then she experiences more fully the joy of making music regardless of external outcomes. Furthermore, her practice will be more efficient as she loses less time and energy to petty concerns, unnecessary anxiety, and procrastination over factors beyond her control. The more she focuses on the immediate significance of the present moment of practice, the more her progress is accelerated. Finally, when she does perform as an accomplished virtuoso, being true to her original vision, she realizes the deep significance of her humble beginnings; she is able to reflect on the long way that she has come but also appreciate what it has meant to follow through with her initial moment of inspiration.

In real life, of course, things are even more complicated. There are musicians who are criticized for achieving virtuoso status by being overly ambitious, and those who are praised for the purity of both music and personality. Nevertheless, it is easy to understand how obsession with a future goal can hinder progress toward the realization of inward potential.

In like manner, Myōe believes that profound practice of the Mantra of Light entails the simultaneous realization of the efficient cause (faith) and its effective result (buddhahood): "When the meaning of this is suddenly grasped in the midst of samādhi, cause and effect are simultaneous.... It is difficult to express in words." In returning to Myōe's thinking, then, the later stages do not exist without the earlier ones, and since emptiness is fully present at each stage, the earlier are more essential than the later. He continues,

> Since the exoteric schools also speak of the sudden teaching, and the teachings leading up to it end up there, this appears profound but is not profound; that which embodies both the sudden and the gradual truly represents the profundity of the dharma. Thus, there are two types of sudden [awakening] in the view of attaining buddhahood in this very body. The profundity of the sudden and profound is the sudden teaching [of esoteric Shingon]. Thus, in the Huayan [teaching], sudden and gradual are both explained as profound, and this is also [the teaching of] attaining buddhahood in this very body.[18]

In other words, seeing the sudden significance within the gradual process of actual practice is, for Myōe, superior to the *rhetoric* of the sudden teaching of the exoteric schools. Whether one regards it as highly creative or merely idiosyncratic, here we see just how singular his interpretation is. In Japanese Shingon esotericism, the progression of practice is traditionally defined in terms of Kūkai's *jūjūshin*, the ten abiding stages of mind. Myōe, however, refers to the stages of bodhisattvahood defined in Huayan. In doing so, he takes a taxonomy that has historically been defined as exoteric in order to describe an esoteric ritual process. Furthermore, although the sudden/gradual distinction originating in Chinese Chan eventually came to be the norm for all schools of East Asian Mahāyāna, Japanese Shingon did not really adopt this distinction until the emergence of Tendai esotericism, whose interpretation Myōe criticizes. Although in Shingon Buddhism there is the concept of "attaining buddhahood in this very body" *(sokushin jōbutsu),* Kūkai formulated this idea as an accelerated view of practice, not as an all-at-once, sudden notion. Myōe's view is simultaneously gradual, sudden, and accelerated, a view that reflects practical concerns as well as his attempt to synthesize Mahāyāna thought.

By combining ideas from Shingon, as well as Zen, Huayan, and the other exoteric schools, Myōe attempts to resolve issues of practical concern for his own understanding of the Mantra of Light. In doing so,

he asserts the superiority of his particular esoteric understanding of emptiness and the twofold truth as it relates to such contemporary doctrinal
and hermeneutical concerns as attaining buddhahood in this very body,
stages of practice, sudden versus gradual awakening, and exoteric versus
esoteric understanding. Of course, an open pluralistic approach to practice does not necessarily mean that all practices are treated equally. Ideas
arise dialectically in historical context, so that some practices are advocated over others even within an egalitarian, pluralistic framework in order to correct what are perceived to be sectarian excesses and imbalances.

In a sense, Myōe's own inclusive yet hierarchical view of practice
was quite typical of the established sects. Jien's Tendai, for example, catalogued multiple valid practices including Pure Land *nembutsu,* meditative visualization, and even Zen meditation. Likewise, Jōkei recognized the Pure Land practice of *nembutsu,* the yogic practices of his own
Hossō School, and devotional incantations to Maitreya. Jien, Jōkei,
Myōe, and others thus advocated an inclusive approach based on their
own classification schema and criticized the Pure Land master Hōnen's
exclusive *nembutsu* practice as contradicting the spirit of *upāya,* or skillful means. Myōe's criticisms, as set forth in his *Breaking the Circle of
Heresy (Zaijarin)* and its supplement, *Breaking the Circle of Heresy—
Elaboration (Zaijarin shōgonki),* were among the harshest. However, it
can be argued that Myōe was more thoroughgoing in applying the emptiness critique to his own views than others such as Jien and Jōkei. Although
he criticized Hōnen for the exclusivism of the Pure Land views articulated in his *Passages on the Selected Primal Vow of Amida Buddha
(Senchaku hongan nembutsu shū),* Myōe seemed to recognize that, however justified his criticisms may have been at the level of conventional or
relative truth, an inclusivism that excludes exclusivism still falls prey to
the pitfalls of linear, dichotomous logic. Perhaps illuminated by the vast
awareness of emptiness, Myōe seemed to lament the fact that he had
been caught in the thicket of dogmatic opinions in his own criticisms of
Hōnen: "By nature I am pained by that which is harmful. I feel this way

about writing the *Zaijarin*."[19] Neither Jien nor Jōkei seemed to have reflected on their own views in such a manner.

One must be careful here, however, in claiming that Myōe's view of *upāya* was more faithful to the logic of emptiness than that of his contemporaries, for to assert any view as finally superior to that of another falls prey to the divisive effects of dichotomous thinking. According to Myōe's own statement in the *Commentary*, any discursive view represents a partial, incomplete position:

> There are two main tenets to the Tathāgata's esoteric words, the meaning that can be explained, and the meaning that cannot be explained. The former, because it is responding to the capacity and circumstances [of the practitioner], summarizes the incalculably profound meaning and principle *by taking one part out of it* and causing wisdom and understanding to arise within a person. The latter, because it is the esoteric language of the Tathāgata, *does not reside within the realm of conception;* one should simply believe and hold this within one's mind [italics added]. [20]

•

THE LOGIC OF ILLUSIONS

OUR ATTENTION IS NOW directed to Myōe's understanding of the twofold truth as it appears in his *Kōmyō Shingon dosha kanjin ki* (Recommending Faith in the Sand of the Mantra of Light; hereafter Recommending Faith), a work written in *kana*-syllabary mixed in with Sino-Japanese ideographs and addressed to a lay or novice audience. Written in more accessible terms than the scholarly exposition of the *Commentary* or the *Lectures* and focusing on the problem of faith, it is more of a beginner's text. Yet, as we have seen, for Myōe the faith of the beginner is just as or more important than the sophisticated knowledge of the expert. Indeed, he cautions that learning without faith is counterproductive. Knowledge driven by faith is what really empowers practice: "Thus it is said that knowledge without faith only leads to greater heterodoxy. Knowledge [by itself] is like a scavenger scrounging around

hither and dither.... In the Buddha Way, one should first of all obtain
the appropriate amount of knowledge such that it will empower one's
practice. To know the appropriate amount is to be the one who [truly]
knows."21

This is echoed in the *Kyakuhai mōki* (Chronicle of Things Not to
Be Forgotten): "Although one cannot enter the Buddha Way without the
two dharmas of faith and understanding, if one is to be missing, then
just faith is to be taken."22

To understand Myōe's views on the twofold truth and its relation
to faith in the Mantra of Light, it is helpful to juxtapose a passage from
Recommending Faith by Myōe to a similar passage from the Daoist text
Zhuangzi, a classic work that was a standard subject of study for intellectuals in thirteenth-century Japan.23 The passage from the *Zhuangzi*
is the well-known episode involving Zhuangzi's dream of the butterfly;
in *Recommending Faith* there is an episode involving a monk's hallucination after ingesting some mushrooms.

Although there are no direct quotations from the *Zhuangzi* in
Myōe's extant works, he almost certainly studied it as part of his classical education. In fact, the archives of Kōzanji, where Myōe served as abbot, contains a commentary on the Zhuangzi titled *Various Discussions
of the Zhuangzi (Sōji zōron;* Ch. *Zhuangzi zalun).*24 It is found alongside copies of two other Chinese classics, the *Analects of Confucius* (Ch.
Lunyu), dated 1303, and sections of the *Chronicle of History* (Ch. *Shiji*),
dated 1211. The *Various Discussions of the Zhuangzi* is undated but very
likely in line with the other classics, indicating that the study of the
Zhuangzi was part of the life of Kōzanji during Myōe's time.

As mentioned earlier, comparisons involving Myōe's practice of
the Mantra of Light have been dominated by juxtapositions with Hōnen's
practice of devotion to Amida Buddha. Yet there are no references to
the Pure Land *nembutsu* practice of intoning the name of Amida or
Hōnen in any of Myōe's writings on the Mantra of Light, or even within
eight years of any works on the Mantra of Light. Certainly, Myōe was

aware of Hōnen's ideas and had criticized them. Furthermore, comparisons with Pure Land *nembutsu* help to illuminate the context of medieval Japanese Buddhism. Yet for the same reasons that too much focus on a conventional lineage-based view of Myōe's intellectual and institutional lineage can obscure important aspects of his perspective on religious authority, overemphasis on parallels with and divergences from Pure Land *nembutsu* can similarly obscure key facets of his Buddhist thought. For example, there is virtually no discussion of the mushroom episode in any of the major modern studies on Myōe, even though it is key to understanding *Recommending Faith* and his logic of emptiness.[25] Just as breaking with stereotypical approaches to questions of lineage opened the way to alternative interpretations, so too can juxtaposing Myōe with Zhuangzi rather than Hōnen remove him from the shadow cast by Hōnen's Buddhist thought without taking him out of historical context. In fact, as Sueki Fumihiko points out, Myōe interpreted the Mantra of Light independently of any need for specific devotion to Amida.[26]

In comparing the Daoist thought of Zhuangzi as presented in the butterfly episode and the Shingon and Huayan Buddhist thought of Myōe as presented in the mushroom episode, notable similarities and differences come to light. The similarities provide the basis for identifying common issues for comparison, while the differences hold the promise of mutually illuminating insights that might go overlooked if either text or figure were examined in isolation.

Specifically, both Zhuangzi and Myōe share a view of reality in which discursive reason and its expression in language are limited with regard to grasping or realizing the most profound reality, that of the Dao for Zhuangzi and that of emptiness for Myōe. Nevertheless, both figures find language to be an indispensable tool for approaching the depths of reality. Indeed language may even be a vehicle for embodying the highest truth when the bonds of discursive language and reason are broken. Furthermore, both are advocates of various practices designed to enable the Daoist or Buddhist, respectively, to cultivate the awareness of the Dao or the twofold truth of form and emptiness in everyday life. Despite these similarities, there are important differences in their uses of language, methods, and the larger worldviews of which the two episodes are emblematic. As we shall see, there are significantly different notions of selfhood, time, moral destiny, and the structures and practices by which each seeks to attain his highest ideals. There are diverse consequences not only for theoretical understanding but also for living in the world.

•

THE BUTTERFLY AND THE MUSHROOM: THE ILLUSION OF REALITY AND THE REALITY OF ILLUSION

From the *Zhuangzi:*

> Once Chuang Chou [Zhuangzi] dreamt he was a butterfly, a butterfly flitting and fluttering around, happy with himself and doing as he pleased. He didn't know he was Chuang Chou. Suddenly he woke up and there he was, solid and unmistakable Chuang Chou. But he didn't know if he was Chuang Chou who had dreamt he was a butterfly, or a butterfly dreaming he was Chuang Chou. Between Chuang Chou and a butterfly there must be some distinction! This is called the Transformation of Things.[27]

From *Recommending Faith:*

> Last year one of the monks living here [at Kōzanji] became intoxicated after eating some mushrooms. After he awoke he related the following story. He said that the lowly monk who picked the vegetable and gave it to him had come with his mother and would not leave his side. I thought he should return to his home, but he would not leave. [The monk who had fallen ill] said that he found it a difficult situation.
>
> This is a remarkable event. Although he was affected by the mushrooms and fell ill both mentally and physically, why would a

monk have picked the mushrooms and come to his side? And even if a monk had been seen picking the mushrooms, why would his mother be at his side? Although one might be an ignorant monk full of doubt and stupidity, one can come to know the principle of Buddhism through hearing of such events and be influenced by the virtuous mind and heart of the Tathāgata. In the *Weishizhang* (Treatise on Mind-only), the Great Master Zhixiang gives the following interpretation: "One ought to know, the principle expressed by the scriptures is that the various phenomena do not exist, there is only suchness." Furthermore, nonself as the real nature [of things] is the ultimate [reality], and [the realization of this fact] is the way to be cured from the intoxication of these mushrooms.

If one inquires into the origin of this intoxicated mind, [one sees first that] the monk's mother [of the story] gave birth to the monk. The monk then picked the mushrooms and came. Someone ate the mushrooms. These various conditions combined to produce the intoxicated mind. If the mother had not given birth, then there would have been no monk to pick the mushrooms. If there were no monk, then he would not have picked the mushrooms and come. If the mushrooms had not existed, then [no one] would have eaten them. Then the original mind would neither have become intoxicated, seen the monk, nor seen the mother. This is the true and real original mind. Truly one ought to know. This intoxication was like a dream or phantasm. This is what the Great Master Xiangxiang (Fazang) states is the mind of dreams of the three realms and four phases (of arising, abiding, changing, and perishing). According to his exegesis, they are all "due to the power of fundamental ignorance," and it is of this mind that he speaks. One should ponder the principle of the buddha-dharma in these terms.

This is no different from believing in this sand and obtaining its virtue. The sand is like the mushrooms. The Buddha who thus expounds [on the sand] is like the monk [who picked the mushrooms in the story]. The various buddhas of the three worlds are [really] expounding the teaching of the singular equality [of things]. They are like the mother who gave birth to the monk. Sentient beings believing [in what they say] is as though they eat the mushrooms. To believe, accept, and obtain virtue is like becoming intoxicated with the mushrooms. The person who is protected by all of the tathāgatas of the ten directions is like the one who had the monk and his mother at his side. When conditions overturning this come together, then one becomes a sinner. All of this is due to the power of interdependent origination difficult to fathom.[28]

The illusion of reality. Whatever else one might say about these passages, there are certain striking similarities in the ways that Zhuangzi and Myōe circumscribe the relationship between language, distinctions made in waking reality, and the deeper truth that calls these distinctions into question. Specifically, both Zhuangzi and Myōe see the distinctions of ordinary waking reality as illusory and therefore questionable. At the same time, they do not deny the waking world of distinctions. Rather, the various phenomena and creatures of this world come to be seen for what they truly are precisely because one sees through the clumsy, artificial boundaries set up by the fixed categories of dichotomous logic.

The truth or reality they seek to illuminate is neither illogical nor irrational. Rather, there is a different kind of logic at work in the dream of the butterfly and the intoxication from mushrooms, one that cannot be captured in or reduced to propositional terms. More specifically, there is a paradoxical logic involving identity and difference: One's true identity is discovered through calling differences into question or dissolving differences. Yet, paradoxically, this does not obliterate differences but rather heightens one's vivid perception of difference.

Zhuangzi identifies himself with the butterfly during the dream, but once awake, he distinguishes himself from it. However, he has neither left the dream state entirely behind (since it is alive in his memory), nor can he return to the state of wakefulness before he fell asleep. His center of awareness has shifted to a point of intersection between the dream and waking states. On the one hand, he is aware of the interpenetration of identities that can take place in the fluid dream-realm that calls into question the boundaries of waking reality. On the other, he becomes vividly aware of the otherness of the butterfly as a component of his own experience. That is, his sense of identity is heightened in such a way that he sees himself as at once both the butterfly and not the butterfly, both Zhuangzi and not Zhuangzi: "But he didn't know if he was Chuang Chou who had dreamt he was a butterfly, or a butterfly dreaming he was Chuang Chou. Between Chuang Chou and a butterfly there must be *some* distinction!"

Myōe's monk suffers a bout of intoxication due to some mushrooms he ingested that were brought to him by another monk and this monk's mother. Yet in the original mind out of which this entire episode arises, there is no mother, no son of hers who is a monk, and no mushrooms. In that sense, the entire episode is like a dream or intoxication: "Truly one ought to know. This intoxication was like a dream or phantasm."

This makes it clear that the distinctions between mother, monk, mushrooms, and the monk who ate the mushrooms are themselves hallucinatory, illusory. Yet, this realization would not have been possible unless the monk ate the mushrooms, which were surely distinct from him. From the perspective of discursive logic, this contrast presents the reader with an aporia: How could the monk have become intoxicated by mushrooms that were nothing more than a hallucination? Myōe's point, however, is that, to see the distinct reality of the mushrooms for what they truly are, one must see that the attempt to grasp them on the sole basis of discursive logic is delusory; only by becoming immersed in a deeper awareness of the "intoxicated" state does one become more intimately aware of the mushroom's reality, a reality that is at once an intimate part of Myōe's own identity and vividly distinct from it.

Discursive logic cannot bridge identity and difference, which for both Zhuangzi and Myōe operate in a complementary relationship.

The reality of illusion: Zhuangzi. Some have described the Zhuangzi of the butterfly episode as a language skeptic,[29] the Daoist who calls into question the ability of language to capture reality but who believes that the awakened spiritual adept can in fact accurately discern the difference between the dream state and waking reality, the butterfly and Zhuangzi, within a realm of wordless intuition or awareness. It may be true that Zhuangzi (and Myōe) does use language skeptically, but he is not a language skeptic in the sense of someone who is merely skeptical about the ability of language to render reality faithfully. Rather, it is a matter of knowledge; as far as Zhuangzi is concerned, he knows that language cannot capture the Dao that he believes in. However, if he clings to this knowledge, then he becomes trapped in the very mode of linear thinking that he is trying to call into question. If he were to assert that language cannot grasp reality, then he would be caught in the very language of "this" versus "that" of which he had just made a mockery in the passage preceding the butterfly episode:

> The Way has never known boundaries; speech has no constancy. But because of [the recognition of a] "this," there came to be boundaries.... There is left, there is right, there are theories, there are debates.... The sage embraces things. Ordinary men discriminate among them and parade their discrimination before others. So I say, "those who discriminate fail to see."[30]

Thus, the problem is not with language but with the mode of logic and with his mind. Not with *his* mind, actually, but with the mind of the reader. Zhuangzi is trying to help the reader break out of the endless morass of discursive thought and to move her into another mode of logic. He calls into question the distinction between the butterfly and himself in order to call into question the distinctions assumed in the reader's mind. Ultimately, this is done in order to evoke in the reader a more intimate relationship with reality, her own and that of the world around her (the two being ultimately inseparable). It is a reality in which "heaven and earth were born at the same time I was, and the ten thousand things are one with me."[31]

The difference between saying that Zhuangzi is a language skeptic and that he uses language skeptically may seem subtle, but the significance of this difference becomes apparent in examining alternative translations to the last line of the butterfly episode. A. C. Graham, for example, offers this translation: "Between Chou and the butterfly there was necessarily a dividing,"[32] while Burton Watson renders the same line as: "Between Chuang Chou and a butterfly there must be *some* distinction! [italics Watson's]" The difference between the two translations is that while Graham's translation appears to be flatly declarative, Watson's translation is potentially conjectural or ironic: "there must be some distinction," although one cannot (discursively) determine what that distinction is![33]

Two other translations leave the question open. Victor Mair renders the same sentence as "Now there must be a difference between Chuang Chou and the Butterfly,"[34] which could be taken to support either Graham or Watson. The Japanese Sinologist Kanaya Osamu renders it as, "*Sōjō to chō to wa, kitto kubetsu ga arudarō,*"[35] which is closer to Watson—though since Watson often follows the work of Japanese scholars, it is probably more appropriate to say that Watson is closer to Kanaya.

Both readings are possible, not only grammatically but also due to the ambiguity of possible intent. That is because the presence of irony or conjecture is often as much or more a function of *voice* as of sentence *logic*. This is especially true in the *Zhuangzi,* where sentences that begin in a rather analytical fashion end up being exercises in parody or self-parody, not by virtue of logic per se but by implied *tone* and comic disparity.

Of course, the question of voice and tone is more ambiguous than the logical relations defined by the grammar on the page. Yet the *Zhuangzi,* like so many other texts of early Chinese Daoist and Confucian thought, relies on the depiction of virtuous persons who embody the Way. For the early Chinese, virtue is necessarily embodied. Whoever might be behind the name Zhuangzi, the literary significance of the text relies on the function of embodied voice as much as on logical relations to convey a sense of virtue.

Watson's translation allows Zhuangzi to be seen as someone who uses language skeptically. By leaving the door open as to whether there is a distinction between Zhuangzi and the butterfly ("there must be *some* distinction"), he is opening the way for the reader to see that the more doubtful the distinction becomes, the more clearly she sees the butterfly and herself for what they are: distinct yet intimate and inseparable. Propositional *logic* may fail to capture the Dao, but the *voiceless voice* that states that "there must be *some* distinction" expresses and to some extent embodies the spirit of the Dao.[36] In that sense, language turns out to both be incapable and capable of capturing the Dao. But since such a proposition regarding language is useless by itself in *conveying* the Dao, Zhuangzi seeks to give voice to his reality by using a skeptical or conjectural tone rather than a merely logical analysis. Of course, there are passages in the *Zhuangzi* where he does use logical analysis to make his point, such as his examination of "this" and "that" in the pages preceding the butterfly episode. But in doing so he not only deciphers the logic of the Dao but shows in a self-mocking *tone* just how silly his analysis is: "But I don't know whether what I have said has really said something or whether it hasn't said something."[37]

In this way, Zhuangzi plays on the boundary between the ordinary waking reality of distinctions and the more fluid realm of the Dao, the boundaryless boundary where identity intersects with difference to enable a paradoxical recognition of both of these aspects constitutive of selfhood in Zhuangzi's Daoism.

The reality of illusion: Myōe. We can see a similar logic operating in Myōe's episode of the intoxicating mushrooms. Whereas Zhuangzi often uses language skeptically in a kind of Socratic irony to loosen the boundaries of discursiveness, Myōe stays with a more staid logical analysis. Beyond that, a sense of ironic humor can be found in some of Myōe's writings, but he appeals more often to a sense of devotion and faith to carry the reader to a deeper level of intuition or awareness. This is especially true in *Recommending Faith,* which is, after all, about faith: "To believe, accept, and obtain virtue is like becoming intoxicated with the mushrooms," and "Wisdom is to deeply believe in the preciousness of this mantra." As we shall see, logical analysis is used to loosen the grip of the discursive mind; the language of belief and faith is used to inspire the reader to a nondiscursive awakening.

One of the keys to understanding the original mushroom episode is the term *doku,* translated here as "intoxicating." *Doku* in a conventional sense is simply "poison," but "intoxicating" is a more apt translation in this case because it is the cause of a hallucination or vision. Furthermore, "intoxicating" carries both the positive connotation of "inspiring" or "entrancing" on the one hand, and the negative connotation of "poisonous" on the other. This ambiguity in meaning is crucial to understanding the mushroom episode, much like the ambiguity of Zhuangzi's sense that there must be *some* distinction (but maybe not!).

In order to understand the significance of the dual function of the term "intoxicating" as it appears in the mushroom episode, it is important to note a central feature of the twofold truth of form and emptiness, a cornerstone of Myōe's Huayan thought: Emptiness as a critical notion has as its object all manner of conceptual attachments, including attachment to the notion of emptiness. This aspect of emptiness becomes clearer when juxtaposed with a contrasting notion, such as "the sacred." Since "God" is no longer considered universally appropriate for referring to the ultimate reality in religion, the term "sacred" has gained currency. Mircea Eliade, for example, claims that the sacred is a *sui generis* category that is absolute and irreducible to other terms.[38] Emptiness, in contrast, while pointing to a higher truth, is not a *sui generis* category. Ultimately, there is no fixed realm of truth apart from the ordinary world of distinctions, and even the distinction between form and emptiness is illusory.

Paradoxically, however, one cannot attain this realization without the teaching of "form" and "emptiness" or some other functionally homologous notions. The danger, ever present, is that no heuristic device—or to use the Buddhist term, no skillful means (Skt. *upāya*)—is free from potential abuse. In the right hands, the twofold truth and the entire array of skillful means serves, on the one hand, to intoxicate the believer, that is, to entrance her in the samādhi of emptiness beyond all distinctions and inspire her to realize the realm of formless awakening, and on the other, to enable the believer to live in the world of distinctions without becoming entangled by them. In the wrong hands, the same ideas and practices become dangerous intoxicants that ensnare the believer in the trap of his own discursive delusions. More precisely, one must allow oneself to be entranced by the intoxicating "mushrooms" of the Buddhist teachings in order to see that all distinctions, including those of the Buddhist teachings themselves, are provisional and illusory, no matter how powerful they are as expressions of highest truth. That is, one must grasp the dual nature of the intoxicating mushrooms *simultaneously*, that they are both the means to religious awakening and the poison to be avoided.

A further implication of this understanding of language and reason is that there can be no final awakening, at least not in any solely discursive sense. When one realizes that the episode of intoxication was itself a dream, one is not fully awakened; rather, one's awareness from the perspective of discursive consciousness is that one has reemerged into the limited world of ordinary waking consciousness. However, since one is now aware that this is not all that there is, one is no longer merely blinded by discursiveness. In Myōe's own words from the mushroom episode, one is aware of being a sinner: "The person who is protected by all of the Tathāgatas of the ten directions is like the one who had the monk and his mother at his side. When conditions overturning this come together [to reveal the dreamlike character of this Buddhist world], then one becomes a sinner."

Zhuangzi might point out, however, that the foregoing analysis, while logically sound, is nothing more than another case of "this" and "that." Where, he might ask, is the person who embodies this logic? Or, in the terms with which we examined Zhuangzi above, where is the positive voice that corresponds to the logic that has just dismantled the discursive intellect? The answer, for Myōe, is the Mantra of Light. The practitioner who grasps the logic of the mushrooms' twofold truth, has faith in the dharma, and intones the Mantra of Light, *On abogya beiroshanō makabotara mani handoma jimbara harabaritaya un*—such a practitioner cultivates the virtue of the Mantra. In thus becoming one with the mantra, the practitioner embodies the voiceless voice of emptiness, the unborn mind of awakening: "Although the minds of sentient beings are unborn by nature, they nevertheless form the mental bases for the realization of all the Tathāgatas."[39]

As we have seen, both Zhuangzi and Myōe circumscribe a framework of language in which discursive language and logic are of limited use for attaining knowledge of the world. While the common, naïve realist use of language may be fine for the ordinary waking world of distinctions, it is insufficient for attaining awareness of the Dao or emptiness. In order to realize the depths of reality, one must enter that dreamlike world of butterflies and mushrooms, where rigid distinctions are called into question, dissolved. Then one can reawaken to this world transformed and begin to live freely and intimately in and with the world, one foot in the heavens—emptiness—and the other one on earth in the conventional world of form. In such a world language is also renewed, and the one who embodies the Way speaks with a new voice, attuned to the subtle illusion of reality and the complex reality of illusion.

•

TRANSFORMATION AND KARMA-TEMPORALITY AND CAUSALITY

AS STRIKING AS ARE the similarities between the worlds of Zhuangzi and Myōe and the ways in which they employ language and reason, there are significant differences as well. One of the most important differences lies in their respective understandings of the manner in which the world of distinctions and the fluid world beyond are linked. This becomes particularly apparent when we pay attention to the attitudes of Zhuangzi and Myōe toward time and causality. Although their views are complex and require a more extended treatment than I give here, it can be said that both thinkers hold that events in time appear in at least two ways: momentarily and sequentially.

In their momentary aspect, events reveal the transiency of phenomena, and this very transiency becomes a portal to the infinite expanse of the Dao or of emptiness. Concretely, this often finds expression in Myōe's poetry. Just to cite one example, the following is a poem that he composed after his evening meditation upon seeing the moon emerging from behind the clouds:

> Shingetsu no sumu ni mumyō no kumo harete
> Gedatsu no mon ni matsukaze zo fuku

> In the clear moonlight of the mind, the clouds of ignorance have
>   dispersed
> Through the gate of deliverance blows the wind in the pines[40]

In the *Zhuangzi* there are many passages that illustrate the momentary character of time. For example, the Daoist adept Wangtai is described as someone who accepts the transitory nature of existence against the vast backdrop of the Dao, someone who "takes it as fate that things should change…[and] holds fast to the source." Thus, he is able to regard "the loss of a foot as a lump of earth thrown away." In this way, the True Person of the Dao "knew nothing of loving life, knew nothing of hating death. He emerged [from the vastness of heaven] without delight; he went back in without a fuss. He came briskly, he went briskly."[41]

In terms of the sequential aspect, Myōe tends to emphasize the causal, karmic relationship between events as the nexus of human action. Zhuangzi, in contrast, tends to use sequential time to depict "the transformation of things," the unfurling of transitory phenomena against the impersonal background of nature and the Dao. Zhuangzi's view is evident in the butterfly episode, where in one moment he is the butterfly and in the next Zhuangzi. Another vivid illustration can be found in his description of his wife's death: "I looked back to her beginning and the time before she was born.... In the midst of the jumble of wonder and mystery a change took place and she had a spirit.... Another change and she was born. Now there's been another change and she's dead. It's just like the progression of the four seasons, spring, summer, fall, winter."[42] Contrast this with Myōe's description of the monk's intoxication, quoted earlier: "If one inquires into the origin of this intoxicated mind, [one sees that] the monk's mother gave birth to the monk.... If the mother had not given birth,...[i]f there were no monk,...[and if] the mushrooms had not existed,...[t]hen the original mind would neither have become intoxicated, seen the monk, nor seen the mother. This is the true and real original mind."[43]

Although both episodes trace a sequence of events originating from a point beyond the reach of the discursive intellect, Zhuangzi locates this point in the "jumble of wonder and mystery" of an impersonal Dao whereas Myōe locates it in the original unborn mind of awakening;[44] moreover, Myōe's concern is with the causes and conditions leading up to the monk's eating the mushrooms. The causal nexus rooted in the personal, that is, in the mind, points to an important difference between the two. As Benjamin Hawes notes, "the mushroom episode's stress on [personal] origins and karma contrast with Zhuangzi's butterfly, which symbolizes the wonder of *transformation* considered strictly on its own terms. Cause and effect do not interest Zhuangzi nearly as much as following effortlessly along in harmony with the constant flux of phenomena."[45] While Zhuangzi seeks to become one with the flow of heaven and earth, Myōe seeks to realize the oneness of human nature and buddha nature, of yogic practitioner and cosmic deity:

Like the heart and mind (of truth), so also the Buddha;
Like the Buddha, all beings.
The mind, the Buddha, and all beings,
[Ultimately] no difference among these three.[46]

It is not that Zhuangzi never speaks in personal terms; his descriptions of the Daoist Sage are sometimes mythic in scale. Conversely, Myōe is famous for his nature poetry. However, this difference in emphasis between Zhuangzi's focus on the impersonal transformation of things and Myōe's concern with the oneness realized between the Buddha and himself in personalized terms reflects a larger difference in their respective understandings of the world as a whole.

For Myōe the problem of liberation is rooted in the profound burden of evil karma accumulated over lifetimes. Ultimately, this entire problem is illusory, but saying so does not make it go away. The practical reality of human experience is daunting, a sense that was amplified for Myōe historically because he believed that he lived in *mappō*, the age of the final dharma, a particularly degenerate age. He pined for the Buddha like a lost child looking for his mother:

Pity me as I think of you, oh my enlightened one.
Other than you no one knows...
Birth upon birth, age after age
I will not be parted from you, even for a moment,
Oh great mother, dear mother.[47]

On the one hand, this means that an arduous path of self-cultivation is required to extricate the practitioner from the bonds of blind passion; on the other, human beings are helpless by themselves to overcome this burden. Although it is the responsibility of the individual practitioner to eradicate his own evil karma, he cannot do so without the aid of the buddhas' mystic power residing in the three actions of body, speech, and mind *(sanmitsu kaji)*. The Mantra of Light and the sand empowered by this mantra are precisely the means through which the body, speech, and mind of the buddhas become one with the body, speech, and mind of human beings: "When the wisdom of the buddhas [and the power of the mantra are] added to the sand of foolish beings, the sand radiates light by taking on the wisdom of the buddhas. This is the meaning of mystic power."[48] Initially, however, since the practitioner is so blinded by his attachments, he cannot see this light and must be convinced to place his faith in the Buddha's teachings.

> For this reason, when a person possesses the mind of faith in nothing more than this mantra, the seed of this wisdom is planted in that person's mind. It is like the flourishing growth of vegetation that takes place when the seeds of grasses and trees are planted in the great earth where there are no stones. Although the minds of sentient beings are unborn by nature, they nevertheless form the mental bases for the realization of all the tathāgatas. If the stone of disbelief gets in the way, the seeds of virtue will not grow. If there is faith, myriad goods will flourish like the verdant earth.[49]

Myōe is known for his attempts to revive the monastic precepts, for setting out a strict regimen of ritual practices for his followers and himself, and for generally seeking institutional reforms within the Kegon and Shingon Buddhist organizations of his day.[50] The sense of ritual propriety, institutional hierarchy, and faith in the wisdom of the ancients is in some ways more resonant with the Confucian officialdom that Zhuangzi so strongly criticizes, but for Myōe all of this is necessitated by his view that the source of spiritual malaise lying within can only be overcome by entrusting oneself to the teachings of the Buddha.

Zhuangzi, however, sees the spiritual malaise and moral chaos of his day as residing primarily without. First, the problem is external to the individual in the sense that it is adventitious and not a problem intrinsic to human nature. Second, Zhuangzi is not looking to take responsibility for those who have perpetuated the problems, such as the bumbling Confucian officials with their conniving ways. He is not seeking reform but is instead content to go on his own way while the establishment crumbles around him. He in fact believes that the Dao is near at hand; those who are excluded from the hierarchical structures of Confucian society are often predisposed to be attuned to the Dao, such as the Crookback Woman and Crippled Shu. Those who are lower on the Confucian hierarchy such as Cook Ding and Woodworker Qing,[51] who tend to be engaged in repetitive manual tasks, are less likely to be distracted by intellectual static and can apply their whole being to inconspicuously immersing themselves in the Way.

•

OPTIMISTIC INDIFFERENCE AND COSMIC COMPASSION

BOTH ZHUANGZI AND MYŌE seek spiritual freedom from the bonds of discursiveness, but because of their different assumptions about the nature of the self and the world, their attitudes toward society and other beings also differ. For Myōe, who sees sentient beings (including himself) as burdened with countless lifetimes of evil karma, faith in the Cosmic Buddha's compassion is needed to expiate karma in this life and achieve liberation in the afterlife. For Zhuangzi, the Dao is nearer at hand, but one still needs to choose. One can either "forget the years, forget distinctions,…[l]eap into the boundless and make it [one's] home!"[52] or one can become like the calculating, bumbling Confucian officials who, in the name of virtue and benevolence, become mired in the desire for wealth, status, and fame.

It is not that Zhuangzi does not care about others in society, but he optimistically believes that the inept will bring about their own self-destruction while those who truly follow the Way will live out their lives peacefully and flourish, finding usefulness in what the status quo regards as useless. In this manner, the true oneness of the Dao may eventually become manifest in the world of distinctions. Myōe, on the other hand, follows the Mahāyāna ideal of the bodhisattva who actively makes the suffering of others his own in order to realize emptiness or oneness on a cosmic scale.

Both Myōe and Zhuangzi see a dynamic, fluid world unfolding beyond the artificial boundaries of the discursive intellect. For Zhuangzi, the goal is to blend with the impersonal flow of heaven and earth; for Myōe, the world of emptiness is a place filled with sentience, not only that of human beings and animals, but also trees, rocks, and grasses,[53] a cosmos in need of great compassion to heal its endless suffering. If Zhuangzi's attitude can be characterized as one of optimistic indifference, then perhaps Myōe's can be seen as one of cosmic compassion.

•

A QUESTION OF PRACTICE: HOW MUCH AND WHAT KIND?

THE DIFFERENT ATTITUDES of the two figures are apparent in their conceptions of praxis. Myōe's emphasis on the need to overcome evil karma is reflected in his advocacy of the Mantra of Light and the rigorous cultivation of virtue, while Zhuangzi's sense of flowing with the Dao is reflected in his sense of *wuwei,* or doing nothing, a paradoxical mode of engaging the world in which one frees oneself from pursuing goals that society deems worthwhile.

This contrast between engaged compassion and optimistic indifference, however, does not mean that Myōe implements an elaborate system of practices while Zhuangzi's stance is *laissez-faire.* Figures such as Woodworker Qing and the Crookback Woman describe contemplative exercises that are designed to quiet the mind and free it from the entanglements of the world. Others, such as Cook Ding, seem to use the ordinary activities of their profession or life as the arena of self-cultivation. Still others, such as the humpback Master Yu and the one-footed Wangtai reflect on their disabilities to deepen their awareness of the Dao. Harold Roth suggests that the *Zhuangzi* is part of a larger constellation of texts in early China that reflect the existence of a loosely knit community of like-minded Daoists who engaged in specific kinds of meditative practices.[54] At the same time, it is important to remember that Zhuangzi's suspicion of highly structured organizations makes it unlikely that the author of the *Zhuangzi* saw himself as competing in the same arena as the Confucians and Mohists.[55] Zhuangzi was a married farmer, not a celibate guru or a sage advisor to kings and nobleman, roles eschewed by the protagonists of the *Zhuangzi*.[56]

Myōe is well known for advocating a wide range of ritual practices to be found among the various schools of Mahāyāna Buddhism. For the last decade of his life, however, he concentrated much of his energies on the Mantra of Light and made the practice of the mantra integral to the daily regimen of Kōzanji where he served as abbot. The Mantra of Light essentially came to form the core of a set of highly structured practices designed to alleviate the suffering of sentient beings in this life and the next. Unlike Zhuangzi, Myōe was a celibate monk, the abbot of a large monastery, and the founder of a convent; he was a prolific scholar-monk, whose fame was widespread among the religious leaders and literati of his time; and he became a respected advisor to the rulers and nobility of his day.

Like Zhuangzi, Myōe did have a mischievous, spontaneous side to him, and Zhuangzi, like Myōe, was a highly literate man who had a deep reverence for cosmic forces and sought to express the subtleties of the Way in intricate detail. In general, however, the Daoist world of Zhuangzi is free-wheeling, iconoclastic, and tends to be distrustful of officialdom. Myōe's practice of the Mantra of Light, like so much of East Asian Mahāyāna, is devotional, and its philosophy of nondualism is inseparable from a highly organized, hierarchical system of ritual practices and institutions designed to lead the practitioner out of the morass of blind passions and evil karma and into a world of awakening.

•

IN THIS SECTION on the Logic of Illusions, we began with the premise that Zhuangzi and Myōe, two figures working within related yet distinct strands of East Asian religious thought and practice, share some strikingly similar views about the province of language and reason but also differ significantly in their understandings of selfhood, morality, and praxis. Both hold to a view of reality in which fixed, discursively bound categories of thought give way to the dreamlike flow of reality at a deeper level. Poised on the fluid boundary between the distinctions of the ordinary waking world and the reality of oneness, they both see themselves as living in a dream within a dream, where, ultimately, difference and identity inter-penetrate to reveal the vastness of the Dao or of emptiness.

For all that they share, they also differ in their views on time, moral agency, and causality, which in turn inform their attitudes toward the world and the practices by which they traverse the illusory divide be-tween the "solid" mundane world and the fluid dreamlike world. Zhuangzi's momentary view of time unfolding against the background of an impersonal Dao leads him to adopt a skeptical, ironic attitude of optimistic indifference. Myōe's view of karmic causal connections in a cosmos filled with feeling lead him to seek the path of compassion.

Social and moral decay, institutional corruption, and spiritual las-situde plagued China in the fourth century B.C.E. as much as in thir-teenth-century Japan, albeit in different forms. The oneiric episodes of the butterfly and the mushrooms help us to see both their similarities and their differences. In particular, they help us to understand that for all his otherworldly, dreamlike orientation to Buddhist life and thought in thirteenth-century Japan, Myōe's practice of the Mantra of Light is articulated within a structured, discursively defined framework of de-votional and yogic practices. Yet, precisely the kind of complex, hierar-chical system of ritual practices needed to counteract blind passions and enter the world of boundless compassion stands in tension with Myōe's free-flowing vision of emptiness.

•

¹ See C. W. Huntington, *The Emptiness of Emptiness* (Honolulu: University of Hawai'i Press, 1990).

2 See, Paul L. Swanson, *Foundations of T'ien-T'ai Philosophy: The Flowering of the Two Truths Theory in Chinese Buddhism* (Berkeley: Asian Humanities Press, 1989); Ming-Wood Liu, *The Teaching of Fa-Tsang: An Examination of Buddhist Metaphysics* (Ph.D. diss., University of California: Los Angeles, 1979).

3 As James Foard notes, it was this sense of hierarchical and sometimes exclusive communal and institutional membership that helped to define the contours of Japanese Buddhist life thereafter (James Foard, "In Search of a Lost Reformation: A Reconsideration of Kamakura Buddhism," *Japanese Journal of Religious Studies* 7, no. 4 [December 1980]: 280–281).

4 IBJ, 334a.

5 MSS, 2:817, 889.

6 MSS, 2:883.

7 MSS, 2:856.

8 MSS, 2:856.

9 *Kōzanji Myōe Shōnin gyōjō*, MSS, vol. 1. This is my own translation as it appears in Hayao Kawai, *The Buddhist Priest Myōe: A Life of Dreams* (Venice, Calif.: Lapis Press, 1992), 47. Although this statement is taken from a hagiographic source, it is consistent with Myōe's general openness to the plurality of practices and, in fact, the highly syncretistic character of his own understanding and practice as well as that of his community. Nevertheless, there are complexities that emerge in various contexts including the Mantra of Light as discussed below. In fact, it may be easier to depict Myōe as pluralistically open and egalitarian within a hagiographic context because such a context allows the author/compiler to be more anecdotal and not have to deal with the complexities of historical conflict.

 Of course, Myōe was not unique in his pluralism. The established schools of the Tendai, Shingon, and the various Nara schools also took pluralistic approaches to practice. However, they generally tended to have their own set of pluralistic practices arranged according to their respective *panjiao* hierarchies. Thus, they were not always open to incorporating ideas from the other schools; their differences even became violent at times, when monks from one school forcibly entered and wreaked havoc on temples from other schools. Later on in this study, I examine in greater detail Myōe's pluralistic approach to practice.

 Others who were pluralistic in a more egalitarian, open sense often did not have an integrated understanding of how disparate practices fit together and failed to articulate a compelling soteriology for themselves or for others. One such example can be found in the case of Mujū Ichien. As Robert Morrell suggests, Mujū took a genuinely open approach to a multitude of practices but may have lacked the religious zeal to achieve a focused soteriology (Robert E. Morrell, *Sand and Pebbles* (Shasekishū): *The Tales of Mujū Ichien—A Voice for Pluralism in Kamakura Buddhism* [Albany: SUNY Press, 1985], 55).

10 For a discussion of Sanlun thought, see Taitetsu Unno, "Philosophical Schools—San-lun, T'ien-t'ai, and Hua-yen," in *Buddhist Spirituality*, ed. Takeuchi Yoshinori (New York: Crossroad, 1993), 344–350.

11 MSS, 2:857, 856, 856.

12 MSS, 2:852. The fifty-two stages are given in groups of ten followed by two individual stages: ten stages each of faith, abiding, practice, merit-transference, and

bhumi; and then the stage equal to awakening (enlightenment), and finally the stage of marvelous awakening.

13 Three wisdoms *(sangen):* In the Tendai classifications, this refers to the following three groups of ten stages in the fifty-two stages of bodhisattvahood: ten abidings, ten practices, and ten merit-transferences (BGDJ, 461c).

14 MSS, 2:852.

15 The ten *bhumi* stages are called: joy, purity, emitting light, fiery wisdom, difficult to attain, manifest before [one's eyes], far reaching, imperturbable, good wisdom, and dharma cloud.

16 The expression "pure mind of self-nature" may be somewhat puzzling, since emptiness discourse tends to emphasize the absence or emptiness of any intrinsic self-nature (Skt. *niḥsvabhāva*), but it is easy to see that there is no contradiction here since self-nature is equated with emptiness. The question then arises, If self-nature is empty, then how can there be a mind of self-nature? On the one hand, there is no mind as we conventional conceive it, that is, as some kind of independent entity that is enclosed in the physical encasement of the body. The true nature of mind cannot be equated with any finite, relative entity. On the other, the emptiness of mind does not mean that the mind does not exist; rather, the true mind is the mind that is empty of preconceived notions and therefore one with everything.

17 MSS, 2:150–151. This is my own translation taken from Kawai, *The Buddhist Priest Myōe,* 187–188.

18 MSS, 2:852.

19 *Kyakuhai mōki,* KKB, 122.

20 MSS, 2:887; italics added.

21 MSS, 2:807.

22 *Kyakuhai mōki,* MSS, 2:529.

23 As Fukunaga Mitsuji notes, the influence of Daoist thought in Japan generally and that of Laozi and Zhuangzi in particular can be seen as early as the seventh century ("Nihonjin to Rōsō shisō" and "Heian jidai no Dōkyōgaku," in Fukunaga, *Dōkyō to Nihon bunka* [Kyoto: Jimbun Shoin, 1982], 188–191, 86–100). Although Daoism did not establish the independent institutional presence in medieval Japan that they had in China, the study, translation, and interpretation of Chinese classics and the influence of Daoist practices was an integral dimension of medieval Japanese cultural and religious life in the thirteenth century.

    Although Myōe does not quote the *Laozi* or *Zhuangzi* directly, other figures of his time such as Shinran and Mujū Ichien do refer to the *Zhuangzi* (See, for example, Shinran, *Kyōgyōshinshō,* in *Shinran chosaku zenshū,* ed. Kaneko Daiei [Kyoto: Hōzōkan, 1964], 326, 330; Morrell, *Sand and Pebbles,* 95–97, 161). In the fourteenth-century, the Zen monk Musō Soseki, following the thought of the Chinese Zen monk Tsungmi, whose thought Myōe had also studied, advocated the unity of the three great traditions *(sankyō itchi)* of Confucianism, Daoism, and Buddhism. Even today, the study of the Confucian and Daoist classics is a standard part of the curriculum of those who are preparing for monastic training in various Japanese Buddhist sects.

24 Murakami Sodō, *Toganoo-zan Kōzanji Myōe Shōnin* (Kyoto: Kōzanji, 1937), 339.

25 One of the problems that sometimes plagues modern scholarship is the replication of dominant institutional ideologies. For example, Hakamaya Noriaki's *Hōnen to*

Myōe (Hōnen versus Myōe) asserts that Hōnen's Buddhism is egalitarian and orthodox while Myōe's is discriminatory and deluded with the heterodoxy of a self-powered outlook. Although dressed in modern terminology, Hakamaya's views tend to reinforce contemporary Pure Land sectarian orthodoxy in a way that is overly simplistic.

There are several studies available for those who wish to compare the Mantra of Light and Pure Land *nembutsu*, including George Tanabe, *Myōe the Dreamkeeper: Fantasy and Knowledge in Early Kamakura Buddhism* (Cambridge: Council on East Asian Studies at Harvard University, 1992); Kawai, *The Buddhist Priest Myōe*; and Frédéric Girard, *Un Moine de la secte Kegon à l'époque de Kamakura: Moye (1173–1232) et le "Journal de ses rêves"* (Paris: École Française d'Extrême-Orient, 1990).

26 Sueki Fumihiko, *Kamakura Bukkyō keiseiron* (Kyoto: Hōzōkan, 1998), 257.

27 Burton Watson, trans. *Chuang Tzu: Basic Writings* (New York: Columbia University Press, 1964), 45.

28 *Kōmyō Shingon dosha kanjin ki*, SAZ, 2:21.

29 Philip J. Ivanhoe, "Zhuangzi on Skepticism, Skill, and the Dao," *Journal of the American Academy of Religion* 61, no. 4 (1993): 642–643.

30 Watson, *Chuang Tzu*, 39.

31 Ibid., 38.

32 A. C. Graham, trans., *Chuang Tzu: The Inner Chapters* (London: Mandala, 1991), 61.

33 Grammatically, the problem of interpretation revolves around the function of the final particle *yi*. Edwin Pulleyblank states that *yi* functions to denote the perfect past, similar to *le* in modern Chinese. This seems to confirm Graham's reading. According to Bernard Karlgren, *yi* is "a final particle denoting finality, deciding subjective opinion." This suggests that A. C. Graham is correct but does not exclude Watson's reading, since Karlgren states that *yi* is indicative of "subjective opinion" and leaves the possibility open for objective uncertainty. Axel Schuessler states that *yi* functions as an injunctive and denotes the sense of "should" or "must... indeed." This is closer to Watson's translation than Graham's. From the work of these Sinologists, it is unclear whether Graham or Watson is preferable. See Bernard Karlgren, *Analytical Dictionary of Chinese and Sino-Japanese* (1974), [183] p. 79; Edwin G. Pulleyblank, *Middle Chinese: A Study in Historical Phonology* (Vancouver: University of British Columbia Press, 1984).

34 Victor Mair, trans., *Wandering on the Way: Early Taoist Tales and Parables of Chuang Tzu* (New York: Bantam Books, 1994), 24.

35 Kanaya Osamu, trans., *Sōshi*, vol. 1, Iwanami Bunko, Ao 206-1 (Tokyo: Iwanami Shoten, 1971), 88–89.

36 I use the expression "voiceless voice" here to suggest that it is the wordless Dao speaking through the voice of Zhuangzi.

37 Watson, *Chuang Tzu*, 38.

38 Mircea Eliade, *The Sacred and the Profane* (New York: Harcourt Brace, 1987), 16.

39 *Kōmyō Shingon dosha kanjin ki*, SAZ, 2:15.

40 Kubota Jun and Yamaguchi Akiho, eds. *Myōe Shōnin shū*, Iwanami Bunko 33-326-1 (Tokyo: Iwanami Shoten, 1981), 30.

41 Watson, *Chuang Tzu*, 65, 74.

42 Ibid., 113.

43 *Kōmyō Shingon dosha kanjin ki*, SAZ, 2:21.

44 It is important to note that the sense of "impersonal" here does not signify a cold and unfriendly universe. Rather, the Daoist sage has an intimate sense of the vivid and dynamic workings of heaven and earth. The ancient Chinese did not have the sense of a cold world of dead matter described by modern natural science with which the impersonal is often associated today (for the perspective of natural science, see, for example, Steven Weinberg, *The First Three Minutes: A Modern View of The Origin of the Universe* [New York, Basic Books, 1977]).

45 Benjamin Hawes, "Dreaming and Awakening in the Writings of Myōe Kōben and Zhuangzi" (Providence: Brown University, 1996, unpublished), 6.

46 Kawai, *The Buddhist Priest Myōe*, 42. This is a verse from the *Flower Ornament Sutra*, on which Myōe wrote his commentary *Kegon yuishin gi* (Commentary on the Significance of Mind-Only in Huayan). Historically, both Huayan and Shingon thought have been heavily influenced by the mind-only orientation of Yogacara, a trend that is clearly evident in this verse as well as in the earlier discussion of the "pure mind of self-nature."

47 Kawai, *The Buddhist Priest Myōe*, 72.

48 *Kōmyō Shingon dosha kanjin ki*, SAZ, 41.

49 Ibid., 15.

50 See Mark Unno, "As Appropriate: Myōe Kōben and the Problem of the Vinaya in Early Kamakura Buddhism" (Ph.D. diss. Stanford: Stanford University, 1994).

51 Watson, *Chuang Tzu*, 62, 78–80, 46–47, 126–127.

52 Ibid., 44.

53 In one interesting episode, Myōe writes a letter to an island and tells his disciple to deliver it to his companion. See Kawai, *The Buddhist Priest Myōe*, 98–99.

54 Harold D. Roth, "The Inner Cultivation Tradition of Early Daoism," in *Religions of China in Practice*, ed. Donald S. Lopez Jr. (Princeton, N.J.: Princeton University Press, 1995), 123–148.

55 The Mohists, the followers of Mozi, represented another movement seeking to address the social and political ills of ancient China. Briefly, the Mohists proclaimed a doctrine of universal love based on providing for the material needs of people, especially the downtrodden. They organized themselves into militia-type groups to combat what they saw as the oppressive rule of the powers that be. The Mohists were critical of the Confucians whom they saw as advocating expensive, wasteful rituals and frivolous activities such as making music.

56 Aaron Stalnaker has pointed out in a personal communication with the author that the relationship between Liezi and his master Huzi depicted in chapter 7 of the *Zhuangzi* reflects a formal guru–disciple relationship. This may be true, but it is important to note that this does not lead Liezi to become a Daoist master with a large following. Instead, he makes himself inconspicuous and lives out his life as a married householder (Watson, *Chuang Tzu*, 92–94).

---- |CHAPTER 4|----

PURITY AND DEFILEMENT IN THE MANTRA OF LIGHT

If one's heart is pure, the truth can be found in wiping one's behind.

—Myōe

LOCATED IN THE NORTHEAST CORNER of Sekisui'in, in the compound of Kōzanji where Myōe served as abbot, is a wooden tablet with inscriptions rendered in Myōe's own hand. It bears the heading in seven Sino-Japanese characters, *Arubekiyōwa*, "As Appropriate."[1]

The text of *Arubekiyōwa* is divided into three parts: first, the daily schedule of temple activities; second, rules of comportment while in the temple study hall including the handling of scriptures and meditation cushions; and third, rules of comportment while in the buddha-altar hall, including care of the altar and handling of ritual implements. "As Appropriate" is actually the heading for the first section only, and there are separate headings for the other two sections, "Etiquette in the Temple Study Hall" and "Etiquette in the Buddha-Altar Hall," respectively. Murakami Sodō refers to the entire tablet as *Nichiyō shingi* (Daily Regulations),[2] drawing on the similarities between the contents of this tablet and the *shingi* (Ch. *qinggui*) or monastic regulations of the Zen schools, first formulated in Chinese Chan and reformulated in Japan. One of the most prominent examples among Myōe's contemporaries is Eihei Dōgen's (1200–53) various *shingi,* collectively known as the *Eihei*

111

Shingi (Regulations of Eiheiji), which contains instructions on everything from the description of administrative offices to instructions for the Zen cook.[3] Although a brief document, a close examination of Myōe's *Arubekiyōwa* tablet reveals much about Buddhist life at Kōzanji and Myōe's practice of the Mantra of Light.

The daily schedule lists various meditative activities including seated meditation, or *zazen,* chanting of various scriptures, and, at mid-morning, forty-nine recitations of the Mantra of Light. Thus, we know that the mantra was a staple of daily practice at Kozanji.

Turning to the two sections of the wooden tablet concerning etiquette in the study hall and buddha-altar hall, one finds rules having to do with the use of texts, tools, and implements such as scriptures, ink and brush, and meditation cushions. A surprising number of these rules explain in minute detail things having to do with cleanliness and ritual purity. In just three lines from the etiquette in the study hall, one finds the following proscriptions:

> During the summer, do not use day-old water for mixing ink.
> Do not place scriptures under the desk.
> Do not lick the tips of brushes.[4]

At first glance, one might take such admonitions to be a matter of hygiene, but in fact they are part of a larger view of religious purity, as we shall see.

Purity and the sand of the Mantra of Light. Purity is a central component of Myōe's practice of the Mantra of Light. In *Recommending Faith in the Sand of the Mantra of Light* (which Myoe presents in a question-and-answer format), he goes to great lengths to explain that the sand used in conjunction with the Mantra of Light must be extremely pure: QUESTION: Let us say there is a Shingon master living deep in the mountains where fine-grained sand is not available. If there is a person who hears of its efficacy and desires some sand, obtains it from an impure place, sends it deep into the mountains, and requests that the mantra be intoned to transfer its mystic power [to the sand], is this to be rejected? ANSWER: Such a thing should never, never happen. The teaching of the mystic power of the Mantra is exceedingly pure and comes to fruition. If it is defiled, then Vināyaka and other deities will gain a foothold and hinder the realization (Skt. *siddhi*) of [mystic power]. Even if there are obstacles to be overcome such as mountains to be climbed and valleys to be crossed, sand from the purest place should be placed in a new container and sent to the Shingon master.[5]

He instructs the practitioner to cull all impurities out of the sand including seashell fragments:

> Only sand from the purest of places should be used.
>
> This fool [Myōe] has made this a matter of the greatest importance, and at first I went to gather sand from an island located very far from any human habitation. However, there were broken shells mixed in, and I discarded it [all] and did not use it. Sekisuiin, one of the buildings of Kōzanji, is located at the source of water for various other buildings. The rocks there are craggy and soar up high, and there is little sand there, but it is very pure.[6]

Myōe then sets up a dialogue with an imaginary interlocutor who asks him how he knows what "pure" sand is. As Myōe answers a series of questions, he declares that even bits of gold mixed in with sand are not to be treated as pure sand:

QUESTION: What is this sand?

ANSWER: [The various grains] of sand differ in color, being blue, yellow, and so on; likewise, they differ in shape, being rectangular, round, and so on. [Together] they form a mass of tiny, hard [particles]. This is called "sand."

QUESTION: But then, grasses and trees also differ in color, being blue, yellow, and so on; likewise, they differ in shape, being rectangular, round, and so on. Why are they not regarded as sand?

ANSWER: They are larger and not hard. Sand is hard and small.

QUESTION: But then, dried grains of rice that have been ground into pieces are also hard and small. Why are they not regarded as sand?

ANSWER: Those grains were originally soft and only later dried and hardened. Sand is hard and small from the beginning.

QUESTION: But then, gold, iron, and the like are also hard and small. Why are they not regarded as sand?

ANSWER: It is so. Thus, people call [bits of gold] *sagon,* "sand-gold." They are not sand.[7]

Turning the question of the nature of sand back to the imaginary interlocutor, Myōe states that gold bits are not sand because of human valuation. People value the bits of gold, and so even if they are mixed in with the sand, people upon seeing them regard these bits not as sand but as gold:

QUESTION: You originally said that the various grains of sand differ in color, being blue, yellow, and so on, that they differ in shape, being rectangular, round, and so on, and that they are hard and small. Since sand-gold and earthen sand both have these qualities, how do you distinguish the two?

ANSWER: Golden sand is a rare treasure, stored wrapped up in the bottom of a [jewel] box. Earthen sand is not a treasure and fills the whole earth. The two are not comparable.

QUESTION: Why is it that sand-gold found where it is dug up, not wrapped up in the bottom of a box, but found everywhere in the earth, is not regarded as treasure?

ANSWER: It is, in fact, a treasure.

QUESTION: It already fills the earth. It is not kept in a storehouse, nor is it accumulated in a box. Who regards it as treasure? Again, it is people who gather and store it. Thus, if people merely gather and store sand, is it regarded as treasure? And if golden sand is scattered all over the earth, is it not regarded as treasure?

ANSWER: Sand-gold would still be treasure.

QUESTION: Various meanings have been examined exhaustively. There is no [way to ascertain which is] greater or lesser, golden sand or earthen sand. Who would still assert that sand-gold is [inherently] better?

ANSWER: Although one has listened to this discussion of equality, *if one still desires sand-gold and does not desire ordinary sand, then one still regards sand-gold as treasure* [italics added].[8]

Thus, it is the mind or consciousness that desires and values gold that makes it gold instead of sand:

> The sand contains the most minute subtleties which are synthesized provisionally. If they are scattered, then they lose their reality [as sand].

Mind-consciousness transforms them, and causes and conditions bring them together.[9]

The very value of ordinary sand, which, illuminated by the Mantra of Light, becomes pure sand, lies in its ordinariness. What is valueless to most people is precisely thereby of infinite value to Myōe because it functions to release them from their attachments. Herein lies the secret to the practice of gathering and transferring the sand. It is not in the sand per se but in the consciousness of the sand. Both the chanting of the mantra and the gathering of sand serve to purify the mind of the practitioner.

Similarly, in the daily life of the monks at Kōzanji, the process of constant purification establishes a ritual hierarchy of the sacred and the profane, indexed in descending order from Buddhist deities at the top to human bodily functions and secretions at the bottom. Specifically, at the top of the hierarchy are found images of buddhas and bodhisattvas, followed by those of the patriarchs, sacred scriptures, various ritual implements, outer garments, inner garments, and bodily fluids at the bottom. Thus, offerings for Buddhist deities and for patriarchs are to be kept separate from one another, rosaries and other ritual implements are not to be placed on top of scriptures, and no ritual implements are to be placed on the floor, which is sullied by human feet. Monks are not to enter the temple study hall wearing only white undergarment robes, they are not to lick the tips of calligraphy brushes, and nose tissues should certainly not be placed under the cushions.

This logic of purity, implicit in the hierarchy of ritual actions prescribed by the *Arubekiyōwa* tablet, mirrors the logic of purity pertaining to the sand of the Mantra of Light described in *Recommending Faith in the Sand and the Mantra of Light.* Like the process of gathering pure sand, the practice of observing rules of ritual purity in the monastic setting requires mindful awareness. Furthermore, the sacred hierarchy of the rituals serves to invert the ego-centered logic of the mundane world, in which human beings find it convenient to leave tissues nearby, to lick brushes rather than prepare clean water, and so on. Likewise in the case of the sand of the mantra, specks of gold, representing objects of ego-centered attachment, must be removed from ordinary sand in the process of ritual purification.

The picture is slightly complicated by the fact that, in the case of the mantra and sand, it is the very ordinariness of the sand that places it above gold specks in the ritual hierarchy. Myōe explains that, although images of buddhas and bodhisattvas are more obviously sacred, the sand carries the same significance:

QUESTION: Faith is easy to awaken when gazing upon the images of buddhas, for the various details and auspicious marks have been carved into them. But in the case of grains of sand that have no such form, it is difficult to awaken faith even though one might hear of the profound efficacy of the sand. If faith is not fully realized, then the efficacy [of the sand] also fails to be realized fully. [How should one properly understand this matter?]

ANSWER: There is no one who [does not] have faith in the images of buddhas.[10] Why do they not have faith [in the sand]? Both [images and sand] come from the sutras. Why is one taken and the other discarded? Images of buddhas are painted and carved in wood. The knowledge of the senses is based on the discrimination of mind-consciousness. Foolish beings [i.e., unenlightened humans] are called "those of ears and eyes."

Their minds only discriminate the realm of the senses. The knowledge of the sages [i.e., the awakened] is that of the principle of the dharma [unbounded by the senses]. If sentient beings strive [to understand the buddha dharma] and awaken the mind [of aspiration], then they will believe and come to know [the significance of the sand]. Thus the connections formed through the senses are not in vain. [They] will ultimately lead to the unexcelled fruit of buddhahood.

The great emphasis placed on ritual purity, however, raises questions about the problem of discrimination or discursive distinctions discussed in this passage. In Myōe's Mahāyāna thought, everything is said to be equal: equally empty and equally significant. Thus, the Mantra of Light is designed to cultivate the wisdom of intuiting the equality of all things:

> Maṇi is the wisdom of equality. It is bright and pure like the maṇi jewel. This wisdom can purify the defilements of the discriminations of the two types of innate attachments, namely, to self and to phenomena. It authenticates the principle of the equal nature of all things. Thus, this wisdom arises from the Buddha Ratnasaṃbhava.[11]

Everything should be embraced equally, whether they be specks of gold or ordinary sand, images of buddhas or nose tissues. Although this might hold at the ultimate level of highest truth, distinctions are still necessary at the conventional level of practice due to human beings' attachments. In order to attain the highest realization of nonattachment in which everything is seen to be equal, the practitioner must first detach from his or her attachments. To effect this movement from attachment to detachment and then to nonattachment, the false ego-centered hierarchy of values that places gold above ordinary sand must be canceled out by imposing on it precisely the opposite hierarchy in which ordinary sand is placed above specks of gold:

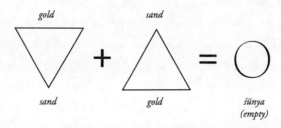

The empty or nondual realm of equality is realized through the mutual cancellation of the profane and sacred hierarchies. Similarly, the placement of buddhas and bodhisattvas above human bodily functions is designed to purify the consciousness of the practitioner of attachments to the human realm.

Ideally, it is this salvific scheme that informs Myōe's logic of purity and the social hierarchy of his monastic world, a world where pure, enlightened monks who embody the buddha virtues are found at the top, followed by less virtuous (and lower-ranking) monks and nuns, lay followers who are not allowed to enact rituals or touch ritual implements, and so on.

Considering himself to have been befallen with the unfortunate circumstances of *mappō,* the final age of the dharma, Myōe did not see the monks of his day as conforming to this ideal. In facing these circumstances, the symbolism of the sand also helped Myōe to establish critical distance from the corrupt ecclesia. References to gold along with other precious metals and jewels appeared frequently in Buddhist literature as symbols of spiritual opulence. Lavish descriptions of pure lands and celestial beings were designed to help evoke the mood of transcendence. These textual references were realized visually in the design of elaborate temple altars, statuary, and paintings. While the mythological landscape thus depicted no doubt helped to inspire many a devotee's faith, elaborate temple adornments also became indices of social and political power. In a world of ever larger temples and competition within the priesthood, Myōe's exaltation of the sand served equally to unmask the decadent Buddhist establishment as much as the mundane greed of the laity.

This, however, did not mean that Myōe abandoned the use of buddha images. For Myōe, both beautiful images of celestial beings and sand were proper objects of ritual devotion: "Both [images and sand] come from the sutras." In fact, the more one penetrated the logic of the sand, the more one could appreciate the true beauty of buddha images adorned with gold. This again shows that Myōe used the purifying power of the sand not to abandon the traditional monastic and social hierarchy but to attempt to revive its pure implementation. As the *Arubekiyōwa* tablet shows, Myōe held this social hierarchy as essential to his ideal of Buddhist practice. For him, the visible forms of institutional hierarchy were useless without the purity manifested through the mindful practice of ritual forms.

Myōe recognized the inadequacy of current practices quite early on in his career. Armed with an understanding of the logic of ritual purity and its relation to institutional hierarchy, he used a rhetorical inversion of this hierarchy to comment upon the priesthood of his day. At the age of thirteen, he composed the following verse:

Yamadera mo hosshi kusaku wa itakarazu
Kokoro kiyoku wa kuso fuku nari to

I do not wish to stay in this mountain temple
Which stinks of so-called dharma masters.
If one's heart is pure,
The truth can be found in wiping one's behind.[12]

Even the basest actions involving bodily excretions, if carried out correctly, could better represent the true practice of the dharma than monks whose offices were assigned a high symbolic value but were carried out poorly. Unless one takes the logic of purity into account, one is apt to read this verse as a rejection of existing institutions. Closer reading, of course, reveals the opposite to be the case. Myōe's rhetorical inversion of the existing hierarchy assumes its basic validity. Dharma masters ought to be pure in all aspects of their practice *including* the basest actions. Because these so-called dharma masters are so impure, they cannot see the truth of emptiness in wiping their behinds, let alone buddha images. The purity of ritual actions is to be maintained from the buddha-altar hall to the toilet, a point reiterated by Myōe in the *Chronicle of Things Not to Be Forgotten (Kyakuhai mōki):* "It is deplorable that the toilet next to the Great Gate is not well maintained. There are unsightly urine stains. It is shameful if people come to the temple and say, "The atmosphere of that temple has changed." Upon seeing anything that has fallen into disrepair, everyone should clean and make [the necessary] repairs. It is a great transgression to live in the temple but lack the heart to maintain it."[13] By rhetorically inverting the usual hierarchy of practices, Myōe sought to unmask the hypocrisy of the visible hierarchy and point the way to true practice. Yet, this rhetorical inversion served the purpose of confirming the validity of the established hierarchy and Myōe's attempt to revive its deeper significance.

There were times, however, when mere rhetoric was insufficient to communicate the force of his criticisms. Actions speak louder than words in a corrupt age, so that even if it meant transgressing the bounds of ritual purity, Myōe found it necessary at times to take action. The most vivid example of this is Myōe's amputation of his own ear. In the time of *mappō*, taking the tonsure had lost its significance as a symbol of renunciation: The shaved head had lost its shine. In order to demonstrate the true spirit of renunciation, Myōe went before an image of Butsugen Butsmo (Buddha-Eye Buddha-Mother; Skt. *Buddha Locana*, an embodiment of *prajñā*-wisdom), and cut off his ear.[14] At that moment, blood spurted out, and the stains from this ritual amputation are said to be discernible to this day. Self-mutilation and defilement of a sacred image with blood transgress the bounds of ritual purity, yet Myōe used this transgressive act to invert and subvert what he perceived to be the false hierarchy of the ecclesia. A most impure act was used to purify the office of monkhood for which taking the tonsure had lost its symbolic value. The amputation of the ear was an act intended not only for his contemporaries but for Myōe's own sake as well. He needed something to help him realize the true spirit of renunciation as well as point it out to others. According to the account contained in the *Gyōjō,* he felt that not having an ear

> "is like being deficient in the five senses. But unless I become a one-eared [misfit], I will easily give way to the [false] respect of those who come to see me and end up selling myself short. I have to resort to such means since I am weak of determination; otherwise I will certainly end up being lost." [Thinking thus,] he hardened his determination, went before the image of Butsugen, invoked her name, and cut his right ear off with a knife. Blood spurted out and stained the picture as well as ceremonial tools and scriptures that lay nearby. The stains remain to this day.[15]

The hierarchical logic of purity, so carefully laid out in the daily schedule of the monastery as found in the *Arubekiyōwa* tablet, turns out to be much more involved than is apparent at first glance. Through a series of inversions and subversions, rhetorical and real, Myōe sought to variously unmask, confirm, and overturn the practices of his day. The extremes to which he went indicate the profundity of the problem. As the tablet indicates, however, after all these twists and turns of logic and practice, Myōe finally returned to the confines of a strict traditional monastic setting. The stains of blood, then, become the exceptions that confirm the rule, the rule of purity.

With regard to the problem of ritual purity, the conservative character of Myōe's stance regarding the traditional monastic codes can easily be seen by way of contrast with the rule-breaking attitude of the Korean Huaŏm patriarch Wŏnhyo whom Myōe greatly admired. Myōe looked to Wŏnhyo for inspiration on a number of counts, including what he believed to be the latter's advocacy of the Mantra of Light in the *Yusim Allakto* (Playful Heart and the Path of Repose), a work now widely believed to be falsely attributed to him. For our purposes, the authenticity of the work is not important, as we are dealing with Myōe's image of Wŏnhyo, not Wŏnhyo himself. This image was rendered in an illustrated biography of Wŏnhyo composed at Kōzanji while Myōe served as abbot there.[16]

The original source of this elaborated narrative is the *Song gaoseng zhuan* (Lives of Eminent Monks: Song Dynasty Edition) that contains a brief hagiography of Wŏnhyo along with his contemporary Ŭisang.[17]

Wŏnhyo was a prolific scholar-monk who produced numerous treatises and commentaries, and he became the highest-ranking monk in the land, an advisor to the throne. According to the original hagiography, Wŏnhyo had been a pure monk who observed the precepts, but he was told by an elder master that he would not know the full meaning of the dharma as long as he remained attached to purity, and so to realize the true meaning of oneness, he set off into town and the red-light district. He is said to have called himself a "small layman" who went about freely in the monastery as well as in towns and villages.

The account in the *Kegon engi emaki* basically follows the original in the *Lives of Eminent Monks* with a few embellishments added, but there are also some important details left out. Specifically, it makes no mention of Wŏnhyo's frequenting of drinking establishments and brothels, and it contains only general references to his debauchery. It is noteworthy, then, that Myōe, who either composed the text of the illustrated scrolls himself or had someone close to him write it, excluded the most "impure" or transgressive aspects of Wŏnhyo's life.[18] This corresponds with the fact that, even though Myōe apparently recognized the significance of Wŏnhyo's free and open spirit, he himself did not consider this a fit way to live.[19] On the one hand, Wŏnhyo's transgressions take him beyond the monastery walls, and his path of practice becomes a conduit through which his fluids interpenetrate those of the townspeople. On the other, Myōe's fluids stay within the temple walls, and his act of self-amputation is used to reinforce those walls; moreover, his editing of Wŏnhyo's hagiography reflects the difference between the two figures on this point.

Individual and cultural predispositions might account for this difference between Myōe and Wŏnhyo, but one factor that should not be overlooked is their understanding of their times. Wŏnhyo developed his model of practice following a period of the rapid rise of monastic institutions and emphasis on strict adherence to monastic codes. His transgressive style reflects in part a dialectical move to break free from overemphasis on observance of ritual forms and institutional boundaries. Myōe, living in an age he considered to be *mappō,* was moving in precisely the opposite direction to reestablish strict monastic practice as the foundation of Buddhist life and society. Myōe's lamentations of his age and his exhortations to his monks to overcome the pervasive degeneracy of the times is vividly chronicled in the *Final Instructions of Myōe Shōnin (Myōe shōnin ikun),* compiled by his disciple Kōshin in 1235, the same year in which the *Chronicle of Things Not To Be Forgotten* was compiled. It begins with an instruction to comport oneself *arubekiyōwa,* "as appropriate": "People should maintain these seven characters, *arubekiyōwa.* Monks should act as appropriate to monks, lay as appropriate to lay; similarly, emperors as appropriate to emperors, vassals as appropriate to vassals. All that is bad results from turning one's back on what is appropriate."[20] Thus, Myōe's slogan "as appropriate," which heads the daily regimen inscribed on the wooden tablet at Kōzanji and his final teachings to his disciples, has as its basis a logic of ritual purity that is designed to be appropriate for the true realization of emptiness—appropriate, that is, for subverting and inverting the particular perversions of his time. The Mantra of Light, integral to the daily schedule at Kōzanji, lies at the very heart of this logic that is designed to purify the world of *mappō,* lay and monastic.

Plurality of practices. In addition to the hierarchy of ritual purity, another important aspect of the *Arubekiyōwa* tablet is the plurality of practices represented. The daily regimen lists practices that appear to reflect four main sources of sectarian and doctrinal influence: Shingon, Zen, Huayan, and the Vinaya school of Daoxuan.

There are two Shingon mantras listed, the Mantra of Light and the *Goji Shingon* (Five-Syllable Mantra).[21] There is also the liturgy of the *Ritual Repentance Based on the Sutra of the Ultimate Meaning of Principle (Rishukyō raisan)*,[22] a work by Myōe inspired by the *Sutra of the Ultimate Meaning of Principle (Liqu jing)*,[23] a key sutra of Japanese Shingon as noted earlier. The Zen influence is apparent in the two periods of *zazen,* or seated meditation, carried out with the counting of breaths *(sūsokukan).*[24] The influences of the Huayan School and the Vinaya School of Daoxuan are evident in Myōe's instruction that one section from the *Gyōganbon, Rokkankyō,* or *Yuigyōkyō* be recited on alternate days. The *Gyōganbon* is the final section of Prajñā's translation of the *Flower Ornament Sutra,* the *Practice of the Vows of Bodhisattva Samantabhadra (Puxian pusa yuanxing pin).*[25] The *Sutra in Six Fascicles (Rokkankyō)* probably refers to the *Treatise on Matters Pertaining to the Practice of the Dharmaguptaka Vinaya (Sifenlu xingshi chao)* by Daoxuan.[26] The *Yuigyōkyō* is Kumarajīva's translation of the *Sutra of the Buddha's Teachings Bequeathed [to His Disciples at the Time of His] Parinirvāṇa (Fochuipo niepan lueshuo jiaojie jing),*[27] an important work in several schools but especially in Zen Buddhism. In addition to the *Ritual Repentance Based on the Sutra of the Ultimate Meaning of Principle,* two other rituals formulated by Myōe are included for daily practice: chanting *Revering the Three Treasures (Sambōrai)* and the liturgy of the *Manual on the Practice of Contemplating the Mind-Only (Yuishin kangyō shiki).*[28] The latter is an unknown work that may reflect a variety of doctrinal influences including Huayan, Yogācāra, and Shingon.

For our purposes, three characteristics of Myōe's pluralistic approach are significant. First, although the Mantra of Light, along with other Shingon practices, is a prominent part of the daily regimen, it is no more than one practice among many. Thus, while Myōe may have focused on the Mantra of Light more than any other practice in the latter part of his career, he still maintained a pluralistic environment for practice. This contrasts greatly with his Pure Land contemporary Hōnen. In Hōnen's mature practice it is said that he devoted himself so intensively to the *nembutsu* that he recited the name of Amida Buddha upward of sixty thousand times a day, leaving little time for any other practices.

Second, although Myōe's practice as inscribed in the *Arubekiyōwa* tablet is integrated and unified for the entire community, it reflects the pluralism of his monastic community. As the *Chronicle of Things Not to Be Forgotten* indicates, Myōe's followers pursued diverse paths to enlightenment within this setting. Although there is a strong Shingon emphasis in both of these documents, Myōe's references to other practices and ideas clearly indicate the diversity of paths to enlightenment recognized and accepted at Kōzanji. Third, there is a compromise between hierarchical and egalitarian pluralism. As discussed below, Myōe at times regarded esoteric Shingon teaching with its gradual, hierarchical path as the standard by which all other practices were to be measured. At other times, he expounds the equality of all paths. The emphasis on gradual progress through a ritual hierarchy comes from the Shingon. The sense of equality reflects Myōe's appropriation of Huayan thought, in which all practices, indeed all phenomena, interpenetrate and are ultimately one.

The Mantra of Light serves to unify the hierarchical and egalitarian dimensions of Myōe's pluralistic approach to practice. On the one hand, it aims for the highest level of Shingon practices; it is a deity yoga through which the practitioner comes to embody the five wisdom buddhas and the dual mandalas through the three mysteries of body, speech, and mind. On the other, it is the lowest level of practice: simple, accessible, and designed to expiate the negative mental and physical karma of inferior practitioners. Due to this dual character, it can paradoxically be both the starting point for more complex practices and the highest level of attainment. In other words, it is designed as an inclusive framework for practice without negating the individual significance of other paths.

Although Myōe formulated the Mantra of Light to be accessible to all believers, including the laity, it was the monks, not the laity, upon whose shoulders rested the primary task of gathering the sand and implementing the mantra. The *Arubekiyōwa* tablet, when seen in the light of other works such as *Recommending Faith in the Sand of the Mantra of Light,* offers us a unique glimpse into Myōe's daily practice in which the Mantra of Light is placed squarely in the middle of Myōe's ritual hierarchy and pluralistic approach. The religious thought of emptiness seen earlier is thus translated into a hierarchy of purity, one in which the light of the mantra is refracted with the aim of erasing the practitioner's own skewed hierarchy of attachments.

•

[1] This phrase, which was a kind of slogan for Myōe, has been rendered by Robert Morrell as "that which is appropriate," and Rebecca Rasmus as "behaving as we should" (Robert E. Morrell, *Early Kamakura Buddhism: A Minority Report* [Berkeley, Calif.: Asian Humanities Press, 1987], 53; Rebecca Rasmus, "The Sayings of Myōe Shōnin of Togano-o," *Eastern Buddhist* 15, no. 1 [spring 1992]: 89).

[2] Murakami Sodō, *Toganoo-zan Kōzanji Myōe shōnin* (Kyoto: Kōzanji, 1937), 318–320.

[3] See NBSJ, 36a.

[4] Murakami, *Toganoo-zan Kōzanji Myōe shōnin,* 319.

[5] *Kōmyō shingon dosha kanjin ki,* SAZ, 2:45.

[6] Ibid.

[7] Ibid., 38.

[8] Ibid., 38–39.

[9] Ibid., 39.

[10] This may be a mistake in wording. It would make more sense to say, "There is no one who believes in sand," although this, too, is somewhat awkward.

[11] MSS, 2:887.

[12] *Myōe Shōnin shū,* ed. Kubota Jun and Yamaguchi Akiho (Tokyo: Iwanami Shoten, 1981), 33.

[13] KKB, 117.

[14] *Myōe Shōnin gyōjō,* MSS, 1:24.

[15] *Myōe Shōnin gyōjō,* MSS, 1:24. Translation taken from Hayao Kawai, *The Buddhist Priest Myōe: A Life of Dreams* (Venice, Calif.: Lapis Press, 1992), 78.

[16] Kameta Tsutomu, ed., *Kegon engi emaki* (Illustrated Origins of the Kegon), in *Shinshū Nihon emakimono zenshū,* gen. ed. Tanaka Ichimatsu, vol. 8 (Tokyo: Kadokawa Shoten, 1976).

17 *Song gaoseng zhuan* (T, 50:709, #2061).

18 For discussion of the authorship of the *Kegon engi emaki*, see Karen L. Brock, "Gangyōe ni Myōezō o miru," in *Nihon bijutsushi no suimyaku*, ed. Tsuji Nobuo sensei kanreki kinenkai (Tokyo: Perikan, 1993), 355–91. For differences between the image of Wŏnhyo presented in the *Kegon engi emaki* and the *Song gaoseng zhuan*, see also Kawai, *The Buddhist Priest Myoe*, 163–4.

19 As Bernard Faure notes, transgressive acts involving bodily fluids, whether it be through sexual intercourse or self-mutilation, has long been part of East Asian Buddhist discourse (Bernard Faure, *The Rhetoric of Immediacy: A Cultural Critique of Chan/Zen Buddhism* [Princeton, N.J.: Princeton University Press, 1991], 137–138, 234–257).

20 *Myōe shōnin ikun*, MSS, 3:670.

21 Goji Shingon (Five-Syllable Mantra). A Shingon mantra based on the five seed-syllables of *a-bi-ra-un-ken* (Skt. *a vi ra hūṃ kham*).

22 *Rishukyō raisan*. There are no extant copies of this work.

23 T, 8:784–786, #243.

24 Although the counting of breaths in meditation may not be unique to Zen practice, there is good reason to believe that Myōe's adoption of the practice was influenced by his exposure to Zen. Myōe is known to have studied the practices of the newly prominent Zen school. In the *Chronicle of Things Not to Be Forgotten*, Myōe remarks that the Zen teachings are not suitable for laity. Myōe apparently had also had contact with Eisai's Zen community at Kenninji; although now considered to be apocryphal, there are three episodes in Myōe's hagiography, the *Toganoo Myōe shōnin den* (Biography of Myōe Shōnin of Toganoo), that purport to record encounters between the two (*Toganoo Myōe shōnin den*, MSS, 1:308). Myōe's disciple Shōjō also composed the *Zenshū kōmoku* (Survey of the Zen School).

25 *Puxian pusa yuanxing pin* (T, 10:661, #293). I am indebted to Raoul Birnbaum and Evgeny Torchinov for identifying the *locus classicus* of the *Gyōganbon*.

26 The abbreviated title of the *Sifenlu xingshi chao* by Daoxuan (T, 40:1, #1804) is the *Liujuanchao* (Jpn. *Rokkanshō*), but *Rokkankyō* could easily be an alternate name (BGJ, 193b).

27 *Fochuipo niepan lueshuo jiaojie jing* (T, 12:1110, #389).

28 *Sambō rai* is an abbreviation for Sanji sambōrai, a brief ritual practice devised by Myōe, based on the recitation of the three refuges and set forth in the *Sanji sambōrai shaku* (DNBZ, vol. 13). See George Tanabe, *Myōe the Dreamkeeper: Fantasy and Knowledge in Early Kamakura Buddhism* (Cambridge: Council on East Asian Studies at Harvard University; Harvard University Press, 1992), 112–115.

The *Yuishin kangyō shiki* is a work by Myōe that is no longer extant. See Murakami Sodō, *Toganoo-zan Kōzanji Myōe Shōnin* (Kyoto: Toganoo Kōzanji, 1937), 315.

---- |CHAPTER 5|----

GENDERED POWER OF LIGHT: PASSION AND COMPASSION

WOMEN AND THE FEMININE DURING THE KAMAKURA PERIOD

LIKE MOST TRADITIONAL SOCIETIES, medieval Japan was a male-dominated world, and that world certainly included the domain of religion. Yet, as in other societies, women were integral to the religious and social life of the Japanese, often wielding considerable power and influence. Moreover, they were active in a wide range of religious capacities—as Buddhist nuns, Shinto shamans known as *miko*, novelists and poets utilizing religious symbolism, wandering minstrels known as *shirabyōshi* singing of religious themes, and women associated with prominent monks as wives, patrons, devotees, mistresses, courtiers, and the like. In a broader consideration of gender, one must consider images of the feminine as well as the historical records of women who lived during that time. Thus, there are depictions of the feminine in a wide range of media: visual images in painting and sculpture; literary representations in sacred scripture, novels, folk literature, women's records of dreams and visions. These images and representations include the full range of existence both human and nonhuman, mythical and legendary: buddhas, bodhisattvas, kami; human women in the roles of wife, patron, devotee,

129

mistress, and courtier; mythical serpents and female animals and birds associated with, or even transformations of, human women.

Although the accomplishments of women authors such as Murasaki Shikibu, who composed the epic novel the *Tale of the Genji,* have been well known in the West for over a half century, the richness of religious women's lives and religious representations of the feminine have only begun to receive consistent attention during the past few decades. In this sense, one must consider the androcentrism, or male-dominance, of medieval Japanese Buddhism as a problem of *scholarly representation* as well as classical *medieval realities.* That is, the androcentric view of medieval Japan is partially a result of the failure of intellectuals (both Japanese and Western) to represent fully the variety, complexity, and power of women and the feminine. This is not to deny that Japanese religion and society of the Kamakura Period was androcentric in itself. Certainly, historical records indicate that Buddhist institutions, government, and commerce were dominated by men, often to the exclusion of women. Such was the case at the major Buddhist centers of Mount Hiei and Mount Kōya, where women were not allowed to enter the precincts until the nineteenth century.

Nevertheless, recent findings demonstrate that women played a much greater role, that images of the feminine exerted much more influence than previously acknowledged. For instance, in 1990 Barbara Ruch published her finding that a female Zen master was active during the Kamakura Period, a woman by the name of Mugai Nyodai, an accomplished religious with means and education.[1]

Just as we are learning about the depth and complexity of women and gender in medieval Japanese religious life, we are reaching similar findings about the Mantra of Light, especially in relation to Myōe. A number of key points come into relief when we examine the gendered power of light.

Prior to Myōe's time, the records associate the Mantra of Light primarily with men. The main deities of the sutra literature are Dainichi,

Amida, and Fukūkenjaku Kannon (Skt. *Mahāvairocana, Amitābha,* and *Amoghapāśa Avalokiteśvara*), all traditionally male buddhas and bodhisattva. Chinese and Korean references are to scholar monks such as Amoghavajra and Wŏnhyo, who composed translations and treatises dealing with the mantra. Early Japanese references to the mantra involve the performance of funerary rituals by male monks and commentaries composed by them. As recounted earlier, the mantra was used at funerary rituals for noblewomen, but there is little else mentioned in connection with women.

Myōe, in fact, was the first to impute a specifically gendered reading of the Mantra of Light: "Furthermore, the five hindrances affecting women as described in the *Lotus Sutra* can also be transmuted by means of the power of this mantra."[2] The *Lotus Sutra* is famous for Nichiren's reading that the dragon girl attains enlightenment as herself—contrary to the view of other Mahāyāna sutras, such as those of the Pure Land, according to which women must first be transformed into men before they can attain enlightenment. Nevertheless, the *Lotus Sutra* also describes human women as being hindered by the five defilements of being unable to be reborn in the heavenly realms of the gods Brahma, Indra, and Māra or as the Cakravartin (the World Ruler), or as a buddha.[3] Conversely, the Pure Land sutras leave room open for more gender-inclusive interpretations. The *Daimuryōju kyō* (Ch. *Wuliangshou jing,* Larger Sutra of Eternal Life) states that there is actually no one in the Pure Land because the realm of enlightenment is empty, beyond distinctions.[4] The *Kanmuryōju kyō* (Ch. *Guanwuliangshou jing,* Meditation Sutra) features the embattled Queen Vaidehi, who sees that at the heart of the Pure Land vision is the wisdom of "non-origination" or emptiness.[5] These contradictory strains concerning the status of women carry over into the medieval Japanese visions of Buddhist priests such as Nichiren and his *Lotus Sutra*-based Buddhism as well as Hōnen and Shinran and their Pure Land movements. Their views reflect simultaneously a movement toward gender inclusivity and the limitations of their androcentric historical context.

Take, for example, the case of Shinran. On the one hand, he cites the Thirty-Fifth Vow of Amida Buddha, which states that, once transformed into men, women can attain birth in the Pure Land. Such a view, while arguably forward-looking in some sense, certainly would not be regarded as gender-inclusive or acceptable to most of us today. On the other hand, Shinran also states, "When one contemplates the great ocean of entrusting, it chooses not between the rich and the poor, has nothing to do with being male or female, old or young, sudden or gradual, meditative or non-meditative, orthodox or heterodox...but [is found] just in this true entrusting inconceivable, inexplicable, ineffable."[6] To collapse Shinran's views to either the androcentric or the gender-inclusive poles fails to account for the complexity of the social and religious tensions involving women's lives during that time. Shinran's own life reflects these tensions. He taught as a married priest along with his wife Eshinni, who also wore the robes of a religious. Yet, while they were partners in life and in ministry, he was clearly the head, at least in the outer world of religious propagation, reflecting the current androcentric orientation.

Interestingly, the sutra literature that served as sources for Myōe's practice of the Mantra of Light makes no reference to women transforming into men even though these sources follow the Pure Land sutras in promising birth in Amida's buddha-land. There must have been historical circumstances during the Kamakura Period, then, to account for Myōe's references to women's five defilements. A closer examination reveals that the Mantra of Light lies at the intersection of larger forces defining gender during the Kamakura Period. Specifically, these forces unfold at three related levels: (1) Mythically, we find celestial deities such as Dainichi and Fukūkenjaku Kannon, integral to the practice of the mantra, traditionally male but taking on feminine characteristics during the Kamakura Period. (2) Then, there are semilegendary figures, such as Shanmiao (Jpn. Zenmyō), a Chinese devotee of the Korean monk Ŭisang. (3) Finally, there are Japanese women who were contemporaries of Myōe: Kōsanmi-no-Tsubone (Lady Sanmi), a noble-woman and Myōe's lay patron; the Woman of Yuasa (also known as the Lady Tachibana), shaman of the Kasuga Shrine, a relative of Myōe; and the nuns of Zenmyōji, the convent founded by Myōe.

As we shall see, these figures—mythical, semilegendary, and hu-man—while delineating distinct representations of gender, flow in and through one another in the confluence of religious, erotic, social, and political forces that coalesce and congeal in the Mantra of Light. The mantra is not merely some kind of abstraction that exists in a vacuum; even when a practitioner invokes it in physical solitude, it evokes a whole network of relations, celestial and earthly, male and female. The women who were related to Myōe through the mantra were anything but sec-ondary or auxiliary in importance. In fact, in some cases, it was Myōe who submitted to their erotic passion and religious power.

Eros and compassion, familiar love, and dharmic love. Religiously speak-ing, one way to understand the role of women in Myōe's life is that they facilitated his journey between the two worlds of form and emptiness, samsāra and nīrvāṇa, this defiled world and the pure land. He both helped them and was helped by them; they were to him objects of pity and compassion but also his guides and companions. Early Western scholarship created a persisting stereotype of Buddhism as an other-worldly, pessimistic religion that denies all desires. Rather than elimi-nating desires, however, Buddhism has historically advocated transform-ing them. The earliest Buddhist sources of the Nikaya literature make a distinction between desire based on attachment (Pali: *taṇhā*) and selfless desire for the welfare of others (Pali: *metta*).[7] In the Mahāyāna gener-ally, the contrast is drawn between particularistic desire based on attach-ments *(katsuai;* Skt. *taṇhā)* and the universal desire of great compassion for all beings *(daihi;* Skt. *mahākaruṇā).* In East Asia, the same dynamic was articulated in terms of familiar love *(shin'ai)* and dharmic love *(hōai).*[8] While the transformation of familiar, particularistic love into the dharmic love of great compassion is well known, the place of particularistic love has not been as well understood. It is not merely a one-way street going from particular, attached love to universal, nonattached compassion, since dharmic love must be expressed in the world of familiar love. One does not simply leave behind human passion in favor of Buddhistic compassion. For dharmic love to function in the realm of particulars, it must conform to each individual form. For example, a Buddhist master must be attentive to the particular needs of each disciple. "Needs," here, means not what the ego wants but what the disciple needs to cultivate the Buddhist way. The attentive master must meet the disciple where he or she is spiritually, which includes the calls of eros and passion.

Thus, there is an interplay of form and emptiness, eros and compassion, where eros is transformed into compassion and compassion embraces the contours of eros. In the case of the master-disciple relationship, this would seem to mean that the master's compassion embraces and transforms the eros of the disciple. Upon closer examination, however, one sees that such a view is too one-sided. The master, no matter how enlightened, remains a human being with particular needs; the disciple, no matter how seemingly unenlightened, is ultimately an expression of buddha-nature and so also of great compassion. At the deepest level, then, the interplay of eros and compassion occurs not merely between two beings, one superior and the other inferior, but between the erotic and compassionate aspects of each as diagrammed below:

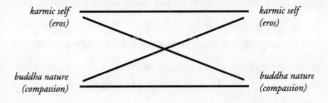

Perhaps this view can help us to understand Myōe's relationship with women.

•

LADY SANMI

AT THE END OF *Recommending Faith in the Sand of the Mantra of Light (Kōmyō Shingon dosha kanjin ki)*, Myōe relates the story of a woman who supposedly saw a dream of her deceased husband.[9] In this dream he said to her,

> My life came to an end and I fell into hell. There was no end to the suffering I underwent. On the first of this month, Master Zhixing of Chandingsi struck a bell, and the reverberations reached all the way down to hell. Those who had been subject to the suffering of the same karmic consequences were immediately liberated and have already been born in a blissful place. In order to repay his kindness, I presented him with ten bolts of silk and told him of my aspirations.

According to Myōe, there was a similar episode in the life of one his patrons, Lady Sanmi: "On the first day of the eleventh month of the first year of the Jōkyū Period (1219–21), Lady Sanmi, the great patron [of this temple], made offerings to the monk of the Bell Hall [Myōe]. She said, 'The sound of the bell can be heard [even] in the evil destinies. My [deceased] son the *shōshō* (lower-rank court noble) must listen to this.'"[10] *Sanmi* means "third rank," and is not the woman's name; as was often the case in medieval Japan, women were not referred to by their name but by their social station. In any case, Karen Brock has carefully researched the figure of Lady Sanmi,[11] and we now know that she was a noblewoman with means and one of the principle patrons of Myōe and Kōzanji. In learning of the foregoing episode, one might be skeptical and say that Myōe simply related the story of the virtuous wife in order to encourage donations from his patron. But Brock shows that the depth of the relationship between Myōe and Lady Sanmi was beyond the merely financial. She points out that Myōe not only had the connection to Lady Sanmi's son recounted in this episode but that Myōe went to minister to her ill daughter, Zenni, a nun, in 1218.[12] Myōe, in turn, praised Lady Sanmi with words that show not only his gratitude for her generosity but respect for her religious virtue:

> Our patron [Lady Sanmi] showed no hesitation concerning poverty or suffering in making her generous offerings to the temple; the monks took joy and gathered before the Buddha[-image] to express their gratitude to her. This fool [Myōe], filled with faith, inscribed inside of the bell various mantras such as the Hōrōkaku, Bodhi-Maṇḍa, and Mantra of Light, as well as passages from the *Flower Ornament Sutra* and other scriptures. When I began to strike the bell dedicating my whole being to the task, faith spontaneously arose and permeated my very bones; I knew that I had encountered the compassion of Vinaya Master Zhixing [from the episode cited above] and the benefit he brings to sentient beings.[13]

As Brock states, "The praise that Myōe lavishes on Lady Sanmi's contribution is deeply felt."[14] If we accept Myōe's account, then one can say that Myōe and Lady Sanmi related to one another both at the level of the familiar love of mutual friendship and at the level of dharmic love in which they saw each other as spiritual beings. Of course, one cannot know what they really thought, but Brock suggests that there is further evidence of their genuine mutual devotion.

•

ŪISANG AND SHANMIAO

IN CHAPTER FOUR we saw the way in which the account of the Korean monk Wŏnhyo originating in *Biography of Song Dynasty Masters* (Ch. *Song gaoseng zhuan*) was altered for the text of the *Illustrated Origins of the Kegon [Patriarchs] (Kegon engi emaki)*.[15] Brock suggests that Lady Sanmi may have been a principal patron for these scrolls, and furthermore, that she, or at least women in positions similar to her, inspired some of the content of these illustrated biographies. Specifically, Brock points to the relationship between Ūisang, the other Korean monk depicted in the scrolls, and the Chinese maiden Shanmiao. Like Lady Sanmi, Shanmiao was a laywoman, of apparently noble upbringing, who fell in love with Ŭisang but came to elevate her eros to Buddhist com-passion. She gathered together sacred scriptures to give to Ŭisang as a parting gift, only to miss him as he left port. Instead of grieving her missed opportunity, she turned herself into a sea serpent to carry Ŭisang's boat back to Korea and then into a massive stone slab to ward off het-erodox monks. The character of Shanmiao is much fuller as she appears in the illustrated scrolls than in the brief entry in the *Biography of Song Dynasty Masters.* She expresses personal and religious sentiments, she is human and legendary, and she is by turns vulnerable and invincible.

The earliest complete dating for the six scrolls of the *Illustrated Origins of the Kegon [Patriarchs]* is 1250, but work on the scrolls on Shanmiao may have begun as early as 1220.[16] In that year Myōe had a dream of a young Chinese woman strikingly like Shanmiao, and he even identified her as such once he awoke from the dream. In this dream he finds a Chinese figurine in the form of a maiden, who is a upset at hav-ing come to Japan. Once he gives her his assurance that all will be well, she turns into an actual human being:

> I took her in my palm, and she suddenly transformed into a live maiden. I thought, "I must go to another place tomorrow to perform a Buddhist ceremony. I want to go there to deepen karmic ties. We should go together." She was happy to accompany me.
>
> I told her, "There is a lady there who has some connection with you." (I was thinking that the Nun Sakiyama would be there. We would go to hear her since she was Saburō's mother. I thought of this because Saburō had brought the figurine.) We arrived together.
>
> Jūzō was there and said, "This woman consorts with snakes." When I heard this I knew she did not associate with snakes sexually, but that she hid the body of a snake. While these thoughts passed through my mind, Jūzō continued, "This woman is also a snake." I then awoke.
>
> *Commentary:* The woman is Shan-miao. She was a human dragon and had the body of a snake. The tea bowl [symbolizes] her stone body.[17]

One could argue that here is just another case where the woman merely submits to the dominant patriarchy, or that the dream carries some Freudian significance. While anything is possible, one must take into account that Myōe depended upon the prestige and personal virtues of women like Lady Sanmi as much as they may have depended on him. As Brock states, she was one of the most important patrons, not only for the direct financial support that she provided Myōe but for the many other patrons she brought with her to Kōzanji.[18] And, while it is not unreasonable to think that there may have been some personal feelings between Myōe and Lady Sanmi, one would have to be quite cynical to dismiss *all* of Myōe's religious attitudes toward her as sublimated eros. As the diagram above suggests, it could be that Myōe and Lady Sanmi related to one another simultaneously at both levels, at the level of eros and friendship as well as dharmic love and compassion.

The dating of the dream of Shanmiao in 1220 coincides with the beginning of Myōe's work on the Mantra of Light. Myōe built the convent of Zenmyōji, named in honor of Shanmiao, in 1223. Many of the nuns there were war widows on the losing side of the brief but bloody Shōkyū War of 1221, the result of a failed coup by the retired emperor Gotoba, who had originally sanctioned Myōe's abbotship at Kōzanji; as Brock notes, however, the nuns were not merely taking refuge in Myōe's protection but also were bringing support to Myōe and Zenmyōji through the attention they drew from other court nobles.[19] The episode of Lady Sanmi and her deceased son appears in *Recommending Faith in the Sand of the Mantra of Light* that Myōe composed in 1228.

Thus, both in spirit and in material means, the women surrounding Myōe played key roles in his life during the period of his most intense concentration on the Mantra of Light. Is it any surprise, then, that when the central deity of the mantra Vairocana appears in Myōe's vision of 1221, she appears in the form of a queen? It seems quite possible, and even likely, that Myōe, invoking the mantra, was mindful of the women who had touched his life, both as those to whom he ministered and as those from whom he received institutional and spiritual sustenance.

•

VAIROCANA, THE QUEEN

Between four and six in the afternoon on the third day of the eleventh month [of 1221], I went to sleep as planned. In a dream I saw the figure of the Buddha Vairocana [seen in meditative contemplation]. On either side of the image there were ornaments of golden beads strung together which shone forth from under the raiments draped over the ears.

In a dream seen on the night of the sixth day of the eleventh month (during my early evening meditation when I wished to perform esoteric practices) there was a dignified and beautiful lady in a room. She was dressed exquisitely, but she showed no sign of worldly desire. I was in the same place, but I did not feel any affection for her. She was quite fond of me and did not wish to be separated. I ignored her and left. She still showed no sign of worldly desire. The lady was holding a mirror around which she wrapped some wire. She also had a large sword.

Interpretation: The woman was Vairocana; she was no doubt the queen.[20]

Mahāvairocana (Dainichi) as he appears in the sutra literature is generally rather neutral in terms of gender associations because his cosmic scale tends to overshadow any sense of concrete personality. He is usually depicted as an illuminating presence rather than as an active personality.[21] This is also true of his iconographic representations. The statue of Dainichi in the great Kegon temple of Tōdaiji, for example, is so enormous that its head had to be built disproportionately large; otherwise, those looking up from below would see a pinheaded buddha. Nevertheless, this great cosmic Sun Buddha is almost always depicted in male form. Thus, it would normally be rather surprising that Vairocana appears as a queen in Myōe's vision, but based on the context outlined above, it seems to make perfect sense that Vairocana would appear as the queen.

Tanaka Takako identifies a key feature of this queen image of Vairocana that others have tended to overlook.[22] She appears holding a mirror and a sword, two of the three regalia of the imperial court. The regalia are symbolic and function as the jewels of the throne. Thus, Tanaka identifies this Vairocana with the motif of the jeweled woman that began to appear regularly in the dreams of prominent monks during the twelfth and thirteenth centuries. This image of her as the jeweled woman is amplified by the dream preceding the dream of Vairocana as the queen; although her gender is not made explicit, there is a decidedly feminine air surrounding the image in which Vairocana is draped in ornaments made of golden beads. As Tanaka notes, in many cases, elements of both sexual eros and maternal compassion were present in the images of these jeweled women.[23] Even though Vairocana shows no worldly desire toward Myōe, her evident beauty and affection carry a distinct impression of erotic power. It is possible that he left her side because he sensed the danger of transgressing appropriate boundaries from his side.

In 1206 by the imperial decree of the retired emperor Gotoba, Myōe was given abbotship of Kōzanji.[24] However, as Brock notes, it was Lady Sanmi whose "patronage was crucial to the construction and support of Kōzanji, and her family connections eventually led to even more support for the Kōzanji community after the Shōkyū War."[25] Symbolically, Vairocana as the queen bears the imperial regalia, images easily associated with the retired emperor. As the queen, however, the real power of the regalia seems to rest with the feminine dimension of nobility. Myōe associated with nobles and warriors from all sides; even though he was appointed abbot by Gotoba, Myōe became close friends with Yasutoki, Gotoba's nemesis. The support he received from women such as Lady Sanmi may have made it easier to associate with different factions within the patriarchal culture because he did not have to depend on any one faction for his institutional survival.

In the earlier discussion of lineage, it was noted that Myōe "may have been *ordained* in orthodox historical lineages, but he considered that the real dharma was *transmitted* to him by cosmic and celestial beings."[26] Perhaps it should be added here that he was *bequeathed* institutional support through the noblewomen and nuns of Kōzanji and Zenmyōji.

•

THE WOMAN OF YUASA
AND THE KASUGA DEITY

EARLIER IT WAS MENTIONED that twice, in 1203 and 1205, Myōe planned his pilgrimage to India, the homeland of his beloved teacher Śākyamuni. Both times he abandoned his plans, but he did not do so of his own accord. Instead, he followed the dictates of the Kasuga Deity. Of concern for us is the first attempt, when the deity, or kami, stopped Myōe by delivering a dramatic oracle.

Accounts of the oracle can be found in the *Himitsu kanjin chō* (Secret Book of Shrine Pledges), a work by Myōe chronicling the founding of a shrine that he built in Kishū, where he was engaged in intensive practice; in the *Kasuga Myōjin takusen ki* (Chronicle of the Oracle of the Kasuga Deity), by Myōe's closest disciple, Kikai, as well as in later hagiographic sources.[27]

According to these accounts, Myōe went to pray for an oracle concerning his desire to go to India in early 1203. There were a number of people present, and his cousin, the Woman of Yuasa *(Yuasa no onna)*, the wife of his uncle Yuasa Munemitsu, had been preparing for this occasion by fasting for seven days. She was about the same age as Myōe, who was thirty at the time. At one point she suddenly entered a trance and declared that she was the Kasuga Deity who had come to tell Myōe not to go to India. In order to receive further confirmation, the prayers continued, until three days later, she entered a trance once again:

> When she spoke a thick odor accompanied her breath, and it covered everything, reaching a distance of more than four hundred yards.

The Kasuga Deity spoke to Myōe through her and said, "I love you as I would my own dear child. But it is to be regretted that you have been neglecting your studies of late, and I wish that you would pay more attention to the holy scriptures.... Many suffering beings are waiting for you, so do not isolate yourself but go live near the imperial palace. I also feel a deep sympathy for Gedatsubo Jōkei, but unfortunately, he has gone into seclusion in Kasagi. Please relate my feelings to him. You are under the protection of various deities, but the Sumiyoshi Deity and myself are your constant guards, and I am like your father. You are assured of being born in the Tuṣita Heaven in your next life, but you should serve as a teacher for humans while you are in this world. Your desire to go to India is a great source of concern for me.... You should come to the Kasuga Shrine and live in Nara....

After the deity had finished speaking, he lifted Myōe up by his hands and cradled him. Tears filled his eyes as he looked into Myōe's face with tender affection. He said, "Do not go against my word no matter what happens."[28]

According to Myōe's account in the *Himitsu kanjin chō,* the Kasuga Deity exuded a sublime sweet flavor on its hands, feet, and mouth, and the people present licked this off her body and became enraptured.

Myōe was descended on his mother's side from the Yuasa clan that identified itself as a branch of the Fujiwara. This clan identification may have been contrived for political purposes, a common practice in medieval Japan.[29] Regardless of the origin of this affiliation, it had led both Myōe and his cousin to form close ties with the Kasuga Shrine, the clan shrine of the Fujiwara. As in previous cases, there appear to be elements of both maternal care and erotic passion expressed by the Woman of Yuasa in her relation to Myōe. She was obviously some kind of female shaman, her emotions exhibiting a powerful, numinous quality.

As in the case of many other shrines, the deity of the Kasuga Shrine was an instance of the Japanese phenomenon of the *honji suijaku,* literally "fundamental ground and flowing traces." According to this idea, the deity, or kami, of the shrine was the manifestation or flowing traces of a higher Buddhist deity, the fundamental ground or essence. In the case of the Kasuga Shrine, the kami was the manifestation of two Buddhist figures: the Buddha Śākyamuni and the Fukūkenjaku Kannon (Skt. *Amoghapāśa Avalokiteśvara*), one of the main deities of the *Bukong zhuan-suo shenbian zhenyan jing* (Sutra of the Mantra of Divine Transformation of the Unfailing Rope Snare), translated from Sanskrit to Chinese by Bodhiruci (ca. sixth century).

Thus, for Myōe, it was as though the two Buddhist deities spoke to him through the words delivered by his cousin as the medium. Although it would be another seventeen years before he began to devote himself to the Mantra of Light, he would not have remained in Japan to do so had it not been for the intervention of the deity of the mantra, Fukūkenjaku Kannon, who spoke to him along with Śākyamuni through the Woman of Yuasa. On his part, Myōe maintained a close association with the Kasuga Shrine throughout his life, and he worked to spread the universal Buddhist spirit behind the Kasuga deity by opening up shrine affiliation to people outside the Fujiwara clan: "Myōe Shōnin became the first spiritual leader to urge Kasuga devotion upon people outside of the Fujiwara clan. In his activity,... one may see the trend toward popularization that is...apparently responsible for the development of the Kasuga *kō,* or devotional 'confraternities' [religious communities], which were common in Yamato and nearby areas."[30]

•

FEMALE POWER OF LIGHT

IN EACH OF THE CASES examined above, there are paired images of the male and the female. At first glance, it might appear that the male figure dominates the female, but upon closer examination one might well argue that it is the female figure that empowers Myōe's life, powerful female figures behind the overt male image: Lady Sanmi, the real driving force in the development of Kōzanji (rather than the retired emperor Gotoba, who merely gave initial sanction to Myōe's abbotship); the Chinese maiden Shanmiao, the real focus in the hagiography of the

Korean monk Ŭisang; the queen, the real image of the regal Vairocana; and the Woman of Yuasa, whose shamanic power kept Myōe in Japan. Myōe rejected much of the male Buddhist establishment; his advocacy of the Mantra of Light, then, can be understood in part as empowered by the women and feminine images that inhabited his world, both mundane and mythological, both historical and cosmic, and both really imagined and imagined to be real.

•

1 Barbara Ruch, "The Other Side of Culture in Medieval Japan," in *The Cambridge History of Japan*, vol. 3, *Medieval Japan*, ed. by Kōzō Yamamura (Cambridge: Cambridge University Press, 1990) 500–511.

2 *Kōmyō Shingon dosha kanjin bekki*, SAZ, 2:72.

3 *Hokkekyō*, T, 9:35.

4 T, vol. 12, #360.

5 T, vol. 12, #365.

6 Shinran, "Shin kan," *Kyōgyōshinshō*, in *Shinran chosaku zenshū*, ed. Kaneko Daiei (Kyoto: Hōzōkan, 1964), 119–120.

7 See, for example, the *Metta Sutta* (Sutra on Loving-Kindness), in *Khuddaka Patha* of the *Khuddaka Nikaya (The Minor Readings and The Illustrator of Ultimate Meaning)* (Oxford: Pali Text Society, 1991).

8 See Hayao Kawai, The Buddhist Priest Myōe: A Life of Dreams (Venice: Calif.: Lapis Press, 1992), 165–6.

9 *Kōmyō Shingon dosha kanjin ki*, SAZ, 2:50.

10 Ibid., 51.

11 Karen Brock, "Chinese Maiden, Silla Monk: Zenmyō and Her Thirteenth-Century Japanese Audience," in *Flowering in the Shadows*, ed. Marsha Weidner (Honolulu: University of Hawai'i Press, 1990), 185–211.

12 Karen Brock, "Chinese Maiden, Silla Monk," 204.

13 *Kōmyō Shingon dosha kanjin ki*, SAZ, 2:52.

14 Brock, "Chinese Maiden, Silla Monk," 204.

15 See p. 122 above.

16 Karen Brock, "The Case of the Missing Scroll: A History and Reconstruction of the *Tales of Gishō and Gangyō*," *Archives of Asian Art* 41 (1998): 6–31; Brock, "Chinese Maiden, Silla Monk," 205.

17 Kawai, *The Buddhist Priest Myōe*, 159.

18 Brock, "Chinese Maiden, Silla Monk: Zenmyō," 202.

19 Ibid.

20 Myōe, *Yume no ki*, MSS, 1:155.

21 See, for example, the *Huayan jing* (Flower Ornament Sutra) (T, 9:395–788), and the *Dari jing* (Skt. *Mahāvairocana Sūtra*) (T, 18:1–55).

[22] Tanaka Takako, "*Gyokunyo no seiritsu to genkai:* Jichin musōki *kara* Shinran muki made," in *Shiriizu josei to Bukkyō* 4 *Miko to joshin,* ed. Ōsumi Kazuo and Nishiguchi Junko (Tokyo: Heibonsha, 1989), 106.

[23] Ibid., 121.

[24] Tanaka Hisao, *Myōe* (Tokyo: Yoshikawa Kōbunkan, 1961), 87–88.

[25] Brock, "Chinese Maiden, Silla Monk: Zenmyō," 204.

[26] See p. 60 above.

[27] Kawai has summarized the main points in *The Buddhist Priest Myoe,* 102–104.

[28] MSS, 1:237–243. Translation taken from Kawai, *The Buddhist Priest Myoe,* 102–103.

[29] Matsumoto Hochio, *Yuasatō to Myōe* (Wakayama, Japan: Uji Shoten, 1979), 28–29.

[30] Royall Tyler, *The Miracles of the Kasuga Deity* (New York: Columbia University Press, 1990), 58.

CHAPTER 6

CONCLUDING BEGINNINGS

CONSIDERING THE IMPORTANCE of the Mantra of Light in Japanese Buddhist history, it is somewhat surprising that this is the first monograph devoted to the topic in Western-language scholarship. This sense is further reinforced when one considers the importance of the practice in the life and thought of Myōe Kōben, who has been gaining increasing attention in recent years. As an initial offering, the present study is necessarily limited in its focus. While I have attempted to place Myōe's articulation of the mantra in the larger context of the religious and cultural life of thirteenth-century Japan, there are dimensions of his life and of the practice that remain beyond the scope of this effort.

In terms of the history of the Mantra of Light, this study focuses only on its history from the earliest beginnings up through the time of Myōe. I plan to devote a second volume to the development of the practice thereafter. Even in terms of its prior history, however, the focus on Myōe has meant that coverage of earlier periods and texts is selectively organized around key relevant moments. The fact that Myōe played a pivotal role in formulating and advocating the practice for his Japanese context and that he wrote more extensively on the topic than perhaps anyone else before him certainly justifies the attention that I have tried to give to his contributions. Nevertheless, many significant questions remain for further study in relation to the early history of the Mantra.

In terms of the texts of the Mantra of Light, further inquiry into the status of the Chinese translations as they relate to their purported Indian origins potentially opens up new areas of knowledge concerning not only this particular practice but also the development of Amitābha worship, mantra practices, and East Asian tantrism. Much still remains unknown concerning the history of East Asian tantra, whose influence has tended to be underestimated. In the context of the Buddhism of the Kamakura Period, Kuroda Toshio was the first scholar of prominence to document the widespread influence of tantric or esoteric practices in the religious and cultural life of the times. However, his critical formulation of what he called the "exoteric-esoteric establishment" *(kenmitsu taisei)* has tended to lend a negative connotation to medieval tantrism. While more recent scholarship has called his ideas into question, they often continue to paint a picture of Japanese tantric Buddhism as being in collusion with the corrupt powers of the status quo. While there is certainly an important truth to this view, and some of Myōe's own views of his contemporaries tend to confirm it, tantric practices including the Mantra of Light cannot simply be reduced to instruments of the state, the aristocracy, and the ambitions of Buddhist institutions—and nowhere is this clearer than in the case of Myōe.

While Myōe himself may have struggled with the contradictions within the Buddhist institutions of his day, his writings on the Mantra of Light show not only a profound awareness of the problems of Buddhist thought and practice during the Kamakura Period but also a creative response, a positive vision. His is a view that takes into account karmic limitations and potentials at both the individual and communal levels, addresses the specific needs and demands of women and men, lay and ordained, and places the Mantra of Light in the pluralistic context of the burgeoning practices during his time.

In order to provide a framework for understanding Myōe's contributions, I have selected works from his opus that place his practice of the mantra in the larger context of his pluralistic vision as well as those that are devoted specifically to the mantra. There remain other works by Myōe relevant to the Mantra of Light, but it is my hope that the selections for the present study offer a suitable balance between specific attention to the details of the practice and its place in the larger scope of his life and thought. Myōe, drawing upon the scriptural legacy of the mantra, articulates a practice that is designed to alleviate suffering and to cultivate virtues at all levels: physical and spiritual, individual and social, in this life and the next.

Of course, one of the problems of Mahāyāna Buddhism throughout its history has been the difficulty of fulfilling the great cosmic vision of universal salvation it offers. Myōe in his time and those who have followed have surely thought about this difficulty in relation to the Mantra of Light. As well, however, we historians must recognize that our very historical consciousness tends to attenuate the mythical and cosmic dimensions of life, leaving us to ponder the religious and spiritual meagerness of life seen primarily on the stage of history. History, with all of its tragedies and abominations, rarely seems to live up to the promise of a world transformed into a buddha land or pure land, but perhaps to someone like Myōe, even such a world appeared bathed in beatific light.

This study will have more than fulfilled its purpose if it serves as a useful beginning to ponder this and other issues specific to Myōe's implementation of the Mantra of Light as well as broader questions concerning the Buddhism of the Kamakura Period and beyond.

PART II

TRANSLATIONS: ILLUMINATING TEXTS

ARUBEKIYŌWA
(AS APPROPRIATE)[1]

6:00-8:00 P.M.

Liturgy: *Yuishin kangyō shiki* (Manual on the Practice of Contemplating the Mind-Only).[2]

8:00-10:00 P.M.

Practice once. Chant the *Sambōrai* (Revering the Three Treasures).[3]

10:00 P.M.-12:00 A.M.

Zazen (seated meditation). Count breaths.

12:00-6:00 A.M.

Rest for three [two-hour] periods.

6:00-8:00 A.M.

Walking meditation once.[4]

(Inclusion or exclusion should appropriate to the occasion.[5]) Liturgy: *Rishukyō raisan* (Ritual Repentance Based on the Sutra of the Ultimate Meaning of Principle) and the like.[6]

8:00-10:00 A.M.

Sambōrai. Chant scriptures for breakfast and intone the *Kōmyō Shingon* (Mantra of Light) forty-nine times.

10:00 A.M.-12:00 P.M.

Zazen. Count breaths.

12:00-2:00 P.M.

Noon meal. Chant the *Goji Shingon* (Mantra of the Five Syllables) five hundred times.[7]

2:00-4:00 P.M.

Study or copy scriptures.

4:00-6:00 P.M.

Meet with the master (Myōe) and resolve essential matters.

•

ETIQUETTE IN THE TEMPLE STUDY HALL

Do not leave rosaries or gloves on top of scriptures.

Do not leave *sōshi* [bound] texts on top of round meditation cushions or on the half [*tatami*]-size cushions [placed under the round cushions].[8]

During the summer, do not use day-old water for mixing ink.

Do not place scriptures under the desk.

Do not lick the tips of brushes.

Do not reach for something by extending one's hand over scriptures.

Do not enter [the hall] wearing just the white undergarment robes.

Do not lie down.

Do not count [pages] by moistening your fingers with saliva. Place an extra sheet of paper under each sheet of your *sōshi* texts.

•

ETIQUETTE IN THE BUDDHA-ALTAR HALL

Keep the cloths for wiping the altar separate from that for wiping the Buddha[-statue].

During the summer (from the first day of the fourth month to the last day of the seventh month), obtain fresh water [from the well] morning and evening for the water offerings.

Keep the water offerings and incense burners for buddhas and bodhisattvas separate from those for patriarchs.

When you are seated on the half-size cushions, do not bow with your chin up.

Do not place nose tissues and the like under the half-*tatami* size cushions.

Do not let your sleeves touch the offering-water bucket.

Do not put the [altar] rings on the wooden floor; they should be placed high.

Place a straw mat at your usual seat.

The regular sutra for recitation is one fascicle of the *Flower Ornament Sutra* (or half a fascicle). The three sutras should be read alternately every day.

When traveling, you should read them after returning.

The *Gyōganbon* (Chapter on Practice and Vow), *Yuigyōkyō* (Sutra of the Buddha's Last Teachings), and *Rokkankyō* (Sutra in Six Fascicles) should all be read alternately one fascicle a day.[9]

—The Kegon School Shamon Kōben

COMMENTARY ON THE SIGNIFICANCE

OF THE SYLLABLES OF THE MANTRA OF LIGHT OF THE BAPTISM OF THE BUDDHA VAIROCANA OF THE UNFAILING ROPE SNARE[10]

REFLECTING ON THE INTENT of commentators, [it is apparent that] there are two main tenets to the Tathāgata's esoteric words: the meaning that can be explained, and the meaning that cannot be explained. The former, because it is responding to the capacity and circumstances [of the practitioner], summarizes the incalculably profound meaning and principle by taking one part out of it and causing wisdom and understanding to arise within a person. The latter, because it is the esoteric language of the Tathāgata, does not reside within the realm of conception; one should simply believe and hold this within one's mind. Now, regarding the first gate, [I] will take one meaning filled with multiple significations and set forth a little of the faith of one who holds this [i.e., the faith I possess]. [I] pray that you will bring forth the light of the Buddha's wisdom and break through the long night of ignorance. Compiled by Shamon Kōben, who holds these thoughts on the nineteenth day of the fourth month of Jōō [1222]. The mantra states,

157

*Oṃ amogha vairocana mahāmudrā maṇi padma jvāla pravart-
taya hūṃ*[11]
*On abogya beiroshanō makabotara mani handoma jimbara
harabaritaya un*

COMMENTARY: [The syllable] *Oṃ* is the basis and mother of all
mantras. The significance of the fulfillment of the three bodies through
the synthesis of the four syllables *A o ma aṃ* and the like is as it is usually expounded.

A mo gha vairo ca na ma hā mu drā is the great mudrā of unfailing
Vairocana. Namely, this is the unfailing great mudrā of the Tathāgata
Vairocana.

As for *maṇi padma jvāla,* *maṇi* is said to be the *maṇi* jewel, the collective gate of all of the tathāgatas' blessings and virtues, that is, the virtue
that arises from the great wisdom and compassion described below.
Padma means "Lotus blossom" [and signifies] the *dharmakāya* (dharma
body) of all the tathāgatas; again, this is great compassion.[12] *Jvāla* signifies the light, namely, the great wisdom of all the tathāgatas. The above
three seed-syllables comprise the substance of the unfailing great mudrā.

Again, *Amogha vairocana* [signifies] the wisdom of manifesting the
full nature of the dharma-realm. By means of the wisdom of manifesting the full nature of the dharma-realm, the Tathāgata Vairocana makes
wisdom [the basis] for unfailing wisdom.

Mahāmudrā is the great mirrorlike wisdom. The multitudinous
oceanic assembly of those such as the Thirty-Seven Honored Ones becomes manifest on the basis of the wisdom of the dharma-realm.[13]

Next, *maṇi* is the wisdom of equality. It is bright and pure like the
maṇi jewel. This wisdom can purify the defilements of the discriminations of the two types of innate attachments, namely, to self and to phenomena. It authenticates the principle of the equal nature of all things
(i.e., equality of all things in emptiness, as equally empty). Thus, this
wisdom arises from the Buddha Ratnasaṃbhava.

Next, *padma* is the lotus wisdom of discerning marvelous being. This wisdom deeply examines [both] the self and common aspects of the various dharmas, severs the various doubts and uncertainties, and opens the flower of the mind.[14] Thus, of the five divisions [corresponding to the five wisdom buddhas], this is the wisdom of the Lotus Division.

Next, *jvāla* signifies light, namely, the wisdom of completing all actions. Great wisdom is fulfilled and manifests innumerable divine powers. The previous four wisdoms correspond to substance. This divine wisdom corresponds to function. Its function is likened to light. Or, because this light is foremost of the divine powers, it is said to contain all of the other divine powers.

Next, *pravartta* means "easy." It [also] means "to turn over." The various virtues mentioned before are easy to realize based upon the efficacy of this mantra. Thus, the various aforementioned virtues are easy to realize based on the power of this mantra. Also, the aforementioned virtues are turned over [to one] and permeate one's being. Sin and defilements are overturned and extinguished; blessings and virtues are turned over and attained.

Maṇi is to eliminate impoverished karma and attain great wealth. Within, eliminate the evil of greed and realize the good roots free of covetousness. *Padma* is to realize respect and love and to receive the love and respect of the people. Within, eliminate anger and realize compassion. *Jvāla* is to embody great force and vanquish the enemy of hate. Within, eliminate stupidity and doubt and attain great wisdom. In these ways one eliminates the defilements and hindrances of this world and the next; this is [what it means] "to turn over." To fulfill the innumerable great vows; this is the meaning of "easy."

Next, *ya* is the fourth turning, namely, voice, the great wisdom and compassion of the Tathāgata Vairocana, the unfailing great seal that has been sealed. The innumerable virtues of the Tathāgata are manifest in the mud of these three roots of non-good.

Thus, sentient beings, just barely hearing these syllables, immediately attain the mystic power of the tathāgatas. Upon [invoking the power of] incantation on the grasses, trees, and sand, the buddhas' virtues are attained. It is broad, as explained elsewhere.

Next, *hūṃ* is the seed-syllable of this mantra. In the *Liqu shi* (Commentary on the Ultimate Meaning of Principle) this is called the mantra of the original vow-mind of the unfailing *samaya* of the vajra of great ease.[15] According to the great signification of this mantra, this is none other than the mantra of the mind of the unfailing great seal of the Tathāgata Vairocana. "Great Seal" refers to the original vow. They are two names in accord with one another. According to the *Liqu shi, hūṃ* signifies the cause. "Signifying the cause" means to signify *bodhicitta* [the mind of aspiration for enlightenment] as the cause. Namely, this is the *bodhicitta* of all of the tathāgatas; again, this is the unaccompanied wondrous body of suchness of all of the tathāgatas.[16] The virtues as innumerable as the sands of the Ganges all arise from this [*bodhicitta*].

In this one syllable is contained the significance of four syllables. The syllable *ha* is the fundamental substance. The syllable *ha* arises following the syllable *a*. As all dharmas are unborn with *a* as their basis, the cause of all dharmas is unattainable [cannot be grasped discursively].

Within this syllable lies the voice of the syllable *ū*. The voice of *ū* signifies that the destruction of all dharmas cannot be realized. On top of the script for this syllable there is the marking for the *anusvāra* and the *anunāsika*.[17] This is the syllable *ma*. The syllable *ma* [signifies] that of all the dharmas the meaning of "self" is unattainable. There are two types of selves: the personal self and the dharmic self. These two types are both [the products] of attachments to delusory affect and are [thus called] "inflated extremes."[18] If one is able to free oneself from ideas of denial and obsession, then one enters into accord with the middle way. Now, if we understand this according to the great meaning of this mantra, then the great accumulation of inexhaustible blessings and virtues of the unfailing great seal of *maṇi* of the Tathāgata Vairocana arises by means of the great compassion of *padma* and the great wisdom of *jivāla* as the causes.

By entering the gate of the syllable *a* [one realizes that] these three dharmas are all originally unborn. It is said that, engulfed in delusory affect, one receives the [karmic] retribution which is like a phantasm on the basis of attachment to self. This self-retribution, [which takes place] as one stands within the confines of the ten directions, gives rise to the discrimination between self and other, this and that. [Out of this, in turn,] arises the abusive [language] of denial and obsession. Someone says, "I have this thing, he does not have this thing." In this way everyone slanders their dharma-nature.

There is originally no master among the four great elements [of earth, water, fire, and air] or the five aggregates [of form, sensation, thought, volition, and consciousness]. For whom are the ten directions established? Their original nature is the body of emptiness that is self-evident. That which illuminates the nature of the ten directions is called great wisdom. That which encompasses sentient beings from without is called great compassion. Thus, if this great compassion and wisdom are present and one can be said to know and to have mercy on the place where dharma-nature [is manifest], then sentient beings, as myriad dharmas of nature, are the true sentient beings as sentient beings, and true sages as sages.

There is neither attainment nor karmic retribution. Then, the various buddhas do not teach and transform, and sentient beings are not taught and transformed. This is the principle of no teaching or transformation. Thus, the various dharmas are separated [freed] from the being of obsession, the nonbeing of denial, the distinction between being and nonbeing, and the idle speculation of "not-two." Thus, to speak of the originally unborn is to be empty of the being of obsession and to be freed from the remaining three [types] of slander. When one is thus freed from the four [types] of slander, then the four significations are [properly] established. Thus, it is said that the meaning of the cause of the syllable *hūṃ* is for the nature of mind to be free of these four types of slander. This is none other than the *bodhicitta* of all of the tathāgatas. This is also the unaccompanied wondrous body of suchness. This is why there is the pure mind as self-nature. (This establishes the significance of being.) The nature of this mind is originally unborn. (This establishes the significance of nonbeing.) These natures are established mutually. (This establishes the significance of being as well as nonbeing.) In juxtaposing them relative to one another, they are neither being nor nonbeing. (This establishes the significance of neither being nor nonbeing.) Thus the various buddhas and sentient beings exist. The way of those who teach and of those who are taught is based upon severing doubt and authenticating the principle as that which is originally unborn, and everything is established on this basis.

This is the significance of the causal meaning of the syllable *hūṃ*. Also, according to one explanation of the ritual protocols the syllables *hūṃ pha ṭu svā hā* signify the following: exorcising curses, stopping calamities, and fulfillment. They are said to exorcise various evils, to fulfill various goods, and to eliminate the three types of sundry defilements.[19] The foregoing is a separated interpretation.[20] In the *Bukong zhuanso jing* (Sutra of the Unfailing Rope Snare) there are two types of interpretation based on textual evidence, separated and united.

First, the textual evidence for the separated interpretation is the following, which can be seen in various places in the scriptures: the wish-fulfilling jewel, the seal of the esoteric mandala of the great baptism. Namely, it refers to the *maṇi* syllables of the mantra. Again, it is what is described in various places in the seven great good dreams of the holder: the family of the great lotus of all of the tathāgatas. Namely, it refers to the *padma* syllables of the mantra. Again, the scriptures in various places speak of the great lotus family *(padma),* the great *vajra* family ("great *vajra*" signifies wisdom; namely, the *jivāla* syllables signify light, and light signifies wisdom), and the great *maṇi* family.

Next, according to the meaning of the united interpretation, the three syllables *maṇi padma jvāla* in the mantra taken as a whole are said to be the light of the jeweled lotus. The originating passage is the "Twenty-Eighth [Fascicle] Pure Lotus Bright-King Section, Sixty-Seventh Part" which states that drops of sweet dew emanated from the fine white hair in the brow of the Bodhisattva Kannon (Skt. *Avalokiteśvara*).[21] It streamed like a burning star and was very bright. It passed like a brilliant crystal and was pure and clear. It fell from the sky and came to rest before the Buddha, transforming itself into a many-jeweled, thousand-petaled lotus blossom. This stem was made out of pure lapis lazuli. Its luminescence was greater than the light emanating from millions of suns, radiating afar. Once the bodhisattvas' mantra had been expounded, the lotus blossom opened, and there appeared on the [lotus] dais the Bright King of the Pure Lotus of the King of the Mind of the Unfailing Rope Snare. ([The following] takes the meaning [and restates it].)

Again, the "Sixty-Seventh Part, the Section on the Fulfillment of the Baptism and the Mantra," expounds on this Mantra of Light as aforementioned and goes on to say that in all the lands of the ten directions, all of the tathāgatas of the three worlds (in the rest of the scripture it is stated that the likes of [Bodhisattva] Samantabhadra are called the future tathāgatas) including the Tathāgata Vairocana expounded on this mantra and bestowed the baptism on the crown of the Bright King's head.

Then, in all the lands of the ten directions, the Tathāgata Vairocana and all of the tathāgatas of the three worlds at one time expounded this baptism and the mantra. By means of all of the divine powers, the wish-fulfilling jewel, the seal of the secret mandala of the great baptism, and the *samaya* baptism, each [of these tathāgatas] bestowed upon the Bright King of the Pure Lotus: the various families, the wish-fulfilling jewel, the great baptism, and the fulfillment of the *samaya* baptism of the seal of the secret mandala.

With this understanding it is said: In the *Avataṃsaka Sūtra* [Flower Ornament Sutra] a lotus flower arose before the Tathāgata. All of the dharmas and the Bodhisattva Victorious Sound emerged from the brow of the Tathāgata and sat in this lotus blossom. In their exegesis those of this school (the Huayan) explain the meaning as follows: The lotus signifies the meaning expounded, and the bodhisattvas are the ones who expound the teaching. The third fascicle of the *Tanxuanji* [Treatise on Fathoming the Mysteries] states that, according to the One Vehicle, this bodhisattva is called Seeing-Teaching-Body. The complete teaching is revealed due to the non-obstruction of person and dharmas. The *Shenbianjing* [Divine Transformation Sutra] is largely in agreement with this.[22]

Following this, one should also know regarding the *Avataṃsaka:* The lotus before Kannon is the meaning that is expounded, and the Bright King is the one who expounds the teaching. Thus, all of the tathāgatas call this mantra the Lotus-Bright-King. By baptizing the crown of the head of the Bright King, one becomes a [full] person by means of this dharma which is received on the "crown" of one's mind. Thus becoming properly embodied, the substance of the Mantra of Light [is realized].

The name and meaning of the Mantra of Light of the Great Baptism of the Buddha Vairocana of the Unfailing Rope Snare are thus established. [Knowledge of] the mudrā of the original deity of this mantra and the like should not carelessly be made available.

Thus it is recorded elsewhere.

—Commentary on the Significance of the
Syllables of the Mantra of Light

This concludes [the commentary on] the excerpts by the Vajra Son of the Buddha, Kōben.

For the sake of those who are unable to read the Devanāgari script [used in Sanskrit], Sino-Japanese characters have been provided alongside. Thus the Sanskrit and Chinese scripts are both given.

An exposition [on this text] was concluded on the twenty-first day of the eighth month of the first year of the Kanki [1229] / a gathering of more than twenty people.

An exposition [on this text] was concluded on the twenty-first day of the eighth month of the first year of the Kanki [1229] / a gathering of more than twenty people.

This work had been copied and presented to Toganoo on the seventh day of the fourth month of the third year of Karoku [1227].

[This work] was ceremonially expounded to Mikawa Sōzu on the dharma-drum dais on the seventeenth day of the sixth month of the first year of Kanki [1229].

LECTURES ON THE COMMENTARY
ON THE SIGNIFICANCE OF THE SYLLABLES OF THE MANTRA OF LIGHT[23]

FIRST FASCICLE

• [Commentary on] the passage "The meaning that can be explained and the meaning that cannot be explained [...] taking one part out of it and causing wisdom and understanding to arise within a person":

"The meaning that can be explained and the meaning that cannot be explained" refers to the fact that, with respect to the mantra, there are ample grounds for stating the meaning. At the same time, there is the aspect of the Tathāgata's profound dharma in which one should have faith [beyond discursive understanding] and that one should cultivate through practice. "Taking one part out of it" refers to that which can be explained. If it goes unknown, then the way is diluted; by preparing explanations of the syllables and phrases, one causes the [mind of] wisdom and understanding to arise within a person. In the Great Master Xiangxiang's (Fazang's) commentary on the *Heart Sutra* where [the phrase] "*Gya tei, gya tei*" (Ch. *Jie di, jie di*) occurs, the venerable truth comes out. This venerable truth can be found in various scriptures such as the *Mahāvairocana Sūtra* and the *Vajraśekhara Sūtra* (Diamond-Peak Sutra).[24]

167

Thus, one should know how to distinguish between those places where one should not speak and where one should explain. One should not let it hang from the tip of one's tongue, as found in the exoteric schools; one should not speak lightly of that which is beyond explanation, as found in the commentaries on the *Mahāvairocana Sūtra*.

• The passage "The latter, because it is the esoteric language of the Tathāgata, does not reside within the realm of conception":

"The latter" refers to the meaning that cannot be explained. All mantras manifest the profound source of the buddha-dharma. Because the Tathāgata *is* the Tathāgata, even bodhisattvas who have attained virtual awakening must not speak of carrying out practice on [the pretense] of knowing everything. Even if one says that something ought to be known, this can be overdone, as the [following] statement indicates: "If one desires to attain discursive thought, then there is confusion and the mind becomes crazed"; to seek to know completely that which cannot be known completely [in any discursive sense] is actually harmful. Although something may be good, one should reflect whether one has sufficient stature to know [the good in its true sense].

Thus it is said that knowledge without faith only leads to greater heterodoxy. Knowledge [by itself] is like a scavenger scrounging around hither and thither. Just like a degenerate person speaking, one fails to be straightforward and instead wanders around so that wisdom becomes twisted, and it becomes difficult to enter into the truth. In recent times the mundane is presented in an entertaining way so that even the seat of straightforward truth becomes forlorn, and students end up taking a liking to that which is warped.

However, as the phrase "in the buddha-dharma wisdom is at the head" states, if the mind reigns supreme, then even [such gods as] Skandha and Śakta will study, thinking this is [to be left] out, this is [to be taken] in; thus beginning properly, the true buddha-dharma will arise. In India those who were determined to be wise were all clear about the five illuminations.[25] As far as what one ought to know is concerned, even in these parts [Japan], one should [still have time to] attain mastery if one is thirty [years old] or less. Those who do things generally do four or five [variations].[26] As far as wisdom is concerned, those whose minds grasp the scriptures within [Buddhist scriptures] also grasp the scriptures without [non-Buddhist scriptures]. Again, if one is able to write Chinese characters, then one should also be able to write in the Devanāgari script. Then, it is not much to think about the sixty or seventy fascicles of the Tendai school, and if one reads through ten fascicles of the various other schools, then one should be able to grasp the essence of their traditions. Things like earth and trees cannot be forced, no matter how hard one pushes, but there are things that, upon hearing about one, one knows about ten, in which case their [knowledge] is easily nurtured.

No matter how much they hear from good persons [i.e., capable teachers], those who are not naturally endowed are really like the starving who do not eat and do not even wear clothes. (It is like the fact that the natural endowment of children [born] to wealth in this world lead them to become poor. Truly this is lamentable.) Those who are naturally endowed should above all attain thorough knowledge and then realize this in practice. This refers to those who have the requisite allotment [of karmic dispositions] to act.

Bodhicitta alludes to those who go beyond their allotment and become extreme [in their pursuit of] illumined mind, knowing mind. Thinking that the world, one's wife, [and the like] have been so good to one, one becomes obsessed that one must repay one's debts. One crowds things together in the mind to such an extent that there is no room in one's mind, and this becomes a hindrance to the practice of the Buddha Way.

In order to deal with this, one should practice the Buddha Way in life after life, in this world and the next, seeking to repay one's karmic debts. Yet, it is difficult to make progress in the mind which has become congested with too many things pieced together. The so-called "illumined mind" is the mind that seeks to elucidate everything. For example, it is as though, seeking to know one's ancestors, one goes to the trouble of seeking out the names and abodes of one's grandfather, great-grandfather, and those who came even earlier. To know one's ancestors, however, it is sufficient to know and to repay one's debt to one's grandfather and one's great-grandfather. To go to the trouble of finding out about even earlier generations leads to a confused mind, and one will eventually go mad.

Thus, [this example of] thoroughly knowing one's ancestry shows how one can become overly obsessed to the point of insanity. In the Buddha Way, one should first of all obtain the appropriate amount of knowledge such that it will empower one's practice. To know the appropriate amount is to be the one who [truly] knows. If one knows that the buddha-dharma is great, then, as the passage states, "one abides pure, sitting on grasses and leaves that have been laid out under the tree among the craggy rocks on a blissful mountain where there is nothing." One who knows seeks to act in this manner.

Saying that one should know thoroughly and then act, one ends up going to the trouble of pursuing idle knowledge, and this is what is ill-regarded as "illumined mind, knowing mind." Ordinary beings should not try to seek complete knowledge; trying to know too much, they instead end up becoming confused about the characteristics of the dharma. Yet, it is also in excess to set aside this life and to say that one will seek knowledge in the Pure Land [in the next life]. It is bad to try to know everything; one should know just the right amount.

In ordinary learning, gathering [information] and memorization are considered to be the end result. Even if one does not memorize everything, if one is able to attain faith by opening up the text and delving into the meaning, then [the words] will have taken root, and it is good.

[In Buddhist logic] there is a [proper] method for carrying out the three-part syllogism of thesis, reason, and instantiation.[27] If only the skillful articulation of these [ideas] is taken as the basis, then there will be confusion, and the wisdom-eye will be forsaken; if one makes too much ruckus, the wisdom-eye will become hidden and lost. It is like wearing oneself down by felling too many trees with an ax. Knowing things well is for the sake of breaking down ignorance. One will know well if ignorance is removed. Those who know well always desire to act. This is what it really means to know well. It is deleterious to say that the realm of academic inquiry [by itself] is like this. This is being said for the likes of Jigon-bō.[28]

(Jigon became a monk late in life. Someone said, "Those who attain omniscience are buddhas. As for those who try to know everything completely, what could be more harmful? Buddhas bestow the dharma in response to the capacity and circumstance [of each person]. Right before my eyes the world is being filled with people who are losing out because they seek for that which is beyond their capacity with regard to both this world and the beyond. If one studies until one attains the mind of the three treasures, of faith and reverence, then one will hurry to establish one's practice and vanquish the mind [of attachment]. If one is bound by doubt, then one should study more. If in studying [further] the ego becomes even more entrenched, then how will one tackle this? The pain [of this predicament] is not limited to Jigon-bō alone. Those who are immersed in study should be especially careful on this point.)

• The passage "Compiled [...] on the nineteenth day of the fourth month of Jōō [1222], hour of the rabbit":[29]

This work was compiled at the request of the late retired emperor Jimyōin [retired emperor Takakura],[30] but because there was some hesitation involved, the reason for the request has not been recorded.

• The passage "[The syllable] *Oṃ* is the original mother of all mantras":

QUESTION: What is the meaning of "original mother"?

ANSWER: "Original mother" signifies the original body. This syllable is placed at the beginning of all mantras; it is the body of that mantra.

• The passage "the synthesis of the four syllables *A o ma aṃ*":

Oṃ is the syllable that constitutes these four syllables. The diacritical marking for *a* is the crown of the script for *o*. The crown of all syllables is the diacritical marking for *a*. The *matra*, or vowel modifier marker, is the crown of the script for *o*. The syllable *ma* is the *anunāsika* on top of he script.[31] *Anunāsika*, according to the *siddaṃ* experts, simply refers to an embellishing element. Of course, it appears that there is something else in relation to the mantra, namely the syllable *ma*. The *anusvāra* is the syllable *aṃ*. The explanation for the Sanskrit lies in the singular way. This is related to the phenomenal aspect of the mantra; if it is applied to something else, then it will be harmful. Jishin-bō said, If one knows a little Sanskrit, then one is something of a *siddaṃ*-mantra master; if one is [somewhat] learned, then one is a scholar-mantra master, and so on. As for mantras, they are all in Sanskrit, and the experts on the phenomenal aspect should know the meaning of the Sanskrit, and so forth.

QUESTION: Is the body of the syllable *oṃ* the syllable *o?*

ANSWER: Thus is the case without going into too much detail. It is likewise with giving explanations of the *gyō*-style script.

• The passage "The significance of the fulfillment of the three bodies [...] is as it is usually expounded":

The explanation of the fulfillment of the three bodies can be found elsewhere.

• The passage "*Amogha vairocana mahāmudrā* is the great mudrā of unfailing Vairocana":

QUESTION: How are the Sanskrit and the Chinese correlated?

ANSWER: *A* is the negative prefix. *Mogha* is "empty [fail]." For *Vairocana* no translation is used. *Mahā* is "great." *Mudrā* is "mudrā." In general, the practice of providing translations for the Sanskrit-Chinese correspondences does not [always] match syllable for syllable, but phrases are often taken one at a time and provided with a translation. One should know this in reading the texts.

• The passage "Namely, this is the unfailing great mudrā of the Tathāgata Vairocana":

QUESTION: Following the above translation, [the text] states, "the unfailing great mudrā of the Tathāgata Vairocana." Why is the explanation focused on the great mudrā of the Tathāgata Vairocana?

ANSWER: In Sanskrit, the word order is like that when writing in the [Japanese] *kana*-syllabary. In following Chinese syntax the word order is reversed. Thus, [if one were to follow the Sanskrit] it should properly be *"Birushana Nyorai fukū dai'in"* (Skt. *Vairocana-tathāgata-amogha-mahāmudrā*).

QUESTION: What is the meaning of "great mudrā"?

ANSWER: It is to press on the hands. It is customary with respect to the mudrās that one press red clay on the hands; then the hands manifest the [proper] form [of the mudrā]. It is also like this in carving the image of the Buddha in wood. Anything carved into wood will manifest that shape, and this is called a mudrā or seal. It is like the fact that if one presses a piece of wood with the shape of a horse or an ox [carved into it], then the shape of a horse or an ox will appear. The unfailing great mudrā of the Tathāgata Vairocana signifies the Tathāgata, the one whose very being is great compassion, great wisdom, the various virtues.

Thus, this Tathāgata impresses broad and great samādhi-wisdom and virtue on sentient beings like a wood-seal and makes manifest the virtue of great wisdom and compassion. That is why it is called the unfailing great mudrā of the Tathāgata Vairocana.

• The passage *"Maṇi* is said to be the *maṇi* jewel":

QUESTION: Is this *maṇi* a metaphor, or does it directly point to the substance of the dharma?

ANSWER: It is not a metaphor. It is called *maṇi* [as an expression of] the collective gate of all of the tathāgatas' blessings and virtues. The form of *samaya* embodies this virtue. It is the likes of the Maṇi Lotus.

We can sense [touch] ordinary *maṇi* jewels that are the livers of the Garuḍa.[32] There may be something to the saying that those who ingest poison face a bad death. The Garuḍa devours dragons for food, so that when the Garuḍa approaches death, its body weakens and gives off the heat of a dragon. Unable to bear the heat, it flies through rings of earth and water, arriving at a ring of wind. Blown back by the wind, the intense heat burns the [Garuḍa's] body, leaving only its liver. The Ring King takes it and makes it a jewel. Indra also obtains it and makes it a jewel.

[The *maṇi* jewels] of bodhisattvas are not like this. [For them] *maṇi* signifies the manifestation of the collective gate of all of the tathāgatas' blessings and virtues. In general, there are two gates [types] to the virtues of the buddhas and bodhisattvas: wisdom and blessings. *Mañjuśrī* is wisdom; the likes of *Ākāśagarbha* are the collective gates of all of the tathāgatas' blessings and virtues. If placed in the framework of the six transcendent virtues, the first five virtues are blessings; *prajñā* is wisdom.

In the Shingon [school] *maṇi* is given form as a round object in visual depictions. (According to one explanation, some are actually round.) Seals are [often] made with corners. This is not the liver of a Garuḍa. It is the manifestation in form of the collective gate of all of the tathāgatas' blessings and virtues. Thus, that which is called *maṇi* here refers to the form of *samaya*. The form of *samaya* refers to all of the virtues of the buddha and bodhisattvas gathered into a unity. When there are eyes and nose, and one expounds on the dharma,[33] there are differences between master and disciple; [yet,] all of the virtues are gathered together, and this is called the *maṇi* blade.

Uniting this with the *maṇi* of the realm of sentient beings, it is called the *maṇi* jewel. If this *maṇi* (the *maṇi* of the realm of sentient beings) is contemplated as a *maṇi* (the *maṇi* of the buddha-realm), then it becomes a *maṇi* (the *maṇi* of the collective gate of all of the tathāgatas' blessings and virtues). Also in the exoteric schools, they speak of the body of sentient beings, the body of the land, and they render these bodies of sentient beings and land as the buddha body.

The *maṇi* held by buddhas and bodhisattvas is the basis out of which the *maṇi* as one actuality is taken up. Thus, this *maṇi* is the virtue of the buddhas and bodhisattvas. (When the virtue of the collective gate of all of the tathāgatas' blessings and virtues is correlated with the *maṇi* jewel of this world so that the two become of one substance, then they are said to be made into one actuality.)

The interdependent origination of the various dharmas is inconceivable. First, one's self as part of this realm of foolish beings was born into this world through the causes and conditions constituting mother and father. This is to be born among the four types of birth: from egg, womb, moisture, and metamorphosis. Birth by metamorphosis refers to those who are born seeking the scents of the heavens. Birth by moisture refers to those who are born seeking to be born in a ditch or a sewer. Thus, nothing manifests its own body; it is as though all beings are simply pulled about by a rope. Those of egg, womb, moisture, and metamorphosis are born dependent upon [other] things. Because this chain of dependence is so pervasive, it is said that a mountain potato becomes an eel and animal glue becomes a leech.[34] It is also like this for other things. Truly [such a thing as] one's own body does not [really] appear, for the body [one] acquires is nothing more than a temporary assemblage. [One attains] the realm of buddhas and bodhisattvas by abandoning this [temporary abode] and manifesting the original nature of mind. One leaves behind the four types of birth, and with this as the causal stage, one attains wisdom and awakening.

Furthermore, one comes to know the nature of the unborn in terms of the two aspects of active and passive [subject and object]. This becomes increasingly subtle and is said to [manifest] the *dharmakāya* [dharma body] as the point where [the two aspects] unite as the unborn. When this unborn nature becomes pervasive, [one realizes that] things are in the east even as they are in the west although one hears and sees something [in particular].[35]

When this unborn nature is manifest, it appears subtly, inconceivably, and to speak of buddhas and bodhisattvas is no different from speaking of peacocks, flowers, and the moon appearing as images in a mirror. It is not something whose bodily nature one can characterize in terms of long, short, and the like. Even beings in the intermediary state [between death and rebirth] cannot be hindered by Mount Kongō.[36] This is not a cultivated attainment; it is simply acquired by birth, but it can be like this before one has received the coarse effects of karmic retribution. How much more so, then, if the various dharmas are not meaningless. When the inconceivable nature of mind is manifest, the smallest nature coincides with the dharma-realm; even the smallest particle of dust fuses with the dharma-realm. Thus, it is inconceivable.

• The passage "*Padma* means 'lotus blossom'":

This lotus is also the samādhi of the aforementioned *maṇi*. Buddhas, bodhisattvas, and anything else among them are also in this samādhi. Buddha-nature exists within this realm of sentient beings, and the fact that they are undefiled is like the lotus that is undefiled in mud. Mindful that [they] may be undefiled like this lotus blossom, and thus loving them, the lotus arises within the buddha-realm. This is the meaning of the phrase "by means of one's virtuous power, the mystic power of the tathāgatas." This means that the lotus arises for the sake of the sentient beings one must love. (Sentient beings' love for the realm of buddhas corresponds to "by means of one's virtuous power.") (The lotus of the buddha-realm arises by means of the tathāgatas' mystic power. This is one explanation. There is also [an explanation of] the meaning of three powers with respect to the lotus of the realm of birth. Think about this.)

If one wishes to stay home with regard to this, there is a palace that is even greater than paradise, a towering mansion. If one wishes to play in a chestnut grove, then in the Pure Land there is a tree of seven-layered jewels. Thus, this lotus is none other than the lotus of the buddha-realm. ([To state this] in terms of the dharma, this is the *dharmakāya* [dharma body] [manifest] as great compassion. One should know the meaning of this.)

• The passage "Again, this is great compassion":

There are three types of compassion: compassion based on the karmic bond of sentient beings, compassion based on the karmic bond of the dharma, and compassion based on the karmic bond of no-self. The karmic bond of no-self refers to wisdom, the wisdom of equality. When one sees that sentient beings and buddhas are of one body, [one also sees that] although sentient beings are originally destined to realize their buddha-nature, they continue to wander in the cycle of birth and death as though they are perversely taking a liking to the merciless begging [rounds] of the first part of the twelfth month. If only they would unite with the *dharmakāya,* then [they would realize that] they are one with the buddhas from the beginning (like the first part of the twelfth month).

Sentient beings sink in the ocean of suffering (as though begging) because they are confused. Buddhas, being enlightened, have mercy on them. (They have mercy because they see them as of one body with the buddhas and their equals.) If one unites with the phenomenal aspect, then the buddhas have [manifest] great compassion, and sentient beings are saved; namely, if one divides this into active and passive [subject and object], then there are the two [aspects of] phenomena and principle. If they are brought together, then they are finally one. (Although it seems as though there is a difference between the savior and the saved in light of the phenomenal aspect, there is the compassion of identical body and the karmic bond of no-self in light of the principle; there is the great compassion of nondual equality when they are brought together.)

• The passage "*Jvāla* signifies the light":

The light of the Buddha is wisdom. (Although the two illuminations of person and wisdom are not the same, they both make wisdom their body.)

• The passage "The above three seed-syllables comprise the substance of the unfailing great mudrā":

"Great mudrā" refers to pressing on the hands. Just as pressing a shape on to something makes that shape appear, what must be carved in order to make great wisdom, great compassion, blessings and virtues [appear]? One must carve into the wood block the great wisdom, great compassion, blessings and virtues of the jeweled seal of the oxen-king of the Tathāgata Vairocana.

• The passage "*Amogha vairocana* is the wisdom of manifesting the full nature of the dharma-realm":

The wisdom of manifesting the full nature of the dharma-realm is the pure dharma-realm comprising the virtue of the Tathāgata Vairocana of which the exoteric schools speak. In the Shingon, the wisdom of non-arising and non-extinction are established on the basis of the wisdom of that which realizes. This wisdom of manifesting the full nature of the dharma-realm is the source of innumerable virtues.

QUESTION: What is "unfailing virtue"?

ANSWER: The wisdom-power of the Tathāgata Vairocana is decisively realized and thus unfailing.

• The passage "*Mahāmudrā* is the great mirrorlike wisdom":

Mahāmudrā is the great mirrorlike wisdom. Just as a mirror effectively receives the image of a thing, the wisdom of manifesting the full nature of the dharma-realm is applied from behind so that all dharmas are impressed upon and manifest in this wisdom. (The wisdom of manifesting the full nature of the dharma-realm is said to be applied from behind because it depends upon the mirrorlike wisdom. This wisdom is the great mirrorlike wisdom. The great mirrorlike wisdom effectively manifests the Thirty-Seven Honored Ones.[37] According to the explanations of the exoteric scholars, the great mirrorlike wisdom is that which makes manifest, and the remaining three kinds of wisdom are that which are made manifest. According to the mind [as understood in] Shingon, the wisdom of manifesting the full nature of the dharma-realm is that which makes manifest, and the four [other kinds of] wisdom are that which are made manifest.)

The Buddha has embodied these virtues from the beginning (the meaning of the wisdom of manifesting the full nature of the dharma-realm). To impress and manifest the virtues of this Buddha also signifies the mandalas of the two realms (the meaning of the great mirrorlike wisdom). The five wisdoms according to the Shingon are the wisdom of manifesting the full nature of the dharma-realm, the great mirrorlike wisdom, the wisdom of equality, the wisdom of discerning marvelous being, and the wisdom of completing all actions. Thus are established the five wisdoms.

• The passage "The multitudinous oceanic assembly of those such as the Thirty-Seven Honored Ones becomes manifest":

QUESTION: What is the meaning of "oceanic" in "oceanic assembly"?

ANSWER: There are various meanings. First, explained in terms of phenomena and principle, phenomena refers to multitudinous meanings, and principle refers to profound meaning. [There seems to be something missing in the original transcript as this does not adequately answer the question.]

• The passage "*Maṇi* is the wisdom of equality. It is bright and pure like the *maṇi* jewel. This wisdom can purify the defilements":

The wisdom of equality is undefiled like the *maṇi* jewel. It is pure and free from the defilement of the two types of attachment to self and to phenomena. The attachments of sentient beings are of two kinds: attachment to self and attachment to phenomena. There is attachment to self when sentient beings think there is a self even when there is no such thing. Attachment to self is said to exist when one constantly thinks "I... , I... ," even though there is no basis in the five aggregates of form, sensation, thought, volition, and consciousness. To be attached to the body of the five aggregates is called attachment to phenomena.

As stated in the sutras, "It is like gathering parts together in provisional thought to establish [the existence of] a cart." To think of a cart as something that moves around here and there is to make something out of woven bamboo, *tatami* mats, thills, wheels, and so on.[38] The constituent parts are called dharmas. To presume that [the gathering of parts] makes a cart is like the self. Thus, sentient beings presume their existence and think of the self in place of [just] a person; this is attachment to self. To think that there are [such things as] flesh and bones is attachment to phenomena. There is that which is [acquired by means of] discriminating [consciousness] and that which is innate. The sixth consciousness arises on the basis of discrimination; the seventh and eighth are innate.[39] When one is purified of attachment to self and to phenomena, then one sees the equality of self and other, that and this. This is the wisdom of [intuiting] the equality [of all things].

• The passage "This wisdom arises from the Buddha Ratnasaṃbhava":

Ratnasaṃbhava is the buddha of the collective gate of blessings and virtues. Here all of the buddhas' blessings are gathered together. Thus, the *maṇi* jewel is its substance and its name is "jeweled birth." "Jewel" refers to the fact that [this buddha] arises from the collective gate of blessings and virtues of the Tathāgata Vairocana; this is also where the blessings and virtues of all sentient beings arise. It is said, "See the sentient beings of the six realms of rebirth who are impoverished and lack blessings and wisdom"; foolish beings are especially impoverished because they are deficient in the wisdom of equality. The various buddhas gave birth to the Buddha Ratnasaṃbhava because they take delight in this wisdom of equality.

• The passage "Wisdom of discerning marvelous being. This wisdom deeply examines the self and common aspects of the various dharmas":

As for the self-aspect and the common aspect of the various dharmas, the self-aspect is [found in the fact that] this fan is not a *tatami* mat, and the like. The common aspect [lies in the fact that] a fan is a kind of mat, *tatami* is a kind of mat, and *chimaki-ga-ie* is also a kind of mat.[40] Although their respective shapes may differ, the fact that they are all mats of a kind refers to their common aspect.

Thus, the common [basis] that they have in the dharma is differentiated in terms of their shape, and this discriminated aspect is called the self-aspect. In relation to this the suffering and impermanence of all dharmas refers to the fact that the meaning of the self-aspect and the common aspect are thoroughly profound. (The fact that the meaning of the self-aspect and the common aspect are profound is given in contrast with the meaning of the fan and the *tatami*. "In relation [...] to the suffering and impermanence of all dharmas" particular self-nature is taken to be the self-aspect. All conditioned existence [Skt. *saṃskṛta*] is impermanent. All outflows are suffering. Since this unsurpassed meaning applies to all dharmas, it is called the common aspect.)

There are the self-aspect and the common aspect. When students gather together they are boisterous and argue. The venerable monk Jōkei states that the principle of interdependent origination goes with the unconditioned [Skt. *asaṃskṛta*]. When he presents this [teaching] to the lay priests, in his caution he makes them write it down. He busily instructs even the likes of Jigon-bō. Actually, he is able to say all of this because he knows it well.

• The passage "The five divisions [corresponding to the five Dhyani Buddhas], this is the wisdom of the Lotus Division":

The Lotus Division refers to the Lotus Division within the five divisions which include the Buddha Division, Lotus Division, and so on.

• The passage "Great wisdom is fulfilled and manifests innumerable divine powers":

When one speaks of the six divine powers, the five divine powers, and the like, this "divine" signifies samādhi, and "powers [lit. 'penetration']" refers to the lack of obstruction; thus, each character is interpreted separately. Also, one can speak of the divine power of the mind that fuses. To fly is the divine-realm power. Emanating light is also one of the divine powers.

• The passage "*pravartta* means 'easy.' It [also] means 'to turn over'":

In one commentary, this *pravarttaya* is explained as "to turn around." Here, to interpret it as "to turn over" means that it corresponds to the meaning of "to turn around." In the *Kugishaku* (Commentary on the Syllables of the Mantra) I interpret the syllable *ya* separately. In this commentary the syllable *ya* is taken in. Since this *ya* is a part of a larger word, it is taken in and enunciated. Thus, it also happens that one speaks of *pravartta* without saying [adding] *ya*.

When one says, "*mani padma*," and one sees, "*mani renge* [*mani lotus*]," this is easy. When one says, "*pravarttaya*," then there is the interpretation given above. When one must take this to heart as the important matter, suddenly one cannot grasp it. If one cannot easily grasp its meaning, then a diagram is properly [provided to make it] easy.

• The passage "The various virtues mentioned before":

"The various virtues [mentioned] before" are the various virtues of great wisdom, great compassion, and the like. They are easy to realize based on the efficacy of the Mantra of Light.

• The passage "Sin and defilements are overturned and extinguished; blessings and virtues are turned over and attained":

"Overturned and extinguished" and "turned over and attained" mean "to extinguish that which existed before" and "to attain that which did not exist before," respectively.

Again, "to abandon that which is bad" is called "overturn and intercept" and "overturn and extinguish." "To attain ability" can be said to be "to turn over and to attain," "to turn and turn over."

• The passage "*Padma* is to realize respect and love and to receive the love and respect of the people":

Respect and love can also be seen superficially in such relations as those between husband and wife where the benefits are not trivial. The original meaning is that the various buddhas love sentient beings, and sentient beings have faith in the buddhas. This establishes master (buddhas and bodhisattvas) and servant (sentient beings), mollifies the minds of sentient beings, and leads them into the buddha-realm. All of this occurs in accordance with the gate of the buddhas' compassion. Thus, the Shingon masters must also possess compassion and wisdom, and fundamentals do not get lost and confused. (This is the skillful means of the secret dharma of respect, love, and the like of the Shingon.)

One can also lead them in if one has carefully grasped in one's mind the prayers of respect and love in this world. (If one fulfills the wishes of sentient beings in this world, then in the end one can lead

LECTURES ON THE COMMENTARY

them into the buddha-realm.) How can it be otherwise? (Unless this were the case, they would deteriorate to the point of being stained only by the love of [this] samsaric [world], and the time of their emergence [out of samsara] would grow ever farther away; one should carefully secure this in one's mind.)

My grandfather the lay priest (the holy man [Myōe's] grandfather, the lay priest Yuasa Muneshige) said something strange once,[41] "Do not become too familiar with dharma masters and keep your distance. If you entrust your mind to them, they will become Tengu,[42] or they will become merciless."

• The passage "Next, *ya* is the fourth case":

In [examining] this phrase, [one is reminded that] there are eight cases [in Sanskrit]: nominative, accusative, instrumental, dative, ablative, genitive, locative, andd vocative. There are examples such as the following. When the Buddha invokes and expounds this mantra, and one sees his appearance, [one realizes that] he [could] simply expound [on the mantra] and let this flow out to the realm of sentient beings. [Nevertheless,] the buddha prepares [sentient beings] to hear the buddha who truly expounds.

In order to invoke this *pravarttaya*, the Buddha presses into and creates for sentient beings the three roots of good [described] above. However, if he only expounds on the three roots of good, then what ought to be [does not come to be]. In order [to show that] this is for you [sentient beings], the phrase [ends] with *ya*.

QUESTION: Are the *ya* of all mantras the same meaning as this syllable *ya*?

ANSWER: That varies. It is [often] said in bestowing upon sentient beings, [here is] "the great *dhāraṇī* something-or-other *ya*." To be really detailed, this dative case is included. In abbreviating this the *ya* is sometimes left out. Even without saying [*ya*] one should be able to grasp it in one's mind, but [one follows] the details more by having this.

The eight cases are "World Honored One," "this, the World Honored One," "the World Honored One who liberates sentient beings," "World Honored One for the sake of sentient beings," and so on. The first "World Honored One" is nominative "This, the World Honored One" is the accusative of "World Honored One." "The World Honored One who liberates sentient beings" is the instrumental and refers to that which is carried out by the Buddha. "World Honored One for the sake of sentient beings" (dative) means the one who brings benefit to sentient beings. This passage is in the *Mahā-prajñā-(pāramitā Sūtra)*. Again, these eight are also cited in works such as the *Yinmingshu* [Commentary on the Illumination of Logic].[43]

QUESTION: Do the two paths inner and outer use these eight cases the same way? What about this?

ANSWER: That's correct. In the western area (India), one must study these rules when learning the inner and outer texts. In this area (China), it is often said that these cases do not exist. When told to read grammatical points according to the illumination of logic (Skt. *hetu-vidyā*) and so forth, it was necessary to create the [Sino-Japanese] reading *i* where there was no Sanskrit *ya*. Again, it was necessary to raise or to lower; in any case, when the mind could not grasp it, it was called a grammatical point and given some kind of reading. Thus one's mouth would just make noise.

In Chinese there is no *kun*-reading,[44] but if one could grasp it in one's mind, then one could apply a *kun*-reading to something. To grasp it in one's mind in terms of the *kun* meaning, however, might mean that there were actually two or even three meanings; this was because, following the six interpretations or eight cases, one grasped [a particular word or phrase] as far as the principles could be applied. It is a farce to say aimlessly that there are many meanings without knowing this.

One should have a proper grasp in one's mind of what is what to say that one has grasped [all of] this in one's mind.

QUESTION: The illumination of language (Skt. *śaba-vidyā*) presents the forms of communicating the voices contained in [the text]. This (the illumination of language) creates the forms through which one truly [goes] before the Buddha, pays obeisance to the Buddha, and [expresses] one's deepest faith and reverence. This is the reason why the forms have been created to pay obeisance to the voice of things.

QUESTION: When one is ignorant about the text of the teachings, it must be difficult to pay attention to the gate of practice. What about this?

ANSWER: When the Buddha was learning the *dhyāna* [meditation] of the deity Parīttābha-deva,[45] his master passed down to him [the method] of the meditation, whereupon he mastered it immediately. [This shows that] how much or how little one hears does not necessarily matter. Previously it was said that the first priority lies in hearing much, [but only] when there were teachers [to lead one] into the principle could one be taught well.

• The passage "the unfailing great seal that has been sealed":

To seal [means that] there must be that which seals and that which is sealed. As to what seals what, the great unfailing seal of this great wisdom and compassion seal the three roots of non-good.

QUESTION: What are "the three roots of non-good"?

ANSWER: Greed, anger, and stupidity.

• The passage "Sentient beings, just barely hearing these syllables, immediately attain the mystic power of the tathāgatas":

QUESTION: What does it mean to say that one attains the mystic power of the tathāgatas upon hearing these syllables?

ANSWER: When there are sentient beings who even hear just some of the syllables of this mantra, all of the virtues of the tathāgatas' great wisdom and compassion are bestowed on them. [In the Sino-Japanese compound *kaji*, "mystic," the first character] *ka* signifies adding to sentient beings the virtue of the tathāgatas' great wisdom and compassion. [The second character] *ji* signifies that the tathāgatas grasp and hold the sentient beings. The meaning of *ji*, "to hold," should also be applied to the sentient beings [who hold what has been added to them]. (This is the usual meaning of that which bestows the mystic power and that which receives the mystic power.)

QUESTION: What does it mean that [to invoke the power of] incantation on the grasses, trees, earth, and sand is to impress and manifest the buddhas' virtues?

ANSWER: When one turns toward the grasses, trees, and the like and invokes this mantra, the grasses and trees in their entirety become the mantra. The meaning of mystic power is as given above. When one invokes the mantra on the trees and grasses, this mantra becomes that which bestows the mystic power, and the grasses and trees signify that which grasps and holds it. "To hold" also refers to that which is passive or the object.

• The passage "'Great Seal' refers to the original vow. They are two names in accord with one another":

"Great Seal" means to press upon the hands. "Original vow" is the first. If one reduces this to the mind of the Buddha, then this is the original vow; if one reduces this to that which is acted upon, then this is the great seal.

• The passage "According to the *Liqu shi* (Commentary on the Ultimate Meaning of Principle), *hūṃ* signifies the cause":

Hūṃ signifies the seed-syllable of this mantra. According to the *Liqu shi*, this is called "the mantra of the *vajra* unfailing original vow-mind." The *Liqu shi* is a commentary on the *Liqu jing* (Sutra on the Ultimate Meaning of Principle) by the Tripitaka Master Amoghavajra. As he states repeatedly, "When the abilities of monks are gathered together, this constitutes a mandala. (This meaning is repeatedly indicated with respect to the five secrets. It is as noted elsewhere.)

In the *Liqu shi*, [Amoghavajra] sets forth seventeen stages for practitioners to contemplate and to create a mandala. The practitioner should sit in the middle and contemplate being ensconced in the original deity. He should enter into each gate of the ultimate principle and bond himself to the pure phrase of the ultimate principle, filling the dharma-realm and so on until he attains the seventeenth stage. He should circumambulate and begin again. All of this must take place within the context of having maintained the precepts.

It is only then that the mandala can be created. If the precepts are broken, then everything [evil] will befall one. (Due to breaking the precepts, one will be cut off with respect to the profound dharma.) This matter is unlike [mere] academic study. If I say too much now, then there will be painful consequences on one side.

Since this *Liqu jing* (Sutra on the Ultimate Meaning of Principle) is the section on the ultimate principle of the *Prajñā-pāramitā,* Shingon masters may criticize it, but the text and the words are all quite similar to one another [in this scripture and those of the Shingon]. It all points to the esoteric section of the exoteric teachings and is a normal part of the Shingon teachings. Those such as Annen were fond of commenting on it.[46] Thus have Shingon masters received it.

[The Shingon teachings] so closely resemble the phrases and entirety of the section on the ultimate principle with its statements referring to the jeweled crown of baptism and so forth. They are largely the same in substance, as can be seen when one opens the text of the commentary on the section on the ultimate principle.

QUESTION: There are those who say that the venerable monk Gedatsu [Jōkei] has stated that the commentary on the section on the ultimate principle is deeper than the teachings of the Hossō school. What about this?

ANSWER: This is found in the Hossō (Yogācāra) school because Cien interpreted it. To say that it is more profound than the Hossō school's [teaching, one must clarify the meaning of] "profound," which corresponds to the teaching of the middle way within the teachings of the three times.[47] That is that, but then he states that Jiaxiang's commentary on the lotus is more profound than the Sanlun.[48] Again, in Great Master Xiangxiang's (Fazang's) commentary, he states that the commentary of the *Qixinlun* (Awakening Faith in the Mahāyāna) is superficial, and in commenting on the *Avataṃsaka Sūtra* that it is profound. The reason [he gives] is that, among the five teachings, the *Qixinlun*

(Awakening of Faith in the Mahāyāna) is found among the later [Mahāyāna] teachings, and the *Avataṃsaka Sūtra* is the complete teaching.[49] Thus it is customary in interpreting the sutras that profundity is determined according to the sutra schools.[50]

Well now, the so-and-so Tokugō [high-ranking scholar] of Kōfukuji and the Lord of Uji [have stated] that in India there was no Buddha-nature school.[51] [Their arguments are based on the fact, for example, that] in the *Treatise on Mind-Only*,[52] there are dialectical arguments set forth against the heretical [non-Buddhist] views and the Hīnayāna, but none against the Buddha-nature school. However, that is like saying that there was no Yogācāra school in India because it is not named among the twenty divisions of the Hīnayāna.

The *Treatise on Mind-Only* depends on the dialectical arguments of the ten great logicians. In the *Abhidharma-mahāvibhāṣā Śāstra*, [which is] an interpretation of the *Abhidharma-jñānaprasthāna Śāstra*, the dialectical arguments of five hundred great logicians are set forth, but there is no basis for saying that these are not taken into account in the *Treatise on Mind-Only*.

The venerable Gedatsu would say quietly that, generally speaking, if the [problem of] interpretation is left up to the sutra schools, then there may be profound [revelations], but this kind of [superficial conclusion] may also be reached. As I was quietly reading this text *(shien)* yesterday, [I thought that] any monk who reads this will suddenly realize the same thing.

As for the significance of the causal meaning of the syllable *hūṃ*, the cause refers to *bodhicitta*, where cause means reason, and result means to accomplish. To give a metaphor, the cause is like a seed, and the result is like the fruit of a tree [where the character for fruit is *ka*; the character for sweets] *ka* [is different and] has the radical for grass on top.[53] In the dharma, *bodhicitta* is planted like a seed and results in the attainment of the buddha-fruit. In the ancient matter of Devanāgari, first of all with respect to *hūṃ*, the causal meaning comes out in saying *ha* such-and-so.

To say that Amida means *muryōju* (immeasurable life) is to say that each character *mu, ryō,* and *ju* has meaning; [this is] just as Shandao applied his interpretation [that] here Amida should be translated and interpreted as *muryōju*. Interpretations unfold and expand in various ways according to the liking of each person. In the interpretation of the Tendai, [a word] such as *shitakomu (shidagon)* [meaning "once-returner"] is [interpreted according to] the logic of the one hundred *wu* sounds of the study of sounds (this is the study of sounds at Kōfukuji) without any knowledge of the difference between Sanskrit and Chinese.[54] Such seekers of the way are naive to believe in such things.

Not only that, [but there are those who say that] *shintan* (dawn) is about the sun rising from the east where the Shina (China) of Maka-Shina (Great China) is one with *shintan*. Any number of such interpretations are given as translations from the Sanskrit. When there were only a small number of such instances, and [the rules] were broken in this manner, meanings [increasingly began] to be attached so that *shamon* (Skt. *śramana*) was made into *satamon* (the gate of discrimination).

This ancient matter is always found in mysterious interpretations. In the Chinese commentaries, the Sino-Japanese character for the Sanskrit *hūṃ*, which has the mouth radical attached to the phoneme depicting an ox, is said to represent the crying voice of the ox. This is actually read *hūṃ* and in the same manner [as described above], this is said to produce the Sino-Japanese *umu*.

Then, gradually, the meaning was expanded in [this] small country, and *katakana*-syllabary was mixed in. In order to explain the meaning, [things were placed] in the context of the seventy-five dharmas of the Hīnayāna and the hundred dharmas of the Mahāyāna, with people explaining how many dharmas there were. To say that certain letters [and syllables] are to be found therein is [nothing more than] for those of us who have no business knowing to simply identify the letters that we know. Take, for example, the notion of a drum. In the buddha-dharma there are the mundane and highest truths. Before the gate of mundane truth, the Buddha expounds at length in accordance with the knowledge of ordinary people. "Drum, arms and legs" are changed in order to explain their meaning, and "arms and legs, drum" become the written forms.[55] When speaking of *bodhicitta,* "arms and legs, drum" becomes [the form through which] one comes to know the meaning of *bodhicitta* as the basis [of what one is trying to convey].

As far as learning is concerned, one should first of all rigorously make these distinctions clear. One should not ask beginners about these things too much. Sometimes there are women who hear mundane [truths] and try to accrue virtue thereby. The desire to hear begets a desire to hear more. Again, if one hears, then one knows, but then this is gainsaid, and it comes out that one has not heard so much. In this way everything becomes twisted.

[Standing] before novices in learning the way, one may think nothing of believing in the various buddhas in one's mind and go on and on [as if one could grasp it all] right away. Before the various buddhas and bodhisattvas, however, this is actually [expected to be] the case. There are also cases where the explanation is heard deeply before the ordinary person actually comes to know this principle.

To the same degree that one would think learning takes place regularly in the temples, one actually finds [the monks] sleeping. They think that all that is necessary is just to know. People think that it is useless to act without even knowing how to read, but there are times when [acting without the need to know] is actually in accord with the true way.

In the learning and debate that takes place these days, it is not uncommon to find that [people] have fallen into [the rut of lining up concepts,] saying, "Here is one. Here is two." The more they argue, the noisier it becomes. This is the crock of delusion and awakening.

QUESTION: What is the meaning of the statement "'Signifying the cause' means to signify *bodhicitta* as the cause"?

ANSWER: To speak of the *bodhicitta* of all of the tathāgatas is to speak of the syllable *hūṃ* as *bodhicitta. Bodhicitta* means the mind that seeks the

Buddha way. For example, in India, the script for *ha* is pronounced *ha* and signifies the cause. One syllable therein is taken as the cause and [identified as] the seed-syllable signifying *bodhicitta*. This seed also exists in the grasses and trees. The seed for becoming a buddha lies in *bodhicitta*.

First, in all of the dharmas there are that which states and that which is stated. That which states corresponds to name. That which is stated corresponds to form. There is the phrase "aspect and name always mutually follow," which means that there is always a name where there is a form. Again, whenever there is the mind and its function (Skt. *citta-caitta*),[56] there is a name to express that dharma. Even an infant differentiates [between things] when something is present. This is called "revealing the object of name and speech." To say that there is a drum or that there are arms and legs is called "expressing the meaning through names and speech." As stated one day, in this way, the external, objective world always returns to the discriminations of the mind.

As for the two [aspects of] the name which names and the substance which is named, in the Shingon [school], to show the true and real Buddha is said to consist of seeing the eight great events of Prince Siddhārtha's life, [in particular his] awakening; this, in turn, consists of nothing more than seeing the eight great events [for oneself]. In seeking to see the actual Buddha, ordinary people first inquire after the name and then come to know the substance. That true name is established on the basis of the names of the Tathāgata Vairocana and the like. To seek to know the causal meaning, [one must realize that] *hūṃ* has as its basis the syllable *ha*. *Ha* is the causal meaning. Once one knows the name, one should inquire into its meaning. The cause of the Buddha way is *bodhicitta* as its basis.

Human beings are also involved in order to establish the name of the Buddha. In relation to the name of the Buddha, there are such syllables as *a, ba, ra, ha,* and *kha*. The syllables *a* and *ba* are associated with earth and water in India. When *a* is used as a prefix and one inquires into the meaning of [the resulting word] which is named, then [one sees that it has to do with] earth, water, and the like. This earth and water carry a [further] significance. Their names are seed[-syllables]. Earth, water, and the like are the forms of *samaya*. That which is named by those [syllables] *a, ba, ra, ha,* and *kha* are earth, water, fire, wind, and air. Earth, water, fire, and wind correspond to square, circle, triangle, and half moon [semi-]circle. To realize the significance of the square, circle, triangle, and so on [is to realize] the Tathāgata Vairocana.

That which has neither eyes nor nose, that which does not become a buddha, gradually awakens within the practitioner as [his] allotment of wisdom, [and he] sees through to the reality of the Tathāgata Vairocana ([he] sees this through as the seed[-syllable], as the form of *samaya,* as the [Tathāgata's] noble form). [That is how a] *chūjō* (middle-ranking court noble) is said to become a Buddha, the Tathāgata Vairocana, and [how] an image is painted. In a sense this is painfully funny.

Painting such an image [can occur only when] the wisdom to contemplate the depth and source of the appearance of the buddha-dharma [penetrates to] the bottom. [Only] the buddha who sees the mutual realization of cause and effect with the wisdom-eye emerges out into the world to become the buddha who manifests himself to benefit sentient beings. When this happens, the asceticism and life of maintaining the precepts of the causal stage [of bodhisattvahood arises] dependent upon the syllables, *a, ba,* and so forth. (Furthermore, question.) The form of *samaya* [is realized when] this body becomes round and square; this is the form of *samaya*.

To say that the four types of mandala do not separate is to embody the significance of all [of these mandalas]. The way to uncover the secret treasure is to see the water of this world and think of the lapis lazuli of the land of bliss, to see the light of the sun and to contemplate the light of the land of bliss. When the lapis lazuli and so forth of the land of bliss are pulled out of the water and sun in this manner, the seed-syllable and the like are [fully] realized.

The person who paints images fills a covered bowl with water when the land of bliss is beginning to emerge [on the paper]. To acquire the ability to discern things is a separate matter. In India the syllable *hūṃ* is used to say that one should express the seed of something. With respect to things in the world, this is the seed of grasses and trees in terms of the aspect that is bound to the body of that which is expressed and manifest. In terms of the aspect that is bound to that which expresses, this is the syllable *ha*. If one takes the syllable that expresses the seed of grasses and trees and attaches it to *bodhicitta,* then this *bodhicitta* as the seed is revealed in the buddha-dharma. This syllable *hūṃ* is invaluable because it expresses the principle of suchness. To know that the cause of all dharmas is unattainable is itself *bodhicitta.* If [one delves down] deeply enough, then [one sees that] all syllables manifest *bodhicitta.*

QUESTION: Does "the unaccompanied wondrous body of suchness" refer to the significance of *bodhicitta* and suchness taken together and [as expressed by] this syllable *hūṃ?* What about this?

ANSWER: The significance of suchness cannot be realized apart from *bodhicitta.* The unattainability of the cause of this syllable *hūṃ* is the suchness of emptiness; its true reality is the basis for cognition of suchness.

It is like the fact that the pure dharma-realm flows out of the completely awakened nature. On a matter such as this, in the exoteric schools, it is said that if one wishes to grasp the essence, one should pay careful attention to the *Darijing shu* (Commentary on the *Mahāvairocana Sūtra*) by Yixing, who is, after all, a person of the Tiantai school.[57] How could someone who does not know [the teachings of] the exoteric schools compose the *Darijing shu?* In order to check selected passages, if one does not know where they are [from], then one would not know even if one were to go to India; [one's knowledge] would be totally unreliable.

If the exoteric schools are likened to the shore and the Shingon to the offing, then one might wonder where one will end up. The teachings of the Shingon are found in the discussion of the Sanskrit syllables. The ten stages of mind are [also] relevant to the exoteric schools [so that] the teachings of the exoteric schools become mixed. They [end up] actually [talking about] the gates of practicing the dharma according to the various explanations of the syllable *a,* the syllable *hūṃ,* and so forth [even though these] belong to the teachings of the Shingon. On top of that, they do not even know the meaning of the teaching aspect [as opposed to the practice aspect]. Furthermore, their meaning cannot be explained solely in terms of the eight consciousnesses and three natures [of the Yogācāra].[58]

Thinking that is the way things are in the terms of the meaning of the Shingon, there are various people who write on these matters, but I have nothing to do with this. In this way they swear up and down [that they know what they are talking about].

QUESTION: According to [Kūkai's] *Jūjūshin ron* (Treatise on the Ten Stages of Mind) the *a* syllable, *hūṃ* syllable, and so on constitute that which produce, and "principle" is that which is produced. The exoteric [schools] take principle to be ultimate. Here, however, in contrast, to take the syllables *a* and *hūṃ* as the basis is [to see that] the syllables *a* and *hūṃ* are deeper than the principle of suchness. Is this right?

ANSWER: They [the exoteric schools] focus on the meaning revealed through the practice of the nature of [emptiness] as principle. It is like saying that the pure dharma-realm (completed nature) flows out of the mind of sentient beings; I am not trying to speak of deep or shallow.

—Lectures on the *Commentary on the Significance of the Syllables of the Mantra of Light of the Baptism of the Buddha Vairocana of the Unfailing Rope Snare,* [end of] First Fascicle

Manuscript completed on the tenth day of the fifth month of 1259.

Jinshin

•

SECOND FASCICLE

• The passage "The syllable *ha* arises following the syllable *a*":

"Following the syllable *a*" means to become two, like giving birth to a child. It does not become three. To explain the meaning, this is to say that first the mind arises, and with this one comes to know it. The wisdom attained after the fundamental basis refers to before and after [. . .] before and after the explanation of the meaning. When opening [. . .] everything is *a*. This gradually becomes *o*.

• The passage "As [from the fact that] all dharmas are unborn with *a* as their basis":

That all dharmas are unborn refers to what has been written in *kana*-syllabary (this is the *Kanjinki*). This stands apart from eternalism and nihilism. The thoughts of ordinary beings are based on the two attachments to self and to dharmas, and that [. . .] of the actual body [. . .] finally [. . .] confused. If, with respect to person and dharmas, one awakens out of attachment to self and dharmas, then this is the awakening of the Buddha.

QUESTION: Previously, you stated that all syllables have *a* as their basis. What about this?

ANSWER: The head of all syllables is *a*. In the Shingon [school] the contemplation of the seed-syllable is an esteemed practice. The contemplation of the seed-syllable is good for those whose natures are of middling quality. In the *Liqu jing,* (Sutra on the Ultimate Meaning of Principle) there is the phrase, "the *prajñā-pāramitā* [transcendental wisdom] of the light of the various dharmas." This refers to the illumination of emptiness of all dharmas. The practitioner is exhorted to contemplate this; the yoga practitioner must construct the mandala with Mañjuśrī and the other bodhisattvas in repose at the center. Even if Mañjuśrī does not attain repose [during the practitioner's contemplation], one must be in accord with the principle. If this is not achieved, then it will be as though one were dying even though there are no stricken foxes or badgers.[59] This will not end as long as one fails to practice, and one will be born in a world where practice cannot be established, and one's mind will float about [lost]. (If the illness of one's practice in the buddha-dharma does not reach an end, then the deluded affect of the two attachments to person and dharmas will not die. Think very carefully on this.)

• The passage "The voice of *ū* signifies that the destruction of all dharmas cannot be realized":

As for the syllable *ū*, in India this indicates denial, and *ū* is said [...] This is used as a word for denial. As for [the terms] "word-root" and "word-relation," the part of a word that is the base is the "word-root." [For example, the word in Sanskrit for] "knowledge" is *jñāna; jña* is the word-root, and *na* is the word-relation. Similarly, the word for "denial" is *ū*-plus-something.

• The passage "On top of the script for this syllable there is the marking for the *anusvāra* and the *anunāsika*. This is the syllable *ma*":[60]

[...] in the seed-syllable should there be an *anunāsika*, [...] definitely dropped? In this way it is used to interpret in relation to the syllable *ma*. When I saw the great buddha[-statue] being repaired at Tōji, the Great Master was inscribing the seed-syllable of the mantra with his brush, and he put it in [...] even though there was no paper, and he bent the rules by putting in an *anunāsika*.

QUESTION: In the signification of the two syllables, the three syllables of *a, u,* and *ma* are given, but there is no discussion of *aṃ*.

ANSWER: In order to make the allotments to the three bodies, the *ma* and *aṃ* were joined. This is what it means "to join" (the text of the *Liqu shi* [discussed] here [in this forum mentions] *ma* but there is no commentary on *aṃ*). The syllable *ma* in its heavenly nature can be read with an *anusvāra*.

QUESTION: Can [the character for] *u* [also] be read *o*?

ANSWER: As for *u* and *o,* just as the *anusvāra* and the *anunāsika* have an affinity for one another and can be joined, *u* and *o* can be read in accordance with the body.

QUESTION: What about reading *ma* with the *anusvāra?*

ANSWER: There are instances in which *ma* is read *maṃ.* In the world, matters such as this are all [...] definitely, because the syllable *ma* and the syllable *mu* are close to one another.[61]

QUESTION: Is the syllable *ma* the only syllable to which this matter of the *anusvāra* applies? What about this?

ANSWER: The four syllable groupings of soft palatal, palatal, dental, and sibilant can all be read according to the *anusvāra.* Only, [it should be noted that] *ma* easily becomes [this], and the rest [require] some explanation.

• The passage "There are two types of selves: the personal self and the dharmic self":

As for the personal self and the dharmic self: The personal self [is found in] the thought that a master [essence] exists within the dharmas of the five aggregates; not knowing the five aggregates as five [and not a single unchanging entity], one wanders through the cycle of life and death. The dharmic self is found in the thought that there are five [conditioning factors] in the five aggregates.

• The passage "are 'inflated extremes'":

"Inflated extremes" is to arbitrarily negate the existence of the various dharmas. "Negation" is to negate for no reason the interdependent arising of dharmas. This is called the heterodoxy of nihilism. If one becomes free of this, then one enters the middle way. As for the aforementioned significance of the "unattainable," everything [...] creates its own particular significance. Namely, the syllable *ha* [...] within is not [...] *a* [...] within [...] the unattainable significance of the dharmic self [...] As for *ma,* at the beginning [...] gradually, to say like this, *sedara* [...] This is what is called the contemplation of the seed-syllable. One should focus the mind by means of this syllable.

Eventually the precepts and the mantra arise within the mind and form of the buddha-dharma. If one is mindful of this syllable, then one will realize the yoga of the main deity.

• The passage, "The great accumulation of inexhaustible blessings and virtues of the unfailing great seal of *maṇi* of the Tathāgata Vairocana arises by means of the great compassion of *padma* and the great wisdom of *jivāla* as the causes":

If self and dharmas are empty, then one should attain these virtues. Although this may seem to be like a phantasm before the [workings of a] deluded affect, [one only needs to realize that] if one is attached to self and dharmas and is thus born in their midst, then the ten directions are established. Calculating between self and other, here and there, a person thinks, [for example,] that he is an ant, that a horse is one's father [and so forth]. [Seeing] some horse, a word arises in correspondence with it, and thus a dharma is born out of the unborn. [However,] if one loses this attachment to self and other, then one can attain these virtues instantly. Yet, the exoteric schools state that it takes uncountable, innumerable eons to attain them. Thus, the attainment of these virtues becomes far off, but there is a way to attain them immediately. That is the inexhaustible blessings and virtues of *maṇi* with the great compassion of *padma* and the great wisdom of *jivāla* as the causes.

• The passage "Engulfed in delusory affect,…as one stands in the confines of the ten directions, gives rise to the discrimination between self and other":

Within this deluded affect, one is transmogrified due to the delusions of one's mind and emerges out into the world, is born, and then one calculates the expanse of the ten directions. It is as [the following passage] states: "Again, when the various sentient beings come to the end of their lives or have arrived at that long stage of thoughts in which one has not yet sunken into the darkness, the habituated love of self becomes actively manifest. This power is called the self that corresponds to nothing. Then, through self-love one creates the intermediary state and the retribution of [re-]birth." Thus, the dharmas that arise from ordinary beings' two attachments to self and dharmas are all delimited discursively. As long as one is here, the expanse of ten directions also unmistakably seems to exist. Here the various buddhas bestow their compassion, and for the sake of shallow believers, expound upon the five imperial dragon kings and the five imperial *yakṣa* (this is the teaching of the Yin-Yang masters).[62] For the sake of deep believers, they also construct the buddha-ranks of the five directions [five types of wisdom]. If one takes the superficial [aspect] of Shingon as the profound, then, to jump ahead, this is it [the conclusion]. Overturning consciousness and attaining wisdom is also the teaching of the provisional schools.

In the Shingon this is called the overturning and attainment of the five wisdoms as expounded in the *Muli mantuoluo jing* (Sutra of the Mandala of the Jeweled Tower).[63] Since the buddha-ranks of the five directions is the explanation of the overturning and attainment of the five wisdoms, it should be explained in the *Mahāvairocana Sūtra* as well. Also, in speaking of land, the pure land of the mantra of Mahāvairocana is the abode of the bodhisattvas of the eighth, ninth, and tenth stages [and therefore] shallow. However, the profundity of the profound dharma is constant. The Shingon is profound because it expounds the shallow as profound.

In the exoteric schools, according to the explanation of the *Yingluo jing* (Sutra of the Jeweled Necklace), the ten [culminating] stages are profound, and the three [preceding groups of the] wisdom [stages] shallow, and this is constant.[64] Since the *Avataṃsaka Sūtra* is the complete teaching, it teaches that the ten [culminating] stages are shallow, and the three [groups of the] wisdom [stages] are profound.

Since the exoteric schools also speak of the sudden teaching, and the teachings leading up to it end up there, this appears profound but is not profound; that which embodies both the sudden and the gradual truly represents the profundity of the dharma. There are two types of sudden [awakening] in the view of attaining buddhahood in this very body. The profundity of the sudden and profound is the sudden teaching. Thus, in the Huayan [teaching], sudden and gradual are both explained as profound, and this is also [the teaching of] attaining buddhahood in this very body.

• The passage "There is originally no master among the four great elements [of earth, water, fire, and air] or the five aggregates [of form, sensation, thought, volition, and consciousness]. For whom are the ten directions established?"

To construct one's body out of the illusory dharmas of the four great elements and five aggregates is akin to a body of foam and spray; the body is originally empty. The Hīnayāna expounds the four noble truths of suffering, the cause of suffering, the extinction of suffering, and the path, thus quickly moving to exit to the noble truth of extinction. As the basis of Buddhist scripture this is good, but the good resulting from outflows correlates with self and dharmas affirmed as real and existing and thus does not lead to release from the world.

QUESTION: Doesn't this slander the dharma?[65]

ANSWER: As for slander, to speak like this does not lead to accruing sin and falling into hell. It must mean that one does not know the unborn.

• [On the one hand], in the statement, "Their original nature is the body of emptiness that is self-evident," emptiness refers to that upon which the various buddhas and sentient beings are dependent. On the other hand, the existence of the realm of the ten directions arises due to existing within self and dharmas.

Thus, various places each arise in this way, and the provisional explanation is given of self and other, this and that, even before [the eyes] of sagely wisdom, because [all distinctions are resolved in light of the fact that] they inform one another in the emptiness of mind. When there are no [distinctions between] self and other, this and that, self and other inform one another in [their mutual] emptiness. If the five aggregates do not exist, then the ten directions inform one another in emptiness. If this fact fills the realm of the ten directions, then [the nature of] the body becomes self-evident; this is to say that both person and dharmas are empty. Thus, to illuminate the nature of the ten directions within is called great wisdom.

In giving rise to faith and wisdom in accord with this dharma, this seat of learning and hearing whispers and falls silent. To quietly ponder and contemplate this is practice.

To invoke the phrase "My *bodhimaṇḍa* [locus of awakening] here, like an imperial jewel, the buddhas of the ten directions, [their] forms appearing within" all of which is just next door (this is to point to the buddha-lands of the ten directions and call this "next-door"), is like scattering flower petals. This is to practice the profound dharma in a superficial manner. If it is not like this, then is this all just empty words?

The real dharma with respect to the mind [is expressed] in the phrase "Emerging alive innumerably, the lotus blossoms of the dharma, the form of this flower, all truly wondrous." If one invokes this phrase, then one will truly attain its virtue. How much more so if one closes one's eyes and ponders and contemplates it. This is the effective, definitely flourishing buddha-dharma. If people gather together as though they are scooping up hot water with a net, then finally one [enters] the way of debate. Often, if one comes to know this, then there will be a pause [when] the hermit's [life] is truly quiet, and things will get done.

One may polish one's mind for awhile and then emerge [from seclusion]. One may expect some significant result, but nothing all that great comes of it. (There certainly is nothing as great as the karma of the six realms of rebirth and the four types of birth.) All this is extremely frightful, and what I am saying is confidential. To write about things like this within [our circle] is not permitted. Without knowing whether this is good or bad, if this is virtue, then it [must be] inconceivable virtue.

• The passage "That which encompasses sentient beings from without is called great compassion":

When the great wisdom is clearly manifest, one knows and strolls through the realm of emptiness, and all this is directly before one's awakened [mind] as though one cannot help tripping over it. Yet, this is not the case before [the eyes] of [deluded] sentient beings who [live] as though in a dream or phantasm. In trying to make this known to sentient beings, the mind of mercy arises, and this is great compassion. Great wisdom and compassion arise provisionally as manifestations of the originally unborn. Thus, compassion and wisdom are also unborn. If one were to say that compassion and wisdom are truly substantial, then one would want to find great wisdom and compassion and would never become a buddha.

If sentient beings do not have substantial bodies, then sentient beings would be real sentient beings, buddhas would be real buddhas, and it would not be possible to have [the interaction between] those who teach and those who are taught.

• The passage "Thus, the various dharmas are separated [freed] from the being of gain," and so on:

The various dharmas arise from causes and conditions, and their fundamental natures are empty. When one comes to know this, *bodhicitta* arises provisionally. "Provisionally" means arising from causes and conditions. Thus, the various dharmas are provisional and empty. To say upon hearing this that the entirety transcends nonbeing constitutes the slander of denial. Thus, to speak of being and nonbeing is already in error. Next, to think that the various dharmas exist or do not exist constitutes the slander of difference. Furthermore, to think based on this that the various dharmas neither exist nor do not exist is [the exercise of] the useless rhetoric of nonduality.

If one frees oneself from these four types of slander, then the being of the various dharmas inconceivably exists, and the nonbeing also inconceivably exists. (Being and nonbeing inconceivably exist when one is freed from the four types of slander. This means that, with respect to a single dharma there is the meaning of being and the meaning of nonbeing, the meaning of both being and nonbeing, and the meaning of neither being nor nonbeing. Because all of these meanings are realized, [the various dharmas are] inconceivable.)

• The passage "To speak of the originally unborn is to be empty of the being of obsession and to be freed from the remaining three [types] of slander. When one is thus freed from the four [types] of slander, then the four significations are [properly] established":

QUESTION: Does "originally unborn" point to the body of principle?

ANSWER: It means that there is no attachment to self or dharmas with respect to principle.

QUESTION: If that which is devoid of self and dharmas is not the unborn, then the unborn is not the true principle?

ANSWER: That which produces is the unborn, that which is manifest is the true principle. When speaking of the suchness of the manifestation of the two emptinesses [of self and dharmas], the provisional schools [teach] the suchness of the manifestation of the two emptinesses, and the true teaching is that the two emptinesses are none other than suchness. The buddha-nature theory speaks of the suchness of the manifestation of the two emptinesses of self and dharmas, and also speaks of suchness as none other than the two emptinesses of self and dharmas. In the former the two tenets of the provisional and the true share a common basis, but in the latter the true teaching stands alone.[66]

• From the passage "Thus, it is said that the meaning of the cause of the syllable *hūṃ* is for the nature of mind to be free of these four types of slander [...] This is the being of the pure mind of self-nature":

For ordinary beings, the meaning of the cause of the syllable *hūṃ*, like these arms and legs, carries the meaning of cause. To think thus involves the slander of obsession. To think of this in terms of nonbeing [no significance] represents the slander of denial. Thus, in ordinary beings' confusion, to think any thoughts [discursively] is harmful. The nature of this mind is not like that of arms and legs. It stands apart from the four [types of] slander and is inconceivable; this is the pure mind of self-nature.

That "the nature of mind [is] free of these four types of slander" is to say that the *bodhicitta* of all of the tathāgatas [consists of] being free of these four [types of] slander. Also, the body of suchness [consists of] having become free of these four [types of] slander. Thus, if one is free of these four [types of] slander, then being [itself manifests] the pure mind of self-nature, and this is the inconceivable: "the being of the pure mind of self-nature."

Nonbeing is also truly empty in pointing to the nature of emptiness ("the nature of this mind is originally unborn"). Furthermore, there is the significance of the myriad virtues that are inconceivable. Namely, there are both the significations of emptiness and of being ("these natures are established mutually"). If the realm of pure self-nature is the originally unborn [nature] of being, then emptiness is established mutually [in being and nonbeing] so that there is neither being nor nonbeing ("in juxtaposing them relative to one another, they are neither being nor nonbeing"). If one becomes free of the four [types of] slander and comes to abide in the four significations, then the buddhas are noble and sentient beings are bad.[67] Then there are those who teach and those who are taught.

The paths of severing confusion, realizing principle, and the like are all inconceivable. This is all constructed with the originally unborn as the basis. It is just as ordinary beings' constructing [their world] with self and dharmas as the basis. If even one of the significations above is missing, then it is like rot [that spreads] beginning with even one grain of rice.

• The passage "*hūṃ pha ṭu svā hā*":

The *Amoghapāśa Sūtra (Sutra of the Unfailing Rope Snare) is up to *hūṃ*. The ritual protocols of this different version are explained a little too neatly. There is also where [one finds] this *hūṃ pha ṭu svā hā*. *Hūṃ pha ṭu* means exorcising curses and stopping calamities. *Svā hā* signifies fulfillment. To exorcise curses means to exorcise the blind passions that are difficult to regulate. It also means to subdue the enactment of these evils by that person. Stopping the calamities means to extinguish the misfortune of the three sundry calamities. The three sundry calamities are blind passions, karma, and suffering. *Svā hā* is interpreted as the incantation of fulfillment. Thus [we have] the meaning of exorcising curses, stopping calamities, and fulfillment.

• The passage "The foregoing is a separated interpretation":

"Separated interpretation" means to separate and interpret. It is to separate and interpret *maṇi padma jvāla* and the like.

• The passage "The wish-fulfilling jewel, the seal of the esoteric mandala of the great baptism":

This passage is associated with the virtue of this mantra. Namely, [it means] to embody all of the virtues. Baptism means to bestow this mantra on all sentient beings. The seal of the esoteric mandala refers to the great seal that bestows this mantra on all sentient beings. The seal is the body of decisive realization. If one establishes *maṇi* separately, then this is a separated interpretation.

• The passage "The family of the great lotus of all of the tathāgatas":

The significance of the lotus family and so on are given in the *Kanjinki* (Recommending Faith in the Sand of the Mantra of Light). The above separates these three phrases (the lotus family, the great *vajra* family, and the great *maṇi* family) and interprets them. Next is the united interpretation.

• The word "*sphaṭikā* [crystal]":

Sphaṭikā is signified by the place where the red insect emerges. Like the place where the red insect emerges, this jewel is red and very beautiful. However, the *sphaṭikā* of Mount Sumeru cannot [be found] where the red insect emerges.

• The passage "fell from the sky":

That drops of sweet dew fell from the sky refers to [the drops] falling from the brow.

• The passage "radiating afar":

Radiating afar means that it is so great as to be vexatious.

• The passage "all of the tathāgatas of the three worlds":

Future buddhas refers to the bodhisattvas. Samantabhadra is called a future buddha because he will become a buddha in the future. [The fact that this statement does not seem to address the meaning of the quoted passage reflects the content of the original transcript.]

• The passage "the divine powers, the wish-fulfilling jewel, the seal of the secret mandala of the great baptism":

It is always said, the words of the mantra carry many meanings, and explanations are linked together at length to reveal the meanings.

• The passage "Various families":

"Families" refers to the wisdom family, the *maṇi* family, and so on; the buddha family embodies all of the buddhas' virtues.

• The passage "great baptism," and so forth:

As for baptism, the original body is the bodhisattva of the tenth stage who receives the virtues of the buddhas. When the bodhisattva of the tenth stage attains supreme awakening, there will be a great lotus blossom that is as large as ten quintillion worlds. [The bodhisattva's] body will be of commensurate size. [When the bodhisattva] sits on the lotus blossom, innumerable rays of light will emanate from the various sense organs [such as eyes, ears, nose, tongue, and body].[68]

To give a diagrammatic outline, [imagine] a million rays of light emanating from this back that illuminates śrāvakas (due to betraying the buddha, the monks frolic). Rays of light from the hands illuminate the heavenly realms and the realm of *asura,* the angry god.[69] The light from the abdomen illuminates the *kiṃnara,*[70] the *gandharva,*[71] and the like; the *kiṃnara* are musicians and, hitting their drums, [one is reminded that] the abdomen is like a drum.

The monk Kaidō could give an artless reading like this: The light at the peak illuminates all the buddhas. This is quoted in the *Shōgonki* (Elaboration on the Tract [Destroying Heretical Views]):[72] The light from the crown illuminates all of the buddhas and reaches under their feet. The light of divine power and the amplification of all wisdom emanates from the brow of the buddha and enters the crown of the bodhisattvas. The amplification of all wisdom means that all wisdom is amplified, that the light of the buddha enters [into one]. This is similar to the protocol for the proper incantation of the mantra in which the baptismal [fluid] falls and is sprinkled [on the head].

(There is a further question:) With regard to the baptism, in the Great Country, even Uma-no-Jō Hyōe-no-Jō underwent the baptism. The baptism occurred when the scented water of purification was poured on him, and he [took the vows of] renunciation. At the instant that the light of the Buddha enters the crown, it is said, "The ten powers in full array descend as the buddha-seed." This means that the virtue of the ten powers of the Buddha enters the body, and one attains awakening.
• The phrase "*samaya* baptism":

The *samaya* baptism refers to the fact that this amplification of all wisdom entering the crowns of the bodhisattvas' heads is like pouring water. Baptizing the Great King means that the water of the four great oceans and all the rivers is poured on the head of the previous king and the present king. [This is similar to] the matter of the crown of the story of the heavenly being of the southern mountain. (This refers to the baptism.) Thus, if one had thought that the Buddha simply awakened under the Bodhi Tree and opened up [this truth to the world], then one would have been surprised by the unexpected signs that appeared.
• The passage "all of the families":

"All of the families" refers to the fact that all of the tathāgatas ultimately make buddhas. ("All of the families" refers to the *maṇi* family, lotus family, *vajra* family, and so forth aforementioned. The character *shu* [in the Sino-Japanese compound] *shuzoku,* "family," refers to species, [the second character] *zoku* refers to genus. The Buddha ultimately fulfills the *maṇi* family and so on. They are also bestowed upon Kannon (Skt. Avalokiteśvara) and realized. Again, when we receive this mantra, [this is the same as] the buddhas attaining the *maṇi* jewel, and we become relatives of the buddhas' *maṇi* jewel family, and so on. If we are relatives of the buddha, then this is the same as being buddhas. Thus it is said, "make buddhas.")

• The passage "bestowed…the *samaya* baptism of the seal of the secret mandala":

"Seal" signifies that which is decisively realized and does not change. *Samaya* signifies the equal, original vow; stupendous awakening; and elimination of hindrances. Just like the buddhas, the bodhisattvas become buddhas when the virtues are bestowed. Thus, when this mantra of light is invoked, the buddhas are led to bestow this baptism [on all beings] until it reaches us. [This is why it is called] the incantation of Vairo[cana's] baptism.

• The passage "In the *Avataṃsaka Sūtra*…Victorious Sound emerged from the brow of the Tathāgata":

The throng of the lion throne [that appears] in the *Avataṃsaka* refers to the throng that emanates from the brow of the Buddha who is seated on his lion throne. Namely, this refers to all the dharmas and the Bodhisattva Victorious Sound who sat in the lotus blossom.

• The passage "according to the One Vehicle":

"According to the One Vehicle" means that this bodhisattva is the body of the teaching of Huayan. The body of the proper teaching is called the body of the names and phrases. This is shared by both the Mahāyāna and the Hīnayāna and is the body of suchness. It stands as the substance of language and as that which encompasses all aspects and returns them to their [undiscriminated] nature.[73] The substance of the person and teaching is not anything vague. This becomes ever more profound. As the teaching says, it is as the *Avataṃsaka Sūtra* expounds. Namely, victorious sound is the sound given off by all the dharmas. If left alone, teaching [remains] apart from person, [but] this reveals the [mutual] non-obstruction of person and dharma. This is the meaning of the One Vehicle that is complete. The lotus blossom on which this

Bodhisattva Victorious Sound sits is the meaning. The bodhisattva is the teaching; namely, the bodhisattva is found in the words and letters. (Again, question.)

• The passage "The lotus before Kannon is the meaning that is expounded":

The lotus blossom of sweet dew is the significance of the Mantra of Light. The Bright King is the substance of the teaching. Thus this lotus blossom and the Bright King [as the teaching] adorn the mantra. The teaching that expresses this is the unfailing rope snare which in turn is the Buddha. They are suspended from the rope of the various buddhas by means of the Buddha's great mercy and compassion. Then it follows that this mantra bears forth Kannon. To bestow the mystic power on Kannon is to bestow the mystic power on all sentient beings. This Kannon is the result of uniting all sentient beings as one to make Kannon. All sentient beings attain virtue when they hear this Mantra of Light.

(To say that to bestow the mystic power on Kannon is to bestow the mystic power on all sentient beings is to say that all those who receive and attain the Buddha's great mercy and compassion are Kannon. All Shingon *ajari* are called Vajrasattva;[74] similarly, when seen from the side of the Buddha, Vajrasattva is the body of Vairocana that is received and used by the other. When seen from the side of implementing the mandala, Vajrasattva is called *ajari*. All those who receive and hold the mantra like this are to be called Kannon. When seen from the side of the person who bestows [the mantra], this appears as the body of Vairocana that is received and used by the other. When seen from the side of the person upon whom [the mantra] is bestowed, this is Kannon. Thus, those who receive and hold this mantra have already had the rope snare of the Buddha's great mercy and compassion wrapped around them. That is why we [sentient beings] united as one are said to be Kannon.)

QUESTION: What is this thing called a *kenjaku* (rope snare)?

ANSWER: It is a rope.

QUESTION: What is the significance of this name?

ANSWER: It is the Buddha's compassion made into a rope. However, now, the Bright King of the unfailing rope snare sits before Vairocana, so that the explanation of the rope snare is distinct.

• The passage "The mudrā of the original deity of this mantra and the like":

I have virtually no strength [left] now, and I thought I would stop writing before this point, but I thought, this ends with the phrase "are thus established."

This concludes with the above.

The home of the wealthy man Karamori is similar to the dharma-gate. If I know well, then I will really enter [the dharma-gate]. If I only say I know but do not really know, then I cannot enter.

At the back of the *Kugishaku*,[75] [Myōe] has written an excerpt from the *Shien [shū]*. The Ajari Shōdatu-bō said that there was something at the back of the *Dosha gi* (Significance of the Sand).[76]

The high priest stated that, apart from the words on the title page, he had also written on some [other] paper.

—Lectures on the *Commentary on the Significance of the Syllables of the Mantra of Light of the Baptism of the Buddha Vairocana of the Unfailing Rope Snare*, [end of] Second Fascicle

Manuscript completed on the tenth day of the fifth month of 1259.

RECOMMENDING FAITH IN THE SAND OF THE MANTRA OF LIGHT[77]

FIRST FASCICLE

THE EARTH AND SAND of the Mantra of Light is the great secret dharma of all of the buddhas. The Mantra of Light spreads throughout the world and protects all people, lay and ordained. This is the secret mantra that is used by all buddhas and bodhisattvas. All buddhas are included in the five buddhas. They are Vairocana, Akṣobhya, Ratnasaṃbhava, Amida, and Amoghasiddhi.[78] Their virtues are contained in the five wisdoms.[79] That is, the wisdom of manifesting the full nature of the dharma-realm, the great mirrorlike wisdom, the wisdom of intuiting the equality of all things, the wisdom of the discernment of marvelous being, and the wisdom of completing all [liberating] actions.

This mantra constitutes the substance of the five buddhas, or again, the secret words completely containing the five wisdoms. Namely, *amokabeiroshanō* is the wisdom of manifesting the full nature of the dharma-realm, that is, the substance of the Tathāgata Vairocana. *Makabotara* is the great mirrorlike wisdom, the substance of the Buddha Akṣobhya. *Maṇi* is the wisdom of [intuiting] the equality [of all things], the substance of the Buddha Ratnasaṃbhava. *Handoma* is the wisdom of discerning marvelous being, the substance of the Tathāgata Amida. And *jimbara*

211

is the wisdom of completing all actions, the substance of the Buddha Amoghasiddhi.[80]

For this reason, when a person possesses the mind of faith in nothing more than this mantra, the seed of this wisdom is planted in that person's mind. It is like the flourishing growth of vegetation that occurs when the seeds of grasses and trees are planted in the great earth where there are no stones. Although the minds of sentient beings are unborn by nature, they nevertheless form the mental bases for the realization of all the tathāgatas. If the stone of disbelief gets in the way, the seeds of virtue will not grow. If there is faith, myriad goods will flourish like the verdant earth.

Now, the mantra's mystic power augments the mystic power of things. The method for doing this is learned and transmitted by the practitioners of the mantra. If the mantra is used to augment the mystic power of the sand, this sand becomes transformed into each of the mantra's syllables, becomes replete with the significance of each character, and fulfills the meaning of the phrase.

If this sand is sprinkled on the corpse or grave of the deceased, then, even if the deceased had committed grave sins throughout her life, had failed to cultivate the slightest good, and had fallen into the Avīci Hell,[81] the sand will immediately release the light of the mantra and reach the place of sin and suffering. The sin will dissipate spontaneously, and the deceased will attain birth in the Land of Bliss.[82]

Thus the Patriarch Ch'ŏnggu Taesa (Wŏnhyo) composed the *Yusim Allakto* (Playful Heart and Path of Repose) in which he asks,[83] "There are abundant scriptural passages that attest to the attainment of birth [in the Pure Land] by those who, through the establishment of good karmic bonds, fall into one of the nine classes of beings.[84] However, is there a skillful means of saving those sentient beings who have accumulated only bad karma, failed to cultivate the roots of good, and are already suffering from the retribution of the three evil destinies? Is there some way to effect their birth in the Land of Bliss?" To this Wŏnhyo answers

by drawing on the benefits of the sand of the Mantra of Light. Citing the
Amoghapāśa Sūtra (Sutra of the Unfailing Rope Snare), he states,

> Suppose there are sentient beings that have committed various sins
> such as the ten evils and five transgressions and have fallen into the
> evil paths.[85] If the sand of the mystic response of this mantra is sprin-
> kled on their corpse or on their graves, then, even though the de-
> ceased abide in hell, among the hungry ghosts, the angry gods, or the
> beasts, the light will reach them, and the various forms of evil retribu-
> tion will be eliminated; [this is accomplished] by the sand empow-
> ered by the mystic response of the great baptism of the Mantra of
> Light of the Buddhas' true and real original vows. They will go to the
> Land of Bliss, be born in a Lotus blossom, and go on to attain unex-
> celled awakening.

Having thus cited scripture, he goes on to say,

> Although there is no principle that speaks of receiving what has only
> been [karmically] accomplished by the other, the power of interde-
> pendent origination difficult to conceive does exist. Truly know that
> evil people who do not encounter this incantatory sand cannot rise
> up from their plight. Fortunately, [it is possible] to encounter this
> Mantra of Light. It is not difficult to harmonize with this sand. Who
> among those that aspire to do so fail?

This master was a patriarch of the Huaŏm (Ch. *Huayan*) School, and
the virtue of his practice is difficult to fathom. When the queen of Silla
fell gravely ill, no medicine could cure her, and the king's physician could
do nothing. In this impasse a fortune-teller was called in, and he said,
"This nation does not have sufficient resources. There will be some auspicious sign if you visit another country." The king accordingly sent an
emissary to Tang China. As the emissary crossed the ocean, a dragon
god appeared out of the sea and took him to the dragon palace. The
dragon king at that time was named Kûmhae.[86] He split open the side
of the emissary, placed a scripture entitled the *Kûmkang sammae gyong*
(Skt. *Vajrasamādhi Sūtra*) in his body, and said,[87] "This sutra should be
expounded and praised, believed in and listened to wholeheartedly.

However, the meaning of the King of Sutras is deep, and not just any-one can expound upon it. There is only one truly wise person. His name is Wŏnhyo. He is the light of the buddha-dharma, the sun and the moon of the world. He is the one who should be invited to expound on this su-tra." So saying, the dragon king sent the emissary on his way. And mat-ters were carried out according to his proclamation.

This master's mind was especially transparent to the dharma, and he was beyond the compare of ordinary people. Yet he hid his luminous [wisdom] and his virtue, not allowing them to be expressed openly. The king, believing in his wisdom and accomplishments, requested him to appear before the hundred-seat Assembly of the Benevolent King.[88] However, someone who did not know of his accomplishments and virtue interfered [and convinced the king to] withhold [the invitation].

Yet, a proclamation coming from the dragon palace revealed Wŏnhyo's greatness. Not only were the words of scripture beyond doubt, but it was said that the encounter with the incantatory sand of the great wisdom of Wŏnhyo's inconceivable accomplishments and virtue was [the result of] good karma. Who would not think this was auspicious?

"Incantatory sand" refers to the sand [of the mantra]. Although "karmic bonds" are always the result of one's own actions, the actions of the other can also become one's own affair. Thus, when the sands of this mantra of mystic response are sprinkled on the grave, they reach the mind of the one that is being thought of. If there are people whose karma leads them to encounter this sand, it is easy for them to extin-guish [even] grave sins and attain great virtue. It is most important to en-counter this mantra, but a mantra master has already been encountered. Sand is also plentiful. Since mantra masters already exist in this world, it is easy to gain the mystic power of this sand through the mantra.

If the karmic bond for having this sand sprinkled on the grave ex-ists, then it is easy to be liberated from the cycle of samsara and attain awakening. It is beneficial even for those who do not in the least cultivate the roots of virtue during their entire lives. How much greater, then, is the virtue of those who receive and maintain this mantra? And the benefit for the person meeting such sand? Even if one does not receive and maintain this mantra, the roots of virtue of those who benefit from the surplus are again immeasurable and boundless.

The virtue of the buddha-dharma seen and heard is truly profound. The mountain known as Sumeru is made of the four jewels of gold, silver, lapis lazuli, and crystal.[89] Various birds fly around the mountain, but their color does not remain the same. When they fly around the northern face, they become golden in color. They become gold as they fly along the north face. It is similarly the case for the other faces. The virtue of this mantra is also like this. The sand gains the mystic power of the mantra and immediately becomes replete with the virtue of the mantra. When sentient beings approach the sand, its virtue is transferred to them. That is why I find Great Master Wŏnhyo's interpretation, "The encounter with the sand is the fruition of karmic conditions," highly apt. While the lack of a karmic connection with the buddha-dharma is to be lamented, it is easy to create a karmic bond between sentient beings and the buddha-dharma by the skillful means of this sand.

The great master's statement regarding the existence of the power of interdependent origination difficult to fathom is derived from the fact that the meaning of all of the Buddha's teachings of the three realms,[90] both Mahāyāna and Hīnayāna, exoteric and esoteric, have as their [central] tenet interdependent origination. Among these [teachings] the Huayan School in particular explicates this in detail. The meaning of interdependent origination in all of the various schools is exhaustively explained under the rubric of the six harmonious aspects and the ten mysteries of interdependent origination.[91]

In the *Samantabhadra-caryā-praṇidhāna Sūtra* (Sutra of the Vow-Practices of Samantabhadra), which has been read and chanted throughout the world, there is a section expounding the ten vows, the first being reverence to the various buddhas.[92] It states,

One expresses reverence amidst all the buddhas and their assemblies who are expounding the dharma in the vast and innumerable buddha-lands found on each tip of countless strands of hair, each in turn an oceanlike realm. These acts of reverence follow one after another ceaselessly.

The second, praises of the Tathāgata, also teaches that while one is within the vast Buddhist assembly on the top of a strand of hair, an oceanlike realm, one praises the virtues of the Tathāgata by emitting boundless, marvelous music and activating boundless oceans of eloquence. These acts of reverence follow one another without stopping. Even one or two expressions of reverence and praise resonate throughout the ten directions and permeate the three worlds of [past, present, and future]. Samantabhadra realizes these inexhaustible and manifold acts of reverence and praise on the basis of the power of his deep faith and understanding and the vow power of his practice.

Even this exposition on the completion of these inconceivable acts is based on the power of interdependent origination. It is not due to the divine transformation of the bodhisattvas of the ten *bhūmi* stages or stage of Virtual Awakening.[93] When those of us who are utterly unqualified deeply believe in the dharma of the Mahāyāna and give rise to the mind that devotedly takes refuge in the buddhas' virtue, then these inconceivable acts are accomplished. The religious gatherings of our world are based on this. In the general devotions we chant,

I [am] in this *bodhi-maṇḍa* [this place of awakening], which is like
    an imperial pearl,[94]
The various buddhas of the ten directions appear in its midst,
My person appears before the various buddhas,
I take refuge in obeisance touching head to toe.

Of the ten vows of Samantabhadra, this is the [passage on] "reverential obeisance of the boundless circumference." It is also the principle of the Gate of the Realm of Indra's Net of the ten mysterious interdependent originations.

When the principle of this dharma arises in people's minds abundantly, the fruit of virtue is [already] realized at the causal [intermediary]

stage, and even the ordinary person is the same as a buddha. This is all due to the power of interdependent origination difficult to fathom. Since these actions are realized according to the rare and inconceivable power of interdependent origination, the six sense-objects themselves become the syllables of the mantra.[95] The true aspect, [the emptiness] of all phenomena, is the principle of all that is essential. Sand is none other than a sense object; the sense-object has its true aspect. Their virtues interpenetrate each other according to the skillful means of the esoteric and mystic response. The elimination of the three evil destinies and the realization of the dharmic bliss of the Pure Land are achieved, just as the flavor of what we eat and drink are harmonized by the power of water and fire and enter into a person's body to remove the suffering of hunger and thirst.[96] There is no need to overemphasize this. Let us leave aside for a moment the teachings of the scriptures, commentaries, and biographies [of eminent monks]. There are numerous instances, of the wonders of [the power] of interdependent origination difficult to fathom, that appear before our eyes in this world.

Last year one of the monks living here [at Kōzanji] became intoxicated after eating some mushrooms.[97] After he awoke he related the following story. He said that the lowly monk who picked the vegetable and gave it to him had come with his mother and would not leave his side. I thought he should return to his home, but he would not leave. [The monk who had fallen ill] said that he found it a difficult situation.

This is a remarkable event. Although he was affected by the mushrooms and fell ill both mentally and physically, why would a monk have picked the mushrooms and come to his side? And even if a monk had been seen picking the mushrooms, why would his mother be at his side? Although one might be an ignorant monk full of doubt and stupidity, one can come to know the principle of Buddhism through hearing of such events and be influenced by the virtuous mind and heart of the Tathāgata. In the *Weishizhang* (Treatise on Mind-Only), the Great Master Zhixiang gives the following interpretation:[98] "As one ought to

know, the principle expressed by the scriptures is that the various phenomena do not exist, there is only suchness. Furthermore, nonself as
the real nature [of things] is the ultimate [reality], and [the realization of
this fact] is the way to be cured from the intoxication of these mushrooms.

If one inquires into the origin of this intoxicated mind, [one sees
first that] the monk's mother [of the story] gave birth to the monk. The
monk then picked the mushrooms and came. Someone ate the mushrooms. These various conditions combined to produce the intoxicated
mind. If the mother had not given birth, then there would have been
no monk to pick the mushrooms. If there were no monk, then he would
not have picked the mushrooms and come. If the mushrooms had not
existed, then [no one] would have eaten them. Then the original mind
would neither have become intoxicated, seen the monk, nor seen the
mother. This is the true and real original mind. Truly one ought to
know. This intoxication was like a dream or phantasm. This is what the
Great Master Xiangxiang (Fazang) states is the mind of dreams of the three
realms and four phases (of arising, abiding, changing, and perishing).[99]
According to his exegesis, they are all "due to the power of fundamental ignorance," and it is of this mind that he speaks. One should ponder
the principle of the buddha-dharma in these terms.

This is no different from believing in this sand and obtaining its
virtue. The sand is like the mushrooms. The Buddha who thus expounds
[on the sand] is like the monk [who picked the mushrooms in the story].
The various buddhas of the three worlds are [really] expounding the
teaching of the singular equality [of things]. They are like the mother
who gave birth to the monk. Sentient beings believing [in what they
say] is as though they eat the mushrooms. To believe, accept, and obtain
virtue is like becoming intoxicated with the mushrooms. The person
who is protected by all of the tathāgatas of the ten directions is like the
one who had the monk and his mother at his side. When conditions

overturning this come together, then one becomes a sinner. All of this is due to the power of interdependent origination difficult to fathom.

However, there are those who have had doubts and would say that neither the monk nor the mother actually came, that they were merely hallucinations of the intoxicated mind. The way in which sentient beings obtain benefit depends solely on the power of causes and conditions coming together. The power to take dreams for waking reality belongs ultimately only to the stage of buddhahood. Thus, buddhas who have come into the world all appear as transformation bodies,[100] and the sentient beings who are transformed are foolish beings caught in the cycle of the four phases [of generation, abiding, change, and extinction]. Within this there are still further transformations.

When the Tathāgata [Śākyamuni] was still in this world, there was a general-king who caught five hundred bandits, gored out their eyes, and abandoned them in the woods.[101] Unable to bear the pain, these bandits turned their thoughts to the Tathāgata, whereupon a wind arose that blew medicine from the Himalayas and filled their eyes. They regained clear eyesight and saw the Tathāgata before them. Filled with joy and devotion, they listened to his exposition on the dharma. They became victorious [in liberation], threw away their staffs, and returned home. These staffs [eventually] formed [new] woods to reveal the benefits of [the Buddha's] compassion.

These woods still exist. They are called the Eye-Gaining Woods [near the grove Jetavana]. Many bhiksus have made them the place of their meditation. Realizing that the benefit of opening one's dharma-eye is especially prominent there, they greatly regret that they are separated by the long journey over seas and mountains. About this the Tathāgata states, "This benefit accrues to sentient beings who think of me through the power of my great mercy and compassion. Thus there is no need for me to go there in person." Thus, although the mother and the monk did not actually come, the suffering of the intoxicated mind is not meaningless. How much more so for the mystic response of the inconceivable mantra of the Buddha's virtue, and what is there to argue about provisional realities?

Thus should one have faith in this sand, applying it to one's head when bedridden with illness, grasping it in one's hand and even hanging some from one's neck [in a bag],[102] touched by the illumination of the countless tathāgatas' great radiance. If one thus believes, even if one is distracted by the pain of illness and cannot be mindful of this, is unable to free oneself from attachment to the five spices and meat, and is hindered in purification [practices], one can still extinguish [the effects of] immeasurable [acts] of evil karma, gather boundless virtue, and extend the benefit of the Buddha's radiance into the next life.

Benefits will accrue to even those sentient beings who have accumulated [a great deal] of sin and have no roots of good. How much more so for those who have faith, for it is like thrusting a pole into [an already] rapid current. Once long ago there was a bhiksu who transgressed the precepts and abused the three treasures. Fearing retribution for his acts of evil, he gathered together various treasures and attempted to provide compensation. When his life came to an end, he fell into the Avīci Hell. But right before he fell into the great fire of hell, he felt he had entered a hot-house [or bath house], thinking it was built for human beings. When he intoned the incantatory vow, the sentient beings who heard him all exited from hell, and the bhiksu was reborn in the Trāyastrimśa Heaven.[103] Although this bhiksu was falling into hell because of karmic retribution, by virtue of what little good remained in him, he thought that he was falling into a hot-house built for human beings and intoned the incantatory vow.

It goes without saying, then, that for one who protects herself with the incantatory sand and invokes it in faith continually until the end of her life, the fiery flames of the Avīci Hell will be reflected in the sand hanging below her neck and be transformed into the great radiance of the mantra. It is like the bhiksu who had amassed karmic evil but, by depending on what little good remained, saw the endless smoke [rising up from the Avīci Hell] as nothing more than a heated room for human beings.

There are many such occurrences. When the evil denizens of hell are being punished and they hear the sound of iron containers being struck, some think of the sound of temple bells and, meditating on the Buddha, are able to avoid the pain resulting from their evil acts. One's aspirations should be based on these kinds of episodes. There is no need to look for evidence for the efficacy of sprinkling sand beyond the sutra passage that states, "[The sand] should be sprinkled on the corpse and on the grave." Let us leave aside for the moment the explanations of the sutras.

To give an illustration from among the circumstances of this world, there is the case of Nichizō Shōnin, who lived during the Engi era (901–23). He secluded himself in a stone cavern and fell unconscious while fasting and without speaking. While struggling unconsciously [outwardly], he was touring heaven and hell [inwardly] by the divine power of Vajragarbha-rāja,[104] but he had on his person an image of his main deity and sutra scrolls which he had when he entered the cave, and so when he arrived at the palace of Emma,[105] the Great King [of hell] asked him, "What is it that the meditation monk has on his back?"

[Nichizō Shōnin] answered, "They are the buddha-image and scriptures that I had with me when I entered the mountain."

The Great King further asked, "What sutras, which buddhas?"

[The monk] answered, "Images of Mahāvairocana, Śākyamuni, Maitreya, Avalokiteśvara, and others, as well as both mandalas.[106] Also the *Lotus, Nirvāṇa, Suvarṇaprabhāsottama* (Golden Radiance), *Benevolent Kings, Diamond Samādhi,* Ultimate Meaning of Principle and *Prajñāpāramitā* sutras. Again, the various procedures and rituals involving the three objects of reverence of the great dharma, the various *dhāraṇī,* and other scriptural sources."

Thereupon the Great King put his hands together in *gasshō,* bowed down before the monk, took him by the hand, led him up the stairs, sat him down on a floor carpeted with jewels, praised him profusely, and requested him to expound on the dharma. When the monk had finished with his brief exposition, the Great King stood up, bowed again, and praised him, saying, "How wonderful, how wonderful!"

[This story demonstrates] that if one carries scriptures on the person, then one will surely avoid falling into hell.

QUESTION: Those people who abide in right thought at the time of death and receive the virtue of the sand will surely reap the appropriate benefits. People who become confused and lose the right thought have difficulty engaging the benefits of the sand, [do they not?]

ANSWER: Those who come to the end of their lives without losing the right thought do not necessarily seek the benefit of the sand. But those who are devoid of good [karma] throughout their lives benefit from the sand sprinkled [on them] by others. Those who maintain correct thought without becoming confused need not necessarily invoke [the power of] the sand, saying, "Namu dosha"; rather, they may simply be encouraged to intone the Buddha's name and pray without doing anything else.

However, in the case of one who dies suddenly and in ignorance, those near them should be ready to sprinkle sand on his body. If one is ill and bedridden for a number of days but has deep faith in its virtue, one is certain to benefit from the virtue of the sand when death really takes place, even if one is unconscious. Sinners who have committed the gravest transgressions and are utterly lacking in blessings can be born among the jeweled flowers of the Pure Land by the power of sand sprinkled on them by others. It goes without saying that those who had the slightest faith [in the dharma] while alive and expressed their vow [to realize the teachings] will quickly achieve the victory [of liberation] even if they are sinners.

QUESTION: As for the idea of maintaining right thought at the time of death, there is no doubt about obtaining benefits if one has roots of good such as those of the *nembutsu*. Yet, it is difficult to believe that one will cancel karmic retribution in hell if one has obtained the virtue of believing in the sand before the moment of death. [What is the truth of the matter?]

ANSWER: It is as I have said repeatedly before. The benefit of the incantatory sand is to bring the victory [of liberation] to people who lack the roots of good; the rest is to be inferred. However, the continuation of the retributory effects of the three realms depends upon [the state of one's] mind at the time of death. It is the same with regard to the benefit of the incantatory sand. As the *Yogācāra-bhūmi Śāstra* (Treatise on the Stages of Yoga Practice) states in the opening section:[107] "When the time of death arrives for the various [types of] sentient beings, or when thoughts become turbid and confused, the products of the ego's [self-]love habituated over a long period of time become manifest. By this power it is said the ego is unable to truly become attached to itself, and during the interim existence, the next rebirth is then established." I cite this passage for the sake of expedience. The same understanding will be achieved if ignorant men and women simply think of this as evidence for the assurance of the benefit of the incantatory sand. I should not have to give detailed explanations for the wise.

QUESTION: Let us leave aside for a moment the benefits to be accrued after death. Surely one would believe in the beneficial effects of the sand of the mantra's mystic response after death if, when one wanted something [in this life] and ate the sand, it turned into food and drink. If there are no signs of its benefits in the present, it is hard to believe in its benefits after death. One ought to always wear the Mantra of Light about one's neck. Since the effectiveness of the sand depends upon the power of the mantra, it is hard to believe in the idea of using the sand without the mantra.

ANSWER: This is not the first time [for me] to discuss the effectiveness of the mantra. However, as for the substance of the mantra, in terms of the subject, it is the attentive wisdom of *anāsrava*, [the absence of deleterious outflows]. In terms of the object, it is the emptiness of all phenomena.

Now, the attentive wisdom of *anāsrava* is attained at the first of the ten bodhisattva *bhūmi*. The wisdom of the Buddha realizes the ultimate emptiness of all phenomena. Limitless like great empty space, the eyes cannot see it, and hands cannot grasp it. The letters in ink on paper are merely provisional representations of the [real] dharma-treasure.

Although the benefits of accepting and contemplating them are profound, it is difficult to grasp their significance in the face of deluded emotions and mental discriminations. According to the scriptures, as correlates to religious rules: rituals, and sacred scripture, the grasses and trees, earth and sand, are imbued with mystic power [enabling one] to complete the *siddhi* [realizations]. Among them the sand is imbued with the mystic power of the mantra to eliminate suffering and bestow bliss, leading to the completion of the *siddhi,* thus showing the truly profound nature of the mantra.

Since the nature of sand is such that it becomes manifested through sentient beings' karmic power, it is related to the deluded affect of sentient beings. When the power of the Tathāgata's wisdom, the dharmic power of the Mantra of Light, is added to this, the sand retains [this power] and forms the tathāgatas' bodies as sense objects. The benefits [of the Mantra of Light] are quickly attained because this power becomes one with sentient beings. It is nondual with and indistinguishable from this mantra.

An analogy may be drawn from the waters of the ocean. Since the water is [fluid] and not a [static] thing, it can be poured on sand, drained, and hardened. This is the same as the process of making salt. Again, it is as follows. The nature of the mantra is like the ocean water. The addition of the mystic power of the sand is like wetting the sand and hardening it. Its becoming one with sentient beings, extinguishing sins, and producing good is like using salt as a spice for harmonizing the flavor of soup. This salt is nondual with and indistinguishable from the ocean water. Since the substance of the mantra is the realm of the tathāgatas' realization, [the incantatory sand] is like ocean water that has been made fresh and gentle for the sake of ordinary people. Because the sand is the product of sentient beings' karmic power to make phenomena become manifest, when it becomes one with sentient beings, it is like finding salt that has been dried, hardened, and used as a spice for harmonizing the flavor of soup.

If the virtue of the mantra is believed by the mind of faith in accord with the principle, then it will permeate the mind and produce beneficial results. If one eats it, it is like adding a sense object to one's own sense object [namely, the body], in which case it will be hard, stick in one's throat, and prove a hindrance. By means of [properly] believing in the benefit of this sand, one will obtain a different body in the afterlife, the virtue body. It has nothing to do with the [physical] body that now appears here. The doubt you have raised is nothing more than an error of the deluded mind. The virtuous power of the mantra is in accord with the true nature of suchness. It should not be regarded as the same as [the deluded mind or body of blind passions].

QUESTION: [The effect of] the sand is the result of the karmic power of sentient beings; thus, in accordance with the fact that benefits naturally follow, grass, trees, and the like are also all secondary results.[108] The benefit of the [mantra's] radiance is obtained by adding this mystic power. What is the basis for the mystic power of the sand?

ANSWER: The import of this is the profound secret of this method of practice. One ought to focus one's faith on this. Although it is difficult to express in words, in the method of yogic practice, the mind of contemplation is focused on the exposition on the many methods of praxis. It is as if one purifies objects and manifests one's appropriation of [the virtue] of the honored ones by casting these objects into the fire. If we now take this as our model to discern [the meaning] of these expositions, then the sand blown by the wind can be understood to be like the clouds and mist which refract and reveal the radiance. Again, the many [grains of sand] point to the immeasurable radiance of the tathāgatas. Thus, when the radiance of the fivefold wisdom of all of the tathāgatas is to be revealed, sand should be used as the object of correlation. Again, a similar correlation can be made one-to-one when there is an exegesis on the meaning of the mantra.

When the sutra explains the virtue of one who upholds this mantra, it states, "It becomes the basis of the Great Jewel of all the tathāgatas, it becomes the basis of the Great Lotus of all the tathāgatas, it becomes the basis of the Great Diamond of all the tathāgatas." Great Jewel refers to the *maṇi* syllables of the mantra. It is said that sentient beings cannot accumulate the virtue of having no outflows.[109] It is like the poor not obtaining rare treasures. Although śrāvakas and pratyekabuddhas may attain some of the rare treasure of realizing personal emptiness, free from outflows, they are like those who do not give others their treasure because they fear losing what little they have. Possessing the Great Jewel treasure, all the tathāgatas bestow their limitless treasures, fulfilling the needs of self and others. By maintaining this mantra, foolish, ordinary beings fulfill the immeasurable virtues of the tathāgatas, transcending the realm of foolish beings and followers of the two vehicles.[110]

Thus they join the Jewel of the family of the tathāgatas.[111] The first character [*shu*] of [the Sino-Japanese compound] *shuzoku*, "family," refers to species, and the second [*zoku*], to genus. The family of Great Lotus corresponds to the syllables *handoma* in the mantra. The mud of blind passion does not defile the practitioner of this mantra. [Such a person] will unquestionably emerge from the waters of samsara. The family of Great Diamond corresponds to the syllables *jimbara* in the mantra. The practitioner of this mantra unquestionably obtains the diamondlike wisdom of the Buddha. The wisdom of the Buddha signifies the wisdom which is developed from the time that one comes to have faith in this mantra to the time that one attains buddhahood. It is based upon the fact that the Five Ranks each represent a share of the Buddha's wisdom.[112] For example, when a bird flies through the great empty sky, its tracks across the sky are made up of parts of that great empty expanse. Within it there is no question of having or lacking wisdom [in the conventional sense]. Wisdom is to deeply believe in the preciousness of this mantra. This is none other than the family of the Great Diamond of all the tathāgatas.

Following this, it can be said that, since the sand can be likened to pearl, it expresses the family of the Great Jewel. Since it neither rots nor becomes defiled while lying at the bottom of the water, it manifests the family of Lotus. Its hardness manifests the family of Diamond. In this way, there is a basis for revealing the profound meaning [of the mantra] one by one. Thus, sand is a phenomenal correlate. But if the matter is stated thus, then it may sound as though the dharma is vague.

To state the matter more precisely, according to the Hīnayāna, there are ten functions of the mind and the ten functions of good in the mind.[113] Faith is found among the latter, and wisdom among the former. According to the Mahāyāna, faith belongs among the eleven types of good, and wisdom is one of the five dharmas of the separate functions of the mind.[114] People speak casually of the oneness of faith and wisdom without thoroughly discriminating the [various] aspects of the dharma. Failing to fully appreciate the basis for such criticisms, faith in the sand also becomes neglected.

In answer to the [original] question, in the stage of faith in the sand, the mind that discerns sand as the secret teaching of the tathāgatas is itself wisdom. As stated in the above, wisdom is to know, rather than to believe in, the mantra. The reason for this is to emphasize the function of wisdom that accompanies faith. Within the ten stages of faith [of the fifty-two bodhisattva stages], the ten functions of mind all establish the category of faith, but wisdom is also found among them. Although this matter is taken up in the discussion of the various teachings of both the Hīnayāna and the Mahāyāna, when one awakens the mind of entrusting by virtue of hearing the teaching, faith is understood as arising from the wisdom of listening.[115] This shows the unity of faith and wisdom.

Various meanings become evident based on the teachings of the scriptures. It is just as rough winds cause waves. As long as they are not errant, all of these interpretations express a single correct principle. The correct principle, [in itself] having no nature and lacking any distinguishing characteristic, finds its way into the minds of sentient beings without detection. There are people who have deep faith in the buddha-dharma although they appear to be ignorant. Since I do not know [all] the categories and number of the various teachings, I, too, am a stupid person filled with doubts. But if there is faith in accordance with principle, then that mind has already encountered the three treasures. [The mind of such a person] does not linger in byways because subject and object, host and guest, are in accord with each other. As for this person who first comes to believe in the buddha-dharma, the buddhas protect [her] when even the slightest faith arises. In life after life and age after age, the benefits of seeing the Buddha and hearing the dharma accrue; [she] progresses quickly and does not fall back. Such a person is called the bodhisattva whose original nature is truly settled.

Previously, in order to explain the significance of the family of the Great Diamond, it was said, "Within it there is no question of having or lacking wisdom [in the conventional sense]. Wisdom is to truly believe in the preciousness of this dharma." These words point to the person [described in the preceding paragraph]. Although there may be many men and women in the world who possess the virtue of this faith, they simply are not conscious of them. However, liberation does not depend on that [i.e., on whether or not one possesses virtue]. The dharma-nature of suchness is not located in a particular place but is the realm of awakening of the buddhas and bodhisattvas.[116] Pure faith cannot unfold through one's own [efforts alone]. One must await the opportunity to being opened up by a [good] friend and by listening to the dharma.[117]

To await this opportunity to open up means giving rise to the mind that hears the true dharma and deeply receives it in faith. The opening up [of this mind] is the reason for the appearance of the buddhas. Although [I] silently ponder the words and principles of the true teaching and speak about them, my conventional words are mere semblances [of the inconceivable truth]. To point out just one instance of [this] mind as expressed in the Mahāyāna scriptures: In the twenty-fifth section of the Sixth *Sanmaya* Chapter of the *Dari jing* (Skt. *Mahāvairocana Sūtra)*, it states that the *san* of *sanmaya* refers to the threefold aspects of mind that are present in the mind of sentient beings who seek the buddha-dharma. *Sanmaya* is a transliteration of the Sanskrit [*samaya*] which means "equal." If the threefold aspects are not present, then a petty and heretical mind will be mixed in, and the fruit of buddhahood will not be attained. If, however, the three aspects are equally present, then the mind of three[fold] equality arises, that is, the three *samaya*.

In the scriptural passages that explain the first *samaya,* it states, "The beginner's mind does not see self-nature." In Master Yixing's commentary and in Master Jiaoyuan's *Yanmichao* (Treatise on Performing the Mysteries),[118] it states, "When sentient beings first hear the buddha-dharma, but in [their] samsaric existence they have yet to know the virtue which resides within their fundamental nature, they awaken the mind [of aspiration for enlightenment] for the first time and embrace the way of the Buddha. The existence of this wisdom-nature is the first *samaya.*" Following the mind [of aspiration], the wisdom of knowing reality as it is arises next.[119] [At this stage, the mind is able to] discriminate between that which has virtue and that which does not. This is the second *samaya.* Following the [discriminating] mind [of wisdom], great compassion arises next, so that sentient beings may be taught as though they were the same as oneself, thus guided into the buddha-dharma to become enlightened. This is the third *samaya.* Thus the three types [of *samaya*] are, first, the mind of aspiration; second, wisdom; and third, compassion.

In the main text of the *Commentary* [*on the Mahāvairocana Sūtra*] that interprets the first mind of aspiration in terms of the aspect of practice, it states, "[In the beginning], what the virtue of the fundamental nature of the self is has yet to be thoroughly grasped. However, when there is this wisdom-nature, the mind of aspiration first arises from within samsara and seeks the fruit of buddhahood. This is the first samādhi." This aspect of practice is very superficial. Since the wisdom which illuminates and comes to know the fundamental nature of one's own self does not yet exist, the first stage is [regarded as that of] the mind of aspiration, and the second [stage] that of wisdom. However, it states, "There is this wisdom-nature." This is the same as the foregoing explanation given according to the Huayan school: "Faith arises from the wisdom of listening." To speak of "the three samaya" may be rather daunting, but if one takes deep joy in the virtue of the buddhas, then it quickly becomes one's own treasure.

At the general level the meaning of the three equalities can be seen in terms of the three qualities of sparrow chicks. At first there are just eggs without eyes or beaks. It is the stage equivalent to eggs belonging to the mother and father sparrows. Next, they break out of their shells and come to have eyes and beaks. This is the stage where mother and father care for their chicks. Next, they become adult sparrows, have their own chicks, and lovingly care for them. They are the equals of their mothers and fathers. They become mature sparrows by virtue of this threefold aspect. This is the three samaya of sparrows. We are able to hear this teaching even though we have been born in this defiled world. When we love the virtue of the Tathāgata, this is the first samaya. There is a saying, "Pilgrimage to Kumano by copying others." If there is even one person who sincerely awakens the mind of aspiration, then others should learn [from such a person]. This is to give rise to the tathāgata-nature.

The section on the three samaya in the Yanmichao explains the aspect of practice of the fourth, mind of aspiration, of the four types described in the Yogācāra-bhūmi Śāstra. It is an extensive exposition. To quote briefly [the relevant passage, it states],

A group of sentient beings, although they cannot see or hear the spiritual transformations of the buddhas and the subtle, true dharma, are born in the final age among those who commit great transgressions due to their defilements, great stupidity, and their profound lack of repentance. Yet, they are able to awaken the thought [of enlightenment]. This is now the defiled age, full of grief and confusion of all kinds. Even if [one] gives rise to the inferior bodhisattva mind of the śrāvakas and pratyekabuddhas, it is difficult to realize its meager fruits. How much more so for unexcelled, supreme enlightenment. If we awaken the mind of unexcelled, supreme enlightenment as we should, then the various types of sentient beings will learn from us and also awaken the great mind of enlightenment, *bodhicitta*. This great *bodhicitta* will arise with us, knowing that it is difficult to attain the great, unexcelled dharma in the final age.

If we possess the mind that seeks unexcelled enlightenment, then we should properly enact the meaning of these words. Truly must we endeavor, truly endeavor. That is why I said earlier that one can speak of the family of the Great Diamond, when one knows that the Tathāgata possesses the skillful means of the secret mystic power, and one has the wisdom to regard the sand with reverence. I had been thinking about these statements and principles. It may seem as though the meaning of both nature and manifestation are rather crude, as I only touch briefly on the key points. However, if we discuss directly the benefits of the sand, then we will not need to spend time on tangential matters.

The purpose of explaining matters thus in provisional terms is to satisfy the person who [originally] asked the question [about the meaning of the sand], but the written word tends to fly without wings, and go far without hooves.[120] Although light may appear to radiate from within pearly blinds, the true light of the dharma-lamp is not yet visible. Although time spent under the roof of a hut made of brushwood is enjoyable, its store of holy treasures is meager. Idle play among spring flowers and the fall moon, the happiness of ten thousand autumns—all this occludes the path to liberation free from [self-conscious] activity and opens up the gates to transmigration and samsara.[121] How pitiful, how

grievous! When the turns of fate begin to decline, and this impermanent [life] is about to end, one abandons the music halls and dance pavil-
ions never to return. Elephants, horses, and carriages all become the
property of others [i.e., useless for one's own life journey]. Nothing can
help such a one, not wishes granted by heavenly deities, not the majestic power of the Cakravartin.[122]

Wherever this work reaches, I have humbly submitted the teachings in easily understandable terms and carefully explained belief in the
sand. The secret method [of the sand] has been presented out of great
compassion [for all beings].[123] In faith and entrusting what evil cannot
be extinguished, what virtue not realized? Like planting the seedling of
a rare and valuable tree and waiting for it to flower and bear fruit, I wish
to transmit the dharma by following this esoteric practice that is especially effective in the present and later ages. [All of this is] in order to
quickly attain the benefits of the secret store of the buddha-dharma of
the profound effect of the sand.

The Great Master Wŏnhyo has deeply tasted the truth of these
words. Drawing on them he states in reflection,

> How regrettable! Having created evil karma, the resulting suffering
> follows closely behind like a shadow. How painful! Suffering and wor-
> rying alone, there is no one to protect one. Without the great compas-
> sion of identification and the all-embracing secret method, who will
> return and open the mysterious locks and help one to ascend the lo-
> tus dais [of the Pure Land]? Although there is no law that allows one
> to receive the benefit of actions performed by others, there is the
> power of interdependent origination difficult to fathom.
>
> Truly one ought to know, the encounter with the incantatory
> sand is the result of good karma. If one does not receive [the bene-
> fit of] the sand, then how can one speak of liberation? Upon reflec-
> tion, [it is readily apparent that] great compassion is truly boundless.
> The extensive exposition [of the Buddha] does not confuse others.
> Without faith, [the benefits] will not come to be. There is no rea-
> son to regret. Thus, those who do not place their trust [in the sand]
> waste the great blessing, and the day they repay their debt will be
> far off. The spirit of those who follow the practice will come into

contact with the lotus blossom [of awakening],[124] and their filial devotion [to the buddhas] will be established immediately.

These are correct words. The buddha-tathāgatas have compassion for the suffering of sentient beings. Unless one believes in the secret method of the mantra, the day will not come when the blessings of the Buddha are repaid. If, however, one has faith, then one repays the debt of gratitude to the Buddha and becomes a filial child of the Buddha. The Tantric Patriarch and Tripitaka Master Amoghavajra translated this single utterance and made it the practice of the Zhenyan (Shingon) [teachings]. Thus, it is truly joyous to encounter this esoteric practice. [The benefits of] this incantatory sand will quickly accumulate when the teaching of this mystic power is cultivated before and after the practices of the three times: morning, noon, and night. This sand [should be] placed in a large container for storage and given to those who ask for it, be they dear ones or strangers. May [the sand] be spread in all the ten directions [of the cosmos] and permeate the triple-world so that the benefit of the mantra will never be exhausted.[125] *(end of first fascicle)*

•

SECOND FASCICLE

QUESTION: Faith is easy to awaken when gazing upon the images of buddhas, for the various details and auspicious marks have been carved into them. But in the case of grains of sand, which have no such form, it is difficult to awaken faith even though one might hear of the profound efficacy of the sand. If faith is not fully realized, then the efficacy [of the sand] also fails to be realized fully. [How should one properly understand this matter?]

ANSWER: Sentient beings who do not have the slightest good exhaust their lives and depart. When the sand is sprinkled on their corpses, great benefit is realized. Thus one should not depend on what is heard without faith. However, there is no one who [does not] have faith in the images of buddhas.[126] Why do they not have faith [in the sand]? Both [images and sand] come from the sutras. Why is one taken and the other discarded? Images of buddhas are painted and carved in wood. The knowledge of the senses is based on the discrimination of mind-consciousness. Foolish beings [i.e., unenlightened humans] are called "those of ears and eyes" because their minds only discriminate the realm of the senses. The knowledge of the sages [i.e., the awakened] is that of the principle of the dharma. If sentient beings strive [to understand the buddha-dharma] and awaken the mind [of aspiration], then they will believe and come to know. Thus the connections formed through the senses are not in vain. [They] will ultimately lead to the unexcelled fruit of buddhahood.

It is just as Master Wŏnhyo encourages us. There should be no reason for regret. [Sentient beings] are like fish in shallow puddles or sheep in the slaughterhouse. They are about to die and depart. [They ought to] be diligent and strive hard. But undisciplined encouragement only serves to increase people's doubts. Thus, [I offer] a word to break through the doubting mind: When you see before your eyes the ordinary sand of this world, why do you not entrust yourself to the realm of mystic power in the mind?

QUESTION: What is this sand?

ANSWER: [The various grains] of sand differ in color, being blue, yellow, and so on; likewise, they differ in shape, being rectangular, round, and so on. [Together] they form a mass of tiny, hard [particles]. This is called "sand."

QUESTION: But then, grasses and trees also differ in color, being blue, yellow, and so on; likewise, they differ in shape, being rectangular, round, and so on. Why are they not regarded as sand?

ANSWER: They are larger and not hard. Sand is hard and small.

QUESTION: But then, dried grains of rice that have been ground into pieces are also hard and small. Why are they not regarded as sand?

ANSWER: Those grains were originally soft and only later dried and hardened. Sand is hard and small from the beginning.

QUESTION: But then, gold, iron, and the like are also hard and small. Why are they not regarded as sand?

ANSWER: It is so. Thus, people call [bits of gold] *sagon,* "sand-gold." They are not sand.

QUESTION: That is sand-gold. This is earthen sand. One should say that it is not gold-sand but earthen sand.

ANSWER: Earthen sand does not shine. Sand-gold shines. Thus it is not earthen sand. That [other] is sand-gold.

QUESTION: But then small crystals shine and are small. Why aren't they regarded as sand-gold?

ANSWER: Crystal is white. Sand-gold is yellow. Thus, crystal is not sand-gold.

QUESTION: Since the color of earthen sand is not uniform, there are earthen sands that are yellow and shine. Why aren't they regarded as sand-gold?

ANSWER: Earthen sand is simply not sand-gold.

QUESTION: You originally said that the various grains of sand differ in color, being blue, yellow, and so on; that they differ in shape, being rectangular, round, and so on; and that they are hard and small. Since sand-gold and earthen sand both have these qualities, how do you distinguish the two?

ANSWER: Golden sand is a rare treasure, stored wrapped up in the bottom of a [jewel] box. Earthen sand is not a treasure and fills the whole earth. The two are not comparable.

QUESTION: Why is it that sand-gold found where it is dug up, not wrapped up in the bottom of a box, but found everywhere in the earth, is not regarded as treasure?

ANSWER: It is, in fact, a treasure.

QUESTION: It already fills the earth. It is not kept in a storehouse, nor is it accumulated in a box. Who regards it as treasure? Again, it is people who gather and store it. Thus, if people merely gather and store sand, is it regarded as treasure? And if golden sand is scattered all over the earth, is it not regarded as treasure?

ANSWER: Sand-gold would still be treasure.

QUESTION: Various meanings have been examined exhaustively. There is no [way to ascertain which is] greater or lesser, golden sand or earthen sand. Who would still assert that sand-gold is [inherently] better?

ANSWER: Although one has listened to this discussion of equality, if one still desires sand-gold and does not desire ordinary sand, then one still regards sand-gold as treasure.

QUESTION: If you were the owner of sand-gold, it would be like the landlords who know the details of what they own. You would know the value of sand-gold. Thus I ask you, does the substance of the golden sand consist of [the four elements of] earth, water, fire, and wind? Does it have all of the attributes of form, smell, taste, and texture? Is it a small phenomenon or a large phenomenon? Is it an existent phenomenon, or an empty phenomenon? Is it a defiled phenomenon or a pure phenomenon? Is it an ordinary phenomenon or a holy phenomenon? Just as I have inquired into [the nature of] the sand-gold, the same goes for the definition of earthen sand. If one knows that [the substance in question is] sand but does not entrust oneself to the realm of the Buddha's wisdom, then this principle [of equality] will certainly not pervade one's mind. [Questions regarding this matter] must be answered in detail.

ANSWER: I simply know of the difference between sand-gold and ordinary sand. I merely related what I already know. I do not know of other matters.

In conclusion, if one does not know anything about sand or about incantation, then one should simply believe in the exposition of the Great Sage Śākyamuni. He knows about sand and about the method of incantation. The buddhas rely on the twofold truth when they teach.[127] Although the knowledge of the buddhas' wisdom cannot be derived from the [deluded] human standpoint, the various explanations are tailored to the varying capacities of sentient beings. The various teachings of the Mahāyāna and the Hīnayāna are not the same. The sand contains the most minute subtleties which are synthesized provisionally. If they are scattered, then they lose their reality [as sand].

Mind-consciousness transforms them, and causes and conditions bring them together. When the substance [of the teachings] is related to fundamental nature, it is [called] the one principle of dharma-nature as suchness. When it is related to conditions, it becomes innumerable and infinite dharmas. The buddhas of the triple world [of past, present, and future] abide therein, and the buddha-lands of the ten directions are also to be found therein. They become the syllables of the mantra. Thus, when the syllables of this world are used to expound the way of the mantra, there are mantras of various syllables. When the numerical categories of [the teachings of] both the Mahāyāna and the Hīnayāna are established on the basis of these syllables,[128] then names, phrases, and sentences which do not correlate with each other are all contained within the method of practice. The syllables and phrases with their individual meanings all express the truth of the emptiness of all phenomena. In this emptiness are found profound and inexhaustible virtues.

If one believes in these virtues, then countless virtues of the Buddha will be gathered within the body and mind of [even] a foolish being, and one will become a true child of the Tathāgata. The buddhas are like the fathers and mothers of children in this world who, having received the lifeblood of their parents, come to resemble them. To believe in their virtues is like receiving their lifeblood. When one entrusts the self to the buddhas, one seeks to sever the roots of evil and practice good; this is what it means to become like the buddhas.

Now, I explain the truth of phenomena as emptiness in terms of the meaning of the syllables and phrases of this Mantra of Light. When [the power of] this mantra is transformed into sand, then its meaning with respect to the word *amoka* is this: When the sound *a* is heard, the foolish come to know nothingness, and the wise likewise come to know nothingness.[129] Attachment to [ideas of] permanent being and permanent nothingness arise due to the fact that foolish beings cling to [notions of] a fixed nature. This is deluded attachment. The wise know that phenomena arise in interdependence and are not based on permanent being. Being and nothingness are both of one nature. Thus, before [the eyes of] the wise, this sand is originally uncreated.

When the sound of the syllable *mo* is heard, then one comes to know the unattainability of the "I." What is called "I" is one with the substance of the sand. Its substance is empty because it is originally uncreated. When the sound of the syllable *ka* is heard, one comes to know the unattainability of the whole as one.[130] Due to the fact that the true substance of the sand is originally uncreated, the various conditions that gather and are gathered together to create the sand are [themselves] uncreated. This is the true meaning of the sand.

Foolish beings are confused about this, but the tathāgatas know it. In fact, the tathāgatas' wisdom is found precisely at the point of foolish beings' confusion. Thus, I say to you, my friend, that the tathāgatas' great wisdom is to be found precisely at the point where you doubt the meaning of the sand. It is like the [relationship between] reality and its appearance. The tathāgatas teach in accordance with the deluded attachment of foolish beings.

The meaning of the phrase *amoka* as "unfailing" is based upon the following: When sand is understood in terms of the deluded attachments of foolish beings, [and attachments are] emptied by means of the import of the three syllables, the true and real meaning of the sand illuminated by the wisdom of the sages becomes manifest. This is the wisdom of the buddhas. When the wisdom of the buddhas is added to the sand of foolish beings, the sand radiates light by taking on the wisdom of the buddhas. This is the meaning of mystic power.

There is likewise a deep significance to each of the remaining phrases. This is thoroughly attained by the yogic practitioners. The sand already contains innumerable meanings and principles, and when the power of the buddhas and dharma are added on top of this, how can anything prove too difficult for the understanding, no matter how miraculous things [may appear to] be.[131]

QUESTION: If that is true, then this realm of the mystic power of the mantra should be manifest [for all to see] before our eyes. If not, then doubts easily arise regarding the afterlife.

ANSWER: The fruit of karmic retribution in this life is the result of past karma. Thus, our minds and the objectified world are clouded, and we do not know about the past and the future. However, if one enters samādhi and acquires spiritual powers, then through skillful means one gains that knowledge. It goes without saying that the realm of buddha-wisdom is profound and subtle. Evil karma occludes, and virtue is the cause [for liberation].

There is a reason why [all of this] does not easily appear before one's eyes, and why one must engage in the practice of the six transcendent virtues, the accumulated practices of countless eons. The wondrous fruit of the three points and four virtues has a beginning yet no end.[132] To aspire for this is called *bodhicitta,* and whosoever seeks it is called a bodhisattva. It may not be so easy to attain the unexcelled stage [of supreme awakening]. However, when the discrimination of phenomenal consciousness subsides even a little, the luminous vision of the wisdom-eye easily appears.

He who resides in the mountain fastness and makes his mind transparent to the dharma sees the moon within the mind as the light of the dharma-wheel and hears the wind as the turning of this wheel. When one increasingly distances oneself from the attachment of deluded passion, the mind gradually advances on the path toward the fruit of awakening. There is the saying, "It is as if a great expanse of [pure] white becomes spotted. [Or] as if great perfection is [equivalent to being] flawed." [This means,] "Who can measure [the significance] of one who achieves this [supreme awakening]?" It is not always possible. Even if one does not fully realize the fruit of awakening, when the karma of this life is already beginning to decline and the afterlife approaches ever closer, one can glimpse the realm of the mystic power of the mantra as though in a dream.

When this fool [Myōe] was residing on Mount Takao, there was a plague, and many people fell ill. Among them was someone who was diagnosed as terminally ill, the son of a lay priest, one Saishō Ajari Shōken. He is now deceased. He lived on Mount Takao when he was a child. He unexpectedly fell gravely ill and lost consciousness. The High Priest [Jōgaku-bō] Gyōji, my former teacher, came to his side, transferred the mystic power to a melon, and wetted [Shōken's] lips with it, whereupon he revived and said, "If I had died, I was destined to be born as a fish. While I was immersed underwater, a sweet delicacy entered my mouth. As I revived and came out of my unconscious state, I remembered the taste extremely well. Afterwards I became clearly aware that the sweet substance was the melon to which the High Priest had transferred the mystic power and had placed in my mouth." Being immersed in water, he thought he would become a fish. This [episode] reminds me that I, too, was once revived by being wetted with a melon to which the mystic power of the mantra was transferred.

In ancient times the deep faith of King Ajātaśatru was likened to the great ocean.[133] When he heard of the Parinirvāṇa of the Tathāgata [Śākyamuni, he became so upset] that his face became flushed [with anguish]; he felt as though he was being torn apart. He had a wise minister who, applying skillful means, created a pond lined with copper. He filled it with pure, scented oil and told his king to bath in it. He placed an image of the Tathāgata as he appeared during his life on an altar of sandalwood. He had paintings made of the career of [Śākyamuni], including the time of his birth when he descended from the Tuṣita Heaven and entered the body of Queen Maya, his attainment of true awakening under the Bodhi Tree, the first turning of the dharma-wheel in Deer Park, to the Parinirvāṇa in the Sala Grove outside Kusinagara.[134] [The minister] showed all of this to King [Ajātaśatru], and when he came to gaze upon the scene of the Parinirvāṇa, his heart began to race, his very being was transformed, and one-fifth of the fragrant oil in the pond seeped in through his skin. It was like pouring water into a dry lake. The Great King's life was saved by the application of this skillful means.

It is as though, by putting a piece of melon to one's lips, one feels that one is immersed in water. Because the mind is distracted by the phenomenal world before one's eyes, it is not possible to see that the karmic recompense in the present world is the result of accumulated effects of past karma. However, when the effects of karmic recompense are already leaning in one direction, and they are about to bear fruit in the present, the mind becomes aware of their benefits as they appear before one's eyes.

There was a monk named Jōryū in attendance under me who maintained [the practice of the Mantra of Light] for many years. On the twentieth day of the eighth month of the first year of the Jōō Period (1222–24), he fell gravely ill.[135] He was delirious for several days during which he imagined he was traveling a great distance in distress, making his [lonely] way toward Enji [in the afterlife].[136] There he saw many criminals who were in shackles. There was a large scale where they were being weighed. The sight of this filled him with terror, and he single-mindedly intoned the Mantra of Light. There was someone resembling a giant youth about eight feet tall with a red face and disheveled hair.[137] He tried to put Master Jōryū on the scale, but a layman carrying a bow and arrow prevented him from doing so. Thereafter, he treated Jōryū with great respect and told him, "You should go home right away." Greatly relieved, Jōryū turned to go, whereupon he saw that it had suddenly become dark, and he could not see where he was going. He began to intone the Mantra of Light, trying to regain his composure.

With each intoning a bluish-white light appeared before him coming from all directions. As he continued to repeat the mantra rapidly, the light intensified and filled the air. When he tried to return home after this event, he felt physically exhausted and did not have the will to walk. But when he tried to intone the mantra again, his body levitated into the air. He awoke when he felt himself return home by flying through the air. In the years since then this young monk has been an upholder of the Mantra of Light by which he overcame his difficulties. This is the victory [achieved by] the Mantra of Light. The efficacy of the sand is the same.

QUESTION: One should believe in the efficacy of the mystic power of the mantra above all else. However, if a corpse is found in a field of excrement and defilement, should I refrain from sprinkling the sand of mystic power on it?

ANSWER: Although I have not yet seen any textual evidence for this [concerning the sand], there are passages on the mystic power of the mantra saying that the *pharmakon* of the Mantra does adhere even to bodies in impure places.[138] Based on this, before it is scattered the sand should be revered like the relics of the Buddha. If one happens near a corpse, one should sprinkle the sand even on impure places. This is the evidence of the scriptures. Based on the teachings of the Buddha, the eye that sees impurity sees the sand only as a sense object. One should not hesitate to sprinkle the sand, since the effective power of the mantra will not be hindered by impurities. The skillful means of the mystic power of the sand is the expression of the great compassionate original vow of all the tathāgatas. For that reason, the sand is not averse to either the pure or the impure, and it should simply be sprinkled where the corpse is found. Of course, one should refrain from casting the [sacred] syllables of the mantra into a place that is filled with ordure. This again demonstrates the singular efficacy of the sand [which can be sprinkled in such places].

QUESTION: Let us say there is a Shingon master living deep in the mountains where fine-grained sand is not available. If there is a person who hears of its efficacy and desires some sand, obtains it from an impure place, sends it deep into the mountains, and requests that the mantra be intoned to transfer its mystic power [to the sand], is this to be rejected?

ANSWER: Such a thing should never, never happen. The teaching of the mystic power of the Mantra is exceedingly pure and comes to fruition. If it is defiled, then Vināyaka and other deities will gain a foothold and hinder the realization (Skt. *siddhi*) of [mystic power].[139] Even if there are obstacles to be overcome such as mountains to be climbed and valleys to be crossed, sand from the purest place should be placed in a new container and sent to the Shingon master. If this is done, then he will awaken to the great vow, abide in compassion, and pray assiduously before the image of the main deity. Although the Mantra of Light is the core [of this practice, also integral to it are the various] yogic practices, the forming of hand gestures, the intoning of mantras, and not just one or two but numerous corresponding mudrās.[140] Furthermore, abiding in the profound samādhi corresponding to great wisdom and great compassion, [the Shingon master] will strengthen his resolve, bring his mind to [the task of awakening], and perceive the signs of fulfillment such as are found in dreams and auspicious marks.[141] Thus, only sand from the purest of places should be used.

This fool [Myōe] has made this a matter of the greatest importance, and at first I went to gather sand from an island located very far from any human habitation. However, there were broken shells mixed in, and I discarded it [all] and did not use it. Sekisuiin, one of the buildings of Kōzanji, is located at the source of water for various other buildings. The rocks there are craggy and soar up high, and there is little sand there, but it is very pure. In accordance [with this sand] this foolish monk accumulated the practices of the voluminous exoteric and esoteric teachings, of benefiting self and others, in this place for many years.

I removed the rough rocks from there, built an *akai* in the [cleared] area, and washed them.[142] After soaking them in water and sifting out the larger stones, I collected the fine sand and used it. Although this was troublesome, a couple of people of the same mind and faith also undertook this task. The Kiyotaki River which runs in front of here is filled with fine sand. It is very easy to gather, but I do not use it because it is defiled.

Those who would believe in this sand should first distinguish between pure and defiled. This is the first manifestation of pure faith, and devotion is manifest for the first time here. One will thus attain the fulfillment of the *siddhi* of the mantra's mystic power. As this [practice] spreads, one must be careful that unorthodox methods are not introduced. Thus, this exchange of question and answer is especially important.

QUESTION: Is the fruit of birth in the pure land by this mantra limited to that of the [Western] Paradise, or can it also be a cause for birth in the other pure lands?

ANSWER: In the scriptural passage where the holder of this mantra is said to attain seven great dreams when the *siddhi* are fulfilled, it states, "The gates to all the buddha-lands in the ten directions open at once, and the holder of the mantra is able to come and go freely and delight [in the various lands] at will."[143] Also, since it is the secret mantra of all the tathāgatas, the fruit of [birth in] the pure land is not limited to that of the [Western] Paradise; the holder of the mantra may freely be born in the pure land of her own main deity.

QUESTION: Suppose the mystic power [of the mantra] is transferred to sand for the sake of a particular person. Will that sand only benefit the deceased and return to ordinary sand afterward? Also, will the sand to which the mystic power has been transferred retain the power of the mystic mantra and always remain effective?

ANSWER: If a drop of water falls into the great ocean, then it will [only] dry up when the ocean dries up. Likewise, once the buddha-dharma has entered the ocean of sentient beings, it will unfailingly permeate all sentient beings. There are monuments to the Tathāgata in various locales in India. They remain even through the end of the world-cycle and serve as refuges for sentient beings.

When the Tathāgata was a prince, he engaged in a competition with the other members of the Śākya clan. At that time seven iron drums were set out, and he pierced them with arrows, which went into the ground. Later, water came pouring out of the holes of this relic, and when the sick drew this water and used it, their illnesses were cured. There are also footprints of the Buddha imprinted in stone. There was once a *rakṣasa* who struck a stone against them to crush it and ate the broken fragments.[144] When someone questioned the *rākṣasa,* he replied, "This is medicine taken to cure an illness."

These things simply result from people entrusting themselves to the Tathāgata, believing in the relics of his life. Thus, they used the water of the "arrow-springs," and the [flesh-eating] *rākṣasa* also had faith in the relics of the Tathāgata and used as medicine the stone which had come in contact with the pair of wheels [of the dharma].[145] The immediate benefits were accrued [to the *rākṣasa*] through his faith, but the water from the "arrow-springs" is simply the residue of the Tathāgata's power manifest when he was still a prince. The stone with the wheel is simply a symbol of [the disciples'] devotion [to the Tathāgata] after his entrance into Parinirvāṇa. No direct correlation exists with either the sick or the *rakṣasa.* Yet the benefits derived by virtue of their faith was not insubstantial. Moreover, [these benefits] are not limited to the elimination of illness in the physical body. There are further benefits that ultimately lead to the extinction of sins, the production of good, and the realization of great awakening. The relics of the Tathāgata are truly auspicious when devotion is demonstrated at such times.

The wheels of the dharma imprinted in stone radiate light, and water springs forth from the ground through the holes left by the arrows. If one were to go to these places and worship the remains, what pathos and compassion one would feel. However, the Tathāgata does not thereby say, "This water is for the sentient beings' extinction of sins and creation of good. And this stone is for their liberation from suffering and the attainment of bliss." Nevertheless, the benefits are clearly as has been described. How much more [are the benefits, then, of] this [incantatory] sand, even though it consists merely of ordinary sand. The tathāgatas of the three worlds [of past, present, and future] of all the [innumerable buddha] lands all extend their hands, stroke the bodhisattvas' heads, expound upon this mantra, and bestow it to all sentient beings.

They also teach the skillful means of the sand, extinguish sentient beings' evil karma, and establish this as the secret technique of bestowing vast benefit. Once one has received the mystic power of the mantra, [its power] will not be limited to one person or be exhausted at once. It will produce benefit in accordance with the appropriate circumstances. Where mole crickets, ants, mosquitoes, and horse flies crawl about, and where lions, wolves, and foxes seek out corpses, there is a foul smell. If they come into contact with the sand as they begin to fight over corpses, the torment of transmigration will be eliminated, and the seed of awakening will be planted.

How pitiful, how grievous! As we have been born in this tiny country in the borderlands at the end of the evil last age, evil karma easily accumulates before our eyes, and the roots of good are difficult to nurture in the depth of our hearts. Moreover, we are two thousand years removed from the Buddha [Śākyamuni], and several thousand miles from the sites commemorating his life. Although we face his likeness here and there, the thirst of devotion remains unquenched. The pages of scripture are opened, but practice according to his [true] teachings remains but a distant thought.

When I ponder on my misfortune, I seem to hear the workings of the compassionate skillful means of the buddhas and bodhisattvas and the protective thoughts of the dragon-gods and heavenly deities, which I do not deserve. The golden words [of Śākyamuni], as expressed through the metaphors of the original state and examples of beasts never err as [their truths] become manifest in my person.[146] For what should I lament to the point of tears, for what should I feel joy that a smile breaks across my face? [How fortunate that] I am able to encounter the superior practice of the sand, and can truly rely upon the accumulation of good past karma. Just as Master Wŏnhyo states in his words of encouragement and warning, those who believe are the filial children of the Buddha, and those who do not believe invite regret. People with aspirations should carefully examine the gains and losses.

Long ago, in the eleventh month of the fifth year of the Daye Period (605–17), the Chinese Vinaya Master Zhixing climbed atop the bell platform and struck the bell. Someone had died. In a dream this man said to his wife,

> My life came to an end and I fell into hell. There was no end to the suffering I underwent. On the first of this month, Master Zhixing of Chandingsi struck a bell, and the reverberations reached all the way down to hell. Those who had been subject to the suffering of the same karmic consequences were immediately liberated and have already been born in a blissful place. In order to repay his kindness, I presented him with ten bolts of silk and told him of my aspirations.

When [the wife] awoke from the dream, she told some people about it, but no one would believe her. She saw the same dream several times. About ten days later she received another sign. It reinforced what she had already seen in the dream. As her faith deepened she decided to present [Master Zhixing] with bolts of silk. The Vinaya master accepted the silk and divided it among the monks. Surprised by such a gift, they asked him about it, whereupon he replied,

> There is nothing special. I awakened deep faith in the virtues of the bell after reading the profound exposition of the scriptures of the *Bufazang zhuan* (Record of Transmission of the Dharma-Treasure) and *Agama* extolling its virtues.[147] Although the winter winds cut into me as I climbed the bell platform in the middle of winter, I resolved to carry out the [bodhisattva] vows. First the sages would be invited to enter the *bodhi-maṇḍa,* [practice hall of awakening]. Next, sentient beings in the evil paths would simultaneously be liberated from their suffering. I could sense this coming true as I made the vow and struck the bell.

On the first day of the eleventh month of the first year of the Jōkyū Period (1219–21), Lady Sanmi, the great patron [of this temple], made offerings to the monk of the Bell Hall. She said, "The sound of the bell can be heard [even] in the evil destinies. My [deceased] son the *shōshō* (lower-rank court noble) must listen to this."[148]

When I heard that offerings had been sent even though the day [for the ceremony] had not been set yet, I decided that we should begin today, and told the temple monks that they should gather before the buddha-altar in the main hall. I, Kōben, entered the Bell Hall and began to strike the bell myself. An attendant said, "The monks have already begun to gather in front of the hall for the assembly." When I opened the Vinaya text which describes the proper procedure for ringing the bell, I noticed the record of this episode concerning the benefit derived by Vinaya Master Zhixing ringing the bell. I saw that the date of this occurrence was given as the first day of the eleventh month of the fifth year of the Daye Period.

In the past it had not occurred to me to look into this chronicle. But when I did, the significance of faith left a deep impression upon me. More precisely, I saw this chronicle as I called upon the buddhas and bodhisattvas on behalf of our patron. Although China and Japan are far apart and the present differs from the past, the expression on the faces of the participants changed visibly as the mutual response of feeling and intuition [between practitioners in the present and the buddhas of the past] was realized. The Vinaya text comments upon the freedom from suffering and the attainment of bliss brought about by the sound of the bell as follows: "The sinner's encounter with good is the primary cause. The vow made by the one who strikes the bell is the supporting condition. Thus, the sound is carried [into hell], suffering is extinguished, and the mutual response of feeling and intuition occurs spontaneously."

Our patron [Lady Sanmi] showed no hesitation concerning poverty or suffering in making her generous offerings to the temple; the monks took joy and gathered before the Buddha[-image]. This fool, [Kōben], filled with faith, inscribed inside of the bell various mantras such as the Hōrōkaku, Bodhi-Maṇḍa, and Mantra of Light, as well as passages from the *Avataṃsaka Sūtra* and other scriptures. When I began to strike the bell dedicating my whole being to the task, faith spontaneously arose and permeated my very bones; I knew that I had encountered the compassion of Vinaya Master Zhixing and the benefit he brings to sentient beings.

The meaning of the statement "The karmic bond of the sinner who encounters the good constitutes the primary cause, and the striker of the bell giving rise to the [bodhisattva] vow constitutes the supporting cause" is the same as that of Wŏnhyo, who writes, "The encounter with the incantatory sand is an [auspicious] karmic encounter." Such is the benefit obtained by ringing the bell. The same holds true regarding the benefit of the incantatory sand.

As I am recording these words, I hear the late evening bell. This is the bell of directing the merit to others, made possible by the [bodhisattva] vow. May the holy retinue of the ten directions enter the practice hall and realize the virtue of the sand, so that sentient beings of the three evil paths can obtain the benefits of the dharma and are liberated from the bonds of negative karma.

This is recorded in the hour of the lion on the ninth day of the eleventh month of the second year of the Antei Period (1227–29), in the hermitage of Zendōin in Kōzanji.[149] The profound meaning of the mantra and the sand is as it is recorded in the *Kugishaku* (Commentary on the Significance of the Mantra of Light), *Dosha* (Significance of the Sand of the Mystic Power of the Mantra of Light), and other related works. *(end of second fascicle)*

RECOMMENDING FAITH IN THE SAND OF THE MANTRA OF LIGHT—SUPPLEMENT[150]

THIS FOOLISH MONK, previously responding to someone's request, authored *Recommending Faith in the Sand of the Mantra of Light*. At one point a couple of people, upon reading this work, asked, "In the text it states that [the sand] should be sprinkled on corpses and on graves. Then it states that [the sand] should be attached to one's body while alive. Won't this make householders fear and avoid it?"

I had anticipated this question. When one is sick and bedridden, [one] cannot maintain the concentration [necessary to invoke the mantra] and, being afflicted, cannot even maintain a period of ritual purity. If at this time one moves close to a person [with the sand], then, through the workings of the mind of faith, one will not fail to receive the benefit of this mantra. Thus have I explained. I have by no means said that one should keep the sand on one's person in the peaceful, healthful times.

QUESTION: I raised this question in relation to just this one passage, but I am as yet unable to comprehend the real meaning. According to what has been recorded in *Recommending Faith in the Sand of the Mantra of Light*, one should [apply the sand] when one has become bedridden

251

with illness. Then surely one ought to avoid sprinkling the sand on one's head when one is free from illness.

ANSWER: For foolish people who lack the mind of faith, it is difficult to become imbued with the mind of the dharma. If in light of this one is unable to reach any resolution [as to whether one should apply the sand], and one recalls [the sand] at the time of being bedridden, then that is to be lauded. However, if doubts arise upon examining the scriptures, then one should certainly discern the real meaning.

When it states in the sutras that [the sand is] to be "sprinkled on the grave," this is intended for those whose evil karma is as deep as the vast ocean, people who possess not even the slightest seed of virtue, who do not believe in the three treasures, and who end their lives having disregarded the law of cause and effect. If you place the sand on the grave and don't scatter the sand on the corpse, then there is no other measure to be taken. If that sinful person only committed transgressions while alive and took no time to entrust himself [to the power of the sand], then he has [no choice but] to await the benefit of the scattered sand until after his life has come to an end.

The sand will protect whoever hears of its benefits and, possessing the believing mind, keeps the sand on one's person while alive. Failing to do so, one might become attached merely to the words, "sprinkle on the grave." Reading the statement, "One should sprinkle sand on the graves of those who have committed the five great transgressions," one might think that one should sprinkle sand on the graves of those who have not committed the five great transgressions. Actually, there can still be great benefit in sprinkling the sand on the grave based on the understanding that, if a sinner can be saved, how much more so a good person. And how much more so for someone who is alive and holds the sand. There will still be benefits after death. How much more so if one has faith in the sand while alive.

The foregoing discussion is in accord with the spirit of the scriptural passage. The fact that you have enacted the five great transgressions after examining the teachings and scriptures is an expression of your own stupidity.

QUESTION: The signs of effectiveness of the teaching of the mantra's mystic power will differ according to circumstance. Long ago, people watched from on high as the Shingon master Amoghavajra trained a frolicking group of great Emperor Elephants. No one would dare go near. The Tripiṭaka master formed a mudrā with his hands, intoned a mantra with his mouth, and stood squarely in the road. The large group of rampaging elephants suddenly stopped and bent down on their knees. Everyone could hardly believe their eyes.

On another occasion, there was a great storm, and the emperor requested Amoghavajra to "calm the wind." The wind died down as soon as the Tripiṭaka master spoke once from the silver vase and followed the method of the mystic power. A goose came walking and bumped into this silver vase, suddenly knocking it over. Then the wind began to blow again even harder than before. The wind ceased as soon as he applied the mystic power to the silver bottle and stood it back up.

The crazed elephants digging up the earth were no match for the ways of the dharma; the goose floated on the water because the incantatory vase was easy to topple. Although the sand will enable one to discard the torturous retribution of hell, how is it that the benefits of the sand in the two worlds are not the same unless one also speaks of applying it to one's person while in this life?

ANSWER: It is as stated in the previous work *(Recommending Faith in the Sand of the Mantra of Light)*. I recommended you remember this when bedridden with a serious illness. I do not necessarily recommend following this method for those who may be quick to learn yet are not ill. But the signs of the elephants and the goose are something else altogether. He (Amoghavajra) was able to demonstrate one aspect of things by invoking sundry techniques involving the mantra. Yet he did not reveal the benefit of extinguishing evil karma. Excluding [those who have committed] the ten evils and five transgressions, [the Mantra of Light] will bestow upon the practitioner the superior birth of the lotus blossom [of the Pure Land].[151] If one attaches the sand to oneself in the present life deeply believing in its benefits, then karmic hindrances will disappear and virtue will be increased. Then one will also enjoin the protection of the throng of the underworld, and misfortune will go unrealized.

Thus the mantra is not maintained without interruption. Also, it is difficult for householders to avoid the defilements of imbibing alcohol, eating meat, and partaking of the five [forbidden] spices. Since [the mantra] is not like relics of the Buddha or buddha-images, one need not hesitate to invoke it even in the lavatory. The mind of faith itself is enough to protect one since that is where the great compassion and mercy [of the buddha] flows. These words are not from the chronicles of the Buddha. It is simply what is sensed in the entrusting mind of sentient beings. In the previous work, *Recommending Faith in the Sand of the Mantra of Light,* I related an episode involving water that poured out of arrow-holes that became medicine for the ill. There was another episode in which a *rakṣasa* crushed a stone against cast imprints of the Buddha's footprints and at the fragments; by doing so [the *rakṣasa's*] pain was alleviated. Neither of these episodes are recorded in the chronicles of the Buddha. [Again, these events result from] what is sensed in the entrusting mind of sentient beings. One should also consider the benefits of the sand [of the Mantra of Light] in the present life in like manner. As it is stated in the scriptures, "When this sand is sprinkled on the grave, the light [of the Buddha] reaches the person [of the deceased], who immediately abandons suffering and is born in the land of bliss."

This radiant light is the light of the mantra. This light of the mantra is the undefiled wisdom of the various buddhas and bodhisattvas and illuminates the significance of the sand which is unborn. When the activity [of the mantra] is added to the sand as a phenomenal manifestation of ignorance, the sand retains [this activity]; the ignorance [associated with the sand] is unsubstantial and does not hinder the buddha-wisdom.

The sand manifests its innate virtue unborn. If one does not see the sand of deluded affect, then one cannot become free of dogmatic views [concerning the ego]. The innate virtue immediately becomes manifest and does not become separated from the severing of views. When the light of the great wisdom of the middle way radiates throughout [the realm of] all sentient beings, the evil darkness which emanates from ignorance is immediately dispelled, and [the practitioner] emerges from the evil paths.

Buddha-wisdom constitutes that which [we] call the light; as the sand holds this buddha-wisdom, the form of the three roots of good are impressed upon the mud of the three poisons.[152] This is the intent of the following three words within the mantra: *mani, handoma,* and *jimbara.* Thus, the sand is like a jewel for the destitute. It eliminates destitution and bestows riches. For offensive people it is like a lotus blossom and bestows the love and respect of the multitudes. For those who are base it is like a radiant light and imbues them with great power. Thus this sand becomes the great unfailing seal, [the original vow,] of the Tathāgata Vairocana and manifests the mark of immeasurable virtue. It gathers together all that which is auspicious and avoids all that which is inauspicious. Since the great light and wisdom [of all the tathāgatas] are the substance of this mantra, grave transgressions, like pitch-blackness, are eliminated by the dharma from which they are [so] different. For the destitute, it is the light of riches [that counteracts] the darkness of destitution. For the base it is the light of dignified virtue [that counteracts] baseness. Again, it is the effective light of good fortune and happiness [that counteracts] the darkness of causes and conditions in the present that seem to invite misfortune and disaster. Thus, there should be nothing for which the mantra is insufficient in protecting one in this world. However, all of this simply depends upon what one wants of one's own heart and mind.

QUESTION: Certainly, one should believe in the efficacy of the sand above all else. However, first and foremost, one must not doubt the inconceivable coming together of causes and conditions. The fruits of karmic recompense are variously superior or inferior depending upon the power of causes and conditions. It is just like the fact that, although [all] fires have the power to burn, their intensity differs depending upon the hardness or softness of the kindling. Does the benefit accrued to the deceased likewise differ in terms of its profundity or superficiality depending upon the superiority or inferiority of the practice, the loftiness or lowliness of the teachings and admonitions,[153] of the mantra master who applies the sand?

ANSWER: With regard to the mantra there are two significations, that which can be explained and that which cannot be explained. Thus, with regard to such an esoteric realm, one should simply believe completely. One should not be so quick to speak. However, in order to solidify the mind of faith with regard to the signification that can be explained, it is important to reflect on further examples. In fact, with regard to the mantra's *siddhi* there is both attainment and nonattainment. This is not a matter of correcting the attainment or nonattainment of the *siddhi;* [rather,] the attainment of liberation is fast or slow depending upon the superiority or inferiority of the practitioner's practice.

For instance, if one relies on the mystic power of a person of superior practice and virtue, then one can emerge from hell with even one sprinkling [of the sand] on one's grave. However, if one receives the mystic power of a practitioner of inferior practice and virtue, then if [the sprinkling is repeated] time and again, and evil karma is dissipated, one will surely emerge [from hell]. However, this is [from the perspective of] the gate of virtue, not the gate of attainment. Even though the practitioner's practice and virtue be inferior, since the virtue of the mantra is deep and subtle, it will leave a mark like that of soft kindling being consumed. If there is such a mark according to the gate of virtue, and if [this virtue] is brought to completion through the various skillful means, then even though the mystic power be that of an inferior practitioner, one will attain the great benefit of the superior class [of rebirth]. That is, [one will attain a superior rebirth] if one continues to practice the mantra during times of good health, maintains good spirits, fulfills numerous repetitions [of the mantra], and carries the sand on one's person. If one is averse to carrying the sand around one's neck, then one can place it in a sutra box and worship it. This helps the inferior practitioner (from whom the sand was obtained), and one will surely gain great benefit.

If one has a karmic encounter with a practitioner of superior practice and virtue, then even the spirit of an evil person who does not believe in the three treasures and disregards cause and effect will easily come to abide in the lotus dais immediately. This may be realized even though one is [relying on] the mystic power of a practitioner of inferior practice and virtue so long as there are numerous supporting conditions to offset his weak virtue. Suppose there is someone who commits the ten evils and five transgressions. This does not necessarily mean that he is committing the five transgressions. He does not recognize the cultivation of good during his whole life. Yet, he works hard to cultivate the roots of good. Again, concerning the roots of good, he had not heard of the efficacy of the esoteric sand. Hearing of this leads him to deep faith. Yet, no one sprinkles sand on his grave after his life has ended. While he was alive, however, he carried [the sand] on his person and had great reverence for it. In this way a multitude of conditions help the inferior person to cultivate his practice and virtues. It is as if one adds a great deal of the soft kindling [to the fire], and the flames rise up abundantly just as the flames of hard kindling burn things. Reflecting on these things, [one realizes that] there is no reason for doubt concerning the benefits of faith and reverence to be attained quickly.

Thus, with regard to the benefits of the buddha-dharma, the wondrous fruits of true realization may be attained even with [apparent] frivolity as the enabling condition. Long ago there was an old monk. He was very old, yet there was no wisdom in his mind. [However,] upon hearing some young monks expounding on the virtue of the four fruits,[154] the mind of faith and reverence was deeply aroused in [the old monk].

Speaking to the young monks he said, "Please, I implore you to bestow upon me the four fruits that you have expounded on."

The four young monks teased him and said playfully, "If you wish to attain the four fruits, then prepare a sumptuous meal for us and serve us. After that we will bestow the four fruits on you."

The old monk happily prepared various delicacies and offered them. The young monks finished eating, whereupon they playfully called him over to a corner and said, "You must sit here. We will first bestow you with the fruit of the stream-enterer," whereupon they hit him in the head with a handball. "We have now bestowed on you the fruit of the stream-enterer." Believing this single-mindedly, the old monk was overcome with joy that penetrated to his very bones and immediately attained the first fruit.

Next, they told him to go over to the corner again, hit him as before, and said, "With this we bestow the fruit of the once-returner." Immediately he attained the second fruit. Again, they sent him over to the corner, and he attained the fruit of the non-returner, and finally arhatship.

As a foolish old monk, he could not attain his goal solely on the basis of his own efforts at practice. Yet, with the playfulness of the young monks as the enabling condition, he was able to sever forever the blind passions of the three realms [of desire, form, and formlessness], attain the awakening of the wisdom of having exhausted blind passions and of the wisdom of no birth, and become as the blessed fields of heavenly beings and dragons. Even if the sand is from a mantra master of inferior virtue and practice, it should not be added to the precepts (as if the sand were insufficient).

That which is invoked through speech is the great mantra felt by sentient beings. That which is formed by the hands is the secret mudrā expounded by the Tathāgata. If one focuses one's deepest faith-mind on them as enabling conditions, then they are no less than the playfulness [of the monks] that served as an enabling condition. How much more so are the benefits of giving rise to the faith-mind in the dharma, believing in the power of the mantra, possessing the mind of caring for suffering sentient beings, and warmly bestowing [the mantra], even if one has no virtue. [The old monk] believed in the [young monks'] idle words and attained the four fruits so difficult to realize in this life. There is nothing that can be compared to believing in the esoteric dharma and becoming free from the three [evil] paths that are easy to emerge from in the afterlife.

QUESTION: I am happily able to encounter the mantra by examining the commentaries of Ch'ŏnggu Taesa (Wŏnhyo): "It is not difficult to unite with the sand. Who among gentlemen would not want to devote themselves to this practice?" In the next passage he states, "By sprinkling the sand on the grave surely one can play in that land [of bliss]. How much more so for one who invokes the mantra and wears it on his robes, who hears the voice and intones the syllables." If it is as the commentary states, then "it is sufficient after death to sprinkle the sand on the grave and during life to believe in the mantra and invoke it on one's robes, hear the voice of the mantra, and intone the syllables of the mantra." What fault could there be in not carrying the sand while alive as long as one solemnly applies it for benefit after death?

ANSWER: It is as I have stated repeatedly before. There should be nothing lacking if the likes of the lofty nobility and the stately rich take it to heart as you describe and believe that one should intone the mantra while alive and have the sand sprinkled on their graves after death. The fundamental intent of the present contemplation on faith is to reveal the principle to which one should deeply entrust oneself, knowing simply that there is this inconceivable Tathāgata's great esoteric teaching. Insofar as having faith is concerned, one should truly [attain] faith in accordance with the circumstances of the present life.

However, [one should be aware that] when one speaks of the time from the present onward, the time [it takes until] one is lying ill in bed, one's flowerlike figure shrivels, and one's moonlike face darkens [is all too brief]. Those who are born must die; those who meet must part. Although one celebrates "the longevity of a thousand, ten thousand years," even the thousand-year life span [said to belong to] those in the Northern Lands [Russia] passes like an arrow piercing its target. The great expanse of the formless realm that lasts for eighty thousand eons is nothing more than a flash of lightning.[155] Suppose one is fortunate enough to live eighty or ninety years, yet one has fallen ill and is waiting aimlessly for the end; a person of mercy who believes in the efficacy of this sand will approach the dying person, but he will be repulsed because he is used to the trappings of wealth and power. With all that in mind [the sand and the mantra] was designed to reveal its power to protect [the practitioner] in this life. Again, the profound efficacy [of the mantra] is shown for the sake of those with the mind of the Way and in order to solidify benefits for the future [rebirth]. Since doubt arose concerning the previous unvirtuous monk's ability to wield the mystic power [of the mantra, all of this has been stated] in order to establish the significance of the fact that there is certain to be great benefit even if there is a lack of virtue.

Buddha images and the like are made by lay sculptors and painters; they are not necessarily made by virtuous monks who have renounced this world. The only condition [of their profession] is technical skill. [Nevertheless], even if an evil person creates the image, there is superior benefit once one gives rise to the mind of faith. If one does not have faith, then one creates karmic evil. This sand which becomes [one with] the mantra on the basis of mystic power is like the figure created by the evil person which becomes [an authentic] buddha image. If one adds faith while alive, then there will no doubt be benefit after death; this is absolutely certain. Thus, the reason why Ch'ŏnggu Taesa (Wŏnhyo) recommended faith [in the mantra] is his compassionate mind of benefiting both self and other. [The benefit] is not necessarily limited to the grave of another person. In terms of benefiting oneself, after death I will have no consciousness. If others will not necessarily handle [the sand for one], and instead one simply follows [the practice oneself], then the virtue of one's faith will be all the greater. "Who among the virtuous could not devote themselves to this practice?" The one who uttered these words [Wŏnhyo] possesses a truly broad mind. It is not necessarily the case that one must make others promise [to take care of the practice] after one's death.

One may be asked if following [the practice of the mantra in this life] will not actually lead to a shorter life and deleterious effects. If one has grasped the great intent, and one has deep faith and virtue, then one will be able to answer by producing the superior benefits for this life. Having to engage in such dialogue is irritating. In short, if one is mindful of the mantra in this life and reveres the superior benefits of the sand for the afterlife, then one will have grasped the essential intent of contemplating faith [in this practice of the sand].

QUESTION: This matter is truly as you say. However, I have rarely heard of the earlier explanation [you gave] regarding the gate of attainment and the gate of virtue. Surely it seems that if one has not completed the *siddhi,* then there is no virtue. How, then, is it possible that there is virtue even though there is not attainment. Please explain the points of convergence and divergence.

ANSWER: That is a different matter. Although virtue always accompanies attainment, attainment does not always accompany virtue. I have heard that in the world there are people who try to make foxes speak. Although such people may have some *siddhi* attainment, they do not have virtue based on the roots of good. There are also people who chant the *Kannon gyō* in order to attain their desires but are unable to do so as they are burdened by grave defilements in the present;[156] [in this case] the *siddhi* are not attained, but the virtue and benefits are not lacking. Of course, it does happen that everything is attained due to [one's] deep virtue. This can often be found [both] among those who rank as ordinary people and as sages. With regard to this matter there is what is called the classification of the fourfold logic.[157] It can also be said about this matter. Thus, when one intones the mantra, one can become the king of various heavens in the present body or open the cave of Asura.

The reason for speaking at length on such inconceivable phenomena is that it is necessary to clarify the gate of *siddhi* attainments. The details of this have to do with knowing the method of maintaining the mantra and practicing in accord with the dharma. Or [more precisely], one manifests the aspect of attainment when one places the vajra scepter, ring, and sword on the altar and practices mindfully according to the dharma. Or, a voice emanates from the implements, a flame appears, or one rises high into the sky and abides in empty space. In this manner, the practitioner comes to embody these inconceivable and freely manifested virtues according various aspects: superior, middling, and inferior. These methods have not been transmitted to our tiny land. The subtlest causes and conditions combine to [make these] attainments [possible]. They are called the *siddhi* attainments. It is like harmonizing various foods and drinks to create a delicious dish.

Virtue is acquired by simply believing in and maintaining the mantra, by revering, respecting, and submitting to it to eliminate evil hindrances, and to attain the roots of good. It is like maintaining one's life by eating and drinking even though one does not prepare the various foods and drinks. Thus, in intoning the mantra, one should not doubt the virtue for the hereafter just because one does not see any visible signs [of its efficacy].

When I discard life in this body and make the transition to the hereafter, I will receive the recompense that is in accord with the power of karmic actions I have effected. I create the fruit of karmic effects that I myself experience. If I believe in this cause and effect, then what could I believe that would cause me to discard [the understanding of what is] good? How much more so, then, that if I deeply believe in good karma, then evil karma will easily dissipate, and good karma will increase all the more. Benefit and loss will become apparent immediately. Thus, one ought quickly to put a stop to thoughts of doubt. This point is only reinforced in the sacred scriptures which state, "Although bodhisattvas wield [such] power freely, they do not scatter and sprinkle the seven rarities, since, being considerate of the mind of practice of sentient beings, they do not want to cause them to be distracted and to abandon [their practices].[158] Again, in order to illuminate the significance of great compassion which works by embracing suffering in place [of another], it is stated, "Bodhisattvas will accept the suffering of sentient beings in their place if it will lead to benefits."

Truly the foolish think that, as long as the various buddhas and bodhisattvas are compassionate, then even if one does not cultivate the causes [the sources] of the myriad practices, that we can all still take pride in the wondrous ease of *bodhi* and nirvana. In the buddha-dharma, "without action, there is no accomplishment," [a statement that illuminates] the primacy of the profound principle of interdependent origination. Since the virtue of the various buddhas fills the dharma-realm, the realm of the Avīci Hell is reduced to twenty-thousand *yojana*,[159]and the seed of buddhahood can be fixed in the mind of blind passion of sentient beings. The practice of disliking suffering and rejoicing in ease takes place within such a realm and constitutes the skillful means of cultivating the causes and turning it toward the effects. Its beginning is called the stage of faith and its end is determined to be the fruit of buddhahood. In contrast, there are two vehicles for enlightenment. Corresponding to the two vehicles there are the causes and the effects of [the realm of] human beings and of the heavens. Turning this over, there are the causes and the effects of evil karma. The ten evils are the causes, and the retribution of the three evil destinies are the results. Turning this over, there are the causes and effects of [the realm of] human beings and of the heavens. Turning over the realm of human beings and of the heavens, there are the causes and the effects of the two vehicles. Turning over the two vehicles, there are the causes and the effects of the myriad practices of the bodhisattvas. The myriad practices are fulfilled, and there is the fruit of unsurpassed buddhahood.

Thus, were it not for the virtue of the buddhas and bodhisattvas, everything would probably be destroyed, and only the Avīci Hell would remain. Thus, the suffering and ease that exist at [any one] time of the three evil destinies, the realm of human beings, and of the heavens is due solely to the principle of cause and effect. Discarding this by wearying of the myriad practices and still seeking the fruit of buddhahood is like wringing a horn in search of milk from a breast. If [everyone acted] according to the tastes of ordinary sensibility, then the various teachings would all be severed and destroyed.

Thus one should just take joy in being able to encounter the teachings and single(-mindedly) concentrate on one's faith without contriving the various dharmas in the mind of stupidity. Then the karmic recompense [of one's actions] will become manifest in the present, and one will be on the brink of [realizing] the current fruits [of one's practice]. The power of deep faith will surely [enable one] to attain and sense the benefits of the sand. If, in this manner, one repeatedly sprinkles the sand on the grave of the deceased in order to solidify one's virtue and dissipate such doubts [as has been discussed in the foregoing], then all of the power of the Tathāgata's great secret dharma will not be for naught.

QUESTION: Having heard the various explanations given above, all my doubts have dissolved. However, might there be any basis for the idea that virtue is not attained even if one intones the mantra? If so, then there still remains some doubt regarding the gate of virtue.

ANSWER: Even if the sun and the moon were to fall from the sky, one could not fail to attain virtue by intoning the mantra. The reason for this is, as stated previously, that the substance of the mantra, taken in terms of the expression, is the wisdom-mind of the undefiled thoughts of the various buddhas and bodhisattvas. Taken in terms of the principle, it is the true reality of the various dharmas. Since it is the definitively true and real dharma, such manner of profound and inconceivably great benefit is realized. This is what produces all of the mantra's substance and function. When the substance and function of the mantra are manifest, it is as though a prince ascends the throne, his vassals take their positions, and the [positive] signs therewith are visible everywhere. [It is as though] a letter is sent down from on high, and the messenger carrying the reply spreads the news in the streets so that people learn of its contents and talk to one another everywhere. At night the light of the lanterns will be linked together [like a chain], and during the day horse-carriages follow one another in their tracks. Things will be established in this manner thereafter. The ritual whereby sentient beings sense and attain this sand will also be like this.

In examining the sutra one finds the following statement:

> Drops of sweet dew fall from the fine white hairs in the middle of the brow of the Bodhisattva Kannon. Truly, abiding before the Buddha, [the dew] turns into a lotus blossom of a thousand petals and a multitude of jewels. Its great illumination is greater than one hundred trillion suns. The lotus blossoms as soon as the Bodhisattva Kannon intones the Dhāraṇī of the Lotus Deity of the Unfailing Rope Snare. The Lotus Deity appears in the midst of this blossom. All of the tathāgatas of the ten directions extend their right hands and rub the top of this bodhisattva's head; they intone the Mantra of Light and baptize this deity.[160]

In the commentaries of this school, the light of the Bodhi Tree is said to be the light of wisdom, and the *maṇi* jewels that are made to rain down in this light are said to be the dharma treasure. The existence of the multitudes of bodhisattvas in these *maṇi* jewels is said to be [none other than] great wisdom and great compassion. Based on this example, commenting on the preceding sutra passage, one could say that the benefit accrued to sentient beings by the dharma expounded by all the various buddhas is the working of great compassion. Thus, the Bodhisattva Kannon is the main deity and the reason for the teaching to have arisen.

The "middle brow" is none other than the great wisdom of the practice of the Way that never ceases. Great compassion causes the drops of sweet dew to fall. As for the transformation into the jeweled lotus, it is the water of the various buddhas' great compassion that unites with the mud of blind passion of sentient beings, thereby giving rise to the lotus blossom of sentient beings' buddha nature. The thousand-petaled lotus expresses the Mahāyāna. The blossoming of the lotus upon intoning the Dhāraṇī of the Unfailing Rope Snare is [the working of] great compassion that ensnares [sentient beings] and prevents them from falling into the evil and heretical paths; truly it blossoms like buddha nature. The emanation of the Lotus Deity of the Unfailing Rope Snare in the [lotus] dais is [the manifestation] of the great compassion of the oneness [of buddhas and sentient beings]. The fact that that which gives birth and that which is born are both Kannon is the [working of] the great compassion of the condition of no-self. This great compassion only the Tathāgata realizes fully. It does not exist in any of the three vehicles [of the śrāvaka, pratyekabuddha, or bodhisattva]. Namely, it shows the fact that all sentient beings realize their buddha-nature. All of the tathāgatas of the ten directions extend their right hands and rub the top of this bodhisattva's head; they intone the Mantra of Light and baptize this deity. This is none other than bestowing baptism on all sentient beings. To bestow baptism is to bequeath this mantra upon all sentient beings and to form the seeds of the five wisdoms within them. For example, it is like the way that, in the *Avataṃsaka Sūtra*, Mañjuśrī represents the practitioners of the ten faith [stages]. All sentient beings [are able to] encounter the teaching of this mantra due to such power of skillful means and mystic power. Thus, there is no way in which one will not attain virtue through intoning this mantra. If one attains virtue [through the mantra], then the same holds true for the benefits of the sand.

Long ago, when the Tathāgata entered a palace with his monks to beg, there were two children in their path. Let us call one Virtue That Excels and the other Lacking Excellence. They were playing and made a building that they called a storehouse. They filled it with dirt and called it rice, millet, hemp, and wheat. As the two were playing, the Tathāgata passed nearby and saw them. He was majestic, adorned with a myriad virtues, and when they saw his golden form illuminating them, they jumped for joy. As they were young, they were pitifully small. Lacking Excellence kneeled, Virtue That Excels climbed on top of him, took some dirt that he called parched wheat powder and offered it to the Tathāgata. At this the Tathāgata's face beamed like the full moon, and he smiled. When the venerable Ananda asked him the cause [of his joy], he replied

> Due to his offering, this child will become the Cakravartin [Wheel-Turning King] a hundred years hence. He will parcel out my relics and spread them to many places. He will build eighty-four thousand treasure-towers. I give you this [mound] of dirt. You should plaster it into the walls of your abode.
>
> This is [the story of] King Aśoka. The Great Master Xiangxiang [Fazang] refers to this in his analysis of four statements in which he discusses the three superior and inferior objects of field, things, and mind with respect to the act of giving. He brings this out in the verse in which he describes "field" as superior and "things and mind" as inferior. "Field" refers to the field of merit that is the object of reverence. The [field of merit is superior] because the Tathāgata receives it. If the thing given is dirt, that is trifling, a product of frivolity, and the mind of offering [the dirt] is also trifling.

QUESTION: It is said that already "they jumped for joy." How could it be that this is trifling.

ANSWER: Seeing the Tathāgata nearby, the mind of faith and reverence was deep and so [the children] were filled with joy, but they were still young and made an offering of dirt that they called "parched wheat powder"; this is still play. Thus, the master comments, "The mind is trifling because it is only play." The Tathāgata takes the offering made by the child in play and makes it important like this. How much greater, then, is the great secret rare treasure bestowed upon us as the unending great compassion of identification, which is called the Mantra of Light and the Mystic Sand of the Great Baptism of the True and Real Original Vow of All the Tathāgatas. Even if one abandons as many lives as there are grains of sand in the Ganges River [in pursuit of enlightenment], one will not attain the worth [virtue] of even a single grain. We easily sense this. One truly ought to know, this is due to the power of the original vow of the Tathāgata. It is as though one encounters the Medicine King of Good Manifested while one is incapacitated with illness, or one attains the *maṇi* jewel in a condition of destitution,[161] and if one rejoices and reveres the mantra and sand, then, even in the final [degenerate] age when everything remains hidden, this one dharma will be unlike anything else [and attain its virtue].

QUESTION: The ways of this small nation are inferior, and in this final age everything suffers a continual decline. How can you tell people that this one dharma is unlike anything else?

ANSWER: That which is effected in the nexus of cause and effect is not altered by the three times [of true, semblance, and final dharma]. The principle of good and evil is the same in all nations. As I said before, this is unlike anything else because it is the inconceivable dharma within the gate of virtue. In the world there is an incantatory method called the Dhāraṇī of Gandharva. When one perfects this method, one freely ascends into the air. Another incantatory method is called the incantation of Īśāna. When this method is perfected, one can read others' thoughts. Although these are superficial matters, they have not been transmitted to our small nation. They are hard to attain in the final age. Now, however, if one has even the slightest karmic connection with this sand, then even those who do not believe while alive will still reap benefits in the afterlife.

There may still be those who harbor some doubt regarding the ability of the unvirtuous mantra master to convey the power [of the buddhas]. If only the mind of faith is added while one is still alive, then the root of good of receiving the power of belief will not be shallow but instead be decisively established. That is because this mantra is the substance and function of the principle and wisdom which is of the same nature for both buddhas and sentient beings. If one were to say that although one intones the mantra, there is no virtue, then it would be tantamount to saying that a person does not see even though she has eyes and that she does not hear sound even though she has ears, that water does not refresh, and that heat does not cook; that is, it would be irrational.

When the real significance of the sand is stated in this manner, and everything is clearly manifest without any obstruction, this is the light of the sand. Even if foolish people do not fully realize this, as long as they have the mind of entrusting, it will become the efficient cause for receiving the benefit of the light in the hereafter.

The scholars of our school have a work called *Fajie yihai* (Ocean of the Significance of the Dharma-Realm).[162] This is to reveal the inconceivable significance of interdependent co-origination by pointing to the significance of a hundred gates [of the teachings] on one speck of dust. The *Xianguangming Zhang* (Chapter on Manifesting the Light), states the essentials thus: "When one sees the principle and the phenomena of suchness in the speck of dust, that which becomes manifestly clear is the illumination of the wisdom light. One contemplates all dharma-realms by releasing a single illuminating light of the mind. This is what is known as illuminating everything by radiating light." If one uses the term "sand" in place of "dust" in this work, then this [reveals] the significance of the light of the sand. [One could] say, that which is called the light of the sand is the substance of the buddhas' wisdom. For this reason, when the practitioner comes to know the significance of the sand, he gives rise to buddha-wisdom. Thus, when one comes to know the aspects of principle and phenomena, that is, the unobstructed basis of the mantric syllables as the sand, the light of wisdom is clearly manifest. The essential meaning is revealed in the true characters of the *Dosha gi*.[163] This principle pervades the ten directions and remains unchanged for two ages. If it opens up in the properly attuned mind, then it will not disappear in the hereafter.

QUESTION: In that case, the principle transforms itself into light so that the wise can come to know its significance. It should not belong to the measure of the foolish, should it?

ANSWER: Not so. At present, the trunk and the branches mutually assist one another to indicate the significance of the sand that radiates and pervades [the cosmos]. Thus it is said, those who expound on the profound dharma of the sand are the wise. The source of the wise are the tathāgatas, and the bodhisattvas and the sentient beings follow suit. Their virtue even extends to the corpses of the sinners of the five transgressions. However, although the Tathāgata expounds [this dharma], there is no benefit for the inhabitants of the ordinary realm [of sentient beings] if they do not believe or know this. There is benefit if they believe and know it. Thus, the foolish benefit from hearing the various expositions of the wise. Sinners benefit from encountering the compassion of good people. Just as the sun shining in the sky illuminates the mountains and valleys below, the sand spreads and illuminates those in the ordinary realm.

If one examines the significance of the sand by applying the dharma-seal of all of the sacred teachings, then one sees, that which lacks the significance of the light cannot be the exposition of the Buddha. If it differs from the Buddha's exposition, then it does not [contain] the Buddha's wisdom. Without the Buddha's wisdom there is no light. Without the light the darkness of sin cannot be dispelled. However, if each of the necessary conditions are fulfilled, then the light of the wisdom will emanate of itself. What reason is there to doubt that it will dispel the darkness of sin of the hereafter? This explains the basis for the emergence of the sand.

Again, if there is someone capable of expounding on this, then the dharma to be expounded upon will appear. The person who can expound comes to be known by the dharma that is expounded. Person and dharma mutually support one another; separated neither exists. Already the person who can expound exists. The light of the dharma is manifest and illuminates. With the illumination of the wisdom-eye as the efficient cause, the benefit of the light appears as the result.

Summarizing the *Xianrenfa zhang* (Chapter on Manifesting Person and Dharma) from the *Yihai* [Ocean of Significance], it can be said,

> One who realizes the dust is the person. The dust that is realized is the dharma. Person and dharma appear together in mutual support. The dharma appears dependent on the person. The person exists dependent on the dharma. Truly, the person manifests the dharma on the basis of the person having no [inherent] characteristics. Truly, the dharma becomes the person on the basis of the dharma having no [self-]nature. They are two yet not two. They are nondual yet two.

To extrapolate from the exposition of this passage: The one who realizes the esoteric dharma of the sand is the mantra master. The sand that is realized is the esoteric dharma. The person and the dharma manifest virtue in mutual support. The esoteric sand is manifest by means of the mystic power of the mantra master. The esoteric person who applies the mystic power appears on the basis of the esoteric sand to which the mystic power is applied. The esoteric person manifests the esoteric dharma of the sand because no ordinary characteristics appear to obscure this person. There is no deep efficacy to the sand of itself. Truly, the sand becomes what it is by [the hand of] the mantra master because it is the esoteric sand that receives the mystic power of the mantra master. Thus the mantra master who applies the mystic power and the sand that receives the mystic power are two yet not two. If one follows the gate [of this teaching], then the three acts [of body, mind, and speech manifest] light at the time when the mantra master applies the mystic power to the sand. The sand holds the [fruit of the] three acts. The sand does not exist without the light. The significance of the sand becoming the mantra is thus decisively established and utterly complete. The mantra master applies the mystic power of the sand to another person when the one who applies the power and the one who receives it appear to separate from one another by virtue of this nondual mystic power.

The sand receives the mystic power of the mantra master and releases its light and bestows its benefits in the hereafter. If one follows the gate [of this teaching], then the sand is transformed into light, and the ultimate significance of illuminating the darkness of sin is attained. That is why it is said to be unlike anything else. Now one must simply focus one's faith and deeply ponder the benefits that await one in the hereafter. The morning dew vanishes easily; one cannot rely upon the sun at night. Do not lose the great benefit [of the mantra and the sand] by [becoming lost in] the aggravation of empty words and arguments.

This treatise is being recorded now on the twenty-sixth day of the twelfth month of 1228 in the hermitage of Zendōin at Kōzanji. Snowflakes fall gently into the valley. The wind in the pines sound at the mountain peak. The winter skies have already descended, and spring days are approaching. The rays of the sun cannot be stopped, and dewdrops do not linger. This firm, true, and real treasure is attained within a form that is like foam [on the surface of a river].

One ought stop doubting and deeply rejoice. In these three fascicles [including the two fascicles of the *Kanjinki*] I simply recommend faith to householders in *kana*-style designed to reveal the efficacy of the sand.[164] The proper citation of textual evidence and the detailed exposition on the meaning and principle of the mantra is presented in the *Dosha gi* and the *Kugishaku* written in Classical Chinese form.[165] Furthermore, the five hindrances affecting women as described in the *Lotus Sutra* can also be transmuted by means of the power of this mantra. I wrote about this last year, softening the words of this work in *kana* to describe the efficacy of the mantra. This matter is articulated in question-and-answer form.

—The Mystic Sand of the Mantra of Light—Supplement.

Twenty-sixth day of the twelfth month of 1228, noon.

I completed this work in the grass hut of Zendōin in Kōzanji.

Shingon Practitioner, Kōben

CHRONICLE OF THINGS NOT TO BE FORGOTTEN[166]

SECTION I

A record of things heard related by the master of Zendōin [Myōe Kōben] of things in this world and beyond this world.[167]

This record was begun on the sixth day of the ninth month of 1235. These matters are chronicled as they come to mind, and so they are not in chronological sequence. While some statements are out of order and their date remains unclear, I have only recorded his words, and my own words have not been interpolated into the text [of his statements]. As I fear that I may forget what the master has said as the years pass, I am making this record for my own sake. (The master's words begin [flush to the left margin], and my own words are indented.)[168]

> *When [the master] first arrived to take up residence in this mountain [temple], he admonished us, saying,*

A monk must first of all chant the scriptures regularly at the three periods of the day,[169] and his other matters should come after this.

> Again, it has become fashionable in recent years to do things quickly, but this is to be greatly regretted. One should be centered and act quietly, taking as one's guide the words of scripture. Although you may do some things quickly when you are busy, the two basic practices—of contemplating the circle of the seed-syllable and of the self entering [the deity,

273

the deity] entering the self—should be done with care, a settled mind, and thorough contemplation.[170] Herein is found the real meaning of practice.

Once, when I went to see the master at night, I asked him about
some doubts that I had regarding practice. In response he said,
If you study, then your doubts will be cleared.[171] Moreover, if you do some studying and you do not have other matters to attend to immediately, then you should practice what you studied for at least one sitting. If you have a mind to practice mantras, you should read the *Darijing shu (Commentary on the Mahāvairocana Sūtra).*[172]

Once when I went to see the master at his quarters, he said,
I'm glad you came. Even if you don't have anything in particular, it's good just to have you come so that I can see you sometimes.

    If the Buddha [Śākyamuni] were still in this world, then, Jakue-bō [Chōen], you would already have attained the fruit of awakening. Perhaps I am just wasting words on wishful thinking since it is after his Parinirvāṇa.

Once when the master was studying in the meditation hall, I took
a lamp and lit it. At that time the master said,
When you handle a lamp, be sure to wipe your hands with paper or something else before you handle any scriptures. It is so easy to get oil on them.

    The temple is prosperous,[173] and Jakue-bō, you have joined us. You should certainly partake of the bath. (He always said this.)

Once, when he was about to leave for Kyoto to be treated [for ill-
ness], he said,
I should conclude my treatment as soon as possible and begin the preparatory practice of the Kongōkai (Diamond-Realm) for the first time.[174]

With regard to the attainment of buddhahood through the five aspects of the Diamond-Realm, it is said,[175] "You should contemplate the circle of the pure moon as if it were enveloped in a light mist."[176]This means to contemplate in one's mind [the image of] a beautiful moon covered by a thin mist.

"The tathāgatas in midair snap their fingers and startle us into awakening."[177] Such a statement [instructs us] to see the true manifestation of the tathāgatas in midair as they appear before one's eyes.

"Clearly see the nature of the various phenomena."[178] Such statements are the expressions for the two kinds of emptiness, of person and dharmas, of which I so often speak. Although there are differences between the teachings, Mahāyāna and Hīnayāna, exoteric and esoteric, the meaning of these two is constant throughout the Buddhist teachings.

At the assembly of the great offering, the human beings and deities of the ten directions all make offerings of flowers, incense, and light without exception. There is not one of them that does not make an offering, and all of this is due to the power of mudrās and mantras.

Once, when Myōjun-bō and Chōen went before the master, he said,

The third precept [against sexual activity] should be maintained even at the cost of one's life.[179] Due to various ailments, one is liable to be inconsistent with regard to the precept against taking medications for more than seven consecutive days.[180] One should steadfastly maintain this vow regardless of illness or any other condition.

When urinating one must always take off one's robes. But if one is traveling or in the presence of others and is hesitant to take off one's clothes,[181] then it is all right to urinate with the clothes on. In the temple, however, one must always take off one's robes because otherwise urine is likely to stain them.

Once, when we were studying, Jūgen-bō said, "If there is some dirt on the text, should we blow it off with our mouths?"

The master said, "One should never blow the dirt off of scriptures with one's mouth. You must definitely not blow with your mouth."

Girin-bō (Kikai) said, "If we do not blow the dirt off, then the texts will all be sullied and dirty."

The master said, "Then you should endeavor to [find other means]. For the sake of the texts, you must make sure they do not get damaged."

Again, once he said,

Taking the activities of the second and third periods seriously, one should study when there is some spare time. But if you only exert yourself in [intellectual] study, then your mind will become exhausted poring over the dregs of doctrinal differences. In the end you will be pulled in that direction, become restless, and your mind will simply become busy with thoughts. Consider this matter very carefully.

He spoke of this always.

Although one cannot enter the Buddha way without the two dharmas of faith and understanding,[182] if one is to be missing, then just faith is to be taken. If you practice with sincerity, then you should not go awry.[183] That a bright and clever mind occupies itself with matters other than the [real] principles of Buddhism means: Wisdom without faith not only fails to accord with the buddha-dharma but becomes its enemy. Wisdom should be based on the foundation of the mind of faith. Thus, faith should be sought above all else.

If I had been born in India, I would not have had to do anything. I would simply have made a pilgrimage of the holy sites to my heart's content.[184] I would have felt that I was seeing the Tathāgata himself and would have had no need for study or practice.

There are householders who naturally come to have faith. Although dharma-masters may be able to make countless fine distinctions, what is most important are the householders who are incomparable people of faith.[185]

Once, when Jungyō-bō received the instructions for the Diamond-Realm, various instructions were given that were not included in the written text.[186]

The first thing in the transmission [of the teachings] is copying the scriptures. More than anything else in relation to the Shingon teachings, this must not be taken lightly. If it is, it is to be deeply regretted.

While many people were competent with regard to the two mandalas [Jpn. *Kongōkai* and *Taizōkai*; Skt. *Vajradhatū* and *Garbhakośadhatū*; Diamond-Realm and Womb-Realm], not one mastered the mudrās and mantras. There were only words without substance. Studying the two mandalas should have nothing to do with worldly recognition. It is completely useless. [If such be the case,] my place would be accused of destroying the Shingon teachings. In [this] evil age of the final dharma, when there is so much on the rise not in accord with the dharma, the Shingon teaching represents one of the few real teachings that remain. It is truly to be deplored if even this were to be taken lightly. When Zengetsu-bō explained the preliminary practice,[187] it was superb without precedent. This is not all, but in any case one cannot say enough about this matter of not being in accord with the transmission of the two mandalas. This is also written in Jūgen-bō's text on the Womb-Realm Mandala.

Someone else related this matter concerning Jūgen-bō to me.

Due to this, Jungyō-bō returned to the first practice after quite some time, and later, restating the matter, was allowed to proceed.

This is beyond explanation, beyond [all] explanation. Zennin-bō [Myōshin], you should memorize the Diamond Mandala and not miss a single practice on any day.[188] In the first place, it is because there are those who do not act as masters befitting the Way that the causes and conditions for the extinction of the dharma have come about. Although the transmission is received, the teachings are all discarded until there is no one who remembers even a single mudrā or a single mantra. If this is the way things are, then there will be no [qualified] masters after this.

This is a collection of things [the master said] frequently subsequent to the transmission of [the Diamond-Realm].

One who becomes a master to others should be well informed. Water in a full well should be used as needed, and the water should be fresh. When there is only a little water, it becomes stale quickly. If the master is like a full cup, and the disciple is like a full cup as well, then the flavor of the dharma will be rich and full, and nothing bad can emerge.

When choosing a master, one should carefully select from among virtuous teachers. One should not become a disciple carelessly. If you enter into discipleship having chosen a master who embodies all of the virtues, then you should entrust your life with no hesitation.

Once, he said to Kakusen-bō,

Although one cannot help forgetting things, it is truly lamentable. If something has truly entered one's heart and mind, then there is no way to forget it. It is just as one never forgets the precept regarding when to eat and when not to eat. Things that others say, and anything else, for that matter, are all very important and should be regarded in the same way that one does not forget when [to eat] and when not [to eat].

Once, he gave instructions, saying,

When one receives donations from the faithful, one should always endeavor to stay awake. In the palace of Emma, one can speak of not having faults. But everyone must bear the burden of his sins by himself. *(He spoke of this always so skillfully.)*

Whenever greeting people in the guest house, tell them, "There is hot water in the bathhouse, but please do not use the water as usual. Instead, use just enough to wash off the grime, being mindful of the water that is being consumed."

Although there are other things [to attend to], diligent practice is easy to follow. Chanting and [other] practices should be in harmony with each other. Everything else is based upon this. I have practiced since I was young. Although I studied in order to open my mind in the context of practice, I never thought to become a scholar.[189]

If one becomes indolent, then the mind of lascivious desires will arise. In reality, countless transgressions arise out of indolence.

Once, when Zenninbō, Chōen, and others went to see [the master of] Zendōin [Myōe], he said,
Even if one's body is weak with illness, one's mind should be strong. If one follows the path of the Buddha, [one's practice] is true and real, and then one will not be separated from the great spiritual guides. Even if one is headed for the evil destinies,[190] one should know that the encounter with the profound dharma is assured if only one has faith. One should love and seek the unsurpassed great mind of awakening and never forget the vow to encounter the three treasures life after life.

When Jungyō-bō mentioned that Sennen-bō liked [to compose] waka poems, the master said,
It is no good at all trying to make superior waka poems. If one simply composes what one really likes as it comes to mind, then there will be no trouble [writing poems].

Once, during a lecture, he said,
There are no grounds for claiming that there is the slightest difference between a person of the exoteric tenets and that of the esoteric. There is

no distinction between exoteric and esoteric where the meaning is the same.[191]

In Shingon one always takes body and speech as the function of the mind and thereon establishes the equality of the three mysteries.[192] The exoteric does not concern itself with body and speech; it focuses solely on settling the mind. This is the essential difference. There is no distinction concerning the wisdom of contemplation. The doctrines of Shingon are for the most part at the level of the three vehicles' teachings.[193] However, just as an artisan collects odd pieces from here and there and creates something, so too, do [these sundry teachings of the various schools] become the functioning parts of the esoteric school.

Once, he said to Zenjō-bō,[194]
All of the Shingon teachings are wondrous. One contemplates the syllables, and without any particular contrivance, enters the true [formless] aspect of things by means of those syllables; such is the superior [character of the teachings]. The entrance into the *buddha-samaya* of the Diamond-Realm is the first sign of entering into the *buddha-samaya*.[195] The mudrā consists of the moon-circle of the mind with a sword and a flag. The birth of the dharma-realm [consists of] entering into the house of the Buddha, out of which emerges that which is difficult to understand.[196] This is the prior aspect of the fire of wisdom.[197] Thus one forms the mudrā of the fire-circle. Next is the turning of the wheel of dharma. The significance of intoning the Jūni Shingon-ō (Twelve[-syllable] Mantra King) lies in leading one toward the fruit of buddhahood.[198] As it is based on the twelvefold dependent origination, it is [homologous] with continual rebirth in samsara.[199] The significance lies in overturning this [continual rebirth] and turning toward the fruit of buddhahood.

*When Jigon-bō and others were studying, the master said (during
a lecture on the Dosha gi [Significance of the Mystic Power of the
Sand and the Mantra of Light]),*[200]

In examining all aspects, [the heart of] this principle is to single-mindedly practice it with vigor.[201] Everything is satisfied thereby. However,
the one truly important thing is that all this depends on being true and
real.

When he was discussing the meaning of the Shinshugi *(Meaning
of the Seed of Faith in Huayan),*[202]

There are those, such as Kaigyō-bō, who practice [the path of birth] in
the land of bliss.[203] Having heard of the dharma-gate such as this, listen
also to other [teachings]. In the end, this will come about through the
karma of the "best of the superior births."[204]

Once, during a lecture in Zendōin, the master said,

Myōninbō continued to practice [meditation] throughout the night until dawn eliminated indolence. Although there were obstacles, and he
thought of not even waking up, it behooved him to participate at a suitable time, and he said to someone that this was truly divine.[205] In this
way everything becomes clear and distinct. When I practice through the
night, however, [it seems to be] a mistake to say that one should see the
three treasures, and the like. It is especially appropriate to say such things.
In the Vinaya as well, those things that are expressed through bodily
[action] and language are based on these clear distinctions. It is divine
and wondrous.

Once, in relation to something else, he said,

It is unheard of to write in *sō* (grass-style).[206] In one text it is stated that
one should not write in *sō* but should instead write in *shin* (true-style).
In any case, it is a great error to copy the holy scriptures in *sō*. If the

Buddha were in this world, he would surely establish a precept against writing in *sō*.

One should respect the essentials of the two-hundred and fifty precepts. One should act in accordance with these standards. If one takes the two-hundred and fifty precepts as the fundamental framework and patterns one's entire behavior after it, then one will be endowed with boundless dignity appropriate to each occasion and time. Behavior that is true and sincere will naturally be in accord with the precepts.

The Darumashū is not suitable for householders.[207]

[Listening to you] intone the Zuigu Dhāraṇī, one cannot mistake [our] way [of intoning it] in your recitation.[208]

Those who attentively watch over such creatures as worms and cast [the virtue] of the Mantra of Light on them are [Myōe] Kōben's [true] disciples. There are many such followers of our way residing in Zenmyōji. They do not deviate from what I say because they take care to maintain [their practice]. In the *Pusa jieben shu* (Commentary on the Bodhisattva Precepts of the Brahma-Net Sutra), in the section corresponding to nuns, there is an excessively vulgar passage; I could not read it as it is too offensive.[209]

> *Once, Zennin-bō and I, Chōen, went [to see the master] in his res-*
> *idence at Zendōin. [At that time] he said,*

Look at the clouds billowing out at the base of that mountain; there are such interesting things in this world.

> *Once, during a lecture the master said,*

When the person who should take my place emerges, I will stop everything. It will be impossible to do so at the time of death. If one is determined to die in another's place when that other person is to be beheaded, then everything must be halted, including study. If there is the least aspiration for awakening which turns one toward the path of the Buddha, then it is nothing [to sacrifice] one's life. Everyone knows what was in their minds when Prince Mahāsattva gave his life to the tiger, and the youth of the Himalayas gave his life to the *rākṣasa* for half of a verse.[210] Things ought not be as I think.[211] Just as the ordinary person takes joy in eating soup with *hiyo* and rice, so, too, the things that come to my mind.[212]

There is nothing as noble and pure as the myriad practices of the causal stage of the bodhisattvas.[213]

It is deplorable that the toilet next to the Great Gate is not well maintained.[214] There are unsightly urine stains. It is shameful if people come to the temple and say, "The atmosphere of that temple has changed." Upon seeing anything that has fallen into disrepair, everyone should clean and make [the necessary] repairs. It is a great transgression to live in the temple but lack the heart to maintain it. If that is the case, such people should [go] to the charnel grounds in the mountains.[215] As long as you are in [this] temple, you should protect against [all] that which might be bad.

Once, during a lecture the master said,
Those who focus on a single practice and think, "I will read only the Zuigu Dhāraṇī," should be able to explain it clearly. It is hard work. If one haphazardly thinks of it as [no different from] worldly rituals, laughs at it from the side, and makes it into something it is not, this is a grave error. [Such an attitude] is not in accord with the principle of transcending the world.

Once, he said,
How should one understand the precept on eating only at times allotted?[216] One may fall ill, or due to an infection be unable to work, and thus not do what one ought to. All the more in such cases must one [maintain the precept on eating].

One evening, he said,
In my early years in Takao when I was still a child, I went to the [meditation] hall to practice in the middle of the night without anyone's knowledge, seeking to attain true faith and wisdom. I prayed and applied myself diligently for several years.

In observing the practices of the masters of the exoteric and esoteric teachings, I was grieved [by their outrageous behavior] about which I did not know what should be done. I did not know what to do to attain true faith and wisdom. Yet, I vowed to attain the same realization as the Great Sage [Mañjuśrī], resolved to live in the mountains or near the sea, secluded myself in the mountains with but a few sacred scriptures, and single-mindedly prayed to the Great Sage Mañjuśrī, whereupon he manifested himself [in a vision].[217]

When Gien-bō [Ryōten] and others went to see the master, I, Chōen, also went.[218] *[At that time the master said,]*
I saw Mañjuśrī right there, and I prayed to him. Something seemed to be afflicting Jakue-bō [Chōen], who is a sincere seeker of the Way. The sky was filled with limitless radiance. The Great Sage [Mañjuśrī] manifested himself in the midst of the luminosity. My joy was incalculable. That I am able to lecture to you now is due to that event.

Again, at that time, I could not do the practices of the three periods. The first night, as the evening progressed and the dawn approached, I left [the meditation] hall in the morning. Later, I entered the meditation hall and exited toward the evening, but I could not manage the second and third periods. Yet, as I contemplated the *ma* and *ta* syllables with both eyes, as if they were manifest before my very eyes, I could perform this each time as it was taught. It has been a long time since I began to do this; recently, everything occurs as it should, appearing within the mind even when I do it quickly, because I have put so much effort into it [over the years].

When the Taizōkai (the Womb-Realm) was transmitted, the master said,[219]

One should receive [this] as though it were bequeathed by Mahāvairo-cana of both mandalas. I am merely the one who recites [the transmission].

You should ask Kūdatsu-bō [Jōshin] about any doubts you have concerning this transmission.[220]

It is unthinkable to ignore the *siddham* [Sanskrit syllabaries] of the Shingon master [certified to transmit] the practices. The *siddham* should be [directly connected] to practice, but people in recent years make it a separate practice which has no basis.

Once, the master said to Shōdatsu-bō Ajari,[221]

You think of the meditation of the past ajari, and you wish to attain the same meditation. I have studied the ritual practices of Huiguo and Kōbō [Daishi Kūkai]. Although they are fond of the same mantras, there are differences between them. *(He spoke of this as a metaphor.)*

•

SECTION II

To carry the vessels for the [ceremonial] virtue-water below the waist is improper.[222] They should be held high.

In the past I carried such things as virtue-water myself and did not make others carry them. When I had urgent matters to attend to, however, I would naturally have others carry them.

There is something that Kenshō-bō said which remains indelible in my memory. He said that when spring comes to an end and summer arrives, Japanese star anise blossoms are in full flower and one's heart is content, then it is like going to see the Buddha. It was touching to see how joyful he was.

I remember once encountering a group of women in the western part of the capital [Kyoto] when I was leaving the city. When one of the women spoke spitefully about someone, another woman said, "When you talk about the faults of others, you should know that you are talking about your own faults." This is real wisdom.

Once, the master said,
As I now approach death, I wish nothing else but to engage in practice as many times [as I can].

Once in the fall [the master of] Zendōin [Myōe] said to Zenjō-bō,
I would like to record and recite the way in which the leaves of this persimmon tree fall here and there, blown about by the wind, similar to the manner in which birds saunter about. Once one begins to talk about such things, they eventually become the words of waka poetry.

This is playfulness.

Once, the master said,
The youngsters Myōjun-bō and Zengetsu-bō should [sit] facing each other and should not be sent out.[223] Again, if people are not obedient, they should be made to stand up.

Once, the master related the following episode:
There was a time I was in the capital for a night to study. In seeking to resolve the question of the true and the provisional with respect to the one vehicle versus the three vehicles, I came across the following passage from the *Yanyi chao* (Exposition on the Meaning in Accordance with the Avataṃsaka Sūtra):[224] "In the Nirvaṇa Sūtra it already states, 'In the morning expound on extinction, at midnight [enter] nirvaṇa. After this is resolved, other sutras are not expounded.'" After reading this passage I was very moved, whereupon I heard birds crying in the distance. At that time I felt deeply for those birds [whose life is so fleeting]. I do not know what causes and conditions came together so that,

just at that moment when I was so moved by the words of scripture, I heard the cries of numerous birds far away, making the pathos of past karma all the more intense.

Once, the master spoke artfully,
The path of the dharma master is outside of the six realms of transmigration.[225] I have fallen into the path of the dharma master and am now afflicted with suffering. What can be done with the evil ways of the dharma master?

Once, the master said,
One praises someone for their mind when there is nothing to praise.

Once, the master said,
There is a reason for people in the world to say that [the monk] performing the liturgy has fallen into evil. More specifically, *ma* [the character for evil] refers to *mara*, which means hindrance [in Sanskrit]. If one practices incantations through the body and speech within the three actions [of body, mind, and speech], then one will not immediately fall victim to the extreme suffering of hell. However, if one lacks the mind of aspiration for awakening in the actions of the mind, then one will fall into the evil paths. Such is the ultimate principle.

There was one time:
By nature I am pained by that which is harmful. I feel this way about writing the *Zaijarin* (Tract Destroying Heresy).[226]

There was one time:
If you intone the Zuigu Dhāraṇī, then you are certainly a member of our school.

When the master transmitted the Zhenyuan jing *(Forty-Fascicle Flower Ornament Sutra) to Kamo Hisatsugu, he said,*

The burning of incense is especially fine. One should always delight in burning incense. The incense smoke fills the ten directions and pays homage to the buddhas and bodhisattvas.

Once, the master said,

It is one thing to be a wandering monk of the "lower-middle birth" and,[227] bound to a group, be unable to follow one's heart freely. If one attempts to attend to one's practice following the regular schedule but is unable to do so in the morning, then [the consequences] are incalculable.

Once, the master said,

The *siddham* belongs to the practice aspect of the mantra. To think that it is a separate path has no basis.

Again,

One should not accumulate grime in one's finger nails. If one places implements for offerings with grimy finger nails, then Vināyaka will hinder [one's practice].[228]

Again,

One should be well centered and act quietly, taking as one's guide the words of scripture. Although you may do some things quickly if you are busy, [the two practices—of] contemplating the circle of the seed-syllable and of the self entering [the deity, the deity] entering self—should be done with great care, a settled mind, and thorough contemplation. Herein is found the real meaning of practice.

Again,

When one receives donations from the faithful, one should always practice the virtue of diligence and endeavor to stay awake. In the palace of
Emma, [he] may explain that it is not his fault, but everyone must bear
the burden of his sins by himself.

•

1   This translation is based on the text contained in Murakami Sodō, *Toganoo-zan
    Kōzanji Myōe Shōnin* (Kyoto: Kōzanji, 1937), 318–319.
2   The *Yuishin kangyō shiki* is a work by Myōe that is no longer extant. See Murakami,
    Myōe Shōnin, 315.
3   *Sambō rai* is an abbreviation for *Sanji sambōrai,* a brief ritual practice devised by
    Myōe, based around the recitation of the three refuges, and set forth in the *Sanji
    sambōrai shaku* (DNBZ, vol. 13).
4   The original text, *"gyōhō ichido"* usually means "walking meditation," but it might
    also mean "practice method." In this case it might refer to any number of practices,
    perhaps those that were individually tailored for Myōe's disciples.
5   This seems to mean that one might omit or substitute another practice in place of
    walking meditation depending on the occasion.
6   *Rishukyō raisan:* an unknown work.
7   *Goji Shingon* (Five-Syllable Mantra): a Shingon mantra based on the five seed-sylla-
    bles of *a-bi-ra-un-ken* (Skt. *a vi ra hūṃ kham*).
8   *Sōshi* texts *(sōshibon).* There are two possibilities: (1) a bound text created with folded
    pages, (2) a text written out in longhand.
9   The *Gyōganbon* refers to the final section of Prajñā's forty-fascicle translation of the
    Avataṃsaka Sūtra, the *Puxian pusa yuanxing pin* (Practice of the Vows of Bodhisattva
    Samatabhadra) (T, 10:661, #293). The *Yuigyōkyō* refers to the *Fochuipo niepan lueshuo
    jiaojie jing,* translated into Chinese by Kumarajīva (T, 12:1110, #389). The *Rokkankyō*
    probably refers to the *Sifenlu xingshi chao* by Daoxuan (T, 40:1, #1804), which is
    also known as the *Liujuanchao* (Jpn. *Rokkanshō*) (BGJ, 193b).
10 The present translation is based on the *Fukū kenjaku birushana-butsu daikanjō kōmyō
    shingon kugishaku,* MSS, 2:883–891. According to Kobayashi et al., the original doc-
    ument is archived in the Ōtani University Library and dated as a copy from the
    Kamakura Period (MSS, 2:884). According to the colophon it is dated 1229 and is a
    copy of the still earlier original by Myōe from 1222.
11 This first rendering appears in the Devanāgarī script used in Sanskrit; the second is
    the Sino-Japanese transliteration.
12 *Dharmakāya.* In the Mahāyāna theory of the *trikāya,* or three bodies of the buddha,
    there are the *nirmāṇakāya, saṃboghakāya,* and *dharmakāya.* The *nirmāṇakāya* is the
    body of form, or the physical body in human form. The *saṃboghakāya* is the body
    of bliss, or alternately, the body of recompense, so named because when the accumu-
    lated merit of karma is recompensed, the blissful body of the cosmic buddhas is

manifest. The *dharmakāya* or "truth body" constitutes the deepest level of the three levels of the buddhas' existence, equivalent to emptiness as such. Since kāya, "body," here includes more than just the material body but a sense of the personhood of the buddha embodied, "dharma-person" may be a closer translation in terms of meaning.

The term *dharmakāya* can be used to indicate the basis of the other two bodies. Thus, for example, the *saṃboghakāya* is sometimes referred to as the *dharmakāya* manifest as compassion or as skillful means.

13 Thirty-Seven Honored Ones *(sanjūshichi son):* the original deities of the Diamond-Realm Mandala, which include the five wisdom buddhas and various bodhisattvas (MJ, 266).

14 Self and common aspects *(jikyōsō)*. "Self aspect" refers to the aspect of a thing in-itself, namely, emptiness, that which is beyond words. "Common aspect" refers to characteristics that a thing has in common with others and can be abstracted into words and concepts (BGDJ, 556a, 285a).

15 Original vow-mind refers to the mind of a buddha when he or she originally made the bodhisattva vows, giving rise to *bodhicitta*.

16 According to the *Kōgonku gishaku chōjūki*, "unaccompanied" actually seems to mean that *bodhicitta* and suchness are so interfused that they are one and the same (MSS, 2:842).

17 The explanations of Sanskrit diacritical marks and pronunciation are not always accurate, and this translation does not correct any errors in this regard.

18 "Inflated extremes" *(zōyakuhen,* Skt. *samāropa-anta)* is the view that holds on to the extremes, for example to the idea that the self exists independently (Skt. *pudgala-samāropa-anta)* (BGDJ, 883a).

19 Three types of sundry defilements *(sanzōzen,* Skt. *saṃkleśa)*. "Three types" probably refers to blind passions, karma, and suffering (BGDJ, 885a).

20 Separated interpretation *(rishaku)*. According to the *Chōjūki,* "separated interpretation" means to "interpret after separating [the syllables from one another]" (MSS, 2:859).

21 This is the twenty-seventh fascicle of the *Bukong zhuansuo shenbian zhenyan jing,* translated by Bodhiruci (T, 20:227, #1092).

22 *Shenbianjing* refers to the *Bukong zhuansuo shenbian zhenyan jing.*

23 The present translation is based on the *Kōgonku gishaku chōjūki,* MSS, 2:805–881. According to Kobayashi et al., this annotated version is based on the Jinshin copy from 1259 augmented by the Eiben copy from 1684 where the latter contains omissions from the former (MSS, 2:733–734). The Jinshin copy is archived at the Ōtani University Library, and the Eiben at Kōzanji.

24 These are the two most important sutras in Shingon Buddhism (MJ, 241): *Mahāvairocana Sūtra (Dainichikyō,* Ch. *Darijing,* T, 18:1, #848) and *Vajraśekhara Sūtra (Kongōchōkyō,* Ch. *Jingangdingjing.* The *Vajraśekhara* is actually a collection of many scriptural sources. See MJ, 241).

25 The "five illuminations" *(gomyō,* Skt. *panca vidya-sthānāni),* originating in ancient India, refer to the five areas of knowledge: (1) linguistics, grammar, and exegesis, (2) logic, (3) sectarian religious knowledge [in Japan], (4) medicine and magic, and (5) technology and craftsmanship (IBJ, 281b).

26 Myōe seems to mean here that people generally tend to take enough interest in a particular activity to try out four or five variations.

27 This syllogism represents the core of the Buddhist logic of *hetu-vīdya* as one of the "five illuminations." The three-part syllogism of thesis, reason, and instantiation are in Sanskrit *pratijñā, hetu, and udāraṇa.* Originally a five-part syllogism, the three-part syllogism became predominant after Dignāga (BGDJ, 464c).

28 Jigon was one of Myōe's disciples in the latter's later years. His name also appears in the *Kyakuhai mōki* (MSS, 2:873).

29 The original character in the text is probably a substitute for *u*, "rabbit," indicating the time between 6 and 8 A.M.

30 "Emperor Jimyōin" is an alternate name for the retired emperor Takakura (MSS, 2:874).

31 The explanations of Sanskrit diacritical marks and pronunciation are not always accurate, and this translation does not correct any errors in this regard.

32 Garuḍa (Konjichō) are birdlike creatures that symbolize the sun in Indian mythology.

33 "Eyes and nose" refers to the aspect of relative distinctions, i.e., when one expounds on the dharma in the realm of form.

34 Animal glue *(nikawa)* (KOJ, 1945a).

35 Although one sees something in the west relative to oneself, one realizes that everything is everywhere in the realization of the unborn mind of emptiness.

36 Mount Kongō *(Kongōzan,* Skt. *Vajramaya-parvata):* in Buddhist mythology, an enormous mountain range made of steel, impenetrable like diamond (IBJ, 288a).

37 Thirty-seven Honored Ones *(sanjūshichi son):* the original deities of the Diamond-Realm Mandala, which include the five meditation buddhas and various bodhisattvas (MJ, 266).

38 Thill *(nagae):* "either of the two shafts between which a horse is hitched to a wagon," *Webster's New World Dictionary of the American Language,* 2d college ed., s.v. "thill."

39 The most influential strand of Yogācāra in East Asia, articulated by Xuanzang among others, held that there are eight levels of consciousness. However, Myōe here refers to the theory of nine consciousnesses set forth by Paramartha, where the eighth is the storehouse, or *alaya-vijñāna,* and the ninth is the pure, or *amala-vijñāna.* The seventh consciousness is *manas,* having to do with subconscious intentionality. See Diana Paul, *Philosophy of Mind in Sixth-Century China: Paramartha's Evolution of Consciousness* (Stanford: Stanford University Press, 1984).

40 *Chimaki-ga-ie* is a mat-like wrapping used to wrap a kind of dumpling called *chimaki,* often containing rice or rice cakes (MSS, 2:876).

41 "My grandfather the lay priest" refers to Yuasa Muneshige, Myōe's maternal grandfather (MSS, 2:878).

42 Tengu is a figure of Japanese mythology filled with cunning and anger. It is a common expression in Japanese Buddhism to say that a priest or monk who has become drunk with power "has become a Tengu."

43 *Commentary on the Illumination of Logic* (Ch. *Yinmingshu*) probably refers to the *Yinming ruzhenglilunshu* by Cien dashi Kuiji (632–82), a disciple of Xuanzang (600–664), one of the earliest scholar-monks of Chinese Yogācāra and the putative founder of Chinese Yogācāra according to the Japanese (BGJ, 146b).

44 *"Kun-reading*" refers to the indigenous Japanese reading and syntax applied to Chinese characters and syntax structures.

⁴⁵ Parīttābha-deva (Haridaten): the first heavenly realm of the second *dhyāna* of the form-realm. The original text here gives the Sino-Japanese *Pari no zen,* literally "the *dhyāna* of Pari," which suggests the Parīttābha-deva (BGDJ, 1093c).

⁴⁶ Annen (841–89 [or 898]): a renowned monk of the Tendai known for mastering esoteric practices incorporated from Shingon (IBJ, 18b).

⁴⁷ This refers to the hierarchical classification or *panjiao* established by Cien, whereby he identifies a progression from the sutras affirming existence of dharmas, to emptiness, to the middle affirming both the existence of dharmas and emptiness. This is said to correspond to the Hīnayāna, the transition from the Hīnayāna to the Mahāyāna, and the true Mahāyāna, respectively (BGDJ, 465d).

⁴⁸ The Chinese Sanlun, or "Three-Treatises" School, is known for its analysis of emptiness.

⁴⁹ Fazang set forth his five-stage classification in his commentary on the *Avataṃsaka Sūtra,* the *Huayanjing tanxuanji* in terms of the Hīnayāna, Early Mahāyāna, Later Mahāyāna, Sudden, and Complete, where the *Avataṃsaka* represents the complete Mahāyāna (IBJ, 263a).

⁵⁰ Sutra schools *(kyōshū).* Alternatively, this term may be translated as "according to the tenets of the sutras" (IBJ, 176a).

⁵¹ Tokugō: a rank given to scholar monks of Kōfukuji (among others) after lengthy study and an oral examination at one of the major assemblies such as the Yuima-e or Hokke-e (BGDJ, 1019d).

⁵² *Treatise on Mind-Only (Yuishikiron)* probably refers to the *Vijñaptimātratāsiddhiśāstra* by Dharma-pāla (530–61), a work that was central to the canon of Japanese Yogācāra, the Hossō, in the time of Myōe and his close colleague in the Hossō School, Gedatsu Jōkei. However, *Treatise on Mind-Only* might also refer to *Vimśatiknā Vijñaptimātratāsiddhiḥ* by Vasubandhu (BGJ, 141b; IBJ, 810a).

⁵³ The original characters in the text read *sōkō,* but according to the annotation, this should be read as *sōkan (kusakanmuri,* "radical for grass") (MSS, 2:878).

⁵⁴ Shidagon (Skt. *sakṛdāgāmi-phala*): once-returner, or one who only has one more rebirth left before attaining nirvana (BGDJ, 546d).

⁵⁵ "Arms and legs, drum" is a translation for *kyōsoku tsuzumi,* where *kyō* is actually closer to "armpit" or "side of the body under the arms." The context here, however, indicates that "arms" is a more suitable translation.

⁵⁶ The concept of the mind and its corresponding function *(shinshinsho,* Skt. *citta-caitta)* is found in the *Abhidharma-kośa* and becomes integral to Yogācāra (BGDJ, 767c).

⁵⁷ The *Darijing shu* (T, 39:579, #1796) is a twenty-fascicle commentary on the first six (of seven) fascicles of the *Darijing* (T, 18:1, #848). Yixing (683–727) compiled the *Darijing shu* based on lectures given by Shan Wuwei (637–735) (BGJ, 217b).

⁵⁸ In Indian Yogācāra, consciousness is analyzed in terms of eight levels, the most fundamental level being that of the storehouse consciousness, or *alaya-vijñāna.* In the *alaya-vijñāna,* thoughts or impulses are planted as seeds (Skt. *bīja*) which then gain momentum through action, creating dispositions in consciousness. Seeds can be either binding, based on attachment and delusion, or liberating, based on nonattachment and awakening.

The three natures of mind in Yogācāra are *paratantra, pariniṣpana,* and *parikalpita:* dependent, complete, and deluded. The complete is manifest dependent upon turning over the deluded.

59 This seems to suggest that one will enter a realm of delusion and dissolution where one could expect to find stricken fox and badger spirits.

60 See note 31 above.

61 In the original there is an extended note inserted here regarding Myōe's discussion of diacritical marks and related matters in Sanskrit. However, there are so many gaps due to illegible and missing characters that it is virtually impossible to piece together an intelligible translation. For this reason, this note is omitted.

62 *Yakṣa* is a forest-dwelling spirit, incorporated into Buddhism as one of its protector gods (IBJ, 806b).

63 *Muli mantuoluo jing (Muri mandara kyō)* (T, 19:657, #1007), translated by Shi. It is the same sutra translated by Amoghavajra as the *Baolouge jing (Hōrōkakukyō)* (T, 19:619, #1005A). It expounds the fundamental *dhāraṇi* of the mandala of the jeweled tower atop Mount Sumeru (MJ, 633a).

64 Three wisdoms *(sangen).* In the Tendai classifications, this refers to the following three groups of ten stages in the fifty-two stages of bodhisattvahood: ten abidings, ten practices, and ten merit-transferences (BGDJ, 461c).

65 This question refers to slandering the teachings of the "Hīnayāna."

66 The true teaching "that the two emptinesses are none other than suchness" means that there is no intermediary logic to bridge emptiness and suchness. Rather, one is to resolve "emptiness" as "suchness" in practice rather than through the mediation of an intellectual syllogism.

67 That is, the meaningful distinction between sentient beings and buddhas is based on freedom from attachment to views. Distinctions are not delusory in and of themselves. Distinctions made free from attachments have a liberating effect.

68 Sense organs *(shokon)* (BGDJ, 689b).

69 Realm of the *asura* is one of the three desirable rebirths according to the scheme of six realms in the Buddhist view of rebirth. Asura was probably of Iranian origin, related to Ahura, but in Indian mythology he came to be depicted as an enemy of Indra (IBJ, 9a).

70 *Kiṃnara* is the musician-god who resides in the heavenly realm and acts as one of the protector gods of Buddhist mythology (IBJ, 194a).

71 *Gandharva* is a musician demigod residing in the heavenly realm along with *kiṃnara* (IBJ, 240b).

72 *Zaijarin shōgon ki* (Elaboration on the Tract Destroying Heretical Views) (MSH, 335–397).

73 "Encompasses all aspects and returns them to their [undiscriminated] nature *(shōsōk-ishō)*" is an important concept of the Hossō school (BGDJ, 739d).

74 *Ajari,* Skt. *ācārya.* The term *ācārya* was originally used by Brahmins to designate religious teachers, but in Buddhism the term was adopted as a designation for monks at various levels. In Shingon the term became especially important and was also used for various ranks, but the highest ideal is the *ajari* as someone who has mastered the three mysteries of body, speech, and mind (MJ, 8).

75 *"Kugishaku"* refers to the *Fukū kenjaku birushana-butsu daikanjō kōmyō shingon kugishaku* (Commentary on the Significance of the Syllables of the Mantra of Light

of the Baptism of the Buddha Vairocana of the Unfailing Rope Snare), MSS, 2:883–891.

[76] *Dosha gi* refers to the *Kōmyō Shingon kaji dosha gi* (Significance of the Sand of the Mystic Power of the Mantra of Light), SAZ, 2:6–14 (KKB, 115).

[77] The present translation of the *Kōmyō Shingon dosha kanjin ki* is based on: SAZ, 2:15–54, which is essentially the same version as found in NDK, vol. 42, and Myōe Koben, *Kōmyō Shingon dosha kanjin ki*, in *Kōsō meicho zenshū 9: Myoe Shōnin hen*, ed. Yamamoto Isao (Tokyo: Heibonsha, 1930), 191–224. This translation is substantially refined from the version I originally published as "Recommending Faith in the Sand of the Mantra of Light," in *Revisioning Kamakura Buddhism*, ed. Richard K. Payne (Honolulu: University of Hawai'i Press, 1998), 167–218. It has also been checked against and benefited from the modern Japanese rendering: Takahashi Shūei, trans., "Kōmyō Shingon dosha kanjinki," in *Daijō butten: Chūgoku-Nihon hen 20 Yōsai Myōe*, co-translator with Nakao Ryōshin (Tokyo: Chuōkōronsha, 1988), 93–151.

[78] There are two cosmic buddhas with similar names: Vairocana and Mahāvairocana. Vairocana is often used as an abbreviation for Mahāvairocana, thus complicating the issue. However, all of Myōe's references to "Vairocana" (Jpn. Birushana) in works relating to the Mantra of Light are abbreviations for Mahāvairocana.

[79] Five wisdoms *(gochi,* Skt. *pañca-jñānāni):* the description of the Buddha Vairocana's wisdom in terms of five aspects, each aspect being assigned in turn to the five meditation buddhas (BGDJ, 372).

[80] The Sanskrit forms of the foregoing mantra syllables are, respectively, *amogha vairocana mahāmudrā maṇi padma jvāla.* The full mantra is *oṃ amogha vairocana mahāmudrā maṇi padma jvāla pravarttaya hūṃ.*

[81] Avīci Hell *(muken jigoku):* the eighth of eight burning hells overseen by Yamarāja, named for the ceaseless suffering to be found there (MSH, 468).

[82] The Pure Land of Amida.

[83] Wŏnhyo (617–86): one of the most important figures in Korean Buddhist history, identified in Zannin's *Song gaoseng zhuan* (Lives of Eminent Monks: Song Dynasty Edition) (T, 50:709, #2061) as the first patriarch of Huaŏm in Silla. Myōe composed an elaborate hagiography based on this entry, the *Kegon engi emaki* (Kameta Tsutomu, ed., *Kegon engi*, in *Nihon emakimono zenshū*, vol. 7, gen. ed. Tanaka Ichimatsu [Tokyo: Kadokawa Shoten, 1959]). The *Yusim Allakto* is falsely attributed to Wŏnhyo.

[84] Nine classes of beings *(kubon).* According to the *Guan wuliangshou jing* (T, 12:340, #365), regarded by Myōe's contemporary Hōnen as the most important sutra, there are nine classes of practitioners destined for the Pure Land of Amida Buddha. They are ranked hierarchically according to the accumulation of their virtues and karma at the time of death.

[85] Ten evils and five transgressions *(jūaku gogyaku).* There are a variety of classifications. Among the more common for the ten evils are killing, stealing, sexual misconduct, telling lies, harsh speech, evil speech, antagonizing speech, greed, jealousy, and anger. The five transgressions are matricide, patricide, killing an arhat, injuring a Buddha, and disrupting the harmony of the sangha. The five transgressions were regarded as so heinous as to cause the transgressor to fall into the Avīci Hell and even to render his eventual escape impossible. This led to the much debated

doctrine of the *icchantika*, one who could never attain awakening no matter how many lifetimes passed (IBJ, 4a, s.v. *aku*).

[86] According to the hagiography of Wŏnhyo in the *Song gao seng chuang*, the name of the dragon-king was Kŏmhae, not Kûmhae, as Myōe has here. Cited in Takahashi, "Kōmyō Shingon dosha kanjinki," 239 n. 14.

[87] Robert Buswell has developed a theory that the *Vajrasamādhi Sūtra* was not translated from the Chinese, as Wŏnhyo claims, but is an apocryphal work of Korean origin, possibly even written by Wŏnhyo himself. See Robert Buswell, *The Formation of Chan Ideology in China and Korea: The Vajrasamādhi-Sūtra, a Buddhist Apocryphon* (Princeton, N.J.: Princeton University Press, 1989).

[88] The incident involves a dharma exposition on the *Renwang banruo jing* (Sutra of the Wisdom of the Benevolent King) to an assembly of a hundred monks. The sutra was based on the legend of a benevolent king who saved his own life by creating a hundred-seat assembly; see T, 8:840, #246. Cited in Takahashi, "Kōmyō Shingon dosha kanjinki," 240 n. 19.

[89] Actually, the four jewels are listed as gold-silver, lapis lazuli, crystal, and an unidentified substance, *kahō*, but I have adapted the translation for readability and to reflect standard lists of jewels.

[90] The three realms *(sangai)* refers to those of desire, form, and formlessness.

[91] Six harmonious aspects and ten mysterious interdependent originations *(rokusō jūgen engi)*. The six aspects and ten mysteries are foundational concepts in East Asian Huayan, developed by Zhiyan and Fazang and elaborated by Chengguan and others. The six aspects refers to phenomena seen in six different ways, which, however, are perfectly in accord with each other according to Huayan (BGDJ, 1456b). The ten mysterious interdependent originations refers to the ten levels of interdependent origination culminating in the dharma-realm of the mutual interpenetration of phenomena and phenomena, meaning all phenomena interpenetrate one another (Ch. *shishi wuai fojie*) (IBJ, 392a).

[92] T, 10:844b, #293. Cited in Takahashi, "Kōmyō Shingon dosha kanjinki," 241 n. 23.

[93] According to Huayan doctrine, there are fifty-two stages in the development of a bodhisattva's career, based on the fifty-two spiritual guides who Sudhana encounters on his spiritual journey as related in the *Gaṇḍavyūha*. The last ten of these are called the *bhūmi* stages and constitute the original ten stages as found in early Indian Mahāyāna. Although Myōe here describes the tenth *bhūmi* stage as that of Virtual Awakening (meaning virtually equal to the awakening of the Buddhas), it is usually the ninth stage that is regarded as the stage of Virtual Awakening *(tōgaku)*, and the tenth as the Sublime Awakening *(myōgaku)*.

[94] Skt. *bodhi-maṇḍa (dōjō)*: the place of awakening; the place of practice.

[95] Six sense-objects *(rokujin,* Skt. *ṣaḍ viṣayāḥ)*. The six sense-objects are form, sound, smell, taste, contact (objects of touch), and mental objects (dharmas) (BGDJ, 1455d).

[96] Three evil destinies *(sanzu no kunō):* the realms of the beasts, hungry ghosts, and hell (IBJ, 321b).

[97] "Intoxication" *(you)* is used here in the dual sense of being mentally affected and of being poisoned. The reference to mushrooms *(kusabira)* is not entirely clear but seems to be to some kind of meaty vegetable such as a mushroom (IKJ, 395a).

[98] Master Zhixiang refers to Zhiyan (602–68), the second patriarch of the Huayan school. The *Weishizhang* is a section from his *Huayanjing kongmuzhang* (Treatise

on Selected Items from the *Huayanjing*), T, 45:547c. Cited in Takahashi, "Kōmyō Shingon dosha kanjinki," 243 nn. 33, 34.

99 The four phases *(shisō)* of all phenomena are arising, abiding, changing, and perishing.

100 Transformation bodies *(hengeshin,* Skt. *nirmāṇakāya).*

101 This episode appears in Xuanzang, *Datang xiyuji,* sixth fascicle. Cited in Takahashi, "Kōmyō Shingon dosha kanjinki," 244 n. 37.

102 Takahashi, "Kōmyō Shingon dosha kanjinki," 244 n. 40.

103 Trāyastriṃśa Heavens *(Tōriten):* the thirty-three heavens at Mount Sumeru, the mythical mountain at the center of the Buddhist cosmos, and the second (group of) six heavens found in the realm of desire (IBJ, 614a).

104 Refers to either the transformation body of Vajrasattva or one of the deities of the Womb-Realm Mandala. In this case it is most probably the latter (BGDJ, 420d).

105 Emma[-o], Skt. Yamarāja. I have left the name in Japanese because, like others such as Jizō, Emma became a prominent member of the Japanese Buddhist pantheon with strong local color. Already by the ninth century, there were instances in which Jizō and Emma came to be mutually identified (KBJ, 82).

106 "Both mandalas" refers to the two complementary mandalas of esoteric Buddhism that are central to both Tendai and Shingon, namely the *Kongōkai* (Diamond-Realm) and *Taizōkai* (Womb-Realm) *mandara.*

107 Xuanzang, trans., *Yuqie shidilun,* T, 30:281. Takahashi, "Kōmyō Shingon dosha kanjinki," 246 n. 51.

108 Secondary results *(zōjōka,* Skt. *Adhipatiphala).* "Effects obtained as a result of power which accompanies or enhances karma. Effects obtained as a result of karmic momentum or surplus power. Thus, eye-consciousness is the *adhipatiphala* of the sight-organ [composed of the physical eye and its mental basis]" (BGDJ, 881d). In the case of the passage in question, the sand obtains its mystic power by virtue of the power of the Buddhas manifested in the human forms of the ritual.

109 No outflows *(muro,* Skt. *anāsrava):* the absence of defilements flowing out of one's being.

110 Followers of the two vehicles *(nijō).* This is a reference to śrāvakas and pratyekabuddhas, i.e., Hīnayāna.

111 Family *(shuzoku,* Skt. *gotra).*

112 Five Ranks *(go'i):* the five stages of practices according to the Yogācāra.

113 The ten functions of the mind and the ten functions of good in the mind *(daijihō, daizenjihō,* Skt. *mahā-bhūmikā [dharmāh], kusala-mahābhūmikāh.[dharmāh])* (BGDJ, 918a, 923d).

114 Dharma *(hō).* The term as it is used here refers to a component of the mind as it is mapped out in the larger scheme of Buddhist theory. This usage of the term "dharma" is found primarily in the Nikaya literature but can also be found in later Mahāyāna treatises, especially in those of the Yogācāra School. Dharma also refers to the Buddhist teachings as a whole, both in its written, discursive form and in an ineffable sense, as the inconceivable.

115 Mind of entrusting *(shinjin).*

116 Particular place *(hōsho,* Skt. *sthāna, desa):* a place occupying a portion of space (BGDJ, 1224c).

[117] Become close to a [good] friend *(kin'yū)*. This appears to refer to forming ties with a spiritual guide, a *kalyāna-mitra*.

[118] Yixing was the first patriarch of the Chinese Tantric school. The commentary refers to the *Darijing shu* (Commentary on the *Mahāvairocana Sūtra*), T, vol. 39.

Jiaoyuan was a Chinese tantric monk of the eleventh century who studied tantra with the Indian Tripiṭaka master Maṇi. Jiaoyuan composed the *Yanmichao* at the behest of Daozong in 1077. The full title of the *Yanmichao* is *Darijing yishi yanmichao* (Treatise on Performing the Mysteries on the *Exposition of the Meaning of the Mahāvairocana Sūtra*) (*Zokuzōkyō* 37). In it Jiaoyuan uses the Huayan thought of Chengguan to expound the purport of the central Chinese tantric work *Darijing yishi*. Thus, it is a natural source of understanding for Myōe. Cited in Takahashi, "Kōmyō Shingon dosha kanjinki," 247–248 nn. 59, 60.

[119] Reality as-it-is *(nyojitsu,* Skt. *yathā-bhūtam)*.

[120] Myōe is trying to warn his reader against mistaking the intellectual understanding obtained by studying the written word for true realization.

[121] Liberation free from activity *(mui gedatsu):* as opposed to the activity of the mind of one who has not clearly grasped the nature of liberation (BGDJ, 1313a).

[122] Cakravartin *(Rin'ō):* World ruler, emperor.

[123] Out of compassion [for all beings]. Literally, "great compassion of identification" *(dōtai no daihi)*, the meaning of this sentence appears to be: The secret method of the Sand of the Radiant Mantra was created on the basis of the great compassion of the buddhas and bodhisattvas who identify with the suffering of sentient beings (BGDJ, 1010b).

[124] Spirit *(tamashii)*.

[125] Triple-world *(sansei):* past, present, and future.

[126] This may be a mistake in wording. It would make more sense to say, "There is no one who believes in sand," although this, too, is somewhat awkward.

[127] Twofold truth *(nitai):* conventional truth and ultimate truth.

[128] Numerical categories *(hōsū)*. This refers to the Buddhist teachings as they are categorized numerically: the four noble truths, the eightfold noble path, the six transcendent virtues, etc.

[129] In Sanskrit *a* is the negative prefix.

[130] Unattainability of the whole as one *(ichigōsō fukatoku)*. The idea of the whole as one refers to the deluded attempt to grasp reality as one permanent objective whole.

[131] The sense here seems to be that one should not be surprised at what can be accomplished by the power of the buddhas and the dharma.

[132] The transcendences *(shoharamitsu,* Skt. *pāramitā):* the six primary virtues of Mahāyāna Buddhism: giving, morality, patience, endurance, meditation, and wisdom.

Countless eons *(sōgikōkō,* Skt. *asaṃkhyeyaiḥ kalpair)*.

The three points *(santen):* in esoteric Buddhism, the three points are principle, wisdom, and phenomena *(richiji)* (BGDJ, 483a).

The four virtues *(shitoku)*. This refers to the four virtues or attributes of awakening: constancy, joy, [awakened] self, and purity (BGDJ, 528c; IBJ, 447a).

[133] The story of King Ajātaśatru is told in the *Guan wuliangshou jing* (Meditation Sutra) (T, 12:340, #365). Influenced by the machinations of Śākyamuni's cousin Devadatta, Prince Ajātaśatru killed his father King Bimbisāra and imprisoned his mother Queen

Vaidehi. Later he repented and became a follower of Śākyamuni. This episode became especially important in Japanese Pure Land Buddhism. See Inagaki Hisao, *The Three Pure Land Sūtras,* 2d rev. ed. (Kyoto: Nagata Bunshōdō, 1995).

[134] The first turning of the dharma-wheel refers to the first sermon given by Śākyamuni after his awakening under the Bodhi Tree.

[135] The date is given according to the lunar calendar as found in the original Japanese. The characters for "Jōō" are given the reading "Teiō" in the text on which this translation is based.

[136] Enji is the road that one walks alone toward the netherworld (Takahashi, "Kōmyō Shingon dosha kanjinki," 252 n. 26).

[137] The text says about eight *shaku* tall *(hachi shaku).* One *shaku* is about a foot, and so eight *shaku* is about eight feet.

[138] *Pharmakon (yakubutsu):* the pharmacologically active agent (of the sand).

[139] Vināyaka is the eldest son of the Indian deities Māheśvara and Umā (BGDJ, 1134d).

[140] Mudrā *(ingon,* abbreviation for *ingei shingon*): the signs of awakening or realization. There are two types, mudrā with form and without form. Those without form refer to the characteristics of realization manifest without forming ritual hand gestures and postures. The term mudrā is used here in this general sense which includes forms and the formless (BGDJ, 68c,d).

[141] Auspicious marks *(kōsō):* the eighty signs and thirty-two marks that are the physical characteristics of an awakened being or Buddha.

[142] *Akai:* a well dedicated to provide water for ritual use in a Buddhist temple (Takahashi, "Kōmyō Shingon dosha kanjinki," 253 n. 32).

[143] Buddha-lands *(bussetsu,* Skt. *buddha-kṣetra)* (BGDJ, 1195c).

[144] *Rākṣasa (rasetsu):* a mythical Indian demonic creatures known to eat human flesh.

[145] The "pair of wheels" refers to the wheels of the dharma that are engraved or painted into footprints which in turn symbolize the Buddha himself.

[146] Original state *(honryō):* literally, "original estate," as in land which originally belongs to one. This appears to refer to the dharma, as in dharma-dhatu, i.e., "dharma-realm." "Beasts" here refers to the realm of beasts in the cycle of transmigration.

[147] *Bufazang zhuan.* This is most likely an abbreviation for *Bufazang yinyuan zhuan* (T, 50:297, #2058) (see BGDJ, 1175b).

[148] *Shōshō:* officer of the Lower Rank (see KOJ, 1269a).

[149] Hour of the tiger *(tora no toki):* between 3 and 5 A.M.

[150] The present translation of the *Kōmyō Shingon dosha kanjin bekki* is based on the following text: SAZ, 2:55–73, which is essentially the same version as found in NDK, vol. 42, and Myōe Kōben, *Kōmyō Shingon dosha kanjin bekki,* in *Kōsō meichō zenshū 9: Myoe Shōnin hen,* ed. Yamamoto Isao (Tokyo: Heibonsha, 1930), 225–242.

[151] Rebirth in the Pure Land is categorized into nine classes, three each in the superior, middling, and inferior groups, according to one's karmic merit. Birth in the lotus blossom is the highest class.

[152] The three poisons *(sandoku)* are greed, anger, and stupidity, and the three roots of good are their opposites.

[153] The teachings and admonitions *(jōkai)* are categorized into four permutations *(kaijō shiku)* of higher and lower (BGDJ, 751b).

[154] The four fruits *(shika)* are those of attaining the rank of stream-enterer, once-returner (to the cycle of samsara), non-returner, and arhatship (BGDJ, 509b).

155 "Formless realm" here refers to the fourth of the formless realms, the *bhava-agra.* "Eons" is a translation for *kō* (Skt. *kalpa*).

156 *Kannon gyō.* This is a portion of the *Lotus Sutra,* widely chanted in Japan, focusing on the bodhisattva of compassion, Kannon.

157 Fourfold logic *(shikufunbetsu,* Skt. *catuṣ-koṭi).* This is the classic tetralemma of Buddhist logic originating in earlier Indian logic: A exists, A does not exist, A both exists and does not exist, A neither exists nor does not exist.

158 "Seven rarities" *(shichichin)* is a synonym for the seven jewels (Skt. *sapta-ratna).* There are several standard lists taken from the sutra literature, of which one is: gold, silver, lapis lazuli, quartz, giant clam shell, coral, and agate (BGDJ, 585d).

159 Skt. *Yojana:* a measurement of distance in ancient India said to equal forty *li* in East Asia (BGDJ, 1378c). One *li* in Myōe's time was said to be approximately 1.5 kilometers (KOJ, 2676d).

160 *Bukong zhuansuo jing,* T, 20:227, #1092, fascicle 28.

161 Medicine King of Good Manifested *(Zenken yakuō):* a medicine said to be found in the Himalayas that turns into pure healing water by merely being heard, smelled, tasted, or touched (BGDJ, 849a).

162 *Fajie yihai.* This is an alternate title for Fazang's *Huayanjing yihai baimen* (Takahashi, "Kōmyō Shingon dosha kanjinki," 260 n. 36).

163 *Dosha gi* refers to the *Kōmyō Shingon kaji dosha gi* (SAZ, 2:6–14), another work written by Myōe in 1227, a year before he wrote the present work.

164 *Kana*-style refers to the style of writing in *kana* syllabary. Actually, this is a document written in *kana-majiri bun,* or mixed *kana* (and *kanji)* style.

165 *Kugishaku* refers to *Fukū kenjaku Birushana-butsu daikanjō kōmyō shingon kugishaku* (SAZ, vol. 2; NDK, vol. 42).

166 The present translation is based on *Kyakuhai mōki,* KKB, 107–123. The original manuscript is stored in Kōzanji. It is the original document compiled by Myōe's disciple Jakue-bō Chōen in 1235 (Kobayashi Yoshinori, "'Kyakuhai mōki' Kamakura jidai shahon no yōgo," in *Myōe Shōnin to Kōzanji,* ed. Myōe Shōnin to Kōzanji henshūiinkai [Kyoto: Dōbōsha, 1981], 420). A number of notes are incorporated from the version contained in KKB. In such cases, the page on which the original note appears is also indicated.

167 Zendōin is the name of the meditation hall at Kōzanji. It is used several times throughout the text as an appellation for Myōe himself. It was, and is still today, common practice to use the name of a temple to refer to the abbot or head priest of that temple.

168 I have followed the original format of the text, placing statements attributed to Myōe flush to the left margin and indenting Chōen's own statements (which here are set in italics). Some remarks are double-indented, and I have followed the original text for these as well. Within a single section, sentences pertaining to different matters are often set off by the word *mata,* meaning "again," at the beginning. I have omitted most instances *mata* in the translation.

169 The three periods of the day *(sanji):* dawn, noon, and dusk, which are *jinjō, nitchū,* and *nichibotsu,* respectively (KOJ, 1069a).

170 Contemplating the circle of the seed-syllable *(jirinkan).* The Shingon practice of contemplating mantras or Sanskrit seed-syllables housed in the image of the moon

transposed over one's heart (KKB, 108). This and many other notes for the *Kyakuhai mōki* are taken from the annotated text of the *Kamakura kyū Bukkyō* (KKB) volume. These notes are indicated by a reference, as can be seen in this note.

171 Study *(gakumon)*. In this work the term is used to indicate lectures given by Myōe and doctrinal study. Myōe was concerned throughout his life with the relation between doctrinal study and practice (KKB, 430).

172 The *Darijing shu* (T, 39:579, #1796) is a twenty-fascicle commentary on the first six (of seven) fascicles of the *Darijing* (T, 18:1, #848). Yixing (683–727) compiled the *Darijing shu* based on lectures given by Shan Wuwei (637–735) (BGJ, 217b). According to the *Toganoo onmonogatari,* Myōe began giving lectures on this commentary on the nineteenth day of the tenth month of 1213 (KKB, 108).

173 Prosperous *(kōryū)*. The original characters in the text are probably misprinted. (KKB, 109).

174 Preparatory practice *(kegyō):* a preparatory practice preceding the main practice to augment the latter. According to the *Gyōjō,* Myōe went to the Kondō of Jingoji everyday from the age of thirteen to nineteen before he began the initial practice of the Diamond-Realm (KKB, 109).

175 Attainment of buddhahood through the five aspects of the Diamond-Realm *(gosōjōshin)*. This is the meditative practice for attaining buddhahood in this very body according to the practices of the Diamond-Realm. The five aspects are (1) clearly grasping *bodhicitta,* (2) cultivating *bodhicitta,* (3) manifesting the diamond[-like] mind, (4) realizing the diamond[-like] body, and (5) the full and complete buddha body. In the first of these, clearly grasping *bodhicitta,* the practitioner clearly grasps that he or she is fully endowed with the virtue of *bodhicitta* by entering into the samādhi of contemplating the nature of one's own mind, intoning the mantra of fulfilling one's own nature, and visualizing one's mind as a moon-circle that is enveloped in a light mist. The mist symbolizes *avidyā,* ignorance (KKB, 109).

176 This is a quotation from the *Jingangding lianhuabuxin niansong yigui* (Liturgy of Intoning the Mind of the Lotus Section of the Diamond[-like] Head) (T, 18:299, #873), translated from the Sanskrit by Amoghavajra. The phrase preceding the quotation reads, "Contemplate the mind as the circle of the moon." This phrase also appears in Amoghavajra's translation of *Jingangding yiqie rulai zhenshi she dacheng xianzheng dajiaowang jing* (T, 18:207, #865) (KKB, 109).

177 This quotation is also taken from the *Jingangding lianhuabuxin niansong yigui.* "Strike their fingers" appears to refer to the snapping of fingers, which was used as a warning signal or sign of permission (KKB, 109).

178 This quotation is also taken from the *Jingangding lianhuabuxin niansong yigui* (T, 18:299, #873).

179 According to the ten grave prohibitions listed in the *Fanwang jing* (Brahma-net Sutra; see Ishida Mizumaro, *Bonmō kyō: Butten Kōza 14* [Tokyo: Daizō Shuppan, 1971]).

   This refers to the precept against any kind of sexual activity for monks and nuns, which follows the precepts against killing and stealing (KKB, 110).

   On this point, Faure, Girard, and Kawai give differing interpretations of various dreams seen by Myōe with explicit or implicit references to sexuality. Faure suggests a Freudian interpretation in which these dreams are seen as either manifestations of repressed sexuality or as the manifest expressions of latent sexuality

(Bernard Faure, *Chan Insights and Oversights: An Epistemological Critique of the Chan Tradition* [Princeton, N.J.; Princeton University Press, 1993], 111–113; Faure, *The Rhetoric of Immediacy: A Cultural Critique of Chan/Zen Buddhism* [Princeton, N.J.: Princeton University Press, 1991], 222–224). Girard sees in such dreams as the dream of Zenmyō didactic intent (Girard, *Un Moine de la secte Kegon*, n. 340). Kawai gives an extensive Jungian interpretation, seeing sexual imagery in the context of Myōe's relation to the anima (Hayao Kawai, *The Buddhist Priest Myōe: A Life of Dreams* (Venice, Calif.: Lapis Press, 1992).

180 This probably refers to the precept against taking medications for more than seven days. According to the *Sifenlu biqiu jieben* (Book of the Bhiksu Precepts of the Dharmaguptaka Vinaya) (T, 22:1015, #1429), the following medications can be taken for up to seven days: condensed milk, oil, raw milk, honey, and crystallized sugar (KKB, 110).

181 What has been rendered as "traveling" in the translation appears as *tabi* in the text (KKB, 110).

182 Two dharmas of faith and understanding *(shinge nihō)*.

183 What has been rendered as "not go awry" in the translation appears as *yuganuma* in the text (KKB, 111).

184 In the winter of 1203, when Myōe was thirty, he told people of his plans to go to India. However, he abandoned his plans after receiving an oracle from the Kasuga deity. He again sought to go to India in 1205 and calculated the distance between Changan and India, but he abandoned his plans this time as well based on a random drawing he made. In 1215 he composed a work on the remains of the Tathāgata Śākyamuni's life in India, the *Nyorai iseki kōshiki* (See *Shiza kōshiki*, T, 84:898, #2731).

185 Incomparable *(munimusan)* (IKJ, 1256b).

186 Received the instructions for the Diamond-Realm *(Kongōkai denju):* the transmission of the instructions for the incantations of the Diamond-Realm. There is an eight-volume text compiled by Yakushin at Kōzanji that records Myōe's instructions on invoking the Lotus Mind of the *Vajraśekhara Sūtra* (Jpn. *Kongōchō kyō*) (T, 18:207, #865). His disciples copied this text at the time of receiving the transmission (KKB, 111). Apparently, a number of instructions were given to Jungyō-bō that were not included in the text.

187 Preliminary practice *(kegyō):* a preliminary practice before the main practice (BGDJ, 293c). In this case, it probably refers to the practice preliminary to the transmission of the Diamond-Realm (KKB, 112).

188 Myōshin was a senior monk at Kōzanji who was seated after Gien-bō Ryōten and before Jungyō-bō at the Exposition of the Precepts on the fifteenth day of the eighth month of 1203. Myōshin's verse in reply to a *waka* composed by Myōe is included in *Myōe shōnin waka shū* (KKB, 112).

189 In the first fascicle of the *Kana gyōjō*, Myōe is quoted as stating at the age of thirteen, "It has never occurred to me to become a Shingon master or scholar, and I have not wanted [these things]. I have only thought to seek the Buddha's intention [as it is set forth] in the buddha-dharma, and to apply myself and practice according to the teachings of the holy scriptures" (KKB, 113).

190 Evil destinies *(akushu):* the realms of hell, hungry ghosts, and beasts in the six realms of transmigration.

191 In the *Shinmon shū,* fascicle 3, Myōe is quoted as saying, "With regard to the sameness and difference or distinction between one who attains the [exoteric] Lotus Samādhi and one who realizes the [esoteric] Lotus practice, they are the one and the same Lotus Samādhi. Furthermore, there is not superficial or profound. Ultimately, whether [one is speaking of] the exoteric or the esoteric, one enters them by realizing the one mind. Thus, the five wisdoms spoken of in Shingon [esotericism] and the four wisdoms discussed in the exoteric tenets both correspond to the five wisdoms of the pure dharma-realm."

However, in the *Shinmon shū,* fascicle 2, Myōe recognizes the superiority of the esoteric practice while maintaining the equality of the meaning or principle: "Shingon masters who know well the six aspects and ten mysteries of Huayan should be aware of the profundity of the statements regarding practice contained in the *Mahāvairocana Sūtra.* Thus one should not indulge in discussing the superficial and the profound. It is only appropriate to say that Shingon is profound and the esoteric teachings are superficial after one has attained the profound secret of the Shingon teachings. One should carefully consider how one judges and speaks about this matter of the superficial and the profound" (KKB, 431c–432a).

192 Equality of the three mysteries *(sanmitsu byōdō).* The three mysteries refer to the acts of body, speech, and mind through which the power of the buddhas is transferred to the Shingon practitioner. In the seventh fascicle of the *Gedatsumon gi chōjūki* (Records of Things Heard on the Meaning of [Entering] the Liberation [of the Huayan]), Myōe is recorded as having said, "In the esoteric teachings, one purifies the one mind; in Shingon this adorns the three acts [of body, speech, and mind]. One realizes this through the formation of the mudrā with one's hands, the intoning of the mantra with one's mouth, and through the meditative contemplation of one's mind. This practice through which the three acts correlate with each other is called the secret teaching (*Kanazawa bunkō kiyō* 4, 130)" (KKB, 114).

193 Teachings of the three vehicles *(sanjōkyō).* The three vehicles are the paths of the śrāvaka, pratyekabuddha, and bodhisattva. The three vehicles of such schools as the Hossō (Skt. Yogācāra) are contrasted against the one vehicle of the Tendai (Ch. *Tiantai*). In this case, Myōe is indicating that the doctrinal categories of Shingon are roughly those of the three vehicle teachings.

194 According to the *Toganoo sekkai nikki,* MSS, 3:607–644, Endō-bō Shinkei and Zenjō-bō substituted for Myōe to give the lectures on the precepts from the second month to the seventh month of 1230. It is apparent that he was a senior monk from the fact that he is seated next to Shinkei on the fifteenth day of the eighth month of 1230 after Myōe's return. Zenjō-bō also composed a record of Myōe's statements entitled *Shōnin no koto* (Affairs of the High Priest [Myōe], MSS, 1:591–602) (KKB, 114).

195 In the practice of the Womb-Realm as described in the *Taizōkai nenju shidai* (Instructions for the Invocations of the Womb-Realm), there is a section in which one proceeds by practicing the mudrā and mantra of the *buddha-samaya,* followed by those of the dharma-realm birth and the turning of the dharma-wheel. This passage explains the first of these (KKB, 114).

196 "Out of which emerges that which is difficult to understand" *(nangeideku).* (KKB, 115).

197 Fire of wisdom *(chika)*. One of the twelve fires, the fire of wisdom burns off the blind passions with the light of wisdom (BGDJ, 951b).

198 *Jūni Shingon-ō*. The Twelve-Syllable Mantra King is a standard mantra of Esoteric Buddhism. When the practitioner contemplates these seed syllables, forms the mudrā, and intones the mantra, then she receives the mystic power of the buddhas, attains the power to move freely, conquers the four demons, and eliminates evil karma (*Mikkyō daijiten,* cited in KKB, 432–433).

199 Twelvefold dependent origination *(jūnien)*. Usually written *jūni innen,* this comprises the twelve links of dependent origination leading from ignorance to decay and death

200 *Dosha gi*. This is an abbreviation for the *Kōmyō Shingon kaji dosha gi* (Significance of the Sand of the Mystic Power of the Mantra of Light), SAZ, 2:6–14 (KKB, 115).

201 "This principle" refers to the empowerment through the sand of the Mantra of Light.

202 *Shinshugi*. This is an abbreviation for the *Kegon shinshu gi* (Meaning of the Seed of Faith in the Huayan) (T, 72:69, #2330), a monograph composed by Myōe on the twenty-first day of the ninth month of 1221 at Zendōin in Kamo Bukkōji. It is a summary of the *Kegon shuzen kanshō nyū gedatsu mon gi* (Meaning of Entering the Gate of Liberation through the Huayan Practice of Cultivation of Meditative Contemplation of Illumination) (T, 72:74, #2331) (KKB, 115).

203 The meaning here seems to be that those who seek birth in Amida's Pure Land should listen to the teaching of the *Kegon shinshu gi* as well (see preceding note).

204 Best of the superior births *(jōbon jōshō)*. According to the *Guan wuliangshou jing* (Sutra of Meditation on the Buddha of Eternal Life) (T, 12:340, #365), there are nine classes of beings born into Amida's Pure Land depending on the karmic accumulations of the past and present lives, grouped into three groups of each, superior, middling, and inferior, with the same gradations existing in each group. This sutra was translated into Chinese by Kālayaśas sometime between 424 and 442, but it is of uncertain origin. It was the most important sutra for Myōe's contemporary Hōnen and became one of the Three Pure Land sutras central to Jōdo Shinshū (Hisao Inagaki, *Dictionary of Japanese Buddhist Terms,* in collaboration with P. G. O'Neill, 3d ed., with Supplement [Kyoto: Nagata Bunshōdō, 1988], 167).

205 The meaning of this paragraph is not clear.

206 There are three main styles of calligraphy: *shin, gyō, sō,* in order of increasing degree of cursiveness. Myōe is indicating that a loose, cursive style should not be used in copying or writing about Buddhism.

207 Darumashū ("[Bodhi]dharma School"). This probably refers to the Zen schools in general, or to Eisai's Zen in particular. Although the name Darumashū was used with specific reference to Dainichi Nōnin's Darumashū, Myōe and his community used it to describe Eisai's Zen as well. There are references to Darumashū, *Darumatara no shū,* and *Darumatara [zen] kyō* (T, 15:300, #618), in various redactions of both the *Denki* and the *Gyōjō* (MSS, 1:788). In fact, there are a number of anecdotes describing the relationship between Myōe and Myōan Eisai (Minnan Yōsai), the Zen master of Kenninji, but there is doubt about their authenticity (KKB, 433). Although it is uncertain whether Myōe actually encountered any of the key Zen figures of his day, such as Eisai, Dōgen, or Nōnin, Myōe was clearly knowledgeable about Chinese

Ch'an as well as Japanese Zen, from such remarks as contained here, through his references to such figures as Zongmi, and the fact that one of his disciples, Shōjō, composed a major work on Zen, the *Zenshū kōmoku* (Overview of Zen Doctrine), KKB, 159–188.

208 The Zuigu Dhāraṇī is said to destroy all evil hindrances, break through the evil destinies, and immediately bestow blessings according to one's needs. It consists of 290 phrases according to the *Pubian guangming qingjing chicheng ruibaoyinxin wunengsheng damingwang dasuiqiu tuoluoni jing* (Sutra of the Universal Light, the Pure and Full Jewel-Seal-Mind Which Fulfills All Intentions, the Unsurpassed Great and Bright King, the Dhāraṇī of Which Follows All Desires) (T, 20:616, #1153), translated by Amoghavajra (KKB, 116). According to a copy that exists at Kōzanji dated 1842, Myōe copied this sutra at Sekisuiin on the eleventh day of the first month of 1221, and Kikai copied it on the twenty-fourth day of the first month of 1227 (Tanaka Kaiō, ed., *Kainyo wajō gongyōroku,* KKB, 434).

209 *Pusa jieben shu* (Commentary on the Basis of the Bodhisattva Precepts). This is a six-fascicle work compiled by Fazang, and its full title is *Fanwang jing pusa jieben shu* (Commentary on the Basis of the Bodhisattva Precepts According to the *Brahma-Net Sūtra*) (T, 40:646, #1814). It explains in detail the ten grave prohibitions and the forty-eight minor precepts. The section on the precept against sexual activity in the third fascicle contains some vulgar and graphic passages (KKB, 116).

210 See Kawai, *The Buddhist Priest Myōe,* 67.

211 The meaning here seems to be, "I should not expect reality to follow my thoughts; rather, if I am fully mindful of reality, then the truth will naturally become apparent."

212 *Hiyo.* A whitebait, which is a young trout (KOJ, s.v. *hiuo,* 2134d).

213 Causal stage of the bodhisattvas *(bosatsu no in'i).* The period of bodhisattvahood represents the causal stage in contrast to buddhahood, which is the fruit or effect of bodhisattva praxis (KKB, 117).

214 Toilet *(kawaya).*

215 Charnel grounds *(sanchū tsuka no ma).* Literally, among the burial mounds in the mountains (KKB, 117). During the Kamakura Period it was still common to pile up corpses in burial grounds.

216 Precept on eating only at times allotted *(jisai).* According to the *prātimokṣa* from the earliest Vinaya literature, renunciants are only to partake of one meal per day, never after noon.

217 In 1195 Myōe moved from the temple of Jingoji on Takao in Kyoto to the area of his birth in present-day Wakayama Prefecture, where he built a grass hut on Shirakami-no-mine in the Arita District on the Kii Peninsula. Two or three years later, Mañjuśrī appeared in midair in a vision that was to inspire him throughout his life (KKB, 118). According to Myōe's dream diary, "The twenty-fifth day of the same [month and year]. I was practicing the meditation of no-thought before the Lord Śākyamuni. The great sage Mañjuśrī appeared in the sky. He was golden and sitting on the lion king. He was about an arm's length in size" (translation taken from Kawai, *The Buddhist Priest Myōe,* 81).

218 Ryōten was one of Myōe's main disciples and the first abbot of the Ikebō subtemple of Kōzanji. At first he resided at Jingoji as a disciple of Jōgaku-bō Gyōji, Myōe's uncle and sponsor. Eight years younger than Myōe, Ryōten devoted himself to the

construction of Kōzanji when Myōe was installed as abbot. When the latter went to Kii, he followed his master, and Ryōten's name is included with nine other disciples on a wooden plaque entitled *Mainichi gakumon injin shidai* (Daily Instructions for Study and the Seal-Faith [of Transmission]). In 1206 Ryōten was an attendant in a ceremony performed by Myōe for Kujō Kanezane. In Myōe's final years, Ryōten was among five monks in residence at Kōzanji, and after his master's death he was among the leaders of Kōzanji responsible for cataloging his master's work (KKB, 435).

219 It appears that Chōen received the transmission of the Womb-Realm (KKB, 119).

220 Jōshin was the first abbot of the Hōbenchiin subtemple of Kōzanji. At first he was at Jingoji and concentrated on studying Shingon Buddhism (KKB, 119). One year younger than Myōe, Jōshin died in 1250 at the age of seventy-seven after having studied Shingon esotericism with Kōnen and serving as abbot of Kōzanji immediately after Myōe's death in 1232. Many documents pertaining to Myōe and Jōshin bearing the seal of Hōbenchiin are stored in Kōzanji. Two documents composed by Jōshin are of particular significance: *Saigo rinjū gyōgi no koto* (Matters Related to the Final Passing [of Myōe Shōnin]) and *Shōnin onbō onmonogatari-ji Kishū shōnin onbō jōraku unnun* (Notes of Statements Made by Myōe Shōnin as He Traveled from Kii Prefecture to Kyoto) (MSS, 1:543–576, 585–592).

221 Shōdatsu-bō was a resident monk at Jingoji and retired to Kōzanji. Myōe states that Shōdatsu-bō is qualified to be a master of the Shingon teachings pertaining to practice. From the listing of his name among those present at the exposition on the precepts on the fifteenth day of the eighth month of 1230, he appears to have been Kikai's elder (KKB, 119).

222 Vessels for the virtue-water *(akaoke):* vessels for holding water offered to deities installed in altars (KKB, 120). *Aka* is the transliteration for the Sanskrit *argha* (BGDJ, 13c).

223 Should not be sent out *(hashiisasetamaina). Hashii* is probably means either being on a veranda or somewhere nearby outside (KOJ, 2055b). I have taken the latter meaning (KKB, 121).

224 *Yanyi chao.* This is an abbreviation for *Dafangguang huayan jing suishu yanyi chao* (Exposition on the Meaning in Accordance with the *Avataṃsaka Sūtra*) (T, 36:1, #1736), a forty-fascicle work by the Huayan Patriarch Chengguan. The phrase that has been rendered as "already states" is an alternate reading based on a redaction of the sutra that Myōe apparently read (KKB, 121).

225 Six realms of transmigration *(rokudō).* There are several different versions, one of the most common during the Kamakura Period being hell, hungry ghosts, beasts, *asura* demons, human beings, and heavens (KKB, 121).

226 In 1212, the year of Hōnen's death, Myōe composed the *Zaijarin* (KKB, 43–106), severely criticizing the former's *Senchaku hongan nembutsu shū* (Collected Passages on the Nembutsu of the Selected Vow [of Amida Buddha]) (T, 83:1, #2608), for its negation of *bodhicitta*, the aspiration for awakening, and all practices other than Pure Land *nembutsu*. It was a difficult work for Myōe to compose, as he had greatly respected Hōnen previous to his learning of this work and because it meant that Myōe had to go against the spirit of accommodation and criticize another Buddhist master. Myōe also composed a sequel to the *Zaijarin*, the *Zaijarin shōgon ki* (Elaboration on the Tract Destroying Heresy) (MSH, 335–397).

227 See note 204.

228 Skt. Vināyaka *(binayaka)*. The offspring of Maheśvara and Umā, Vināyaka is regarded as a manifestation of Avalokiteśvara (BGDJ, 1134d).

TRANSLATED TEXTS: EDITIONS AND DATING

THE FOLLOWING PROVIDES information concerning editions and dating for the Japanese texts on which the translations included in the present volume are based.

Arubekiyōwa (**As Appropriate**). This wooden tablet, listing the daily schedule practice and rules of etiquette at Kōzanji, is currently on view in a room on the northeast corner of Sekisuiin, a subtemple within Kōzanji. The translation that appears here has been rendered from the text printed in Murakami Sodō, *Toganoo-zan Kōzanji Myōe Shōnin* (The Priest Myōe of Kōzanji on Mount Toganoo).[1]

There is no date on the tablet itself. All one can say is that the likely dating is sometime between 1221 and 1232, when Myōe died. In 1220 he recorded his first major vision involving the Mantra of Light,[2] and in 1221 he completed the *Kegon bukkō zammai kan hihōzō* (Secret Treasury of the Huayan Contemplation of the Samādhi of the Buddha's Radiance),[3] a work on the practice of the Contemplation of the Buddha's Radiance, which contains the first substantial discussion of the Mantra of Light.

Fukū kenjaku birushana-butsu daikanjō kōmyō shingon kugishaku (**Commentary on the Significance of the Syllables of the Mantra of Light of the Baptism of the Buddha Vairocana of the Unfailing Rope Snare**).[4] This treatise is virtually identical to the portion of the earlier

Kegon bukkō zammai kan hihōzō (Secret Treasury of the Huayan Contemplation of the Samādhi of the Buddha's Radiance) devoted to the Mantra of Light. Sueki Fumihiko has made a close comparison between the two showing that there are no significant differences.[5] The present translation is based on the annotated version published in the Myōe Shōnin shiryō (Primary Texts Concerning Myōe Shōnin),[6] which is in turn based on the manuscript currently in the archives of the Ōtani University Library. According to the preface of that work, Myōe completed the work in 1222.

Kōgonku gishaku chōjūki (**Lectures on the Commentary on the Significance of the Syllables of the Mantra of Light**). This is the record of sermons given by Myōe on his *Fukū kenjaku birushana-butsu daikanjō kōmyō shingon kugishaku* (Commentary on the Significance of the Syllables of the Mantra of Light of the Baptism of the Buddha Vairocana of the Unfailing Rope Snare).[7]

There are three extant copies of the *Lectures:* one stored in Kōzanji and copied by the monk Genmitsu-bō Jinshin with a date of 1259, one stored in the Ochanomizu Library collection and from the early Kamakura Period, and one stored in Kōzanji and copied by Eiben with a date of 1684. The present translation is based on the annotated version published in the *Myōe Shōnin shiryō* (Primary Texts Concerning Myōe Shōnin).[8] It consists of the Jinshin copy from 1259 augmented by the Eiben copy from 1684 where the latter contains apparent omissions from the former. The section inserted from the Eiben copy starts at the beginning of the second fascicle and ends in mid-sentence with the following passage:

> The great accumulation of inexhaustible blessings and virtues of the unfailing great seal of maṇi of the Tathagata Vairocana arises by means of the great compassion of padma and the great wisdom of jivala as the causes.[9]
> If self and dharmas...

Jinshin was one of Myōe's highly regarded disciples; he was only fifteen at the time of his master's death, making him forty-two at the time he copied the *Lectures*. At some point between the original transcription of the lectures and the creation of Jinshin's own copy, annotations were made in the text in smaller script. These appear in the present translation in parentheses.

Although the Eiben copy is dated 1684, the colophon is the same as for the Jinshin copy and indicates Jinshin as the one who made the first copy. Apart from the section indicated above, the Jinshin and Eiben copies are virtually identical with only minor differences due to miscopied characters and the like.

The annotated text on which the present translation is based contains notes regarding judgments made concerning illegible or missing characters. These are not indicated in the present translation unless particularly noteworthy. The original text also contains annotations regarding the historical use of names, terms, vocabulary, idiomatic usage, and grammar. Notes are provided where these have been incorporated into the present translation.

Myōe completed two series of lectures on the *Commentary* on the seventeenth day of the sixth month of 1229 and the twenty-first day of the eighth month of the same year according to the colophons of both the versions of the *Commentary* stored in the Ōtani University Library collection and in the *Taishō Shinshū Daizōkyō* (Taishō Tripiṭaka). It is not clear whether all of the *Lectures* translated here were given in 1229, because Myōe often lectured on the same text several times. A reference to *Recommending Faith in the Sand of the Mantra of Light* at the beginning of the second fascicle suggests that those lectures were given after 1228, making it quite possible that all of the lectures were given in 1229.

Kōmyō Shingon dosha kanjin ki (Recommending Faith in the Sand of the Mantra of Light) and Kōmyō Shingon dosha kanjin bekki (Recommending Faith in the Sand of the Mantra of Light—Supplement).

These two works, composed by Myōe in 1228, were written for lay audiences to explain, expound, and advocate the practice of the Mantra of Light and Sand. The original texts in Myōe's own hand are still extant except for the second fascicle of the *Kanjinki* and are stored in the Daitōkyū Kinen Bunkōzō (Daitōkyū Memorial Library).[10] The only extant version of the second fascicle of the *Kanjinki* dates from the Empō Period (1673–81), of which copies are contained in the library collections of Ōtani University and Kōyasan University. Although it is impossible to determine the authenticity of its contents, it is wholly consistent with the rest of the adjoining texts in style, grammar, and content. There is no reason to believe that it does not represent an accurate copy of Myōe's original work.[11]

The combined, complete versions of the two works have been published in *Shingonshū anjin zensho* (Complete Works on the Mind of Repose of the Shingon sect).[12] Virtually the same texts were republished in *Kōsō meicho zenshū* 9: *Myōe Shōnin hen* (Complete Famous Works by Great Monks, vol. 9, Myōe Shōnin), edited by Yamamoto Isao with the addition of *furigana* readings.[13]

The present translations of both texts are based on the versions contained in the *Shingonshū anjin zensho* and Yamamoto's annotated version.[14] They have also benefited from the modern Japanese rendering by Takahashi Shūei.[15]

In contrast to the *Fukū kenjaku birushana-butsu daikanjō kōmyō shingon kugishaku* (Commentary on the Significance of the Syllables of the Mantra of Light of the Baptism of the Buddha Vairocana of the Unfailing Rope Snare), which was written in the more Chinese-based *hentai kambun,* these two works on the Mantra and the Sand were written in the *kana majiri bun,* or "mixed *kana*-syllabary (and Sino-Japanese character) style," and intended for lay audiences as well as for monks and nuns.

Kyakuhai mōki (**Chronicle of Things Not to Be Forgotten**). This posthumous record of Myōe's statements was made by his disciple

Jakue-bō Chōen in 1235, three years after his master's death.[16] Myōe composed all of the works translated in the present study except for *Kyakuhai mōki* and the *Kōgonku gishaku chōjūki* (Lectures on the Commentary on the Significance of the Syllables of the Mantra of Light).

There are two extant versions of the *Chronicle of Things:* the original text compiled by Chōen in 1235, and a copy made by Chikai in 1692.[17] The latter is a copy of the former. The two are virtually identical except for minor differences resulting from miscopied characters. Nevertheless, the latter is useful for identifying illegible characters from the former.

The present translation is based on *Kyakuhai mōki,* contained in *Kamakura kyū Bukkyō* (Old Kamakura Buddhism), Nihon shisō takei 15, edited by Kamata Shigeo and Tanaka Hisao, which is in turn based on the original by Chōen.[18]

$\dashv$ A P P E N D I X 2 $\vdash$

WORKS ON THE MANTRA OF LIGHT BY MYŌE

The following twelve works expounding the significance of the ritual of the Mantra of Light have been attributed to Myōe:[19] Approximate dates of composition (where available) are followed by transliterated titles given in romanization, titles in Sino-Japanese, and an English translation of the title in parentheses. All works consist of a single fascicle unless otherwise noted. Bibliographical information for texts known to be available is given in the notes.

1. 1222 *Fukū kenjaku Birushana-butsu daikanjō kōmyō shingon kugishaku*[20]
(Commentary on the Significance of the Syllables of the Mantra of Light of the Baptism of the Buddha Vairocana of the Unfailing Rope Snare)

2. 1224 *Kōmyō Shingon kōnō*[21]
(On the Efficacy of the Mantra of Light)

3. 1227 *Kōmyō Shingon kaji dosha gi*[22]
(Significance of the Mystic Power of the Sand and the Mantra of Light)

4. 1228 *Kōmyō Shingon dosha kanjin ki*[23]
(Recommending Faith in the Sand of the Mantra of Light), 2 fascicles

5.   1228   *Kōmyō Shingon dosha kanjin bekki*[24]
                (Recommending Faith in the Sand of the Mantra of
                Light—Supplement)

6.   1230   *Kōmyō Shingon no koto*[25]
                (The Matter of the Mantra of Light)

7.   *(n.d.)* *Kōmyō Shingon kōshiki*[26]
                (Exposition on the Mantra of Light)

8.   *(n.d.)* *Kōmyō Shingon saimon*
                (Benediction on the Mantra of Light)

9.   *(n.d.)* *Kōmyō Shingon ryakushiki*
                (Abbreviated Ritual of the Mantra of Light)

                In addition there is a record of his lectures on the
                Fukū kenjaku Birushana-butsu daikanjō kōmyō
                shingon kugishaku compiled by his disciples:

10.   1228–29   *Kōgonku gishaku chōjūki*[27]
                (Lectures on the Commentary on the Significance of
                the Syllables of the Mantra of Light), 2 fascicles

Other works that contain substantial discussions of the Mantra of Light
include:

11.   *(n.d.)* *Kegon bukkō zammai kan hihōzō*[28]
                (Secret Treasury of the Huayan Contemplation of
                the Samādhi of the Buddha's Radiance)

12.   1227   *Shinmonshū*[29]
                (Collected Sayings of Things Truly Heard)

13.   1229   *Toganoo onmonogatari*[30]
                (Tales of Toganoo)

APPENDIX 3

OTHER TRANSLATIONS OF WORKS BY MYŌE INTO WESTERN LANGUAGES

In the list below, items 1 and 5 are both translations of the *Yume no ki,* and items 3, 4, 6, and 7 are all translations of the *Toganoo Myōe shōnin ikun.*

1. Girard, Frédéric. *Le "Journal de ses rêves."* In *Un Moine de la secte Kegon à l'époque de Kamakura: Myoe (1173–1232) et le "Journal de ses rêves,"* 109–200. Paris: École Française d'Extrême-Orient, 1990.
2. Morrell, Robert. "Tenjiku Riteisho" (Calculations on the Distance to India). In *Early Kamakura Buddhism—A Minority Report,* 105–106. Berkeley: Asian Humanities Press, 1987.
3. ———. "Toga-no-o Myōe shōnin ikun" (Final Injunctions of the Venerable Myōe of Toga-no-o), by Myōe/Kōshin. In Morrell, *Early Kamakura Buddhism,* 53–65.
4. Rasmus, Rebecca. "The Sayings of Myōe Shōnin of Togano-o." *Eastern Buddhist* 15, no. 1 (spring 1982): 87–105.
5. Tanabe, George J., Jr. "The *Dream Diary* of Myōe Shōnin." In *Myōe the Dreamkeeper—Fantasy and Knowledge in Early Kamakura Buddhism.* Cambridge: Council on East Asian Studies, Harvard University; Harvard University Press, 1992.

6.———. "The Last Instructions of Myōe Shōnin." In "Myōe Shōnin: Tradition and Reform in Early Kamakura Buddhism." Master's thesis, Columbia University, 1974.

7. Unno, Taitetsu. "The Saying of Myōe Shōnin ikun—*Myōe Shōnin ikun.*" Unpublished manuscript.

•

[1] Murakami Sodō, "Shōnin chosaku mokuroku," *Toganoo-zan Kōzanji Myōe Shōnin* (Kyoto: Kōzanji, 1937), 318–319.

[2] This is the vision recorded in the *Kegon bukkōzammaikan meikan den*. See Sueki, *Kamakura Bukkyō keisei ron* (Kyoto: Hōzōkan, 1998), 259.

[3] DNBZ, vol. 13.

[4] Unless otherwise noted, the following information regarding the textual and philological background of this text is taken from the preface to the annotated version found in MSS, 2:733–744.

[5] Sueki, *Kamakura Bukkyō keisei ron,* 262–263.

[6] MSS, 2:883–891.

[7] Unless otherwise indicated by a reference, the following information regarding the textual and philological background of this text is taken from the preface to the annotated version found in MSS, 2:733–744.

[8] MSS, 2:745–881.

[9] *Shingon refractions,* 198.

[10] Tanaka Hisao, *Myōe* (Tokyo: Yoshikawa Kōbunkan, 1961), 240.

[11] *Bussho kaisetsu daijiten,* ed. Ono Genmyō (Tokyo: Daitō Shuppansha, 1938), 3:339.

[12] SAZ, 2:15–54, 55–73. The same texts were also published in NDK, vol. 42, *Kegonshū shōsho.*

[13] MSH, 191–224, 225–242.

[14] Complete copies of the *Kanjinki* and *Kanjin bekki* are stored in the following library collections: Empō Period, 1673–1681: Ōtani University and Koyasan University: Antei Period, 1227–1229: Taisho University (*Bussho kaisetsu daijiten,* 3:339).

The translation of the *Kanjinki* included here is substantially refined from the version I originally published as "Recommending Faith in the Sand of the Mantra of Light," in *Revisioning Kamakura Buddhism,* ed. Richard K. Payne (Honolulu: University of Hawai'i Press, 1998), 167–218.

[15] Takahashi Shūei, "Kōmyō Shingon dosha kanjinki," *Daijō butten: Chūgoku-Nihon hen 20 Yōsai;* Myōe, 93–180.

[16] Kobayashi Yoshinori, "'Kyakuhai mōki' Kamakura jidai shahon no yōgo," in *Myōe Shōnin to Kōzanji,* ed. Myōe shōnin to Kōzanji henshū iinkai (Kyoto: Dōbōsha, 1981), 420–421.

[17] See MSS, 2:579.

[18] KKB, 107–123.

[19] The following works have been used to compile this list: Murakami Sodō, *Toganoo-zan Kōzanji Myōe shōnin* (Kyoto: Kōzanji, 1937), 314–315; MSS, vols. 2, 3; Okuda

Isao, *Myōe—Yume to henreki* (Tokyo: Tokyo Daigaku Shuppankai, 1978), 307–311; *Bussho kaisetsu daijiten*, vols. 8 and 9. Sueki gives a different list in *Kamakura Bukkyō keisei ron*. Murakami lists the *Kōmyō Shingon ryakushiki* and *Kōmyō Shingon saimon* but gives no indication of the sources of his information. Many works of medieval Japanese Buddhism have yet to be located, catalogued, and/or annotated, and we are at a stage of scholarship on Myōe that is far from complete; the present list constitutes all sources that I have been able to identify in the context of modern scholarship on Myōe.

20 SAZ, vol. 2; MSS, vol. 3.
21 Original manuscript stored in Tōdaiji. See Taira Masayuki, *Nihon chusei no shakai to shūkyō* (Tokyo: Hanawa Shobō, 1992), 404–406. Cited in Sueki, *Kamakura Bukkyō keisei ron*, 273n.
22 SAZ, 2:6–14.
23 SAZ, 2:15–54; NDK, vol. 42; MSH, 191–224.
24 SAZ, 2:55–73; NDK, vol. 42; MSH, 225–242.
25 See Sueki, *Kamakura Bukkyō keisei ron*, 261.
26 DNBZ.
27 MSS, 2:729–882.
28 DNBZ, 13.
29 MSS, 3:3–290; see especially 204–209, 282–285.
30 MSS, 3:293–447; see especially 423–430. According to the preface to the transcription, this work consists of records made following Myōe's lectures by his disciple Kūdatsu-bō Jōshin on three occasions, the first in 1213 and the other two in 1229. The third section, dated 1229, is on the Mantra of Light.

GLOSSARY

AUTHORS AND TITLES

PREMODERN WORKS BY TITLE

Arubekiyōwa. By Myōe. 『阿留邊幾夜宇和』、明惠著。

Baolouge jing 『寶楼閣經』。

Ben kenmitsu nikyō ron. By Kūkai. Kōbō daishi zenshū. 『辯顕密二
　教論』、空海著、『弘法大師全集』。

Bukong zhuansuo piluzhenafa daguanding guangming zhenyan jing.
　『不空羂索毘盧舍那佛大灌頂光明眞言經』。

Bukong zhuansuo shenbian zhenyan jing. 『不空羂索神変眞言
　經』。

Dafangguang fohuayan jing suishu yanyi chao. By Chengguan. 『大方
　廣佛華嚴經隨疏演義鈔』、澄觀著。

Dapiluzhenafa jing shu. By Yixing. 『毘盧舍那佛經疏』、一行著。

Dari jing. 『大日經』。

Darijing shu (see, Dapiluzhenafa jing shu). 『大日經疏』。

Darumatara [zen] kyō. 『達摩多羅禪經』。

Datang xiyuji. By Xuanzang. 『大唐西域記』、玄奘著。

Eihei Shingi. 『永平清規』。

Fahua jing. 『法華經』。

Fajie yihai. 『法界義海』。

Fanwang jing. 『梵網經』。

319

Fanwang jing pusa jieben shu. By Fazang. 『梵網經菩薩戒本疏』、法藏著。

Fochuipo niepan lueshuo jiaojie jing. 『佛垂涅槃略説教誡經』。

Fufazang yinyuan zhuan. 『付法藏因緣傳』。

Fukū kenjaku Birushana butsu daikanjō kōmyō shingon kugishaku. By Myōe. 『不空羂索毘盧舎那佛大灌頂光明眞言句義釋』、明惠著。

Gedatsumon gi chōjūki. 『解脱門聴集記』。

Goshōrai mokuroku. 『御請来目録』、空海著。

Guangming zhenyan yigui. 『光明真言儀軌』。

Guan wuliangshoufo jing shu. By Shandao. 『觀無量壽佛經疏』、善導著。

Guan wuliangshou jing. 『觀無量壽佛經』。

Himitsu kanjinchō. 『秘密勸進帳』。

Huayan jing. 『華嚴經』。

Huayanjing kongmuzhang. By Zhiyan. 『華嚴孔目章』、智儼著。

Huayanjing tanxuanji. By Fazang. 『華嚴經探玄記』、法藏著。

Huayanjing yihai baimen. 『華嚴經義海百門』、法藏著。

Jingangding lianhuabuxin niansong yigui. 『金剛頂蓮花部心念誦儀軌』。

Jingangding yiqie rulai zhenshi she dacheng xianzheng dajiaowang jing. 『金剛頂一切如来眞實摂大乘現証大教王經』。

Jūjūshinron. By Kūkai. 『十住心論』、空海。

Kasuga Myōjin takusen ki. 『春日明神託宣記』。

Kegon bukkō zammai kan hihōzō. By Myōe. 『華嚴佛光三昧觀秘宝藏』、

Kegon bukkō zammai kan meikan den. By Myōe. 『華嚴佛光三昧冥觀伝』、

Kegon engi emaki. Edited by Kameta Tsutomu. In Nihon emakimono zenshū. 『華嚴縁起絵巻』、亀田勉編、『日本絵巻物全集』。

Kegon shinshu gi. 『華嚴華嚴信種義』。

Kegon shūzen kanshō nyū gedatsu mon gi. By Myōe. 『華嚴修禪觀照入解脱門義』、明惠著。

Kegon yuishin gi. By Myōe. 『華嚴唯心義』、明惠著。

Keiran shūyō shū. By Kōshū. 『渓嵐拾葉集』、光宗。

Kōgonku gishaku chōjūki. Att. Kōshin. 『光言句義釋聴集記』、高信編。

Kōmyō Shingon dosha kanjin bekki. By Myōe. 『光明眞言土砂勸信別記』、明惠著。

Kōmyō Shingon dosha kanjin ki. By Myōe. 『光明眞言土砂勸進記』、明惠著。

Kōmyō Shingon kaji dosha gi. By Myōe. 『光明眞言加持土砂義』、明惠著。

Kōmyō Shingon kugishaku. By Myōe. 『光明眞言句義釋』、明惠著。

Kōzanji Myōe Shōnin gyōjō (kambun gyōjō). By Kikai. 『高山寺明惠上人行状 (漢文行状) 』、喜海著。

Kōzanji Myōe Shōnin gyōjō (kana gyōjō). By Kikai. 『高山寺明惠上人行状 (仮名行状) 』、喜海著。

Kûmkang sammae gyong. 『金剛三昧經』。

Kyakuhai mōki. By Chōen. 『却廢忘記』、長圓。

Kyōgyōshinshō. By Shinran. In Shinran chosaku zenshū. 『教行信証』、親鸞、『親鸞著作全集』。

Liqu jing. 理趣經。

Liqu shi 理趣釋。

Liujuanchao (see, Sifenlu xingshi chao). 『六卷鈔』。

Lunyu. 『論語』。

Miaofa lianhua jing. 『妙法蓮華經』。

Muli mantuoluo (Jpn. Ju) jing. 『牟利曼陀羅(呪)經』。

Myōe Shōnin ikun. Att. Kōshin. 『明惠上人遺訓』、高信編。

Myōe Shōnin kankei kechimyaku shū. 『明惠上人関係血脈集』。

Myōe Shōnin waka shū. In Myōe Shōnin shū, edited by Kubota Jun and Yamaguchi Akiho. 『明恵上人和歌集』、『明恵上人集』、久保田淳、山口秋穂編。

Nichiyō shingi. 『日用清規』。

Nyorai iseki kōshiki. By Myōe. 『如来遺跡講式』、明恵著。

Ōjōyōshū. By Genshin. 『往生要集』、源信著。

Pubian guangming qingjing chicheng ruibaoyinxin wunengsheng damingwang dasuiqiu tuoluoni jing. 『普遍光明清淨熾盛如意寶印心無能勝大明王大隨求陀羅尼經』。

Puxian pusa yuanxing pin. 『普賢菩薩行願王經』。

Renwang banruo jing. 『仁王般若經』。

Rokkanshō (see, Sifenlu xingshi chao). 『六卷鈔』。

Saigo rinjū gyōgi no koto. By Jōshin. 『最後臨終行儀事』、定眞編。

Sanji sambōrai shaku. By Myōe. 『三時三寶禮釈』、明恵著。

Senchaku hongan nembutsu shū. By Genku Hōnen. 『選擇本願念佛集』、源空法然著。

Shienshū. 『芝薗集』。

Shiji. 『史記』。

Shingon fuhō den. By Kūkai. 『眞言付法伝』、空海著。

Shinmon shū. By Ryūben. 『眞聞集』、隆辨編。

Shiza kōshiki. By Myōe. 『四座講式』、明恵著。

Shōbōgenzō. By Dōgen. Edited by Mizuno Yaeko. 『正法眼藏』、道元著、水野弥穂子編。

Shōnin no koto. By Zenjō. 『上人之事』、禪淨編。

Sifenlu biqiu jieben. 『四分律比丘戒本』。

Sifenlu xingshi chao. By Daoxuan. 『四分律行事鈔』、道宣著。

Song gaoseng zhuan. By Zannin. 『宋高僧傳』、贊寧著。

Sōshi zōron. 『莊子雑論』

Taizōkai nenju shidai. By Kūkai. 『胎藏界念誦次第』、空海著。

Tanxuanji (see, Huayanjing tanxuanji). 『探玄記』。

Toganoo Myōe Shōnin den. Att. Kikai. 『栂尾明惠上人傳』、喜海
　著。

Toganoo Myōe Shōnin shichiju'in kuden. By Raiyu. 『栂尾明惠上人
　七種印口傳』、頼瑜著。

Toganoo onmonogatari. By Jōshin. 『栂尾御物語』、定眞著。

Toganoo Sekkai nikki. By Chōen. 『栂尾説戒日記』、長圓編。

Weishizhang (see, Huayanjing kongmuzhang). 『唯職章』。

Yingluo jing. 『瓔珞經』。

Yinming ruzhenglilunshu. 『因明入正理論疏』。

Yujia shidilun. 『瑜伽師地論』。

Yume no ki. By Myōe. 『夢記』、明惠著。

Yusim Allakto. By Wônhyo. 『遊心安樂道』、元曉 著。

Zaijarin. By Myōe. 『摧邪輪』、明惠著。

Zaijarin shōgonki. By Myōe. 『摧邪輪荘嚴記』、明惠著。

Zenshū kōmoku. By Shōjō. 『禪宗綱目』、證定著。

Zhenyuan jing. 『貞元經』。

Zui'i betsugan mon. By Myōe. In Kamakura Bukkyō zakkō by Tanaka
　Hisao. 『随意別願文』、明惠著、『鎌倉仏教雑考』、田中久夫
　著。

MODERN WORKS

Reference Works

Mizuno Kōgen, Nakamura Hajime, Hirakawa Akira, and Tamak
　Kōshirō, eds. Butten gedai jiten. 水野弘元、中村元、平川彰、玉
　城康四郎編、『仏典解題事典』。

Nakamura Hajime. Bukkyōgo daijiten. 中村元編、『仏教語大辭
　典』。

Ono Genmyō, ed. Bussho kaisetsu daijiten. 小野玄妙編、『仏書解説
　大辞典』。

Ōno Susumu, Satake Akihiro, and Maeda Kingorō, eds. Iwanami kogo
　jiten. 大野晋、佐竹昭広、前田金五郎、『岩波古語辞典』。

Ōno Tatsunosuke, ed. Nihon Bukkyō shi jiten. 大野達之助編、『日本仏教史辞典』。

Sawa Ryūken et al., eds. Mikkyō jiten. 佐和隆研編、『密教辞典』。

Shinmura Izuru, ed. Kōjien. 新村出編、『広辞苑』。

Books

Fujita Kōtatsu. Genshi Jōdo shisō no kenkyū. 藤田宏達著、『原始浄土思想の研究』。

Fukunaga Mitsuji. Dōkyō to Nihon bunka. 福永光司著、『道教と日本文化』。

Hakamaya Noriaki. Hōnen to Myōe: Nihon Bukkyō shisōshi josetsu. 袴谷憲昭著、『法然と明恵：日本仏教思想史序説』。

Hase Hōshū, ed. Shingonshū anjin zensho. 長谷宝秀編、『真言宗安心全書』。

Hieizan Senshūin, ed. Eshin sōzu zenshū. 比叡山専修院編、『恵心僧都全集』。

Kamata Shigeo and Tanaka Hisao, eds. Kamakura kyū Bukkyō. Nihon shisō taikei 15. 鎌田茂雄、田中久夫編、『鎌倉旧仏教』、日本思想体系。

Kameta Tsutomu, ed. Kegon engi emaki. In Shinshū Nihon emakimono zenshū. 亀田勉編、『華嚴縁起絵巻』、新修日本絵巻物全集。

Kanaya Osamu, trans. Sōshi. 金谷治訳注、『荘子』。

Kazue Kyōichi. Nihon no mappō shisō—Nihon chūsei shisōshi kenkyū. 『日本の末法思想—日本中世思想史研究』、数江教一著。

Kōzanji tenseki monjo sōgō chōsa dan, ed. Myōe Shōnin to Kōzanji. 高山寺典籍文書綜合調査団編、『明恵上人と高山寺』。

_____, ed. Myōe shōnin shiryō. 高山寺典籍文書綜合調査団編、『明恵上人資料』。

Kubota Jun and Yamaguchi Akiho, eds. Myōe Shōnin shū. 久保田淳、山口秋穂編、『明恵上人集』。

Machida Sōhō. Hōnen tai Myōe: Kamakura Bukkyō no shūkyō taiketsu. 町田宗鳳著、『法然対明恵：鎌倉仏教の宗教対決』。

Matsumoto Yasuchio. Yuasatō to Myōe. 松本保千代著、『湯浅党と明恵』。

Murakami Sodō. Toganoo-zan Kōzanji Myōe Shōnin. 村上素道著、『栂尾山高山寺明恵上人』。

Nakano Tatsue, ed. Nihon daizōkyō. 中野達恵編、『日本大藏経』。

Okuda Isao. Myōe—Yume to henreki. 奥田勲著、『明恵—遍歴と夢』。

Sueki Fumihiko. Kamakura Bukkyō keisei ron. 末木文美士著、『鎌倉仏教形成論』。

Taira Masayuki. Nihon chusei no shakai to shūkyō. 平雅行著、『日本中世の社会と宗教』。

Takakusu Junjirō et al., eds. Dai Nihon Bukkyō zensho. 高楠順次朗編、『大日本仏教全書』。

Takakusu Junjirō and Watanabe Kaigyoku, eds. Taishō shinshū daizōkyō. 高楠順次朗、渡辺海旭編、『大正新脩大蔵経』。

Takeuchi Yoshinori. Kyōgyōshinshō no tetsugaku. Gendai Bukkyō meicho zenshū—fukyūban. 武内義範著、『教行信証の哲学』現代仏教名著全集—普及版。

Tanaka Hisao. Myōe. 田中久夫著、『明恵』。

Tanaka Kaiō. Kōmyō Shingon shūsei. 田中海應著、『光明眞言集成』。

Toganoo Shōun. Himitsu jisō no kenkyu. 栂尾祥雲著、『秘密事相の研究』。

Ueda Reijō. Shingon mikkyō jisō gaisetsu—shosonhō, kanjōbu. 上田霊城著、『真言密教事相概説—諸尊法、灌頂部』。

Yamamoto Isao, ed. Myōe shōnin hen. Kōsō meicho zenshū. 山本勇夫編、『明恵上人篇』高僧名著全集。

Articles

Akamatsu Toshihide. "Kajin to shite no Myōe Shōnin." Myōe Shōnin to Kōzanji. 赤松俊秀著、「歌人としての明恵上人」、『明恵上人と高山寺』。

Kamata Shigeo. "Nanto kyōgaku no shisōshiteki igi." 鎌田茂雄著、「南都教学の思想史的意義」。

Kobayashi Yoshinori. "'Kyakuhai mōki' Kamakura jidai shahon no yōgo." In Myōe Shōnin to Kōzanji. 小林芳規著、「『却廃忘記』鎌倉時代写本の用語」。

Koizumi Haruaki. "Myōe Shōnin kankei kikigakirui no Bukkyō-shigakuteki ichizuke." 小泉春明著、「明恵上人関係聞き書き類の仏教史学的位置付け」。

Takahashi Shūei, trans. "Kōmyō Shingon dosha kanjinki." In Daijō butten: Chūgoku-Nihon hen 20 Yōsai Myōe, co-translator with Nakao Ryōshin. 高橋秀英訳、「光明眞言土砂勧進記」、大乗仏典：中国日本編 20 『栄西明恵』、中尾良信共訳。

Takagi Yutaka. "Kamakura Bukkyō ni okeru rekishi no kōsō." Kamakura Bukkyōshi kenkyū. 高木豊著、「鎌倉仏教における歴史の構造」、『鎌倉仏教史研究』。

Tanaka Takako. "Gyokunyo no seiritsu to genkai: Jichin oshō musōki kara Shinran muki made." In Shiriizu josei to Bukkyō 4 Miko to joshin. 田中貴子著、「玉女の成立と限界：『慈鎮和尚夢想記』から『親鸞夢記』まで」、シリーズ女性と仏教 4　『巫女と女神』。

PROPER NOUNS

Amida Nyorai 阿弥陀如来

Annen 安然

Arita 有田

Ayuwang, Mount 阿育王山

Bao Siwei 寶思惟

Binayaka 毘那夜迦

Bodhiruci 菩提流志

Bukkōkan zammai 佛光觀三昧

Butsugen Butsumo 佛眼佛母

Caotong 曹洞

Chandingsi 禪定寺

Changan 長安

Chengguan 澄觀

Chōen 長円

Ch'ônggu Taesa 青丘大師

Chuang Chou 莊周

Chūnagon Tomotaka 中納言朝隆

Cien dashi Kuiji 慈恩大師窺基

Daidenpōin 大伝法院

Daigo, Emperor 醍醐天皇

Daigoji 醍醐寺

Dainichi Nōnin 大日能忍

Dainichi Nyorai 大日如来

Daozong 道宗

Daruma School 達磨宗

Daye Period 大業

Ding, Cook 庖丁

Dōgen 道元

Dōhan 道範

Dushun 杜順

Eiben 永弁

Eisai 榮西

Eizon 叡尊

Ejū 惠什

Emma[-ō] 閻魔王

Endō-bō Shinkei 圓道房信慶

Engi 延喜

Enji 琰路

Eshinni 惠心尼

Fazang 法藏

Fujiwara Akiko 藤原彰子

Fujiwara Katako 藤原賢子

Fujiwara Teika 藤原定家

Fujiwara Yorimichi 藤原頼通

Fukūkenjaku Kannon 不空羂索觀音

Ga'un Shamon Eizon 臥雲沙門叡尊

Gedatsu Jōkei 解脱貞慶

Gien-bō Ryōten 義淵房靈典

Gihan 義範

Girin-bō Kikai 義林房喜海

Goji Shingon 五字眞言

Gotoba, Emperor 後鳥羽上皇

Gyōnen 凝然

Hakuin 白院

Hanjun 範俊

Kōbō Daishi Kūkai 弘法大師空
　海
Kōfukuji 興福寺
Kōmyō Shingon 光明眞言
Kondō 金堂
Kongōbuji 金剛峰寺
Kongōkai 金剛界
Kongōkai denju 金剛界伝受
Kongōkai mandara 金剛界曼陀
　羅
Kongōzan 金剛山
Kōryūji 広隆寺
Kōsanmi-no-Tsubone 督三位局
Kōshō Bosatsu 興正菩薩
Kōshū 光宗
Kōya, Mount 高野山
Kōzanji 高山寺
Kūdatsu-bō Jōshin 空達房定眞
Kūkai 空海
Kûmhae 黔海
Linji 臨済
Li Tongxuan 李通玄
Li Wuzhao 李無諂
Maka Shina 摩訶支那
Mongaku 文覺
Mugai Nyodai 無外如大
Mujū Ichien 無住一圓
Myōan Eisai 妙案榮西
Myōe Kōben 明惠高辯
Myōjun-bō 明順房
Myōnin-bō 明忍房
Nara 奈良

Nichiren 日蓮
Nichizō Shōnin 日藏上人
Ninshōden 仁勝殿
Nōnin 能忍
Ōhara Chōen 大原長宴
Ōyama Ninkai 大山仁快
Pari no zen 波利の禪
Raishō 頼昭
Reiyūkai 靈友会
Rennyo 蓮如
Rinzai 臨済
Risshō Kōseikai 立正佼成会
Ritsu 律
Rokuhi Kannon 鹿皮觀音
Rujing 如淨
Ryōten 靈典
Saburō 三郎
Saichō 最澄
Saidaiji 西大寺
Saishō Ajari Shōken 宰相阿闍梨
　性憲
Sakiyama, Nun 崎山の尼公
Sambō'in 三寶院
Sambōrai 三寶禮
Sanji sambōrai 三時三寶禮
Sanlun 三論
Sanmi, Lady 督三位局
Sanron 三論
Sanuki 讚岐
Seiwa 清和
Sekisuiin 石水院
Sennen-bō 專念房

•

TERMS

ajari 阿闍梨

akai 閼伽井

akaoke 閼伽桶

aku 惡

akushu 惡趣

arubekiyōwa 阿留邊幾夜宇和

bodaishin 菩提心

bosatsu no in'i 菩薩ノ因位

bussetsu 佛利

chika 智火

chimaki-ga-ie 粽カイエ

chūjō 中将

daihi 大悲

daijihō 大地法

daizenjihō 大善地法

dōtai no daihi 同體の大悲

dōjō 道場

doku 毒

gakumon 學問

ganmon 願文

gochi 五智

go'i 五位

gomyō 五明

gosōjōshin 五相成身

gya tei, gya tei

hashii 端居

henge Kannon 変化觀音

hentai kambun 変体漢文

hito 人

hiyo ヒヨ

hō 法

hōai 法愛

hongaku 本覺

honji suijaku 本地垂迹

honryō 本領

hōsho 方所

hosshin seppō 法身説法

ichigōsō fukatoku 一合相不可得

ingei shingon 印契眞言

ingon 印言

jiji muge hokkai 事事無礙法界

jiku 字句

jikyōsō 自共相

jinjō 辰朝

jirinkan 字輪觀

jisai 持齋

jōbon jōshō 上品上生

jōkai 乘戒

jūaku gogyaku 十惡五逆

jūjūshin 十住心

jūnien 十二縁

ka 果 (fruits)

ka 菓 (sweets)

kahō 迦寶

kaijō no shiku 戒乘四句

kaiso 開祖

kaji 加持

kana-majiri bun 仮名交じり文

katsuai 渇愛

kawaya 河屋

kegyō 加行

kenjaku 羂索

kinyū 近友

kōan 公安

konjichō 金翅鳥

kōryū 興隆 (orig. text 興立)

kōsō 好相

kun-reading 訓読み

kusabira くさびら

kusakanmuri 草冠

kyōhan 教判

kyōshū 經宗

kyōsoku tsuzumi 脇足鼓

mappō 末法

miko 巫女

mui gedatsu 無爲解脱

muken jigoku 無間地獄

munimusan 無二無三

muro 無漏

muryōju 無量壽

myōgaku 妙覺

nangeideku 難解出で来

nembutsu 念佛

nichibotsu 日没

nijō 二乘

nikawa 膠

nitai 二諦

nitchū 日中

nyojitsu 如實

rasatsu 羅刹

richiji 理智事

rin'ō 輪王

rishaku 離釋

rokudō 六道

rokujin 六塵

rokusō jūgen engi 六相十玄縁起

ryōin 了因

sanchū tsuka no ma 山中ツカ
ノ間

sandoku 三毒

sangai 三界

sangaku 三學

sangen 三賢

sanji 三時

sanjōkyō 三乘教

sanjūshichi son 三十七尊

sankyō itchi 三教一致

sanmaya 三摩耶

sanmitsu byōdō 三密平等

sanmitsu kaji 三密加持

sansei 三世

santen 三點

sanzōzen 三雜染

sanzu no kunō 三途の苦悩

satamon 沙汰門

shamon 沙門

shichichin 七珍

shidagon 斯陀含

shien 乏蘭

shika 四果

shikufunbetsu 四句分別

shin (true-style) 眞

shin'ai 親愛

shinge nihō 信解二法

shingi 清規

shinjin 信心

shinjin datsuraku 身心脱落

shinshinsho 心心所

shintan 晨旦

shirabyōshi 白拍子

shishi wuai fajie 事事無礙法界

shitoku 四徳

shitakomu 斯陀含

shōbō 正法

shoharamitsu 諸波羅蜜

shokon 諸根

shōshō 少将

shōsōkishō 攝相歸性

shūso 宗祖

shuzoku 種族

sifenlu 四分律

sō (grass-style) 草

sōgikōkō 僧祇廣劫

sōkō 草甲

sokushin jōbutsu 即身成佛

sōshibon 草氏本

sūsokukan 数息觀

tamashii 魂

tatami 畳

tōgaku 等覺

tokugō 得業

tora no toki 寅の時

waka 和歌

wu sounds 誤

yakubutsu 薬物

yi 矣

you 酔う

yuganuma ユガヌマ

zōbō 像法

zōjōka 増上果

zōyakuhen 増益邊

BIBLIOGRAPHY

PREMODERN WORKS BY TITLE
(DOES NOT INCLUDE MODERN COLLECTIONS
OF PREMODERN WORKS)

Baolouge jing. T, vol. 19, #1005a.

Ben kenmitsu nikyō ron. By Kūkai. *Kōbō daishi zenshū,* vol. 1. Edited by Mikkyō Bunka Kenkyūjo. Osaka, Japan: Mikkyō Bunka Kenkyūjo, 1968.

Bufazang yinyuan zhuan. T, vol. 50, #2058.

Bukong zhuansuo piluzhenafa daguanding guangming zhenyan jing. T, vol. 19, #1002.

Bukong zhuansuo shenbian zhenyan jing. T, vol. 20, #1092.

Dafangguang huayan jing suishu yanyi chao. By Chengguan. T, vol. 36, #1736.

Dapiluzhenafa jing shu. By Yixing. T, vol. 39, #1796.

Dari jing. T, vol. 18, #848.

Dari jing shu. (see, *Dapiluzhenafa jing shu*).

Darumatara [zen] kyō. T, vol. 15, #618.

Datang xiyuji. By Xuanzang. T, vol. 54, #2087.

Fahua jing. (see, *Miaofa lianhua jing*).

Fanwang jing. T, vol. 24, 1484.

Fanwang jing pusa jieben shu. By Fazang. T, vol. 40, #1814.

Fochuipo niepan lueshuo jiaojie jing. T, vol. 12, #389.

Fukū kenjaku Birushana-butsu daikanjō kōmyō shingon kugishaku. By Myōe. MSS, vol. 2; SAZ, vol. 2; NDK, 42.

Guangming zhenyan yigui, T, vol. 20, #1098.

Guan wuliangshou jing. T, vol. 12, #365.

Guan wuliangshoufo jing shu. By Zhiyi. T, vol. 37, #1750.

Huayan jing. 60-fascicle version. T, vol. 9, #278.

Huayanjing kongmuzhang. By Zhiyan. T, vol. 45, #1870.

Huayanjing tanxuanji. By Fazang. T, vol. 35, #1733.

Jingangding lianhuabuxin niansong yigui. T, vol. 18, #873.

Jingangding yiqie rulai zhenshi she dacheng xianzheng dajiaowang jing. T, vol. 18, #865.

Jūjūshinron. By Kūkai. In *Kōbo Daishi Kūkai zenshū*, vol. 1. Tokyo: Chikuma Shobō, 1983.

Kegon engi emaki. Edited by Kameta Tsutomu. In *Nihon emakimono zenshū*, vol. 7. General editor, Tanaka Ichimatsu. Tokyo: Kadokawa Shoten, 1959.

Kegon shinshu gi. T, vol. 72, #2330.

Kegon shuzen kanshō nyū gedatsu mon gi. By Myōe. T, vol. 72, #2331.

Kegon yuishingi. DNBZ, vol. 13.

Kyakuhai mōki. By Chōen. KKB.

Keiran shūyō shū. By Kōshū. T, vol. 76, #2410.

Kegon bukkō zammai kan hihōzō. By Myōe. DNBZ, vol. 13.

Kegon bukkō zammai kan meikan den. By Myōe. NDK, vol. 41.

Kegon yuishin gi. By Myōe. DNBZ, vol. 13.

Kōgonku gishaku chōjūki. Att. Kōshin. MSS, vol. 2.

Kōmyō Shingon dosha kanjin ki. By Myōe. SAZ, vol. 2.

Kōmyō Shingon dosha kanjin bekki. By Myōe. SAZ, vol. 2.

Kōmyō Shingon kaji dosha gi. By Myōe. SAZ, vol. 2.

Kōmyō Shingon kugishaku. By Myōe. MSS, vol. 2.

Kōzanji Myōe Shōnin gyōjō (kana gyōjō). By Kikai. MSS, vol. 1.

Kōzanji Myōe Shōnin gyōjō (kambun gyōjō). By Ryūchō and Kōshin. MSS, vol. 1.

Kyōgyōshinshō. By Shinran. In *Shinran chosaku zenshū.* Edited by Kaneko Daiei. Kyoto: Hōzōkan, 1964.

Liujuanchao (see, *Sifenlu xingshi chao*).

Miaofa lianhua jing. T, vol. 9, #262.

Muli mantuoluo (Jpn. Ju) jing. T, vol. 19, #1007.

Metta Sutta (Sutra on Loving-Kindness). In *Khuddaka Patha* of the *Khuddaka Nikaya (The Minor Readings and The Illustrator of Ultimate Meaning)*. Oxford: Pali Text Society, 1991.

Myōe Shōnin ikun. Att. Kōshin. MSS, vol. 3.

Myōe Shōnin kankei kechimyaku shū. MSS, vol. 2.

Myōe shōnin waka shū. In *Myōe Shōnin shū,* edited by Kubota Jun and Yamaguchi Akiho. Iwanami Bunko 33–326–1. Tokyo: Iwanami Shoten, 1981.

Pubian guangming qingjing chicheng ruibaoyinxin wunengsheng damingwang dasuiqiu tuoluoni jing. T, vol. 20, #1153.

Puxian pusa yuanxing pin. T, vol. 10, #293.

Renwang banruo jing. T, vol. 8, #246.

Rokkanshō (see, *Sifenlu xingshi chao*).

Saigo rinjū gyōgi no koto. By Jōshin. MSS, vol. 1.

Sanji sambōrai shaku. By Myōe. DNBZ, vol. 13.

Shiza kōshiki. By Myōe. T, vol. 84, #2731.

Senchaku hongan nembutsu shū. By Hōnen. T, vol. 83, #2608.

Shingon fuhō den. By Kūkai. In *Kōbo Daishi Kūkai zenshū,* vol. 2. Tokyo: Chikuma Shobō, 1983.

Shinmon shū. By Ryūben. MSS, vol. 3.

Shōbōgenzō. By. Dōgen. Edited by Mizuno Yaeko. Iwanami Bunko. Tokyo: Iwanami Shoten, 1990.

Shōnin no koto. By Zenjō. MSS, vol. 1.

Sifenlu biqiu jieben. T, vol. 22, #1429.

Sifenlu xingshi chao. By Daoxuan. T, vol. 40, #1804.

Song gaoseng zhuan. By Zannin. T, vol. 50, #2061.

Taizōkai nenju shidai. By Kūkai. This could be any number of works that refer to methods of practice concerning the Taizōkai mandala. (see, Mikkyō Daijiten. Shukusatsuban. Edited by Mikkyō jiten hensankai. Revised by Mikkyō daijiten saihan iinkai, s.v. *Taizōkai nenju shidai.* Kyoto: Hōzōkan, 1983.

Tanxuanji (see, *Huayanjing tanxuanji*).

Toganoo Sekkai nikki. By Chōen. MSS, vol. 3.

Toganoo Myōe shōnin den. Att. Kikai. MSS, vol. 1.

Toganoo Myōe shōnin denki. MSS, vol. 1.

Toganoo onmonogatari. By Jōshin. MSS, vol. 3.

Weishizhang (see, *Huayanjing kongmuzhang*).

Yinming ruzhenglilunshu. By Ji. T, vol. 44, #1840.

Yuqie shidilun. T, vol. 30, #1579.

Yume no ki. By Myōe. MSS, vol. 2.

Zaijarin. By Myōe. KKB.

Zaijarin shōgonki. By Myōe. MSH.

Zenshū kōmoku. By Shōjō. KKB.

Zui'i betsugan mon. By Myōe. In *Kamakura Bukkyō zakkō* by Tanaka Hisao. Kyoto: Shimonkaku Shuppan, 1982. 309–314.

•

MODERN WORKS

REFERENCE WORKS

Inagaki Hisao. *Dictionary of Japanese Buddhist Terms.* In collaboration with P. G. O'Neill. 3rd ed., with Supplement. Kyoto: Nagata Bunshōdō, 1988.

Mizuno Kōgen, Nakamura Hajime, Hirakawa Akira, and Tamaki Kōshirō, eds. *Butten gedai jiten.* 2d ed. Tokyo: Shunjūsha, 1977.

Nakamura Hajime. *Bukkyōgo daijiten.* Condensed version. Tokyo: Tokyo Shoseki, 1980.

Nakamura Hajime, Fukunaga Mitsuji, Tamura Yoshirō, and Konno Tōru, eds. *Iwanami Bukkyō jiten.* Tokyo: Iwanami Shoten, 1989.

Ono Genmyō, ed. *Bussho kaisetsu daijiten.* Tokyo: Daitō Shuppansha, 1938.

Ōno Susumu, Satake Akihiro, and Maeda Kingorō, eds. *Iwanami kōgo jiten.* Tokyo: Iwanami Shoten, 1974.

Ōno Tatsunosuke, ed. *Nihon Bukkyō shi jiten.* Tokyo: Tokyōdō Shuppan, 1979.

Sawa Ryūken et al., eds. *Mikkyō Jiten.* Kyoto: Hozokan, 1975.

Shinmura Izuru, ed. *Kōjien.* 4th ed. Tokyo: Iwanami Shoten, 1991.

BOOKS

Abe Ryūichi. *The Weaving of Mantra: Kūkai and the Construction of Esoteric Buddhists Discourse.* New York: Columbia University Press, 1999.

Berger, Peter. *The Heretical Imperative: Contemporary Possibilities of Religious Affirmation.* Garden City, N.Y.: Anchor Press, 1980.

Bodiford, Will. *Sōtō Zen in Medieval Japan.* Honolulu: University of Hawai'i Press, 1990.

Buswell, Robert. *The Formation of Chan Ideology in China and Korea: The Vajrasamādhi-Sūtra, a Buddhist Apocryphon.* Princeton, N.J.: Princeton University Press, 1989.

————, ed. *Chinese Buddhist Apocrypha.* Honolulu: University of Hawai'i Press, 1990.

Eliade, Mircea. *The Sacred and the Profane.* New York: Harcourt Brace, 1987.

Ellis, Harper Havelock and Ryūgaku Ishizuka, trans. *Hōnen the Buddhist Saint-His Life and Teaching by Shunjō Hōin.* Kyoto: Chionin, 1925.

Faure, Bernard. *Chan Insights and Oversights: An Epistemological Critique of the Chan Tradition.* Princeton, N.J.: Princeton University Press, 1993.

————. *The Rhetoric of Immediacy: A Cultural Critique of Chan/Zen Buddhism.* Princeton, N.J.: Princeton University Press, 1991.

————. *The Will to Orthodoxy: A Critical Genealogy of Northern Chan Buddhism.* Stanford: Stanford University Press, 1997.

Fujita Kōtatsu. *Genshi Jōdo shisō no kenkyū.* Tokyo: Iwanami Shoten, 1970.

Fukunaga Mitsuji. *Dōkyō to Nihon bunka.* Kyoto: Jimbun Shoin, 1982.

Getty, Alice. *The Gods of Northern Buddhism: Their History and Iconography.* New York: Dover, 1988.

Girard, Frédéric. *Un Moine de la secte Kegon à l'époque de Kamakura: Myoe . 1173–1232. et le "Journal de ses rêves".* Paris: École Française d'Extrême-Orient, 1990.

Graham, A. C., trans. *Chuang Tzu: The Inner Chapters.* London: Mandala, 1991.

Groner, Paul. *Saicho: The Establishment of the Japanese Tendai School.* Berkeley Buddhist Studies Series 7. Berkeley: Center for South and Southeast Asian Studies, University of California, 1984.

Hakamaya Noriaki. *Hōnen to Myōe: Nihon Bukkyō shisōshi josetsu.* Tokyo: Daizō Shuppan, 1998.

Hakeda Yoshito. *Kūkai: Major Works.* New York: Columbia University Press, 1972.

Hase Hōshū, ed. *Shingonshū anjin zensho.* 2 vols. Reprint. Kyoto: Daigakudō Shoten, 1973.

Hieizan Senshūin, ed. *Eshin sōzu zenshū.* Kyoto: Shibunkaku, 1971.

Huntington, C. W. *The Emptiness of Emptiness.* Honolulu: University of Hawai'i Press, 1990.

Inagaki Hisao. *The Three Pure Land Sūtras.* 2d rev. ed. Kyoto: Nagata Bunshōdō, 1995.

Kamata Shigeo and Tanaka Hisao, eds. *Kamakura kyū Bukkyō.* Nihon shisō taikei 15. Tokyo: Iwanami Shoten, 1971.

Kameta Tsutomu, ed. *Kegon engi emaki.* In *Shinshū Nihon emakimono zenshū.* General Editor, Tanaka Ichimatsu, vol. 8. Tokyo: Kadokawa Shoten, 1976.

Kanaya Osamu, trans. *Sōshi.* vol 1. Iwanami Bunko, *Ao* 206–1. Tokyo: Iwanami Shoten, 1971.

Karlgren, Bernard. *Analytical Dictionary of Chinese and Sino-Japanese.* New York: Dover Publications, 1974.

Kazue Kyōichi. *Nihon no mappō shisō-Nihon chūsei shisōshi kenkyū.* Tokyo: Kōbundō, 1961.

Kawai Hayao. *The Buddhist Priest Myōe: A Life of Dreams.* Venice, Calif.: Lapis Press, 1992.

Keene, Donald, trans., *Essays in Idleness: The* Tsurezuregusa *of Kenkō.* New York: Columbia University Press, 1967.

Kōzanji tenseki monjo sōgō chōsa dan, ed. *Myōe Shōnin to Kōzanji.* Kyoto: Dōbōsha, 1981.

———, ed. *Myōe shōnin shiryō.* 3 vols. Tokyo: Tokyo Daigaku Shuppankai, 1971–87.

Kubota Jun and Yamaguchi Akiho, eds. *Myōe Shōnin shū.* Iwanami Bunko 33–326–1. Tokyo: Iwanami Shoten, 1981.

Machida Sōhō. *Hōnen tai Myōe: Kamakura Bukkyō no shūkyō taiketsu.* Tokyo: Kōdansha, 1998.

McRae, John R. *The Northern School and the Formation of Early Ch'an Buddhism.* Honolulu: University of Hawai'i Press, 1986.

Morrell, Robert E. *Early Kamakura Buddhism: A Minority Report.* Berkeley, Calif.: Asian Humanities Press, 1987.

———, trans. *Sand and Pebbles* (Shasekishū): *The Tales of Mujū Ichien- a Voice for Pluralism in Kamakura Buddhism.* Albany: SUNY Press, 1985.

Liu, Ming-Wood. *The Teaching of Fa-Tsang: An Examination of Buddhist Metaphysics.* Ph.D. diss., University of California Los Angeles, 1979.

Mair, Victor, trans., *Wandering on the Way: Early Taoist Tales and Parables of Chuang Tzu.* New York: Bantam Books, 1994.

Matsumoto Yasuchio. *Yuasatō to Myōe.* Wakayama, Japan: Uji Shoten, 1979.

Morrell, Robert E. *Sand and Pebbles* (Shasekishū): *The Tales of Mujū Ichien-A Voice for Pluralism in Kamakura Buddhism.* Albany: SUNY Press, 1985.

Murakami Sodō. *Toganoo-zan Kōzanji Myōe Shōnin.* Kyoto: Kōzanji, 1937.

Nakano Tatsue, ed. *Nihon daizōkyō.* 48 vols. Tokyo: Nihon daizōkyō hensan kai, 1919–21.

Okuda Isao. *Myōe-Yume to henreki.* Tokyo: Tokyo Daigaku Shuppankai, 1978.

Paul, Diana. *Philosophy of Mind in Sixth-Century China: Paramartha's Evolution of Consciousness.* Stanford: Stanford University Press, 1984.

Pulleyblank, Edwin G. *Middle Chinese: A Study in Historical Phonology.* Vancouver: University of British Columbia Press, 1984.

Senchakushū English Translation Project, trans. and ed. *Hōnen's Senchakushū.* Honolulu: University of Hawai'i Press, 1998.

Shinran. *Passages on the Pure Land Way: A Translation of Shinran's* Jōdo monrui jushō. Translated by Dennis Hirota. Edited by Yoshifumi Ueda. Shin Buddhism Translation Series. Kyoto: Honganji International Center, 1982.

Swanson, Paul L. *Foundations of T'ien-T'ai philosophy: The Flowering of the Two Truths Theory in Chinese Buddhism.* Berkeley: Asian Humanities Press, 1989.

Stone, Jacqueline. *Original Enlightenment and the Transformation of Medieval Japanese Buddhism.* Honolulu: University of Hawai'i Press, 1999.

Sueki Fumihiko. *Kamakura Bukkyō keisei ron.* Kyoto: Hōzōkan, 1998.

Taira Masayuki. *Nihon chusei no shakai to shūkyō.* Tokyo: Hanawa Shobō, 1992.

Takakusu Junjirō et al., eds. *Dai Nihon Bukkyō zensho.* 150 vols. Reprint. Tokyo: Dai Nihon Bukkyō zensho kankōkai, 1931.

Takakusu Junjirō and Watanabe Kaigyoku, eds. *Taishō shinshū daizōkyō.* 100 vols. Tokyo: Taishō Issaikyō. Kankōkai, 1924–32.

Takeuchi Yoshinori. *Kyōgyōshinshō no tetsugaku.* Gendai Bukkyō meicho zenshū-fukyūban. Tokyo: Ryūmonkan: 1987.

Tanabe, George. *Myōe the Dreamkeeper: Fantasy and Knowledge in Early Kamakura Buddhism.* Cambridge, Massachusetts: Council on East Asian Studies, Harvard University, and Harvard University Press, 1992.

Tanaka Hisao. *Myōe.* Tokyo: Yoshikawa Kōbunkan, 1961.

Tanaka Kaiō. *Kōmyō Shingon shūsei.* Kisarazu, Japan: Tokuzōji Shuppanbu, 1968.

Tanaka, Kenneth. *The Dawn of Chinese Pure Land Buddhist Doctrine: Ching-ying Hui-yüan.* Albany: State University of New York Press, 1990.

Toganoo Shōun. *Himitsu jisō no kenkyū.* Wakayama-ken, Koyasan: Koyasan Daigaku Shuppanbu, 1940.

Toganoo Shōun. *Shingon: The Japanese Tantric Tradition.* trans. Leo Pruden. unpublished.

Tyler, Royall. *The Miracles of the Kasuga Deity.* New York: Columbia University Press, 1990.

Ueda Reijō, *Shingon mikkyō jisō gaisetsu-shosonhō, kanjōbu (jō).* Kyoto: Dōbōsha, 1989.

Unno, Mark Ty. "As Appropriate: Myōe Kōben and the Problem of the Vinaya in Early Kamakura Buddhism." Ph.D. diss. Stanford: Stanford University, 1994.

Watson, Burton, trans. *Chuang Tzu: Basic Writings.* New York: Columbia University Press, 1964.

Weinberg, Steven. *The First Three Minutes: A Modern View of The Origin of the Universe.* New York, Basic Books, 1977.

Yamamoto Isao, ed. *Myōe shōnin hen.* Kōsō meicho zenshū, vol. 9. Tokyo: Heibonsha, 1930.

Yampolsky, Philip, trans. *The Platform Sutra of Hui-neng.* New York: Columbia University Press, 1967.

ARTICLES

Akamatsu Toshihide. "Kajin to shite no Myōe Shōnin." *Myōe Shōnin to Kōzanji.*

Bielefeldt, Carl. "Recarving the Dragon: History and Dogma in the Study of Dōgen." In *Dōgen Studies,* edited by William LaFleur. Kuroda Institute Studies in East Asian Buddhism 2. Honolulu: University of Hawai'i Press, 1985, 21–53.

Brock, Karen. "Chinese Maiden, Silla Monk: Zenmyō and Her Thirteenth-Century Japanese Audience." In *Flowering in the Shadows.* Edited by Marsha Weidner. Honolulu: University of Hawai'i Press, 1990.

———. "The Case of the Missing Scroll: A History and Reconstruction of the *Tales of Gishō and Gangyō.*" *Archives of Asian Art* 41 (1998): 6–31.

———. "Wŏnhyo as Myōe, Myōe as Wŏnhyo."

Foard, James. "In Search of a Lost Reformation: A Reconsideration of Kamakura Buddhism." *Japanese Journal of Religious Studies* 7, no. 4 (December 1980): 261–287.

Hawes, Benjamin. "Dreaming and Awakening in the Writings of Myōe Kōben and Zhuangzi." Brown University, Providence, 1996. unpublished.

Ivanhoe, Philip J. "Zhuangzi on Skepticism, Skill, and the Dao." *Journal of the American Academy of Religion* 61, no. 4 (1993): 639–654.

Kamata Shigeo. "*Nanto kyōgaku no shisōshiteki igi.*" KKB, 528–569.

Kobayashi Yoshinori. "'Kyakuhai mōki' Kamakura jidai shahon no yōgo." In *Myōe shōnin to Kōzanji,* edited by Myōe shōnin to Kōzanji henshū iinkai. Kyoto: Dōbōsha, 1981.

Koizumi Haruaki. "Myōe Shōnin kankei kikigakirui no Bukkyō-shigakuteki ichizuke." MSS, 3:743–744.

Machida Sōhō. "Life and Light, the Infinite: A Historical and Philological Analysis of the Amida Cult." (monograph) *Sino-Platonic Papers* 9. December 1988.

Marra, Michele. "The Development of Mappō Thought in Japan." Parts 1 & 2. *Japanese Journal of Religious Studies* 15. Nos. 1 & 4 (1988): 25–54, 287–305.

Rasmus, Rebecca. "The Sayings of Myōe Shōnin of Togano-o," *Eastern Buddhist* 15, no. 1 (spring 1982): 87–105.

Roth, Harold D. "The Inner Cultivation Tradition of Early Daoism." In *Religions of China in Practice.* Edited by Donald S. Lopez Jr. Princeton, New Jersey: Princeton University Press, 1995.

Ruch, Barbara. "The Other Side of Culture in Medieval Japan." In *The Cambridge History of Japan,* vol. 3, *Medieval Japan.* Edited by Kōzō Yamamura. Cambridge: Cambridge University Press, 1990.

Schopen, Gregory. "Sukhāvatī as a Generalized Religious Goal in Sanskrit Mahāyāna Literature," *Indo-Iranian Journal* 19 (1977): 170–210.

Takahashi Shūei, trans. "Kōmyō Shingon dosha kanjinki." In *Daijō butten: Chūgoku-Nihon hen 20 Yōsai Myōe,* co-translator with Nakao Ryōshin. Tokyo: Chuōkōronsha, 1988.

Takagi Yutaka. "Kamakura Bukkyō ni okeru rekishi no kōsō." *Kamakura Bukkyōshi kenkyū.* Tokyo: Iwanami Shoten, 1982.

Tanaka Takako. *"Gyokunyo no seiritsu to genkai:* Jichin musōki *kara* Shinran muki *made."* In *Shiriizu josei to Bukkyō 4 Miko to joshin.* Edited by Ōsumi Kazuo and Nishiguchi Junko. Tokyo: Heibonsha, 1989.

Unno, Mark. "Myōe Kōben and the *Kōmyō Shingon dosha kanjinki*: The Ritual of Sand and the Mantra of Light," in *Re-visioning "Kamakura" Buddhism,* ed. Richard Payne . Honolulu: University of Hawai'i Press, 1998.

Unno, Taitetsu "Philosophical Schools-San-lun, T'ien-t'ai, and Hua-yen." In *Buddhist Spirituality.* Edited by Takeuchi Yoshinori. New York: Crossroad, 1993.

INDEX

WISDOM PUBLICATIONS

Wisdom Publications, a nonprofit publisher, is dedicated to preserving and transmitting important works from all the major Buddhist traditions as well as exploring related East-West themes.

To learn more about Wisdom, or browse our books on-line, visit our website at wisdompubs.org. You may request a copy of our mail-order catalog on-line or by writing to:

WISDOM PUBLICATIONS
199 Elm Street
Somerville, Massachusetts 02144 USA
Telephone: (617) 776-7416
Fax: (617) 776-7841
Email: info@wisdompubs.org
www.wisdompubs.org

The Wisdom Trust

As a nonprofit publisher, Wisdom is dedicated to the publication of fine Dharma books for the benefit of all sentient beings and dependent upon the kindness and generosity of sponsors in order to do so. If you would like to make a donation to Wisdom, please do so through our Somerville office. If you would like to sponsor the publication of a book, please write or email us at the address above.

Thank you.

Wisdom is a nonprofit 501(c)(3) organization affiliated with the Foundation for the Preservation of the Mahayana Tradition (FPMT).